THE SONG OF
SIMON DE MONTFORT

Dr Sophie Thérèse Ambler is a historian of medieval Europe and the Crusades. She is a Lecturer in Medieval History at Lancaster University and a Fellow of the Royal Historical Society. She has appeared on radio and TV for BBC and Channel 4, and written for *BBC History Magazine* and *The Historian*. She divides her time between Lancaster and London.

'Sophie Thérèse Ambler's engaging new biography will enthral and horrify in equal measure ... *The Song of Simon de Montfort* is a well-researched, elegantly written and lively portrait of a problematic figure.'
Mary Wellesley, *Sunday Times*

'Amid the valley of dry bones, Ambler breathes life into sources that might otherwise seem arid or dull. Her narrative is expertly paced. Whenever the story threatens to sag or falter, she skips over the drier deserts of fact, moving us from the routine to the remarkable ... From Evesham to the killing fields of the Hundred Years' War and the Wars of the Roses, Simon de Montfort's chief legacy was slaughter and woe. This is, therefore, a song more of lament than of triumph. It is a song that Sophie Thérèse Ambler sings supremely well.'
Nicholas Vincent, *Literary Review*

'Riveting ... a vivid psychological portrait of the charismatic knight through small but enlightening details of character ... *The Song of Simon de Montfort* is an engaging foray from a talented historian into one of the most important but least understood eras in English history.'
Emma J. Wells, *Times Literary Supplement*

'A dramatic story, told here with clarity and insight.'
History Revealed

D1328656

'For such a pivotal figure in English history, Simon de Montfort's remarkable story is one that has been sadly neglected by mainstream history books. Ambler's riveting volume redresses the balance brilliantly, recounting the electrifying build-up to the nation's first revolutionary movement and the emergence of a nascent Parliament with page-turning skill.'   Dan Jones, Waterstones Top History Books of 2019

'Gripping, detailed, and ingenious, *The Song of Simon de Montfort* is a compelling and thrilling story of England's very first revolution. With her beautiful prose, Sophie Thérèse Ambler successfully crosses the gap between narrative and academic history and brings Simon de Montfort vividly to life.'

Dr Estelle Paranque, author of
Elizabeth I of England Through Valois Eyes

THE SONG OF SIMON DE MONTFORT

England's First Revolutionary

Sophie Thérèse Ambler

PICADOR

First published 2019 by Picador

This paperback edition first published 2020 by Picador
an imprint of Pan Macmillan
The Smithson, 6 Briset Street, London ECIM 5NR
Associated companies throughout the world
www.panmacmillan.com

ISBN 978-1-5098-3763-2

1 3 5 7 9 8 6 4 2

A CIP catalogue record for this book is available from the British Library.

Map artwork by Global Blended Learning Ltd
Typeset by Palimpsest Book Production Limited, Falkirk, Stirlingshire
Printed and bound by CPI Group (UK) Ltd, Croydon, CR0 4YY

Visit **www.picador.com** to read more about all our books
and to buy them. You will also find features, author interviews and
news of any author events, and you can sign up for e-newsletters
so that you're always first to hear about our new releases.

For Mary and Kate
'Touz beveroms hui de un hanap, come pieça avoms fet.'

Contents

List of Illustrations

1. ENGLAND AND WALES IN THE REIGN OF HENRY III

N

SCOTLAND

North Sea

Irish Sea

Deganwy
Castle

• Chester
Beeston

Snowdon

Lincoln

The Wash

ENGLAND

Norwich

Wigmore • • Kenilworth • Leicester

Cardigan Bay

Northampton

Worcester
• Pershore
Hereford • Evesham
Gloucester

Dunstable

WALES

Pembroke

Oxford • St Albans

Barham
Down

Wallingford
Castle

London
Rochester
Reading
Odiham

Sandwich

Tonge Canterbury
Dover

Bristol Channel

Bristol

Winchester

Romney Hythe

Lewes

Portchester

Hastings
Pevensey

English Channel

| 0 | 40 | 80 miles |
| 0 | 25 | 50 km |

Castles held by the Montfort family

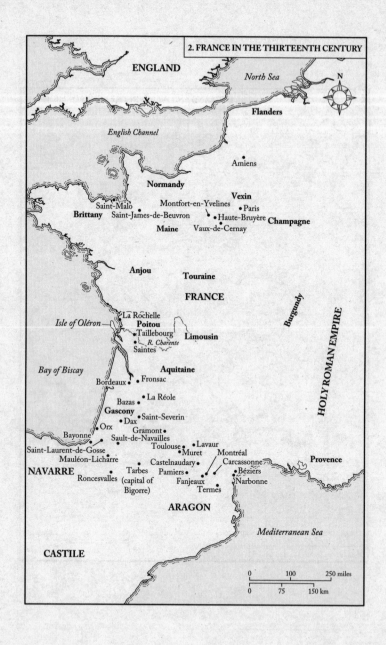

2. FRANCE IN THE THIRTEENTH CENTURY

ENGLAND

North Sea

English Channel

Flanders

Amiens

Normandy

Vexin

Saint-Malo
Brittany   Saint-James-de-Beuvron
Maine

Montfort-en-Yvelines
• Paris
• Haute-Bruyère   Champagne
Vaux-de-Cernay

Anjou   Touraine

FRANCE

La Rochelle
Isle of Oléron   Poitou
• Taillebourg   Limousin
R. Charente
Saintes

Burgundy

HOLY ROMAN EMPIRE

Bay of Biscay

Aquitaine

Bordeaux •   • Fronsac

Bazas •   • La Réole

Gascony   • Saint-Severin
Orx   • Dax
Bayonne   Gramont •
Saint-Laurent-de-Gosse   Sault-de-Navailles
Mauléon-Licharre
Toulouse •   • Lavaur
• Muret   Montréal
Castelnaudary •   Carcassonne
NAVARRE   Roncesvalles   Tarbes   Pamiers •   • Béziers
(capital of   Fanjeaux •   Narbonne
Bigorre)   Termes •

Provence

ARAGON

Mediterranean Sea

CASTILE

0   100   250 miles
0   75   150 km

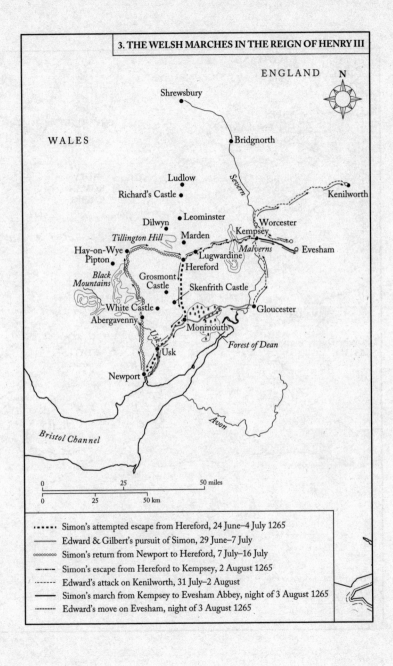

3. THE WELSH MARCHES IN THE REIGN OF HENRY III

ENGLAND

N

WALES

Shrewsbury

Bridgnorth

Severn

Ludlow

Richard's Castle

Leominster

Worcester

Dilwyn

Kempsey

Kenilworth

Tillington Hill

Marden

Malverns

Evesham

Hay-on-Wye

Lugwardine

Pipton

Hereford

Black Mountains

Grosmont Castle

Skenfrith Castle

White Castle

Gloucester

Abergavenny

Monmouth

Usk

Usk

Forest of Dean

Newport

Avon

Bristol Channel

| 0 | 25 | 50 miles |
| 0 | 25 | 50 km |

∙∙∙∙∙∙ Simon's attempted escape from Hereford, 24 June–4 July 1265

——— Edward & Gilbert's pursuit of Simon, 29 June–7 July

ooooooo Simon's return from Newport to Hereford, 7 July–16 July

–∙–∙– Simon's escape from Hereford to Kempsey, 2 August 1265

------ Edward's attack on Kenilworth, 31 July–2 August

——— Simon's march from Kempsey to Evesham Abbey, night of 3 August 1265

∙∙∙∙∙∙∙ Edward's move on Evesham, night of 3 August 1265

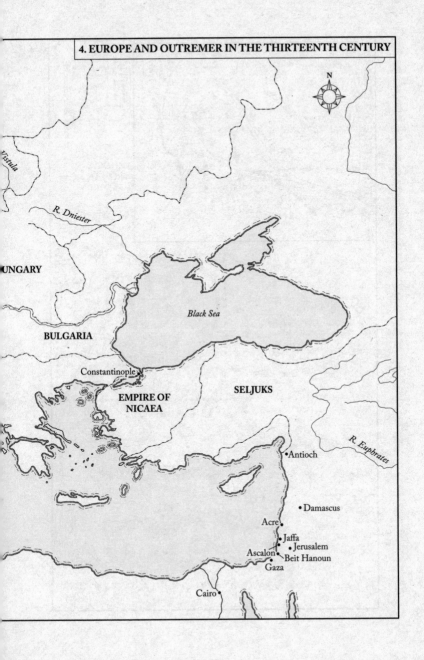

4. EUROPE AND OUTREMER IN THE THIRTEENTH CENTURY

N

Vistula

R. Dniester

HUNGARY

BULGARIA

Black Sea

Constantinople

EMPIRE OF
NICAEA

SELJUKS

R. Euphrates

•Antioch

• Damascus

Acre•

•Jaffa
•Jerusalem

Ascalon•
•Beit Hanoun
Gaza•

Cairo•

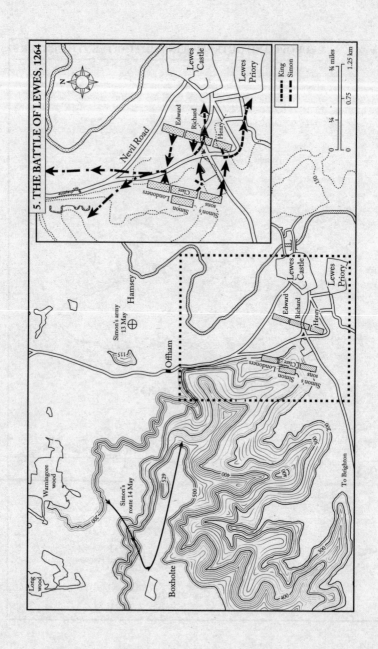

5. THE BATTLE OF LEWES, 1264

King
Simon

0   ¾   1.25 km
0   ¾ miles

Lewes Castle

Lewes Priory

Nevil Road

Edward

Richard

Henry

Clare

Londoners

Simon

Simon's sons

Hamsey

Simon's army
13 May

Offham

115

Warningore
wood

Long
wood

Simon's
route 14 May

Boxholte

To Brighton

529

500

400

400

300

300

200

150

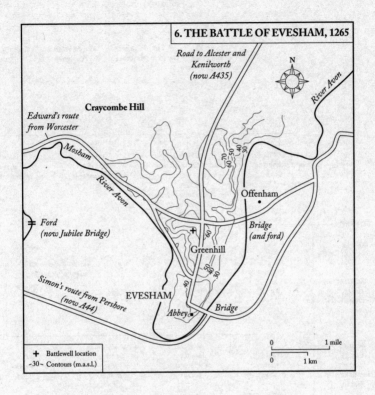

6. THE BATTLE OF EVESHAM, 1265

Road to Alcester and
Kenilworth
(now A435)

N

River Avon

Craycombe Hill

Edward's route
from Worcester

Mosham

River Avon

70
50
40
30

Offenham

60

Ford
(now Jubilee Bridge)

Bridge
(and ford)

+
60

Greenhill

50
40
30

Simon's route from Pershore
(now A44)

EVESHAM

40

Abbey

Bridge

Bridge

0   1 mile
0   1 km

+   Battlewell location
-30~ Contours (m.a.s.l.)

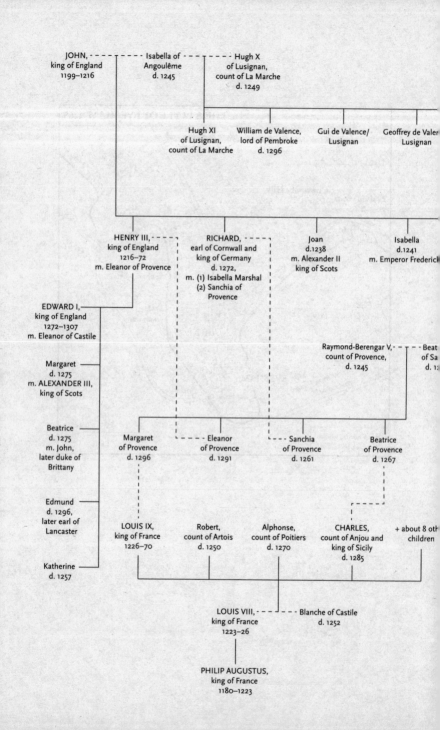

JOHN, – – – – – – Isabella of – – – – – Hugh X
king of England   Angoulême   of Lusignan,
1199–1216   d. 1245   count of La Marche
                                                         d. 1249

Hugh XI   William de Valence,   Gui de Valence/   Geoffrey de Valer
of Lusignan,   lord of Pembroke   Lusignan   Lusignan
count of La Marche   d. 1296

HENRY III, – – – – ⌐   RICHARD, – – – – ⌐   Joan   Isabella
king of England   earl of Cornwall and   d.1238   d.1241
1216–72   king of Germany   m. Alexander II   m. Emperor Frederic
m. Eleanor of Provence   d. 1272,   king of Scots
                          m. (1) Isabella Marshal
                              (2) Sanchia of
                                  Provence

EDWARD I,
king of England
1272–1307
m. Eleanor of Castile
                                                              Raymond-Berengar V, – – ⌐ – – Beat
                                                              count of Provence,   of Sa
                                                              d. 1245   d. 1:

Margaret
d. 1275
m. ALEXANDER III,
king of Scots

Beatrice
d. 1275   Margaret ⌐ – – – Eleanor ⌐ – – – Sanchia   Beatrice
m. John,   of Provence   of Provence   of Provence   of Provence
later duke of   d. 1296   d. 1291   d. 1261   d. 1267
Brittany

Edmund
d. 1296,   LOUIS IX,   Robert,   Alphonse,   CHARLES,   + about 8 oth
later earl of   king of France   count of Artois count of Poitiers count of Anjou and children
Lancaster   1226–70   d. 1250   d. 1270   king of Sicily
                                                                            d. 1285
Katherine
d. 1257

                                  LOUIS VIII, – – – – – Blanche of Castile
                                  king of France   d. 1252
                                  1223–26

                                  PHILIP AUGUSTUS,
                                  king of France
                                  1180–1223

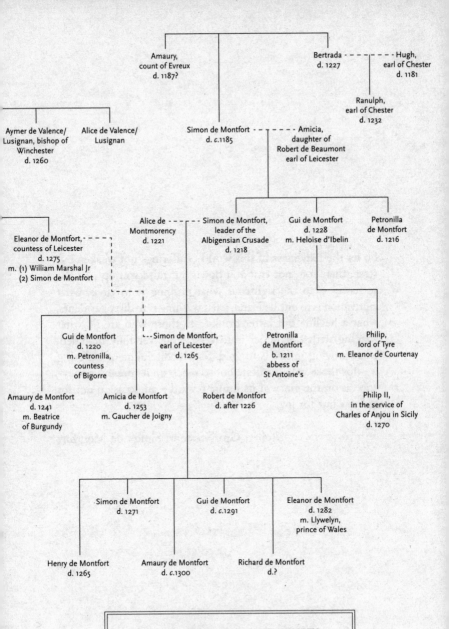

THE MONTFORTS, PLANTAGENETS,
CAPETIANS, SAVOYARDS AND LUSIGNANS
Simplified family tree

- - - - - denotes marriage

So let the harshness of this world's sufferings not weaken but strengthen you, not cast you down but raise you up . . . For suffering is to the righteous what pruning is to vines, what cultivation is to untilled land, what washing is to dirty garments, what a healing but bitter drink is to those who are ill, what shaping with a hammer is to vessels not yet fully moulded, what proving in fire is to gold. So, the discipline of suffering is – for those who meditate not so much on its present annoyance as on the glory of its future reward – an occasion not for sadness but for joy.

Robert Grosseteste to Simon de Montfort

Prologue

It was around 8.30 in the morning, with summer rainclouds weighing heavy in the sky, that Simon de Montfort decided to die. He was sitting talking to his oldest friend, Walter, bishop of Worcester, in the abbey of Evesham when the news arrived: his enemies were upon him. As panic overtook his men, and they rushed to take up arms, Simon did not move. He was exhausted. He and his troops had barely slept or eaten for three days and he had marched them fifteen miles through the night, arriving at Evesham only as dawn broke across the Avon valley. Unbeknownst to him, Edward – dispossessed heir to throne – had also moved his forces under cover of darkness, bringing his army towards Evesham from the west to crest the hill above the town. Now Simon faced a decision. He could take refuge in the abbey and wait to be trapped like a beast in the hunt as his enemies closed in around him. He could withdraw and rush what he could of his forces across the bridge below the town, escaping to the road that led to Kenilworth, his fortress. Or he could fight.

He would be fighting uphill, against a superior force – an option that a general of his skill was loath to choose. He would also be fighting to the death. In normal circumstances, the rules of chivalry ensured that noblemen would not be killed in battle but, rather, captured and ransomed. These were not, however, normal circumstances. Already, fifteen months before, on the battlefield of Lewes, Edward and his father, Henry III, had proclaimed that no quarter would be given to their enemies – for Simon, earl of Leicester, had done what no one before had dared to do: he had disinherited the crown in favour of government by council. At Lewes Simon had taken the king and Edward captive, and for the past fifteen months had been ruling England at the head of a conciliar regime. But at the end of May 1265 Edward, in a thrilling moment of triumph, had escaped and joined his allies, the barons of the March of Wales, to raise an army. Now, on 4 August, he was poised to reclaim his kingdom. Edward was a fearsome enemy, twenty-six and bursting with martial energy – like a lion, as the songs already sung of him proclaimed. No rapprochement would be possible. For Simon, defeat would mean annihilation.

Staying seated as the tumult was raised around him, Simon weighed all this and chose his path: he would make a fight of it and die. The choosing was important. He would give himself to death willingly, in a righteous cause, fighting for God and for justice, knowing that in his martyrdom he would find a place in heaven beside the saints themselves. This is what his father – the renowned crusader and Simon's constant exemplar – had done almost fifty years before, pouring out his blood on the fields of Languedoc in the cause of holy war.

Simon told Walter his decision. The two men rose, and Simon made his farewell with an embrace. The bishop was in tears.

As Simon readied to move his army out, the heavens darkened and the rainclouds burst, soaking his troops. The storm was brief, but a harbinger of what awaited them. One of them tried to stop it all: the men, he pleaded, had gone so long without food or rest that they were shattered, as were the horses. Why not take refuge in the abbey church – its stone walls could be defended – and wait for reinforcements to arrive?

'No, noble friend, no,' the earl replied. 'One should seek knights on the battlefield – and chaplains in churches.'

Simon moved his troops out of the abbey precinct and on into the town. As they passed through the abbey gate, the lance bearing Simon's standard was shattered against the stone. It was another dismal portent, but nothing now would stop him.

'On, on, God help us.'

As they reached the road running north to south through the town, Simon looked behind them, towards the river, and saw that Edward still had not blocked the bridge. He gathered his men around him.

'Worthy lords, there are many amongst you who are not as yet experienced in the world, and who are young. You have wives and children, so think how you might save yourselves and them. Cross the bridge and you will escape the great danger that is coming.'

He turned to Hugh Despenser, another old and dear friend, and member of the revolutionary regime. 'My lord Hugh, think on your great age and on saving yourself. Think that your counsel can still be of great value to all the land, for you will leave behind you hardly anyone of such loyalty and such worth.'

Hugh's reply came without hesitation. 'My lord, my lord, let it be. Today we shall drink from one cup, as we have done long since.'

Introduction

Simon de Montfort, earl of Leicester, was one of a rare species: a man who, uncontent with the world, dared to transform it. Today he is known as a champion of parliamentary power, for in 1265 he held what has been hailed the first House of Commons, inviting representatives of the towns – as well as knights – to gather and discuss the business of government. But he did far more than this: he redrew the entire political order, imagining a means to govern the kingdom that had no meaningful place for kings; instead, England would be ruled by a council, whose powers were sharply defined and decisions carried by the vote of the majority. The radicalism of this regime sat unhappily within the culture of medieval politics, which always preferred tradition to the new, and so Simon and his party were sometimes required to hide their government's more controversial aspects or to cast them in creatively occlusive terms to the outside world. But it was clear then, as it is now, that this was revolutionary. For it was not merely a rebellion, which was a customary form of protest against improper government, whose goal was to compel the restoration of good royal rule. It was an attempt to transform the system of government itself. In this respect, the period stretching from 1258, when Simon and his confederates first seized power from King Henry III, to 1265, when they were annihilated on the battlefield at Evesham, stands apart in the medieval age – the closest parallel, before or since, is the English Civil War of the seventeenth century. The revolution required an uncommon leader, possessed of uncommon traits: above all, monumental audacity and charisma. This is charisma not in the quotidian sense, but in the sense that describes the belief of Simon's followers that he was superhuman, even sent by God. Charisma is one of the few forces powerful enough to change worlds.

As a remarkable political and military leader, Simon has already earned two major scholarly biographies. The first was by Charles Bémont in the 1880s, the second by John Maddicott, published in 1994.[1] Bémont's great achievement was to unearth and transcribe a host of documents connected to Simon's career; John Maddicott's was – apart from describing Simon's activities during the revolutionary era with a new level of precision, and analysing his finances and household – to balance an investigation of parliamentary politics with the first exploration of Simon's inner world, considering his spiritual life and friendships and revealing his complexities and contradictions. I have not sought to replicate these earlier and very important works. Instead, I have set out to answer what, for me, were two questions fundamental to understanding how Simon's leadership made the revolution possible: how did he conceive of his role, and how did he appear through the eyes of those who followed him? In order to answer them, I have stepped away from the established context of the telling of Simon's story, which emphasizes English political tradition. This, instead, is a story of holy war, played out on a global stage by the heroes of the thirteenth century's great crusader dynasty.

The medieval world had many heroes – in life, in history and in literature – men who had shown themselves outstanding in their prowess and their daring, their wisdom and their Christianity. Chief amongst them were those who fought and killed, who suffered and offered up their lives in the service of the faith: *crucesignati*, crusaders. They were paragons of knighthood, and those listening to the songs of their great deeds would hope to follow their example and emulate their feats.

In this book, the first hero according to these terms is the father of our protagonist, whose name was also Simon de Montfort (hereafter called simply the Count). The Count created, in his deeds and in the song of them, a pattern for his children, who learned from his example what it was to be a knight, a father, a husband and a leader. When our protagonist – our Simon de Montfort – followed his father in taking command of an oath-bound cause, it was upon his father's pattern that he formed himself and forged his reputation. To Simon – who, like others of his knightly kind, had a strong sense of narrative and his place within it – this was his contribution to the Montfort family history. By the time Simon took up his cause, his father, his mother and his brothers, all crusaders, had all been laid beneath the ground, all but his mother felled by war. In his living, and in his dying, Simon set out to earn his place amongst their mighty company.

Of course, the man who was a hero to his son is often seen in a different light today: the Count is a monster, the zealot who, in the course of the Albigensian Crusade, sent thousands to fiery and bloody death in southern France because they failed to conform in their beliefs. But the Count was not a monster – for a monster, by definition, is anomalous, and the Count was nothing of the kind. He was a member of a society bound by the belief that killing in the service of the Church was not merely acceptable but laudable, and that heroized those who did it best. This was the context in which Richard the Lionheart – always his own greatest advocate – could write proudly home from Acre to describe how he had ordered the killing of 2,700 Muslim prisoners, who had been led out to their deaths in full view of both armies with hands bound behind their backs.[2] The only difference between the Count and Richard – whose statue stands outside the Houses of Parliament – is that the victims of the Albigensian war have found advocates in the modern era, and in the region they came from: their tragedy more moving, apparently, than that of the hundreds of thousands more for whom they stand because they must have looked, and sounded, familiar.

Simon too set out to kill those who did not share his faith, first in Syria and then in England, where hundreds of Jewish people were cut down in the building of the new regime. But his campaign to establish the new political order was also conceived as a holy cause, to be upheld by the taking of life and the giving of one's own. It was the culture of crusaders that fuelled Simon's cause and, most of all, the particular culture of the Montfort family. Without this context, the revolution – and the parliamentary system that it promoted – could never have survived its infancy, nor ever reached such heights. Hence the title of this book, which speaks to the medieval tradition of the *chansons de geste*, the singing of the deeds of heroes.

The bleeding of crusading culture into English politics was part of a phenomenon that transformed Europe during the lifetime of Simon and his children: the terms of holy war came to be applied concertedly to wars between Christians. During the 1250s and 1260s, the papacy offered the spiritual benefits usually reserved for those fighting in the Holy Land to those fighting in Europe, under papal direction, for the defence of the Church and the Christian faithful. In this context, the making of Simon's cause into something sacred, while it lacked official mandate, essentially followed papal precedent. This fluidity of thinking did not, on the whole, present the mental challenge to people of the thirteenth century that it might to modern audiences, for there was no such term as 'crusade' in the Middle Ages, or at least not in common usage (the term was used regularly only from the eighteenth century). There were 'crusaders', *crucesignati*, those who had taken a vow and been signed with the cross, but what they had vowed to undertake was a pilgrimage (*peregrinatio*), journey (*iter*), path (*via*) or expedition (*expeditio*).[3] As Simon's case makes clear, for *crucesignati* what counted was the solemn commitment to a righteous cause and the expectation of spiritual benefits.[4]

But the transplantation of crusading terms to European conflict had drastic, if unintended, consequences. For two and a half centuries, knightly values (what would, in Simon's lifetime, come to be known as 'chivalry') had stayed the hand of noble against noble: knight did not seek to kill knight on the battlefield, but to capture him for ransom, while killings and executions off the battlefield were most rare.[5] This changed in the 1260s and 1270s, as noble society began the slide to lethal violence that would lead to the horrifying noble dead lists of the Hundred Years War. Amongst the episodes that heralded this ghastly alteration was Simon's end at Evesham, in 1265. It was the end of chivalry – or at least the end of chivalry as it had been understood since the turn of the millennium. As I suggest towards the end of the book, it was a consequence of applying the vows and benefits of war against infidels and heretics – in which killing with no respect for status was acceptable – to wars against fellow Christians. The geographical and mental bounds of holy war were collapsed.

The sources for Simon's story are uncommonly rich. In addition to the records of English government, which detail the daily workings of royal administration and allow us to trace Simon's activities during significant segments of his life, numerous chronicles provide narrative detail and opinion.[6] Chief amongst these is the work of Matthew Paris, a Benedictine monk at St Albans Abbey. Matthew had close access to the court – his abbey provided hospitality for those travelling to and from Westminster, and Matthew attended court several times himself – and he describes events in unparalleled detail. His focus is sometimes skewed by his own interests, but where his accounts can be checked they have been found to be accurate.[7] Matthew's death in 1259 leaves a hole in our narrative sources, though it is partially filled by another outstanding chronicler, Arnold fitz Thedmar. Arnold, as an alderman of the city of London, was one of the very few chroniclers of the age not to have worked from within the walls of a monastery. As a leading member of a city tightly bound to Simon's cause, he was in a privileged position to narrate events after 1258.[8] But perhaps our most treasured account comes from a writer who was in the most privileged position of all: an eye-witness to Simon's final hours. His identity is unknown, but he was probably a monk of Evesham Abbey.[9] The account, discovered only a few years ago, has transformed our understanding of the Battle of Evesham, and is remarkable in what it reveals of Simon. It is described fully towards the end of this book.

A further set of sources are a window into Simon's inner world, as opposed to his more public life: letters written to him by his friends Robert Grosseteste and Adam Marsh. Robert was bishop of Lincoln and a leading scholar, and Simon's close friend from the 1230s until the bishop's death in 1253. Only a couple of his letters to Simon survive, selected for preservation seemingly by Robert himself, when he compiled a collection of his outgoing correspondence as a model for future letter writers, but they are important for suggesting Simon's thinking in his early career.[10] Adam Marsh, a Franciscan friar and respected scholar, was their mutual friend. A collection of his letters was made after his death, for which several letters to Simon, and his countess, Eleanor, were selected for inclusion.[11] Again, they represent only a fraction of the correspondence exchanged (and none of Simon's letters to Robert or Adam survive). But they reveal much of Simon's career in the 1250s, before Adam's death in 1259. Such insight can only be provided by those who were close to the earl.

It is the quality of these government records, chronicles and letters that makes them important, but another set of sources is remarkable also in its type. This is the collection of documents produced as a result of Simon's quarrels with Henry III. Simon's relationship with the king deteriorated sharply after 1252, when Henry held an inquiry into Simon's governorship of Gascony. The inquiry produced a number of testimonies, including Simon's own, as did later attempts to arbitrate on their disputes. Perhaps the most important of these is the deposition given by Simon in 1262, which describes his dealings with the king from their first meeting.[12] Its significance lies particularly in providing us with Simon's perception of events, and his perception of the king, perhaps only partially coloured by hindsight. Other documents produced under Simon's aegis similarly allow us to hear his voice. These include his will, which he dictated to his eldest son.

Many of these sources have been available to previous historians, although I have enjoyed the benefit of new analyses and editions of various government records, chronicles and letters produced in the last few years, as well as much recent scholarship, including the biographies of Eleanor de Montfort, by Louise Wilkinson, and the Count, by Gregory Lippiatt.[13] In various cases I have also returned to the original documents, preserved chiefly at the National Archives and British Library in the UK and, in France, the Archives nationales and Bibliothèque nationale, in order to investigate what the manner of their production might reveal. But this book also brings to bear on the telling of Simon's life a constellation of sources that have hitherto been considered only separately: the accounts of his father's expedition to Languedoc and his brother Amaury's to the Holy Land, as well as the records of the nunnery of Haute-Bruyère, which housed the Montfort family mausoleum.[14] It is these sources that, when considered alongside those described above, reveal how Simon conceived of his identity, and his career in England, within the Montfort family tradition. In this respect, this book seeks to contribute to the growing scholarship on crusaders and family

memory led by Nicholas Paul, as much as to that on warfare, political thought, elite and popular politics, and noble culture.[15]

This book was made possible only with the advice, collaboration
and support of many friends and colleagues. First amongst them is
David Carpenter, who ignited my interest in Simon's world when
I was an undergraduate at King's College London, and has been
my guide since, and generously read this book in draft. The book
was begun with the advice and encouragement of Dan Jones and
Georgina Capel, and guided by Georgina Morley at Picador. Marc
Morris has given much support and sage counsel along the way,
and Saul David, Richard Foreman and Mike Ivey have also been
generous with advice and support. I have been fortunate indeed in
that the research and writing of this book coincided with a coming
together of scholars working on the Montfort family, a highly
productive collaboration led by Martin Aurell and Gregory Lippiatt.
Within and beyond this project, I am also most grateful to Alexis
Charansonnet, Lindy Grant, Amicie Pélissié du Rausas, Daniel
Power and Nicholas Vincent, and to the many others who have
generously shared their thoughts, research and time, including
Elizabeth Brown, Richard Cassidy, Stephen Church, Jamie Doherty,
Felicity Hill, Aaron Hope, Lars Kjær, John Maddicott, Simon
Parsons, John Sabapathy, Ian Stone, Henry Summerson and Anaïs
Waag; Elizabeth Brown and Jean-François Moufflet also offered
help in accessing material in the French archives. Research for this
book has been presented at the Institute of Historical Research, the
Leeds International Medieval Congress, the New College of the
Humanities, King's College London, and the universities of Lyon,
Manchester and Poitiers, and the book's development owes much
to the convenors and participants of these conferences and seminars.
The History Department at Lancaster University has been my home
since 2017, and I am very thankful to my students and colleagues,
who have made it a stimulating and supportive environment in
which to finish the book. Most of all, I am thankful to my mother,
Mary Ambler, and to my sister, Kate Ambler – for everything.

A Note on Money

During the period covered by this book, there was only one coin in circulation in England: the silver penny. For the purpose of accounting, people referred to shillings, pounds and marks – there were twelve pennies in a shilling, 240 pennies in a pound, and 160 pennies in a mark (two-thirds of a pound) – but no such denominations existed. Making a payment of £100 (for instance) would involve delivering 24,000 silver pennies, transported in barrels; although when large sums had to be taken over large distances, such as to finance a military expedition overseas, these could be translated into ingot or plate.

In agreeing and accounting for large sums, sometimes pounds were preferred and sometimes marks. In the latter case, I have provided the equivalent in pounds in those instances where it might be particularly helpful.

1

A Way of Living,
and a Way of Dying

The song of Simon de Montfort begins with a death. It was a death in battle, one morning in 1218, in summer. It was the death of his father, and it happened when Simon was about ten years old.

An army of crusaders was encamped outside the walls of Toulouse, in the south-eastern region of the land we now know as France. At the time, the county of Toulouse was a semi-independent territory; the crusaders had come from the north, from France proper – that is, the lands around Paris whose lords followed the Capetian kings. They had come to conquer, and they had come to purge these lands of the heresy known today as Catharism.

For nine years the crusaders had been waging this war, and for nine months they had besieged this town. Now, at dawn on the morning of 25 June, the crusaders faced a new danger. A party of Toulousains had launched a sortie from the town to attack their siege-machines. As the crusaders fought hard to defend both their equipment and their lives, a messenger hurried to alert their leader.

He was Simon de Montfort, earl of Leicester, lord of Montfort and, by God's grace, duke of Narbonne and count of Toulouse, viscount of Béziers and Carcassonne and lord of Albi and the Razès – so went the glistering parade of titles that proclaimed him lord of his dominion. To the crusaders, though, he was known simply as the Count (the French form of 'earl' – the difference is only one of modern translation). His right to bear the title was originally founded upon a family claim to the earldom of

Leicester, even though his possession of that earldom had been forfeit since 1204, when the king of England had been driven from his continental lands, chiefly Normandy, by the king of France. Many nobles holding estates on both sides of the Channel had found themselves owing fealty to two lords, and were forced to choose sides. The Montfort family had chosen France, and so the Count had been severed from his earldom. But the resilience of his title was in part a recognition of his personal stature, a declaration that he was still counted by his fellows amongst the highest rank of nobles.[1] And, if the measure of a great lord was in his following, then he stood as one of the greatest lords of Europe, for he commanded God's army in Languedoc (see plate 1).

When the Count was sought by his men to defend the siege machines before Toulouse, he was attending Mass in the chapel of Château Narbonnais, the crusader-held fortress on the city's southern wall. The messenger found him kneeling, awaiting the sight of the elevated Host: the bread transformed by the miracle of the Mass into the Body of Christ. He refused to leave before he had glimpsed it; once fortified by the sight of his Redeemer, he hurried to join the fight, saying 'Let us go and if needs must die for Him who deigned to die for us.'[2]

Taking up arms, he and his men rode out against the storm of arrows, boulders catapulted from trebuchets and stones hurled from slings, all raining down in torrents 'like thunder and tempest', as one writer described it.[3] The Count and his men took up position around their siege-machines, sheltering from the bombardment behind wicker hurdles.

It was not enough. Gui de Montfort, the Count's brother and comrade, was hit: his horse took a crossbow bolt through its head and, as the creature reared in pain, another bolt speared Gui's groin, soaking his breeches with blood. As he slid from his dying horse, Gui got out a bitter jest – 'This wound will make me a Hospitaller!' (that is, a warrior, but a celibate one) – before breaking into howls of pain.[4]

His brother's words were the last that the Count heard. As he looked upon his brother, a rock smashed through his helm. It was launched from a mangonel and hit home at high velocity, shattering his skull into a mess of brain and bone. As the Count's body dropped to the ground beside his brother, his men hurried to cover him with a cape. But not before panic began to spread throughout the army: the Count – *their* Count – was dead.[5]

A few hundred yards away, the tower of Château Narbonnais provided a privileged view over the scene for those who had, shortly before, watched the Count fetched from Mass for battle: his family. Alice de Montmorency, his wife and partner in the cause; Gui, their second son, who had been badly wounded by a crossbow bolt earlier in the siege, and Gui's wife Petronilla, countess of Bigorre; Beatrice of Vienne, wife of their eldest son, Amaury, who was fighting at his father's side; the Count's nephews and nieces, children of his brother Gui; and his youngest son – Simon.[6]

*

Simon was born around 1208 in the family domain of Montfort, in the French heartlands, some twenty-five miles west of Paris. But when he was scarcely a year old his mother brought him southward to war. As Simon grew, he watched his father become the divinely chosen leader of God's army, champion of the Church, hero amongst knights, and one of the greatest figures of the western world. And, after his father's death, Simon was taught to cherish his memory and follow his example.

In the age in which Simon grew up, young boys of noble families learned the values of their culture, and how to be good knights, from the great heroes of old. In the feasting hall or sitting at their mother's knee they drank in tales of deeds fit for emulation.[7] In this respect, Simon's education was both like and unlike those of other children of his status. He could be inducted into the knightly culture of his homeland in northern France listening to the greatest of such tales, the *Chanson de Roland*. It was from this that he heard of Charlemagne, the mighty ruler of the early Middle Ages whose story had been transformed into legend. He heard in the *Chanson* how Charlemagne marched his armies into Spain to wrest it from the infidel and how he, as was proper for a lord, took no important decision without first consulting with his men and sifting the good counsel from the bad. He heard, too, of Roland,

Charlemagne's nephew, loyal to his lord and bold – too bold, in fact, impetuous, seeking battles he did not know he could win. He heard of Oliver, Roland's friend and vassal, whose prudence tempered Roland's recklessness. He heard of Ganelon, the traitor, who served up Roland and Oliver to the enemy out of spite, and for profit. And he heard how, at Roncesvalles, Roland and Oliver – betrayed by a lesser man, ambushed and surrounded – swung their swords and hacked down enemy after enemy before they were finally cut down themselves. The ideals embodied in Roland, Oliver and Charlemagne were those of *chevalerie*, knightliness. This was not the knights-in-shining-armour-and-damsels-in-distress pastiche of chivalry of the Victorian imagination, but a set of values that made knights of men: fidelity and largesse, toughness and boldness, prudence and forbearance, honour and the necessity of avoiding shame.[8] These were the qualities that made the ideal knight a generous lord, a loyal vassal, a wise counsellor and a fearsome and cunning warrior. The knight who learned these lessons and commanded his character accordingly was a *prudhomme*: a good man.

But Simon, as a boy, had another exemplar of proper conduct: his father. The father Simon knew (and the one we have just met, dying at Toulouse) was the man found in the pages of the *History of the Albigensian Crusade*, written by his friend and follower, Peter, a young monk from the Cistercian house of les Vaux-de-Cernay, some twenty-five miles outside Paris. The Montforts were the principal patrons of the abbey, whose lands marched with their own, and the bond ran deep. The abbot, another Gui, was Peter's uncle and (so Peter tells us) 'had for many years been a close friend of the Count, who had listened to his advice and followed his wishes ever since childhood'.[9] Gui was already abbot in 1185 when the Count, at the age of about fourteen, succeeded to the family estate upon the death of his father and Gui, having seemingly been charged with his care, educated him at the abbey.[10] The two crusaded together in 1202, in the campaign that was to turn notoriously towards the Christian strongholds of the East and is known to us as the Fourth Crusade – according to Peter, Gui and the Count had stood apart, and shoulder to shoulder, in refusing to attack the Christian city of Zara, and had instead travelled together to the Holy Land to fight the infidel.[11] They were to fight together in Languedoc too: Gui's preaching tour of the southern lands in 1207 paved the path for the Count's crusade; he joined the Count on campaign in Languedoc in March 1212 and was soon appointed bishop of Carcassonne.[12] He brought with him to Languedoc Peter, who began writing his *History* during the course of the war.[13]

Peter was, then, very close to the events of which he writes, having been at the Count's side to witness many of his deeds. But this is not the only reason that Peter's *History* is a source of immense value. For Peter's closeness to the Count during the campaign, and closeness to the Montfort family generally, means that in the pages of his *History* we can see the image of the Count established by the man himself, and by his family. This production of a written history of the Count's expedition was particularly important for the Montforts, because the family had little in the way of crusading heritage.[14] Noble families who could claim amongst their ancestors heroes of the First Crusade, or other great crusading ventures, could celebrate their memory, revel in the honour their deeds had brought the family name and aspire to follow their example.[15] The Montforts had no such figure.

As far as we know, only one of the Count's ancestors had taken and fulfilled a crusading vow: his uncle, Amaury, count of Évreux. Amaury led an expedition of his knights to the Holy Land (known as Outremer, the land across the sea) in the spring of 1186. In one of his surviving charters, we catch him in the company there of a host of Templars (together with the Hospitallers, one of the military orders dedicated to defending Outremer), including Gerard de Ridefort, Grand Master of the Temple, as well as two Anglo-Norman barons, Roger de Mowbray and Hugh de Beauchamp.[16] Although we have no other records of Amaury's activities in the Holy Land, the company he kept is telling: Gerard, Roger and Hugh all went on to fight at the Battle of Hattin, on 4 July 1187. This was Salah al-Din's monumental victory, in which the fighting men of Outremer were all but wiped out. The Templars alone lost some 230 knights, many beheaded on the orders of Salah al-Din after the battle (although the Grand Master himself was spared) and the pilgrims who aided them faced a similar fate: although Roger was taken captive, Hugh was killed on the field. Amaury disappears from view around this time, and it is tempting to suppose that he shared Hugh's fate.[17] For the descendants of crusaders tied to the cataclysm that was Hattin, their involvement presented a difficulty. While the fallen might be celebrated as martyrs,* the implication of their ancestors in the disaster and, ultimately, the loss of the Holy City to Salah al-Din three months after the battle, was unsettling. William Marshal, for instance, had campaigned in Outremer for two years between 1184 and 1186; his biographer, writing in the mid-1220s, chose to exclude almost all detail of the expedition from his narrative rather than attempt to explain how his hero had failed to help secure the Christian territories in Outremer.[18] For the Montforts, then, the Count's leadership of the Albigensian expedition was an opportunity to establish the family's credentials as crusaders. Peter's *History* thus served to chronicle the war, but also to establish the Count's heroic status: he was now the protagonist in an epic crusading tale, who could take his place in the pantheon of crusading heroes.[†]

* Even Raynauld de Châtillon – whose unbridled bellicosity led him to be blamed for the disaster, after Salah al-Din beheaded him personally following the battle – received this honour at the time, and a story of Hugh de Beauchamp's fall – in which he carried the True Cross into battle and willingly gave himself to death – circulating in the 1210s suggests that he was remembered positively (for Raynauld, see: Peter of Blois's 'Passion of Reginald, prince of Antioch', in *Petri Blesensis Tractatus Duo: Passio Raginaldi principis Antiochie, Conquestio de dilatione vie Ierosolimitane*, ed. R. B. C. Huygens (Turnhout, 2002), 31–73; for Hugh de Beauchamp, see: '*Ordinacio de praedicatione sancte crucis in Anglia*', in *Quinti belli sacri scriptores minores*, ed. R. Röhricht (Geneva, 1879), 25; C. Tyreman, *England and the Crusades* (Chicago, 1996), 164; N. Paul, 'In search of the Marshal's lost crusade: the persistence of memory, the problems of history and the painful birth of crusading romance', *Journal of Medieval History*, 40 (2014), 292–310, at 303.

† Peter had dedicated his work to Pope Innocent III, but that it was fundamentally concerned with showcasing the exploits of the Count was recognized by later copyists, who renamed it 'Deeds of the noble man lord Simon, count of Montfort' (*Gesta nobilis viri domini Simonis, comitis de Monte Forti*), for an example of which, see: Biblioteca Apostolica Vaticana, Reg.lat.491, f.1r. (a sixteenth/seventeenth-century copy, manuscript E in the classification provided by Pascal Guébin and Ernest Lyon (P. Guébin and E. Lyon, 'Les manuscrits de la chronique de Pierre des Vaux-de-Cernay (texte et traductions)', *Le Moyen Âge*, 23 (1910), 221–34, at 223).

It was family histories such as this – as much as the famous tales of Roland and Oliver – that served as instruction for noble children. Simon was probably tutored at the monastery of les Vaux-de-Cernay, if his education followed the pattern of his father's (for he was perhaps ten when his father died and he returned with his mother to their homeland, and thirteen when his mother followed his father to the grave). He might have come to know Peter's *History* in the schoolroom, or heard its tales sung in the abbey and family hall, or told by the women of the house in the chamber or the garden.[19] Such tellings were a way to cherish the memory of the departed but were also, like the *Chanson de Roland*, an admonishment to those who listened, the holding up of an exemplar and an encouragement to follow. It is in this context that Peter of les Vaux-de-Cernay, in presenting the Count's example to his children, did far more than describe a man who, like the heroes of old, showed those standard knightly virtues. For Peter picked out other traits that made the Count outstanding – not only deeds but also values, values that Simon would be encouraged to emulate.

The Count, in Peter's pages, was a man whose allure was almost numinous. When Peter came to describe the Count's election as leader of the holy army, in 1209, he wrote of it as one would write of the election of a bishop, and the holier sort at that: a council of seven – comprising two bishops, four knights of the army and the papal legate, the abbot of Cîteaux – chose the Count unanimously, without conferring.[20] It was a manner of election that demonstrated that the choice had been made 'with the help of the grace of the sevenfold Holy Spirit'. The Count's status as undisputed leader came, then, not only from his natural authority and personal courage (it was his daring feats of arms at the siege of Carcassonne that had encouraged his nomination), but also from divine disposition: he had been chosen by God himself.[21]

But, to Peter, what set the Count apart even more than divine endorsement was his ability to govern human weakness. No matter the depravation, the suffering demanded, he remained faithful – to God, to the Church, to his cause, and to his men. He showed this time and time again, cleaving to his crusader's oath, and to the pursuit of holy war, though the cost was high. Maintaining the army outstripped his income, even when revenue could be raised from his newly conquered lands. At times the Count could not even afford bread for his own table. Ashamed at his penury, he would find an excuse to go off at mealtimes rather than sit in his tent. Even then, Peter noted, every penny he raised he spent in the cause of the crusade.[22]

But as the Count went hungry and still battled on, lesser men abandoned the cause. Knights who had come from France to prove their faith and forge their reputations returned home as soon as the traditional term of service (forty days) expired; their duty – and their vow – had been fulfilled. Local knights pledged themselves to the Count and to his expedition only to renege on their oaths and ally with southern potentates. Again and again, the Count found himself alone: a beacon of fidelity amongst the faithless.[23] Yet he stood undaunted. 'Any other man', wrote Peter, 'would surely have given up the struggle in the face of such adversity, and yielded to despair . . . but the Count, putting all his faith in God, was not to be borne down by misfortune.'[24]

As the Count was willing to suffer in his cause, he was also ready to inflict suffering on his enemies. Here he and his fellow crusaders stepped outside the bounds of normal knightly culture. An unwritten rule guiding the conduct of the knight was forbearance: stay your hand against your fellow.[25] In the twelfth century and for much of the thirteenth, a knight did not seek to kill another knight. Instead, in battle knights were taken captive for ransom (foot soldiers, of course, were a different matter, as were the enemies of God, as we shall see). This presented an attractive opportunity for profit, and stopped a noble society fractured periodically by conflict from surrendering to self-destruction.

It was a custom that conditioned even the most momentous of battles. In May 1217 – a little more than a year before the Count's death outside Toulouse – when his youngest son was about nine years old, another noble child of about the same age was waiting upon the outcome of a battle. This was the boy king, Henry III, whose father, King John, had died in 1216, leaving his realm in the throes of civil war. The battle was being fought at Lincoln, between Henry's forces and those of the rebel barons who had allied with the French royal house in the hope of placing a Capetian (Louis, son of the king of France) on the throne of England. And it was to be decisive: already half of England had been taken by the alliance between the rebels and the French – this was the best chance the king of England's men would have to reclaim the kingdom.

Our best account of the Battle of Lincoln comes from a biography of Henry's commander, William Marshal, earl of Pembroke. The *History of William Marshal* was commissioned by William's sons, and composed between 1224 and 1226. Its purpose – as well as telling a ripping story – was (much like Peter of les Vaux-de-Cernay's *History*) to demonstrate the rights and wrongs of knightly conduct and hold its hero up for emulation. For by the time of William Marshal's death in 1219, he was being described (at least according to his biographer) as 'the best knight to be found in all the world in our times . . . [and] a good man'.[26]

As the *History of William Marshal* tells us, at the Battle of Lincoln one knight alone was killed. This was Thomas, count of Perche, and his death was a dreadful error. William had engaged the count in combat and was seeking to take him captive when the count collapsed and slid from his horse. William, thinking that his opponent had fainted, ordered his man to dismount and tend to the count. William, too, was soon by his side. Unbeknownst to William, one of the soldiers of his army, Reginald Crook, had killed the nobleman, whether by accident or design plunging his sword through the one weak spot in a knight's armour, the visor of the helm. When William and his man pulled the helm from the count's head, they discovered the ghastly result: the sword had driven through the count's eye and into his brain. There was nothing to be done. 'The sorrow there', the *History of William Marshal* tells us, 'was intense . . . it was a great pity that he died like this.'[27] The count of Perche might have been an enemy, an invader, an aider of rebels, but he was also a knight, and a *prudhomme*. His worthiness, and the value of his life, transcended any conflict.*

---

* Thomas, count of Perche, was buried in the grounds of the hospital outside Lincoln; Reginald Crook was killed in the fray, and buried at Croxton Abbey (Roger of Wendover, *Chronica, sive Flores Historiarum*, ed. H. O. Coxe, 5 vols. (London, 1841–4), IV, 24).

But in the war-ravaged lands of Languedoc, the situation could not have been more different, for here the war was being fought with a brutality otherwise unknown in Europe.[28] Chivalric principles did not apply. The enemy – whether knights or non-combatants (women, children, the elderly, whose persons, if not their property, were in ordinary circumstances protected) – were heretics. As such, they were little different from the Islamic infidels encountered by the crusaders in the Holy Land; indeed, they were worse, the enemy within forming a greater threat than that without.

This was clear from the very beginning of the campaign, in 1209, when the crusaders sacked the town of Béziers and slaughtered its inhabitants. This was not done on the order of the army's leaders – indeed, it happened because no one was in outright command (the Count had not yet been elected leader of the crusade). Discipline was lax, and the foot soldiers and camp followers had unleashed themselves on the people of the town.* While inhumane treatment of heretics was consistent with the attitudes of the leaders of the crusade, the wholesale slaughter of a town was not – it robbed the crusaders of the opportunity to extract taxes from the townspeople, a financial lifeline for their campaign. Targeted acts of violence were to be far preferred. In 1211, when the Count captured the town of Lavaur, he ordered the hanging of some eighty enemy knights (although when the gibbets began to collapse he instructed that they be put to the sword instead), and the burning of some 400 townspeople. Then, on his order, Girauda, ruler of Lavaur, was seized. Screaming in protest, she was thrown into a well and stoned to death.[29]

Young Simon, through the account of Peter of les Vaux-de-Cernay, was learning quite a different lesson from those who listened to William Marshal's exploits at Lincoln. The Count was showing his willingness to act brutally. He was reluctant – he 'never', wrote

---

* Despite the oft (mis)quoted line supposedly delivered by the papal legate at Béziers: 'Kill them all, God will know his own!' In fact, the words he supposedly spoke were, 'Kill them. The Lord knows who are his own' – though this episode is told only in a source written forty years after the events it describes, and so carries limited value. For a review of this episode, see the discussion in *The History of the Albigensian Crusade: Peter of les Vaux-de-Cernay's Historia Albigensis*, trans. W. A. and M. D. Sibly (Woodbridge, 1998) (hereafter *PVC*), 289–93.

Peter, 'took delight in cruelty or in the torture of his enemies. He was the kindest of men and the saying of the poet [Ovid] fitted him aptly: "a prince slow to punish, and quick to reward, who grieved when driven to be hard".' He did these things, Peter explained, because they needed to be done, because the winning of the cause was everything, and in this there was no room for weakness. Peter gave other examples. The Count, having captured the fortified settlement of Bram, had ordered that the eyes of the defenders be put out and that their noses be cut off – an order given 'not because such mutilation gave him any pleasure', Peter insisted, 'but because his opponents had been the first to indulge in atrocities'.[30] Compassion, mercy, forgiveness: these were the luxuries of men fighting ordinary, not holy, wars.

The brutal side of the Count's character was far from domin-ant, however, in Peter's portrayal of him. As we have seen, it was his willingness to endure suffering in order to uphold his oath that made him outstanding. What also emerges plainly in Peter's pages is a man dependent on the love and support of his family. Even as lesser men fell away and abandoned their oaths to pursue the holy war, the Montfort family, alongside the Count, remained committed. Its members could always rely upon each other. Here was another lesson for Simon: making war was, for the Montforts, a family enterprise. Soon after embarking on his expedition in 1209, the Count had sent for his wife, Alice de Montmorency. For the Count, Alice was (in the words of Peter, who knew her) 'a helpmate like himself . . . in short, pious, wise, and caring'.[31] Her chief role was the raising of troops, providing vital fuel for an expedition that was interminably short of manpower. The task required her to endure the same hardships as the men she recruited. In the summer of 1212 she was bringing foot soldiers from Carcassonne seventy miles north to rendezvous with her husband at Penne. The heat was so intense, and the terrain so hard, that the soldiers were struggling to walk. Alice and her companion, the Count's dear friend Gui of les Vaux-de-Cernay, now bishop of Carcassonne, both dismounted to let the soldiers ride their horses, while they continued on foot. On other occasions, Alice could be found at her husband's side facing the dangers of the front line: at the siege of Termes, and at Toulouse in

1218.[32] She was, effectively, one of the Count's great captains.* We cannot know for sure how unusual Alice was in this respect: through the accounts of her written by Peter and by other chroniclers, she received far more attention than any other noblewoman of the time, but this might be only because most other noblewomen did not have writers to tell of their exploits.[33] But the care that Peter poured into his account of Alice, being so unusual, is important – this was the example crafted for the Montfort children. Simon would have heard the tales of his mother's deeds told second only to those of his father, from the pages of Peter's *History*. The pattern set for him was clear: a woman's place in war was at her husband's side.

Count and Countess were leaders of a family unit. The family was often separated physically: the Count, his sons and brother fought sometimes together, sometimes apart, the Count constantly dispatching and recalling troops from one town to the next across the region to confront the inexhaustible torrent of challenges that faced an army of occupation. The separation of the family was, noted Peter, a source of strain. In the autumn of 1211, the Count was besieged at Castelnaudary, while his wife was almost thirty miles north at Lavaur; Amaury, their eldest boy (who was then ill) ten miles south-east of him at Fanjeaux and their youngest daughter, Petronilla, born during the course of the war, at Montréal with her nursemaid. 'None of them could see each other or give each other any support,' writes Peter, emphasizing – and here was another message for young Simon – that the bond of family, parents and children as well as husband and wife, was of the greatest value; and any great enterprise the Montforts chose to undertake was to be pursued together.[34]

---

* No matter how committed Alice was to their cause, watching her husband and her sons head into battle would always be trying: the night before the Count was due to leave her side to ride for Muret, in order to relieve his besieged garrison there, Alice had a dream that terrified her, in which blood gushed from her arms – an omen, she worried, of her husband's fate. When they woke she told him of it, though he dismissed it as superstition. Here Alice was fulfilling an important, and standard, expectation of a wife, advising and supporting her husband (*PVC*, ch. 449; M. Zerner, 'L'Epouse de Simon de Montfort et la croisade albigeoise', in *Femmes – mariages – lignages. XIIe–XIVe siècles. Mélanges offerts à Georges Duby*, ed. J. Dufournet, A. Joris, P. Toubret and D. Barthélemy (Brussels, 1992), 449–70, at 453–4).

In such undertakings, it was inevitable that children would be exposed to danger, for youth did not exempt a member of the crusader army from the recrimination of southern enemies. Simon's eldest brother, Amaury, in his early teens, had once come perilously close to being killed. In the spring of 1212 he had journeyed with his uncle to Narbonne to attend the consecration of the city's archbishop. One day, Amaury was off exploring by himself ('as any boy might', Peter points out), when he wandered into the deserted palace of Narbonne's lord. He began fiddling with a window, trying to get it open, but it was so rotten that it broke in his hands. The boy left the scene and returned to his lodgings in the house of the Templars. But soon the townspeople ('looking for an excuse to commit mischief', writes Peter) were shouting that Amaury had tried to break into the palace, and turned up at the Templars' house in arms. In fear of his life, the boy put on armour, clambered up the house's tower and hid himself until the townspeople eventually gave up on him.[35] Languedoc at war was not a place where children could play safely.

But Amaury was scarcely any older when he was himself required to fight, around the age of fifteen. At this point his parents had him inducted into the warrior elite and offered him to the Church as a martial instrument of divine will.

According to Peter, the Count decided in the summer of 1213 that the time was right for Amaury to become a knight. The ceremony was to be a grand occasion, involving the whole family, to be witnessed by the biggest audience that could be mustered. It was customary, in order to draw the largest possible crowd, for knightings to be held on major feast days, for (as we are told in a description of a model ceremony, set out in a later chivalric manual) 'the honour of the feast' would encourage a greater attendance, and encourage the prayers of the audience for the candidate.[36] The Count chose 24 June, a day that marked both the Nativity of St John the Baptist and midsummer, and was thus a pivotal point in the cycle of the seasons. It was a wise choice: the crowd that gathered to watch Amaury's knighting was so large that it could not be accommodated inside the ruined town of Castelnaudary, and the Count had to order a number of pavilions to be put up in a meadow outside the town.

It was also customary (something Peter omits to mention) for the candidate to keep vigil the night before the ceremony, praying, fasting and honouring the saint on whose feast day he would be knighted. Early the following morning he would take a ritual bath, whose waters would, like those of the baptismal font, wash him of his sin.[37] Clothed in fine garments, he would then, with the assembled audience, attend Mass. At Amaury's knighting the Mass was celebrated by the bishop of Orléans, assisted by the bishop of Auxerre – celebrants whose rank befitted the status of the candidate's father. Together they celebrated the mystery of the Eucharist in one of the pavilions, before the assembled crowd of knights and churchmen.[38]

It is in what happened next – the crucial moment of the ritual – that Amaury de Montfort's knighting departed from custom, as Peter is keen to point out, 'a novel and unprecedented form of induction into knighthood!' The audience expected to see Amaury kneel before the altar, to be knighted by the most senior or celebrated nobleman present – in this case, the Count himself. The senior knight would take the belted sword and gird the candidate, bestowing the chief accoutrement of knighthood. He would kiss him, then slap him hard, on the neck, to remind him of his promises.[39] But the Count insisted that the bishop of Orléans – not a knight but a churchman – perform this role. The Count took Amaury's right hand, and Countess Alice took his left. Mother and father led their son up to the altar, where they 'offered him to the Lord, requesting the bishop to appoint him a knight in the service of Christ'. The bishop of Orléans, aided by the bishop of Auxerre, then girded Amaury with the sword.[40]

This subversion of the ritual was carefully crafted. It was intended to signal two points central to the Count's identity, and to that of his family. The first was that Amaury was to be, like his father, not an ordinary knight but a knight of Christ. The Christian faith was central to the concept of knighthood; the Church hoped that these armed warriors, skilled in shedding blood, would direct their talents and their energies not against their fellow knights but against the enemies of the faith. Not all knights took the crusader's oath, though many wishing to serve God and the Church, and to test their arm and prove their calibre on the grandest stage, would do so. But

Amaury's knighting signified something particular: for the sons of the Count, fighting for the faith was not optional. It was built into the fabric of their status: to be a Montfort is to be a knight is to be a crusader. This was a family for whom the waging of holy war was now the raison d'être.

The second point was equally important: a partnership with the Church. The way in which the Count worked with churchmen in order to pursue his cause was exemplary, embodying a medieval ideal: the symbiotic relationship between the Church and the knightly order, in which the Church provided direction and authority and the knight provided the sword. For the Count, it was a partnership that was both personal and public. Personal, as we have seen, for the Count's oldest friend was Gui of les Vaux-de-Cernay, abbot of the house his family patronized. Such friendships between noblemen and senior churchmen were not unheard of, but to find them testified so prominently in this account, accompanied by remarks on the depth of the attachment, is unusual. In this respect, too, Simon would follow his father: his two closest friends were bishops, Robert Grosseteste of Lincoln and Walter de Cantilupe of Worcester (see plates 2 and 3).*

But as much as the Count's partnership with the Church was based on personal bonds, it was also proclaimed publicly. He was the Church's champion, and it was the Church's support that imbued his leadership with authority. He was careful to stress this whenever the opportunity arose. In December 1212 he had held something of a celebration of his rulership. His dominion over Languedoc was roughly wrought, by sword and fire, but as lord he was expected to be more than a warrior and a general – he was also to be bringer of order and dispenser of justice. And so he 'summoned the bishops and nobles in his territories to Pamiers . . . to develop good customs in the territories he had won and brought under the Holy Roman Church . . . [and] to promote both the observation of the Christian religion and the maintenance of peace'.[41] At Pamiers, the Count established a council of twelve men who would draw up a set of

---

* Adam Marsh, who was friends with all three, had once told Simon that these two bishops 'favour you among all men with their special friendship': C. H. Lawrence (ed. and trans.), *The Letters of Adam Marsh*, 2 vols. (Oxford, 2006–10), II, 339.

laws by which his lands would be governed. The council comprised
four churchmen (the bishops of Toulouse and Couserans, a Templar
and a Hospitaller), four French knights from amongst the crusaders
and four southerners (two knights and two townsmen). This
representative selection was intended, Peter was careful to note, 'to
remove all suspicion from the hearts of men, since both sides had
representatives amongst those responsible for what was decided'.[*]

Yet, in the Statute of Pamiers itself, the emphasis was altered.
In the opening section, in a formula that is unique amongst the
Count's surviving documents and unusual generally, the Count
declares that he issued the statute 'by the counsel of the venerable
lords, namely the Archbishop of Bordeaux and the bishops of
Toulouse, Carcassonne, Agen, Périgueux, Couserans, Cominges
and Bigorre, and of wise men and others of our barons and leading
men'.[42] Affixed to the fold at the bottom of the parchment (again
this is unusual) are the seals of these eight bishops, lined up
alongside the Count's seal (see plate 4). This statute was meant to
read, to sound and to look like a joint enterprise: the audience
should imagine the Count in his mastery flanked by a mitred troop
in their gold-weaved vestments, wielding croziers alongside his
sword. Again, this was an image that Simon, in the manner of his
father, was to summon time and again, launching the most
important acts of his revolution – the Montfortian Constitution
that established rule by council, and the confirmation of Magna
Carta that sought to render it legitimate – in the visible company
of his episcopal supporters.

This, then, was the way of living that Simon learned from his
father, the father whose name he carried, whose birthright – the
earldom of Leicester – he was to secure, and whose example he
was to follow, when he too became the divinely sanctioned leader
of a holy war. From his father he learned how to keep his family
always at his side, how to choose his friends, how to demonstrate

---

[*] *PVC*, chs. 362–3. This was a matter of presentation rather than of reality. The laws
that were introduced were in part an importation of Parisian customs, and in part an
imposition of neo-Gregorian reform (P. Timbal, *Un conflit d'annexion au Moyen Âge.
L'Application de la coutume de Paris au pays d'Albigeois* (Paris, 1949), 173–6; G. E. M.
Lippiatt, *Simon V of Montfort and Baronial Government, 1195–1218* (Oxford, 2017), 161–8.

his authority, and how to endure as lesser men fell away, cleaving to his oath no matter the personal cost.

*

But Simon also learned a way of dying from his father. It was the worst and best of deaths, for it was death by violence, in his fighting prime, but it was also death in a holy cause: martyrdom, messy and glorious. This was a lesson that Simon had the opportunity to learn too well. By the time that he left his homeland in the Île-de-France and sailed for England, in 1229, when he was about twenty-one, he had lost first his father, in 1218, then two years later his elder brother Gui, who at the age of maybe nineteen had been killed in the continuance of his father's fight besieging Castelnaudary: Gui had stood down his men at the end of a night watch when they were surprised by an attack; Gui and two of his knights, not yet disarmed, beat back the assault and chased the enemy to the ramparts of the town – where, finding that their comrades had not followed, they were surrounded and cut down.* Then, in 1228, Simon's uncle Gui took a lethal arrow wound at Varilhes, near Pamiers.[43] Later Simon was to lose his eldest brother, Amaury, as well, after an expedition to Outremer. This was a terrible rate of attrition at a time when, for knights, death in battle was rare. It was a result, in part, of bad luck – but also of the Montforts' choice to dedicate themselves to holy war, in which chivalric principles did not apply and so death was much more likely.

For those who remained to remember those who fell, the loss was made tangible in the family mausoleum. This was at Haute-Bruyère, a nunnery founded by the Count's ancestor near the family

* Gui died on 20 July 1220, according to the necrology of the priory of Cassan (C. de Vic and J. Vaissète (eds.), *Histoire générale de Languedoc*, rev. edn., 16 vols. (Toulouse, 1872–1904), V, c.36). The story of his death was apparently circulating in France – it is found in the Cotton continuation of William the Breton's *Gesta Regis Philippi*, for which see: H.-F. Delaborde (ed.), *Gesta Regis Philippi: Oeuvres de Rigaud et de Guillaume le Breton*, 2 vols. (Paris, 1882–5), I, 330. The continuator puts Gui's age at his death as 'around twenty-two' – I have followed Michel Roquebert, who estimates he was nineteen or twenty or perhaps younger (M. Roquebert, *L'Épopée cathare*, 4 vols. (Toulouse and Paris, 1970–89), III, 239).

lands, and where his mother and father were buried.* The Count
had originally been laid to rest in the basilica of St Nazaire in
Carcassonne (a fragment of his first tomb survives there – see plate
5), but when Amaury left Languedoc in 1229 he had his father's
remains exhumed and translated to Haute-Bruyère. The building
and its tombs are gone, destroyed in the Revolution, but a precious
record of the mausoleum survives: a copy of a list drawn up in the
early fourteenth century of the patrons buried and remembered at
the house. It describes the tomb of the Count 'who died in the
Albigeois, who lies beneath the great tomb which has an effigy on
the right of the altar', and that 'of Countess Alice, his wife, who
lies at his side, on the left'. The list records the death of the Count's
brother, Gui, who was not buried at Haute-Bruyère but whose
anniversary was marked by a service in the house, before noting
that an effigy of Amaury, the eldest son of Alice and the Count

---

* Burial at the Cistercian monastery of Vaux-de-Cernay would have been an option
for the Count and his family; they chose Haute-Bruyère in part, perhaps, because it
was the family mausoleum, and in part because burial in a nunnery was considered
preferable. This was possibly because male Cistercian houses had such strict rules on
the admittance of visitors, who were allowed into the abbey precinct only once a year,
on Palm Sunday. In patronizing a male Cistercian house but choosing burial in a
nunnery, the Montforts were in good company – it was a practice followed by the
Angevin royal family of England (Henry II, Richard I and Eleanor of Aquitaine,
together with Henry III's mother, Isabella d'Angoulême, were buried at Fontevraud,
chief house of the eponymous order), while Cistercian nunneries were founded and
patronized by various aristocratic families of France during this period, as well as
Alfonso VIII of Castile and his queen, Eleanor of England, who founded the Abbey
of Las Huelgas, near Burgos, as their mausoleum in 1187 (it was incorporated into the
Cistercian Order in 1191). Their daughter, Blanche of Castile, queen of Louis VIII of
France, followed them in founding Cistercian nunneries and selecting one, Maubuisson,
for her burial, which became a family mausoleum second to Saint-Denis. For the
burial of the Montfort family, see: J.-M. Bienvenu, 'L'ordre de Fontevraud et la
Normandie au XIIe siècle', *Annales de Normandie*, 25, 3–15, at 5–7, and D. Power, *The
Norman Frontier in the Twelfth and Early Thirteenth Centuries* (Cambridge, 2004), 331–2;
for the royal burials at Fontevraud and Las Huelgas, see: N. Vincent, 'The Plantagenets
and the priories of Fontevraud: old connections, new resonances?', in *Fontevraud et ses
prieurés*, ed. C. Andrault-Schmitt (Presses universitaires de Rennes, forthcoming) (I
am very grateful to Professor Vincent for allowing me to see a copy of this article in
advance of publication); and for patronage of Cistercian nunneries and burial therein
see: L. Grant, *Blanche of Castile* (New Haven and London, 2016), 210–19, 224–5.

and Simon's elder brother, lies on the right of the altar (we shall hear more of this later). It then records 'count Gui of Bigorre, brother of the aforesaid count Amaury, who lies at the feet of count Simon his father' (his remains had been retrieved from the ramparts of Castelnaudary and delivered to his elder brother, on a litter draped in purple, for burial). One last name to be remembered in prayer is listed here: 'count Simon of Leicester, who died in England'.[44]

The Montforts' deaths in holy war were celebrated in the bodies brought together at Haute-Bruyère: a family community, made of fallen *crucesignati* caught in stone. Simon would have visited the mausoleum. Looking upon the faces of his family, he would be reminded that a path had been set before him.[45] Their tombs, like the deeds of his father described by Peter of les Vaux-de-Cernay, were a challenge: to match the feats of those who went before him, so as to stand proudly in their company – in life, and in death.

2

A New Kingdom

Simon almost disappears from our view from the moment of his father's death in 1218 until the late spring of 1229, when he left his home at Montfort-en-Yvelines for England. By this time he was one of the few Montforts left alive. His father, an elder brother, Gui, and his uncle, also Gui, had all died in Languedoc, as we have seen. In 1221, his mother too had died, and his younger brother, Robert, had followed her in 1226. Simon's eldest brother, Amaury, was still alive, as were their two sisters, Amicia and Petronilla, and their cousin, Philip, son of their uncle Gui. The Montfort family army, over which the Count had presided but a few short years before, had been halved.

It was left now to the young survivors to carve for themselves a life, a career and a reputation fitting for their family name. Simon's plan was to head to England. At twenty-one, he was of age, and determined to secure the delivery of the inheritance that his father had never been allowed to hold: the earldom of Leicester. The Count had been recognized as earl and apportioned half the Leicester lands, but his obedience to the king of France meant that he could not assume his inheritance – and so King John had taken the Count's estates into his royal hands, and fed from the welcome profits.* It was a deprivation that neither the Count nor his family

---

* The claim reached back to the point in 1204 when the last man to bear the title earl of Leicester, Robert son of Petronilla, had died without children. His estates had been divided between his two sisters, Amice and Margaret, and Amice was the mother of the Count, so she was Simon's grandmother. Margaret was married to Saer de Quincy, earl of Winchester, who died in 1219 (D. Crouch, 'The battle of the countesses:

ever accepted: decades later, when Simon spoke of it, he told how John had 'taken [the earldom] from my father, without judgement and without it being duly forfeit to the king, but he did it according to his will'.[1]

With the Count's death the claim fell to Amaury, as the eldest son. But Amaury was bound wholeheartedly to the king of France; there was no chance of the English king allowing him to take possession of the earldom. Simon, though, had little land in France, and so he agreed to exchange what he had with Amaury in return for the family stake in Leicester. Half of the earldom's lands were now beyond recovery (having been apportioned to a co-heir in 1206–7) but the other half, and the title, remained to be won.

*

And so Simon came before the king of England, Henry III, son of King John. In the spring of 1229, Henry, too, was just twenty-one and had been governing alone for two short years. He had come to the throne thirteen years before, aged only nine, and so a council of prelates and magnates had been formed to steer the ship of state on his behalf. Henry had not emerged from this period of minority rule, assuming his full regal authority, until the beginning of 1227.

He was governing a land in the throes of a profound transformation. The rebuilding of the kingdom, atop the ashes of John's reign, was still in progress. John's rule had been one of terror and exploitation. On several infamous occasions the king had violated the norms of proper conduct – not only had he executed noble prisoners but he had done so by starving them to death. His daily manner of ruling had been equally resented, distinguished by a willingness to act without taking counsel from his bishops and barons, his levying of taxes without their consent and, overall, a general readiness to rule according to his own wishes rather than the law. This was the point that Simon was making when he complained decades later of his father's dispossession, saying that John had seized his father's lands

---

the division of the Honour of Leicester, March–December 1207', in *Rulership and Rebellion in the Anglo-Norman World*, ed. P. Dalton and D. E. Luscombe (Farnham, 2015), 179–211).

'without judgement' and 'according to his will' – it was a distinction that made John, according to the established definition, a tyrant.[2] The hostility of John's subjects had been such that, in 1212, a band of disaffected barons had plotted to overthrow him (reports of the plot are patchy, but it appears that they planned to kill him on an expedition in Wales or else to abandon him on the field of battle to meet his death at the hands of the unchivalric Welsh). They had chosen a man to replace him, too: none other than the Count, Simon's father.[3] He bore all the qualities that John did not – martial prowess, leadership, fidelity and a willingness to work with, rather than oppose, the Church.

Three years after this failed plot, and following further martial failures, by the spring of 1215 John's barons were in open rebellion. They won sufficient ground to force John to negotiate. The result was a compromise, hammered out in a meadow by the Thames, in which John made a series of promises to be a better king. These were put to parchment as a charter (a legal grant by one party to another): the Charter of Liberties, which was the first incarnation of the document later to be known as Magna Carta. This part peace treaty, part purported act of royal grace was the best that could be achieved in the circumstances, but it contained a threat that was too scandalous to be suffered by the crown: the appointment of a baronial cadre of twenty-five with the power to seize John's lands and castles if he broke the terms of the Charter. This 'security for peace' (as it was called in the Charter) threatened the very order of society, providing ample grounds for John's successful appeal to the pope for its annulment. Faced with the prospect of an unshackled King John, the barons once again placed their hopes for a better kingdom in a new candidate for the crown. This time, it was Louis, son of King Philip Augustus and heir to France.

Louis was, like the Count, everything that John was not, and he boasted the resources of the Capetian crown (newly inflated by the conquest of John's continental lands), which would fund a large-scale invasion. At the invitation of the rebel barons, then, Louis and his army landed on the shore of Kent in May 1216. Before long he had taken half the kingdom, aided by the flocking to his banner of John's own men and ministers. There followed a year of civil war, punctuated by John's death, from dysentery, in October, and the hurried crowning of the nine-year-old Henry. The future of the dynasty was perilous but, fortunately for the child king, a clutch of highly able loyalists was able to rescue his realm (they included William Marshal who, as we have seen, defeated Louis's forces at Lincoln). Over the decade that followed, a cohort of dedicated ministers had stitched the tattered pieces of the kingdom back together. They brought the rebels in and by increments began to rebuild the machinery of royal government, weathering further rebellion and restoring peace.[4]

But the new kingdom they constructed from the ruins of the old was of a different kind, for John's rule and the rebellion it provoked had proved one thing overall: unjust and oppressive kingship would not be tolerated. And so Henry's ministers, with acute political vision, made the foundation of the young king's government the very Charter of Liberties that had been rejected by his father. No sooner had they had Henry crowned than they issued a new version of the Charter, in November 1216. In so doing they transformed the rebels' demands into a royal manifesto, promising a new kind of kingship – a king who would never arrest, nor imprison, nor disseise, nor outlaw, nor exile, nor in any other way destroy any free person of his kingdom, except by the lawful judgement of their peers or the law of the land. At the same time, of course, the ministers removed those chapters that threatened the integrity of the crown (chief amongst them the 'security for peace'): the new king would rule justly, but it would be he who did the ruling. The commitment was reaffirmed in a new version of the Charter, in November 1217, this time with a partner, the Charter of the Forest, which set limits on the scope and brutality of arbitrary forest law (the need to distinguish between the two brought a new title for the senior document: Magna Carta, literally 'big charter').[5] The final, enduring version was issued in 1225. The rebels might have lost the war, but they had won their prize.

The government's acceptance of the Charter was transformative. It set English kingship on an untrodden path, on which king and subjects over the following decades were to test their footing, through impassioned argument and, occasionally, rebellion. This process was a negotiation, the very fact of which demonstrated that the balance of power between king and subjects had shifted irrevocably. In this

unfamiliar world, Henry was still growing into his role. Nobody
yet knew the kind of king he was to be.

*

Simon, then, young and untested, stood before an equally inex-
perienced king. We cannot know exactly when or where their first
meeting took place – but, based on an account that Simon himself
gave some years later, it was between early May and the autumn
of 1229.[6] Simon, as he later recalled, 'asked my lord the king if he
was willing to give me the inheritance from my father'. But he was
to meet with disappointment. The king, according to Simon, 'replied
that he could not do so because he had given it to the earl of
Chester and to his heirs by his charter. On hearing this, I returned
without having found goodwill.'[7]

Although Simon – so keen to recover what he felt was owed to
him – might not have seen it, Henry's response could not have
been otherwise. King John had granted custody of the Leicester
estates to Ranulf, earl of Chester, in 1215; in 1227 Henry had
confirmed the grant by charter, promising at the same time that
'he would not admit into his peace the earl of Leicester, to whom
the aforesaid part [of the Leicester lands] pertains'.[8] The king was
duty bound to uphold the grant – indeed, he was bound to do so
by the terms of Magna Carta, in which he had promised that 'no
free person shall be . . . deprived of their free tenement . . . except
by the lawful judgement of their peers or the law of the land'. For
Henry to rescind the grant simply because he now favoured Simon's
claim would be to act no better than his father ('without judgement'
and 'according to his will', in Simon's words). And Henry would
have no wish, in any case, to act harshly towards the earl of Chester,
who was a resilient supporter of the English crown and well
respected, as well as one of the greatest potentates of England.[*]

---

[*] Ranulf had been amongst the few loyal counsellors who had gathered round John's
deathbed, entrusted with preserving England for the young Henry. When he endorsed
the second issue of Magna Carta at Bristol in 1216, he was named in the list of lay
witnesses second only to William Marshal, and he went on to fight for Henry at the
Battle of Lincoln.

And so it might have ended there, with the young Simon returning, frustrated, to his home at Montfort-en-Yvelines. But he persevered. The situation was not quite so dismal as he later framed it: the king had not, in fact, granted the Leicester lands to Ranulf and his heirs, but only to Ranulf for his lifetime. And Ranulf had no heirs – or, rather, he had no children. Now at the age of sixty, he was pondering how his estates would be divided upon his death. In such circumstances he was considerate of Simon's hopes. So too was the king. By February 1230 Simon had managed to secure recognition of his right from Henry, who issued letters stating that the lands would be Simon's if the earl of Chester would deliver them. Witness to this statement was Ranulf himself: a declaration of his sympathy for Simon's claim.[9] Simon pressed on with his advantage, sending his knight, Amaury de Misternun, to persuade the king that Simon wanted to be his man. The mission was successful. When Henry wrote to Simon in early April 1230, he did so assuming that an agreement would be concluded (even if the timing and specifics were yet to be determined), for he promised Simon an annual payment of almost £270, 'until you receive the earldom of Leicester, according to what is provided when you should be with us in England'.[10] That sum was a little more than half of the income that Simon might expect to raise from the Leicester lands, but it was certainly worth having. It was, moreover, a demonstrable investment in him by the king.

The king's enthusiasm in the early months of 1230 was founded upon his hopes of reclaiming his own inheritance. He was gathering a mighty army, which he would lead across the Channel to retake the lands lost by his father: Brittany, Normandy and Poitou. Fortuitously, Simon had come of age and made his bid at the very time when Henry was in a mood to welcome men who could be succour to his cause.[11] While Simon was not expected to take part in this particular campaign – his relationship with the king was barely kindled, and the matter of the Leicester lands hung undecided – in the longer term his connections amongst the families of France, as well as his manpower, could support Henry's efforts to restore the cross-Channel dominion of his ancestors. From Henry's point of view, Simon also held a precious asset: his name. Simon might have been young and (as far as we can tell) untried in arms, but the name Simon de Montfort was illustrious. The last Simon de Montfort, earl (or count) of Leicester, had been amongst the most distinguished figures of the age and in England he had been so admired that he was chosen in 1212 as a candidate for kingship. Simon, as his son and namesake, bore the air of his celebrity.

Simon's chance to press his claim further appeared almost immediately. At the turn of May 1230 Henry sailed for Brittany with an armada. He had mustered a force of formidable size and status, bringing with him his brother, Richard, earl of Cornwall, the earls of Ferrers, Albermarle and Huntingdon, his chief minister Hubert de Burgh along with the renowned knight Philip d'Aubigny, as well as Ranulf, earl of Chester, and Ranulf's constable of Chester, the great baron John de Lacy.[12] Henry landed in Brittany, at Saint-Malo, on 3 May. He stayed there for a few days before heading south to Nantes, in the latter part of the month, and then by August onward south to the Plantagenet stronghold of Bordeaux.[13] At some point during the course of these summer weeks, the earl of Chester detached from the main body of Henry's army and pressed eastward, towards the border with Normandy and the castle of Saint-James-de-Beuvron, seat of his ancestors, lost to him since 1204. Ranulf managed to reclaim it – we do not know how, but we know it happened because, according to Simon's later testimony, this is where they met.

It was the earl of Chester whom Simon needed to persuade, for the king could do nothing more without Ranulf's gracious acceptance of the young man's claims. Simon, as we have seen, had already been given cause to hope that Ranulf would look kindly upon him. And so he set out from Montfort-en-Yvelines, riding perhaps for a week or more to cover the 160 miles to Saint-James. 'There I asked,' Simon later recounted, 'if I could find his goodwill in having my inheritance', to which Ranulf responded that 'I had a greater right than him . . . and the entire grant that the king had given him in this matter he relinquished, by which he received me as his man'.[14]

It was a generous concession. It might have been based upon a deal – for, at the time of Ranulf's death, some six years later, Simon owed the earl of Chester £200, perhaps a payment for Ranulf's deliverance of the lands, or compensation for the income lost. Yet, since Ranulf also bequeathed to Simon a wardship (the right to administer the estates of the underage heir of one of Ranulf's tenants), he was also granting Simon the means to pay.[15] Certainly, Simon's account of his relations with the earl of Chester is scrupulous in presenting Ranulf in the best of lights. We can readily understand the fondness of his memories: Ranulf was under no compulsion to show kindness, but chose to anyway. And he went further still: Ranulf (Simon later recalled) 'in the following August took me with him to England and asked the king to receive me as his man regarding the inheritance of my father'.[16] Ranulf was acting as Simon's sponsor: introducing him to the court, helping him set his case before the king and adding the weight of his authority to the request.

And so, while Simon waited until the following August to entreat the king again, his elder brother, Amaury, smoothed his path, sending letters to Henry making clear that he had handed his rights in England over to Simon, and reminding Henry that Simon held no lands from the king of France.[17] In early July 1231, Simon was at Ranulf's side readying to depart (we catch a glimpse of him, acting as witness to one of Ranulf's charters at Saint-Aubin, a few miles from Simon's home at Montfort-en-Yvelines).[18] Shortly afterwards, Ranulf took Simon with him onward to Saint-James-de-Beuvron, and thence across the Channel. Together they made their way over the breadth of England, for they were to meet the king on the border with Wales.

Henry was here, in August 1231, reinforcing his defences in the Marches, the region that formed the border zone between English rule and unruly Wales. Simon met him at Castle Matilda (named for the great marcher potentate, Matilda de Hay, who had defended it masterfully from the Welsh on behalf of Henry's father). It was here, on 13 August or shortly before, that Henry received Simon's homage.[19]

This was a transformative act in Simon's life, binding him and Henry until death or diffidation (the official renunciation of fealty, made by either party if the other failed to keep faith). It was probably performed in the hall of the great keep, or perhaps outside, in the castle's courtyard (all that remains now of Castle Matilda are the earthworks, so a feat of imagination is required). As was proper for an act of such importance, the event was witnessed by a great audience: Peter des Roches, bishop of Winchester and formidable servant of the crown; Hubert de Burgh, the king's chief minister and earl of Kent; Ranulf, earl of Chester; the earls of Surrey, Derby, Aumale, and Hereford; John de Lacy, constable of Chester; as well as knights of the royal household and the retinues of the greater men.[20]

The performance of the act would have followed the standard form. As the witnesses looked on, Simon would have knelt before the king, placing his hands palms together and proffering them to Henry to encircle with his own. This was a gesture of a mutual bond: of reverence and service on one side and protection on the other (preserved even now in the English posture of prayer, which symbolizes homage to the heavenly Lord).

'Sire,' Simon would have said, 'I become your man in respect to the tenement I hold of you, and I will bear you fidelity and loyalty in life and limb and earthly honour, and I will bear you fidelity against all men.'

'And I receive you as my man', Henry would have answered, 'and I will bear you fidelity, as my man.'

Henry would then have kissed Simon, as a sign of that mutual fidelity. Simon, then, would have delivered his oath, repeating his commitment to hold faithful to his lord in life and limb, this time with his right hand held to a sacred object – a Bible or relic – calling upon God to bear witness to the promise and staking his soul upon his good faith.*

The two men now were bound by mutual obligation: Simon's to serve Henry – to offer counsel and to provide, should the need arise, knights and men to serve in Henry's army in numbers concomitant with the amount of land he held – just as Henry was obliged to defend Simon's interests as if they were his own, and to be a

---

* This account of the act of homage is based on two texts: the law book known as Bracton (written *c.*1230) (G. E. Woodbine (ed.) and S. E. Thorne (trans.), *Bracton: On the Laws and Customs of England*, 4 vols. (Cambridge, MA, 1968–77), II, 232) and L. N. Rapetti (ed.), *Li Livres de jostice et de plet* (Paris, 1850), 254–5; see too: J. Le Goff, 'The symbolic ritual of vassalage' in his *Time, Work and Culture in the Middle Ages*, trans. A. Goldhammer (Chicago, 1980), 237–87, at 240–3. The exact form of words spoken varied, as the author of Bracton makes clear – the exchange given here is an approximation.

good lord to Simon, seeking his counsel, showing him largesse and treating him with justice.

Their bond was rooted in the land that Simon now held from the king, the Montfort half of the lands of the Leicester earldom. For the right to enter into his inheritance, Simon was expected to pay 'relief', a customary sum owed by the heir to the lord from whom the land was held (the medieval equivalent of inheritance tax). The size of the sum required to enter into an earldom had been set by Magna Carta at £100. Because Simon was entering into only half the Leicester lands, the figure named was £50. This was an equitable sum, though not a trifling one for someone in Simon's position, amounting to around 10 per cent of the annual income of the lands he was receiving. And so here the king was generous: he did not press Simon for payment and, a few years later, in 1242, wrote off the debt entirely.[21]

Simon's position was transformed. He had been a near-landless younger son, and was now a baron of the English realm. His elevation was not yet complete, for Henry had not granted him the right to bear the title of earl (a sensible precaution on Henry's part, since Simon and his loyalty were as yet untested). Henry would not officially bestow the grant until 1238 when, on Christmas Day, he would make Simon the gift of the third penny of Leicester, the customary levy from the profits of the shire due to its earl.[22] Still, this delay would not have been of overriding concern to Simon, for the right to bear the title of earl was one more of acclamation than of royal recognition; Simon's father had called himself count of Leicester to convey his status amongst the highest ranks of Europe's potentates, and the title had come easily to those who knew him; likewise, Simon's brother, Amaury, styled himself 'count of Montfort'. Simon himself would begin to use the designation by October 1236 (two years before he was officially granted it), by which time he had found his feet in England, and the usage was accepted by the king.[23]

Simon now held lands worth around £500 per annum.[24] This put him, in terms of wealth, only amongst England's middling barons. But he had been admitted into England's political elite.

*

His first task was to establish himself as lord of Leicester. He did so, in one of his earliest acts, by ordering the expulsion of Jewish people from his town. This he announced in a charter bearing his seal. It was issued at some point before October 1232, within a year or so of Simon's entry into the Leicester inheritance. It survives in Leicester today, having been kept for almost eight centuries by the people of the town. Written in an elegant though uneven hand, perhaps by a clerk brought into Simon's service or else borrowed for the occasion from the staff of the local diocese, it reads:

> Simon de Montfort, son of Count Simon de Montfort, lord of Leicester, to all the faithful in Christ who will see or hear this present page, greetings in the Lord. You are all to know that I, for the health of my soul, and those of my ancestors and successors, have granted, and in this present charter confirmed, on my own behalf and on behalf of my heirs in perpetuity, that no Jew or Jewess, in my time, nor in the time of any of my heirs until the ending of the world, may live, abide, or obtain residence within the liberty of the vill of Leicester.[25]

The grant is followed by the names of five witnesses, either men whom Simon had taken into his service or tenants of Leicester lands who had recently performed homage to their new lord. The list is headed by Sir Amaury de Mittun, probably the Amaury de Misternun who had represented Simon's case to Henry in 1230, and it includes a chaplain, Sir Roger Blund, as well as a man who (we can assume by his name) was a Leicester tenant who had recently performed homage to Simon, William de Miravall, and one William de Aquila.* These were early members of the compact circle who would be Simon's counsellors, confidants and servants, and who now endorsed the grant recorded in the charter.[26]

The expulsion was inspired by a growing sense amongst those

---

* Miravall or Merevale was the site of a Cistercian abbey in north Warwickshire, about twenty miles west of Leicester ('Merevale' (Warwickshire, Helmingford Hundred, Atherstone Division), in *The Historical Gazetteer of England's Place-Names*, available at: http://placenames.org.uk/id/placename/13/002725 (accessed 4 Nov. 2018).

in authority that Jewish people ought to be segregated from Christian – or, at the least, marked out (see plate 6). This particular form of persecution was quite new. Jewish people across Europe had suffered violence sporadically for centuries, but not at the hands of those who wielded governmental power. It was mobs of knightly or lower status that, in vicious bursts, set upon local Jewish communities, at once venting their antipathy and, through the destruction of legal documents, nullifying the debts they owed to Jewish moneylenders. The results were often lethal. In one notorious episode in 1190, a horde had come for the Jewish inhabitants of York, forcing them to take refuge in the city's castle. Assailed and hopeless, many chose to take their own lives rather than die at the hands of their persecutors, while those surrendering were quickly cut down.[27] But such attacks were never sanctioned by those in authority. The Church strictly forbade such violence, in line with divine decree.* And in England, Jewish people were protected by the king himself, for they were crown property (Richard I, who was king in 1190, had been furious about the York attack – an assault on his property was an assault on his authority).

By the early thirteenth century, however, the dynamic was shifting across Europe, as governments increasingly concerned themselves with the activities of Jewish people.[28] This manifested, firstly, in the attempts of certain lords to convert those of their domain. Henry III was to be committed to this cause – even founding, in 1232, a house for Jewish converts in London.[29] And there is evidence that Simon's mother, Alice de Montmorency, had taken a similar interest. An account written in the later thirteenth century in Languedoc records how, in 1217, she had imprisoned the Jewish inhabitants of Toulouse in order to force them to convert to the Christian faith.

---

* As Robert Grosseteste would explain in the letter discussed below, the Lord had assured Cain (who symbolized the Jewish people, because his murder of Abel prefigured the killing of Christ by the Jewish inhabitants of Jerusalem) that if he were killed his murderer would be punished sevenfold, and had marked Cain so that those he encountered would know not to lay a hand on him. The Jewish people were also, as St Augustine argued, the bearers of the Old Testament, which prophesied the coming of Jesus Christ, and were thus witnesses to the Christian faith (F. A. C. Mantello and J. Goering (eds.), *The Letters of Robert Grosseteste, Bishop of Lincoln* (Toronto, 2010), 67–8).

Those children under six years old were handed over to priests for baptism, while adults and older children were threatened with death if they did not agree to her demand. According to the account, fifty-seven people submitted to conversion, while those who refused were condemned to death. The process was halted, however, when Alice received orders from her husband to desist and release the captives – an order that came from the papal legate.[30]

This episode reflects a tension between the leaders of the Church and those nobles they encouraged to defend the Christian faith. The Church, as we have seen, forbade violence against Jewish people (a mandate that must have prompted the papal legate's intervention in Toulouse). But, at the same time, it was forming legislation that encouraged Christian antipathy. Two years before Alice took it upon herself to convert the Jewish people of Toulouse, in 1215 Pope Innocent III had voiced concern that 'in some provinces a difference of dress distinguishes Jews or Saracens from Christians, but in certain others such confusion has developed that they are indistinguishable. Whence it sometimes happens that by mistake Christians unite with Jewish or Saracen women and Jews or Saracens with Christian.' Innocent decreed, therefore, that 'in order that so reprehensible and outrageous a mixing cannot for the future spread under cover of the excuse of an error of this kind . . . such people of either sex in every Christian province and at all times shall be distinguished from other people by the character of their dress in public'.[31]

The English government had been the first to implement the papal ruling, encouraged by the many bishops who were committed to implementing Innocent's reforms. And so, in 1218, it was decreed by young Henry's government 'that all Jews, wherever they walk or ride . . . should wear on their chest on their outer garments two emblems in the form of white tablets made of linen cloth, or parchment, so that in this way Jews may be clearly distinguished from Christians'. This was the first order in Europe to dictate the wearing of a Jewish badge.[32]

Henry III's government was, in fact, less concerned with implementing the decree than with charging Jewish people money for exemptions. This prompted a stern letter from the pope in 1221, in which Honorius III (Innocent's successor) chastised the royal council and iterated the concerns of his predecessor that the continued lack of distinction in clothing led Christian men to mingle with Jewish women and Jewish men with Christian women.[33] The archbishop of Canterbury, Stephen Langton, dismayed at the royal council's lack of action (it had been he who had obtained the papal reprimand), pushed on himself with the demarcation of England's Jewish population. In 1222 he issued a decree specifying the size of the badge that Jewish people were to wear (two by four inches). And, in an attempt to compel Jewish inhabitants of his province to obey, he apparently forbade Christian townspeople from trading with or selling food to those Jewish people who refused to wear the badge.[34]

It was in this climate, in which those who ruled were encouraged vigorously by spiritual authorities to prevent the mixing of Jews and Christians, that Simon decreed that Leicester's Jewish inhabitants should be banished. Indeed, it is possible that he was working in concert with a senior local churchman. For, shortly after Simon issued his decree, the dean of Leicester can be found writing sternly to the countess of Winchester, Margaret de Quincy: she held the other half of the Leicester lands and had allowed the Jewish exiles to settle on her property in the town's suburbs. The dean's letter contained a vociferous endorsement of Simon's actions and a rebuke for the countess, supported by an extensive scholarly argument.

The author of the letter was Robert Grosseteste. Robert was a celebrated scholar, learned in medicine, physics, mathematics, astronomy and theology. He was also a pastor committed fiercely to his duties, standing apart – even in an age in which English prelates were uncommonly dedicated to their pastoral cause – for the intensity with which he felt his duty to his flock: as he proclaimed to the pope himself, he knew he would have to stand before the Lord and answer for each and every soul under his care.[35] Robert was soon to be appointed bishop of Lincoln, in 1235, and was already in his mid-sixties; his lack of social status (he was from a peasant family) had slowed his advancement, but he would go on to rule the diocese for almost twenty years. By the time of his death in 1253 he would be known as one of the greatest scholars and pastors of the age.[36]

Robert was to be one of Simon's closest friends. Like his father, Simon was forming close friendships with leading churchmen, friendships that would shape both his inner world and his public career. Apart from Robert, he became close to two other churchmen: Walter de Cantilupe (who would be elected bishop of Worcester in 1237), and Adam Marsh, whom Simon would meet at some point in the next few years, when Adam joined the Franciscan Order and took up the study of theology at Oxford under Robert Grosseteste's tutelage. In a later letter, Adam would remind Simon that Robert and Walter 'favour you among all men with their special friendship'.[37]

Simon's first meeting with Robert probably came as soon as Simon entered into the Leicester lands. Robert, as dean of Leicester, held responsibility for the business of the Church in the town, and so was well placed to advise Simon both on spiritual matters and on the ruling of his estates. It was Robert, then, who perhaps encouraged Simon to expel the Jewish people from the town. Indeed, the echo of the advice that Robert might have given can be heard in his letter to the countess of Winchester, who had undermined Simon's decree by allowing the Jewish exiles to settle on her lands: 'it is the duty of a Christian prince to use his power to rescue Christians from oppression by unbelievers . . . It is his duty to respect the Lord's sentence regarding the penalty imposed on the Jews and not to weaken it by exalting them.' Those rulers who failed in their duty ought to beware, for 'princes who indulge them or favour their usurious exactions from Christians should know that they are themselves guilty of the sin of the Jews and thus will share in their punishment . . . And, in the words of all the holy commentators, those who have the power to prevent something and do not do so are to be understood as consenting to it.' It would be worse still if the ruler in question were ever to raise money from the Jewish people of his dominion, for 'princes, too, who receive some of the usury extorted by Jews from Christians, live by robbery and mercilessly eat, drink, and clothe themselves in the blood of those whom they were obliged to protect. From these princes, as the prophet says, *the Lord will avert his eyes when they stretch out their hands to him and, though they multiply their prayers, he will not hear them; for their hands are covered with blood* [Isa. 1: 15].'[38]

The force of Robert's words speaks of the pressure being brought to bear on rulers – both directly by senior churchmen and by the prevailing sentiment of the age – to enforce segregation. Henry III was himself to follow suit, in April 1233. The king issued a decree that 'no Jew may remain in our kingdom unless he is able to serve the king, and find good pledges for his fidelity. Other Jews, who have nothing whence they can serve the king, are to leave the kingdom before the coming feast of Michaelmas [29 September] . . . so that if they delay they are to be taken in chains and not released without special mandate.'[39] Henry probably intended the ruling more as a statement of sentiment than a practical directive, for at this time the Jewish people of his kingdom were still (in his terms) 'useful' to the crown, providing him with funds through tallages (a tax the king could levy as he wished): between 1241 and 1255, the Jewish communities of England were to provide over £73,000 for the royal coffers.[40] It would not be until later in the century, in 1290, that England's Jewish people could be pronounced entirely 'unuseful' to the crown, and their banishment from England be enacted. By this point English kings had wrung the wealth from their Jewish property, overseeing the conversion of all those who chose the Christian faith over destitution, and so whittling the Jewish population down to a fraction of its former size.[41]

Such acts of banishment, great or small, were a demonstration of the aristocracy's credentials as Christian rulers, showing concern for the wellbeing of their subjects and a willingness to follow the instruction of the Church. But they were also a statement of dominion: a public exhibition of the ruler's power to control the population of his lands. Simon's choosing to do this almost immediately upon entering his inheritance, and his ability to have the order executed, impressed his mastery upon his new domain. He had arrived.

3

Love

Simon spent the next three years establishing his place in England and, by 1236, had found his way to court. He had spent a little time there since his accession to the Leicester lands, and had even passed Christmas with the royal household in 1232, at Worcester.[1] But he now began to occupy a regular place amongst the men and women who stood around the king. The beginning came that January, with the king's marriage to Eleanor of Provence. The wedding and the crowning of the queen that followed were to be grand occasions – heralding, it was to be hoped, the provision of an heir to secure the kingdom. The choice of royal bride also boded well. Eleanor, a young woman of around twelve, was one of four daughters and co-heirs of the count of Savoy, and her eldest sister had been married already to the king of France, Louis IX, giving cause to hope that Eleanor's marriage to Henry would open a newly amicable phase of Anglo-French relations. Eleanor and Henry were married on 14 January 1236 at Canterbury, in a ceremony celebrated by the archbishop of Canterbury, Edmund of Abingdon, attended by nobles of the kingdom.[2]

Simon was probably present at the wedding, and he was certainly part of the festivities that followed six days later when, in the most splendid of celebrations, Eleanor was crowned queen of England. London, its streets cleaned of muck, its buildings decked with flags and banners, was bursting with people eager to see the spectacle. Hordes of citizens and visitors pressed towards the royal couple, seeking a closer view. They were kept apart from the parade by John de Lacy, the constable of Chester, who carried a ceremonial staff for the purpose. John's was one of several prestigious formal roles held by a select number of nobles, passed down from father to son. The new earl of Chester, Ranulf's nephew (Ranulf had died in 1232), processed before the king carrying the legendary sword of Edward the Confessor, named Curtein (clasping it not naked as a martial instrument but within its bejewelled scabbard, pointing downwards – see plate 7); the earl of Pembroke, the marshal of England, walked with him, his own staff in his hand, to clear a path for the king as they processed through Westminster Abbey to where the archbishop of Canterbury, with his bishops and the abbots of the kingdom in attendance, would crown Eleanor queen.[3]

It was after the coronation that Simon took his part. He had inherited the honorary title Steward of England and, with it, the right to supervise the washing of hands at the royal banquet. With hundreds of England's most illustrious men and women gathered in Westminster Hall, ready for the revelry to come and thinking of the rich and varied dishes they would soon enjoy, Simon helped the king to wash his hands. This was no menial role, for such an office brought the incumbent close to the monarch and made him essential to the ritual of the feast. Perhaps Simon himself provided the aquamanile and basin, whose material and workmanship would need to be of fitting standard to convey his own prestige to such illustrious company (see plate 8).[4] All those close by would have seen Simon, at the beginning of the meal, pour water over Henry's hands into the dish below. This grandest of occasions pushed Simon to the foreground of the public stage, and showed his right to take his place at the centre of the court.

When the coronation feast was over, Simon remained at Westminster. His presence is recorded in the witness lists to royal charters, which declare the names of the more prestigious or prominent people attending upon the king, from bishops, earls and barons to royal officers and household knights. The lists describe not only Simon's presence amidst this group but also his status within it, for this was a culture concerned acutely with hierarchy, and so the names within each list were carefully arranged: first the archbishop of Canterbury, followed by his bishops in an order negotiated on the basis of their date of consecration, status of diocese and place at court; then the earls, according to the size and status of their earldom and their closeness to the king; and then the barons (those who held sizeable lands directly from the king without grand title) before household officers and knights. The lists produced in the days following the queen's coronation name the archbishop of Canterbury, five bishops, and six earls, before barons and officers: Simon appears at the head of the baronial number, in the highest position possible for a man without an earldom, and pressing close to the greater status.

The witness lists record that Simon remained at court after the greater part of this company departed. They reveal too that he had found a new companion and sponsor, with whom he remained in the king's company: John de Lacy. John, a mighty baron in his own right, had – as constable of Chester – been Ranulf's chief vassal. John, unlike his lord, had joined the rebellion against King John and been named amongst the baronial twenty-five appointed to enforce the Charter at the king's expense. The bonds between lord and vassal were reforged, however, in 1217, when John submitted following the victory of Ranulf and his comrades at the Battle of Lincoln. They journeyed together to Damietta as crusaders in 1218 and, in 1221, John married Ranulf's niece, Margaret. While Ranulf in his later years had been making provision for the transfer of the Leicester lands to Simon, he had also been arranging a bequest for John. Ranulf had been not only earl of Chester but also earl of Lincoln, and he bequeathed this second title to John.[5] John, as earl of Lincoln and constable of Chester, now became one of the most powerful men in the kingdom (and, as we have seen, he, like Simon, had taken his due place at the queen's coronation). It is likely that Simon and John, sharing a bond with Ranulf, had known each other since Simon's coming into England, but it is in the early months of 1236 that we can first see them acting in partnership. John's status and favour with the king would have further helped to establish Simon at court after the coronation.*

*

---

* During the following month of March 1236, there is no record of either man being around the king, but both appear again in late April, together heading a short list of

For Simon, as a young noble with ambition but not rank, the goal of ingratiating himself into the king's circle was to gain Henry's favour and to obtain any opportunity for advancement and security this offered, whether in the form of money, offices, wardships or a profitable marriage. Such rewards might be offered in return for useful and faithful service, which, in the first instance, was through the offering of counsel.

The process of taking and giving counsel was fundamental to the ideal relationship between lord and vassal: a good lord (whether nobleman or king) ought never to make an important decision without garnering the advice of his men, while his men were likewise duty-bound to advise him in good faith. This mutual obligation rested in part upon the fact that vassals would have a stake in any outcome (they would be affected if the king decided, for instance, to raise a tax or go to war), and so had a right to be consulted. But it also worked in everybody's interests on a practical level, because the process of taking and giving counsel prevented the making of rash or damaging decisions.

Crucially, too, the process itself demonstrated transparency in decision-making. The king was not bound to follow the advice of his men: he might favour the line of the majority, or of only one, or disagree entirely, but the important thing was that he was seen to weigh up the advice he received and then explain his chosen course of action. Nowhere is this more clearly set out than in the description of Charlemagne at the beginning of the *Chanson de Roland*. The *Chanson* opens with Charlemagne taking counsel from his men – this prominent position in the story setting out a marker of such an act's importance to his rule. The scene is conjured carefully. King and nobles are gathered in an orchard, the outdoor location allowing everyone to see, literally, how the decision is made. The king, having heard conflicting advice, sits quietly stroking his beard as he decides which counsel holds greater merit. This is Charlemagne's thinking face, worn pointedly to show his rational nature.

When a decision was made in this way, all concerned could be

---

witnesses to a royal charter (M. Morris (ed.), *The Royal Charter Witness Lists of Henry III (1226–1272) from the Charter Rolls in the Public Record Office*, 2 vols. (Chippenham, 2001), I, 156).

assured that it was reasonable and justified, and vassals would be comfortable in supporting the course of action they were required to follow. The worst sort of decision was one made behind closed doors. King John had been guilty of this, and it had been a major cause of resentment amongst his nobles.[6] Henry's early reign was an opportunity to set this right.

There were various venues in which he could do so. It was expected that great matters of state, affecting the whole kingdom, would be discussed in a formal setting – a purposely called meeting of nobles, laymen and churchmen, which since the 1230s had been known as a 'parliament'.* The king also enjoyed the aid of an advisory council, whose members were sworn to serve him faithfully. But the churning of policies was often done in the everyday chatter of the court, as was the appraisal of smaller matters, such as the king's relationship with individual subjects and institutions, represented in the charters to which *curiales* (men of the court) stood witness. It mattered, then, who was in the group that stood around the king. And, in 1236, Simon became a part of it.

As we have seen, Simon's induction came during a fragile period of rebuilding. Part of the process of negotiating the balance of power between king and subjects was the airing of contending views about the proper role of counsellors. In 1232 a court coup had ousted Hubert de Burgh from the office of justiciar (the king's chief minister). Hubert was a steadfast supporter of Henry III, as he had been of King John, and as an adroit politician and a courageous general had been one of the chief architects of the young king's survival and the kingdom's recovery over the past two decades. Yet he had, perhaps inevitably, made enemies, including Peter des Roches, bishop of Winchester, who equalled Hubert in his political and military service to the crown. Peter had choreographed Hubert's overthrow, swept up all available land and office with the help of his nephew, Peter de Rivallis, and become the closest of royal counsellors. But Peter, unlike Hubert, had no regard for Magna

---

* The first official use of the term 'parliament' is recorded in 1236, in a mandate of Henry III. Derived from the Latin 'to speak' and its French equivalent, the term simply meant 'discussion' (D. A. Carpenter, 'The beginnings of parliament', in his *The Reign of Henry III* (London, 1996), 381–408, at 382).

Carta, specifically its underlying principle that the king was obliged to govern by the law and not by his will alone. He had advised the king as much, and under his malign influence Henry had begun to seize estates from subjects simply because he wished to – the sort of action that could see a king labelled a tyrant.

The political community had come together against this outrage. In 1234 the earl of Pembroke entered into rebellion. To do so in such circumstances was generally seen as a legitimate protest, a calling to account of a king who had failed in his lordship and a demand for a return to lawful rule. In parallel with the earl of Pembroke's actions, England's bishops confronted Henry publicly, threatening him with excommunication for his breaking of the Charter. These protests were successful. The king, chastised and contrite, was drawn to admit his error, to restore the lands he had seized illegally, and to cast Peter des Roches and Peter de Rivallis from court.[7]

This episode was the testing ground for Magna Carta: it demonstrated that no king could now rule arbitrarily and get away with it. But it also showed the potential power, and innate vulnerability, of royal counsellors. Their privileged position allowed them influence over royal actions, as well as the chance to win reward, but also made them targets for those jealous of their favour, or laid them open to accusations of corruption (accusations that, in the case of Peter des Roches, were well justified). Counsellors depended on the king's goodwill for their position, but it was now clear that the good opinion of the wider political community – bishops, earls and barons – mattered too. For, in 1234, the bishops and barons had succeeded not only in bringing the king back to lawful rule but also in ousting those counsellors who, they felt, had led the king astray. They had deployed their weapons – rebellion and the threat of excommunication – together in a way that was prodigiously effective, this efficacy signalling the newfound balance of power between king and greater subjects. Their actions also signalled a state of high alert, for bishops and barons were now sensitive to the coming of any counsellor who commanded too much influence over the king or acted in his own interest rather than that of the community of the kingdom. And, as the events of 1234 had shown, the bishops and barons were poised to act. These issues simmered on into 1236 when, in April, complaints were voiced in a great assembly about the influence of a new counsellor, William of Savoy, an uncle of the queen who had come with her to England and soon won Henry's trust. By drawing William close, it was felt that the king was pushing others from his confidence.[8]

In such a febrile atmosphere, Simon soon fell under suspicion of contending for influence over the king, and in a way that was illicit and underhand. In June 1236 his fellow royal counsellor, Richard Siward, became the victim of a malicious plot. Richard was a man of prodigious military skill and courage, knight of the earl of Pembroke's circle and a hero of the overthrow of Peter des Roches (he had freed Hubert de Burgh from gaol in 1234). Richard, according to the generally well-informed chronicler of St Albans Abbey, Matthew Paris, 'unjustly incurred the king's anger, and was taken and imprisoned, but was soon afterwards released with the same ease'. The author of this injustice, according to the chronicler, was Simon, reportedly acting in concert with the discredited Peter de Rivallis (who had recently returned to royal favour).[9]

The report reads as if it is a fragment of the truth, concealing some more complex machination in which Simon might or might not have been involved. Why Simon would have been conspiring to have Richard Siward imprisoned is not clear at all, and for this newcomer to the court to have entered into factional manoeuvring would seem – especially considering the result – clumsy at best. The truth of the matter is further fogged by our knowledge that, within the next few years, Simon would take Richard Siward into his service.[10] Whether Simon was truly involved – in an action that was misguided if, thankfully for all concerned, lacking in consequence – or not, the accusation speaks of the fragility of his position.

*

Simon remained at court throughout July 1236, after which his name drops from the witness lists for the remainder of the year, probably when he left to attend to his estates. He was not party, then, to the planning at Westminster at Christmastide of a great assembly, which began on the feast of St Hilary (13 January) 1237. There a request was put before England's nobles for a tax of a thirtieth (a levy of one part in thirty on moveable property). This provoked much grumbling amongst the barons, who objected both to the king's harassing them for money and to his failure to consult them before spending the money he had previously been given. Eventually the tax was granted, after Henry made efforts at conciliation, promising to uphold Magna Carta and agreeing to add three more of his barons to his official advisory council.[11] Simon is not named in the account of the assembly authored by Matthew Paris (who gives a colourful depiction, probably drawn from someone who was present). Simon was certainly there, for he can be found as one of the witnesses to the confirmation of Magna Carta made solemnly by the king at the end of January.[12] But he was not of sufficient standing to play a major part in the to-and-fro of assembly debate, lacking the authority to raise his voice and have it heard.

In the wake of the assembly, Simon heightened his efforts to carve a place at the centre of the court. He remained with the king until the latter half of February, as the court moved from Westminster to Kempton and then down to Dover, and returned again to court just one month later. From this point onwards he was with the king almost continuously throughout the year. By the end of March he already enjoyed sufficient trust to be named, alongside William of Savoy, as an envoy in peace negotiations with the king of Scots (although in the event they both had to be replaced), and was with the king and other magnates at York in September to meet the Scots king and arrange a peace. In November, he and John de Lacy were appointed by Henry to act as bodyguards to the papal legate, carrying swords as they escorted the cardinal to the council he was celebrating at St Paul's (ready to defend him from malcontent clerics, whose wealth the legate was threatening in his pursuit of Church reform).[13] By this time, Simon was certainly seen as a man who was close to Henry, so much so that he was named, alongside John de Lacy, by Matthew Paris as a counsellor of ill repute, said to have encouraged the king to maladminister the raising and spending of the tax so recently granted.[14] The accusations, against both Henry's mismanagement and Simon's part in it, are vague. But they betray the suspicion, amongst those members of the political elite who did not have privy access to the king, that Simon held Henry under his sway.

By the end of 1237, then, Simon had succeeded in placing himself within the inner circle of the king. The nature of their relationship we cannot see, and the words they shared – in the corridors of Westminster Palace, on horseback as they rode across the kingdom or in the royal chamber (the room whose intimate association with the king made it a privileged forum, accessible only to the most favoured few) – were never common currency to be committed to the pages of chronicles. We can, however, discern something of how Simon built friendships and alliances with others of the court, most notably his continuing closeness to John de Lacy, as well as his forging of bonds of trust with other magnates, alongside whom he stood as pledge for the payment of debts on a couple of occasions in this year.[15] But there is one part of his forging of attachments that lies, frustratingly, beyond our field of vision – for it was during this time that Simon fell in love.

Her name was Eleanor. She was around twenty-two, a few years younger than Simon (who was now about twenty-eight or twenty-nine). They might have met before this time, though it was during 1237, with Simon spending the greater number of his days at court, that they must have become close. For although we cannot trace Eleanor's movements as we can Simon's (as a woman she did not command a place in the witness lists to royal charters) we can know that she would have been at court with some degree of frequency – she was the king's sister. Eleanor was the youngest child, and third daughter, of King John and Isabella d'Angoulême. She had been born around 1215, and thus spent her first two years in the chaos of civil war. Her father had died when she was one year old, and before her second year was done she had been separated from her mother, who – excluded from the business of the kingdom by the council of her son, the king – returned to Angoulême.

Eleanor was brought up under the guardianship of Peter des Roches, schooled in Latin and raised in piety, before she was married off at the age of nine. Marriage at such an early age was fairly normal for a woman of high status, even to a man twenty-five years senior, as Eleanor's husband was. It was not expected that the marriage would be consummated at this stage, with the bride so young, and it was probably not until the autumn of 1229, five and a half years after the wedding, with Eleanor in her mid-teens, that the couple slept together for the first time.[16] Eleanor's husband was William Marshal, earl of Pembroke, eldest son and heir of the famous father for whom he had been named, the victor of the Battle of Lincoln. We know little of their marriage. But, during their time spent together and apart, Eleanor would certainly have learned the attributes required of a noblewoman: the ability to command a household and to run a vast estate, and to be a partner to her husband. This strengthening partnership can be glimpsed in 1230, when Eleanor accompanied her husband on campaign in Brittany in the service of the king.[17] What might have been a promising union was ended, however, within a year of the expedition, by William's untimely death in April 1231. Eleanor found herself a widow, at sixteen.

How Eleanor responded to the loss we cannot know, at least until we meet her again, three years later, when she was perhaps nineteen. It was then that she decided to take a vow of chastity. With no written rendering of her decision, Eleanor's motives here can only be suggested with some caution. They were perhaps both political and personal.[18] In 1234, when she took her vow, England was disrupted by rebellion – led by the new earl of Pembroke, Richard Marshal, the younger brother and heir of her late husband, who (as we have seen) was protesting against the malign influence of Peter des Roches over the king. Meanwhile, the archbishop of Canterbury, Edmund of Abingdon, was working tirelessly for peace. When Richard Marshal died in the midst of his rebellion, archbishop Edmund assumed the task of reconciling Richard's brother and heir, Gilbert, the third son of the great William Marshal, with the king. It is possible that Eleanor was persuaded to take her vow of chastity by the archbishop, as a way of appeasing Gilbert and encouraging him to agree to peace. For, if Eleanor remained a widow, it would be easier for the Marshal family eventually to recover her dower lands (the third part of her late husband's estate, to which she was entitled during her lifetime for her sustenance).

The cause of obtaining peace was, of course, a worthy one, but it is unlikely that Eleanor made such a commitment without her own reasons. By taking the vow she was removing herself from the marriage market, and therefore guaranteeing that she could not become a pawn of her brothers and others of the court, to be married off again in a match in which she had no say. She was also securing her status as a widow – a privileged one that assured her an independence she could not otherwise enjoy, with control of her own lands as well as her substantial dower, and freedom to govern as she saw fit. By 1237, when she was growing close to Simon, Eleanor had been her own mistress for some three years.

Simon had been considering marriage before he became attached to Eleanor, and had explored the possibility of an alliance first with the countess of Boulogne and then with the countess of Flanders.[19] He was aiming high, seeking to match not his current status (he had by now assumed the title of earl, but his title had not been officially recognized) but his famous name, and concomitant ambition.

In this respect Eleanor was a prize, for (as Matthew Paris noted) she was royalty, the daughter of a king and queen, and sister of three monarchs: a king (Henry), an empress (her elder sister, Isabella, was married to the Holy Roman Emperor), and a queen (her eldest sister, Joan, was queen of Scotland). But this is not the first reason the chronicler provides for Simon's eagerness to marry Eleanor. Matthew Paris – whose narrative is habitually punctuated by cutting reprimand and cynicism – was clear: Simon 'received her joyfully, on account of freely given love'. The words were chosen carefully: *gratuitus amor*, unremunerated love, affection that came without interest in wealth or status. Eleanor must herself have been convinced of this, in order to give up her cultivated independence.

The strength of their attachment is betrayed by the nature of their marriage ceremony. Eleanor, as befitted her royal status, should have been married in a public celebration, something akin to the wedding of the king and Eleanor of Provence two years before. But instead her marriage took place in secret, on the day after Epiphany 1238, while the court was at Westminster for Christmas. It was held in the king's private chapel, and was celebrated not by an archbishop or bishop but by the chaplain of St Stephen's.[20]

It was not only the absence of glittering spectacle that made this event irregular. The king, acting alone, arranged the wedding and gave the bride away. He was obliged to hold the wedding covertly, rather than sponsoring a public ceremony, because he had failed to seek counsel before allowing his sister to marry. As a kinswoman of the king, Eleanor was a commodity of international standing, whose marriage might be used to secure friendship with a mighty nobleman at home or a great ruler abroad. Accordingly, the choice of her marriage partner was a matter of regnal concern, and thus merited discussion and debate amongst the prelates and magnates who held a stake in the kingdom's future, and who expected to counsel the king in all such decisions. Eleanor's first marriage had been managed in this way. Indeed, at that time the scrupulous obtaining of consent from the bishops, earls and barons of the kingdom had been a condition of the marriage, and the propriety of the process had been overseen by the pope himself; the betrothal had even been delayed until Ranulf, earl of Chester (who had been concerned about the bestowal of such a gift as the king's sister to one of his rivals), finally provided his approval.[21] Her second marriage ought to have followed the same process.

Henry's avoidance of this path can only have been due to apprehension that consent would be withheld. It was in part a problem of status. On the one hand, Eleanor had been married to an English earl before and (as those advancing the first match had noted) there was clear precedent in France for marriages between royalty and members of the nobility.[22] But William Marshal junior and Simon de Montfort were two quite different prospects. William had been one of the greatest landholders of the kingdom, with estates stretching across England, Wales and Ireland, and he boasted a strong record of service to the king, having commanded successful campaigns against the Welsh (both arguments advanced at the time for his suitability as Eleanor's husband).[23] Simon, on the other hand, had a famous name but only half an earldom, had not yet proved his talents and commitment on the field, and was viewed with some suspicion by those mistrustful of his closeness to the king. If Henry had been pressed to put forth arguments in Simon's favour, he would have been forced to rate Simon's credentials according to promise only – a promise in which Henry evidently placed his faith, but which sceptical magnates and prelates were unlikely to accept as tender.

Why, then, would Henry allow the marriage to go ahead at all? The imperative was hidden at the time, seemingly withheld even from Henry and Eleanor's own brother, Richard, earl of Cornwall

– who, when he heard of the marriage, was furious that his consent had not been sought. The circumstances emerged only later in the course of an argument between Henry and Simon in 1239. When Simon was required to give a narrative of the dispute many years afterwards all he could bear to say was that Henry 'spoke insulting and shameful words to me that are painful to recall'.[24] The chronicler Matthew Paris, however, felt no compunction about repeating the king's words of 1239: 'you seduced my sister before marriage – because of which, when I discovered it, I gave her to you, though reluctantly, in order to avoid scandal'.[25]

A case could be argued for dismissing this account, for Matthew Paris was fond of the lurid, and Henry's facilitation of the marriage would not be the only occasion in his career when he took uncounselled action moved by a willingness to please those he loved. Yet Simon's own reticence about what was said in this encounter with the king suggests that an accusation of such severity had indeed been made. We cannot know whether Eleanor and Simon did sleep together before their wedding – speculating as to how they weighed the social and moral implications of doing so against the hunger of the heart, from this distance and with no written evidence, could never produce an answer – but Henry apparently believed it.

Henry's facilitation of the marriage provoked a vehement reaction, both from Richard, earl of Cornwall, and Gilbert Marshal who, as we have seen, had his own reasons for wishing that Eleanor had preserved her vow of chastity. The two entered into rebellion, and encouraged others to follow. Henry was rightly anxious, but persevered, writing to the people of the Cinque Ports,* instructing them not to obey Richard if he were to issue orders to them in Henry's name, and requesting that they send representatives to discuss the matter with the king.[26]

Meanwhile, Simon remained at Henry's side throughout January and early February, and the king gave him and Eleanor loans to support their transition to married life.[27] As the tempest whirled, the papal legate in England worked hard to broker peace, promising Richard that Henry would placate him with lands in recompense,

---

* Hastings, New Romney, Hythe, Dover and Sandwich, the coastal towns of Kent and Sussex, holding a special mandate to defend the kingdom from invasion.

and advising Henry to give a hearing to the complaints.[28] A conference was called on 22 February in London. There, in order to quiet the earl of Cornwall, Henry promised to take counsel in future, while Simon made a public statement of submission. With the help of mediators, and the presentation of gifts, Richard was persuaded to accept Simon's entreaty. 'Simon humbled himself to earl Richard', wrote Matthew Paris, 'and received the kiss of peace', an act that probably involved Simon prostrating himself at Richard's feet, and Richard lifting Simon from the ground and bestowing upon him the symbolic mark of concord.[29]

*

Once Simon had settled his position amongst his fellow nobles, he determined to obtain an authentication of the marriage. There were two potential issues that might cause others to question the validity of the union: the ceremony's clandestine nature and Eleanor's vow of chastity, which had been usurped by the couple's marriage vows.

Clandestine marriages were legally problematic, though they had become so only recently. In the early decades of the thirteenth century, the papacy was working to provide legal backing for the principle that marriage was indissoluble. The papal measures sought to address a displeasingly common occurrence, whereby one member of a couple (almost invariably the husband) declared, sometimes after years of marriage, that there had always been a legal impediment to the union. If the marriage had never been legal, clearly it ought to be annulled, leaving both parties conveniently free to marry again. This loophole mocked the indissolubility of marriage, a sacrament that symbolized Christ's union with the Church, and so the pope and his advisers began to devise legal means of closing such loopholes. One solution was the reduction of forbidden degrees of family bond from seven (sixth cousins) to four (third cousins), which made it far harder for couples to claim later that they had not known they were related. Another was a decree that banns were to be read before the ceremony, allowing anybody who knew of an impediment to present it for investigation. Because Eleanor and Simon had married in secret, without the reading of the banns, their marriage contravened this ruling.[30] In the minds of some, therefore, the secrecy enveloping the wedding might have called the marriage into question – and, indeed, Matthew Paris complained about its clandestine nature more than once.[31]

Still, this in itself need not have been too serious. Many couples took their vows with or without witnesses – for the fundamental legal requirement for a marriage was the exchange of words of consent in the present tense. The Church would uphold a marriage contracted at home, or even in an ale-house, as long as this criterion was fulfilled.[32] The decree calling for banns to be read had been created only to serve a higher purpose: the prevention of marriages in those cases where grounds for annulment existed. But if there were no legal impediment, then there was no pressing need for the reading of the banns, and so the omission – while technically illegal – was not a threat to the marriage's validity according to the Church's law.[33]

The problem of Eleanor's vow of chastity was potentially more serious, however. She had sworn to remain single and had apparently received a ring, a token of her betrothal to Christ. As a result, her marriage to Simon was opposed by the archbishop of Canterbury, Edmund of Abingdon (who had overseen the vow), as well as an outspoken Dominican friar named William of Abingdon. And, according to Matthew Paris, 'many other experts' also disapproved. But, despite the weight of their authority, in reality the terms of this oath were not clearly defined – was it, for instance, intended to be a commitment for life? As the Montforts were to point out, it was not as if Eleanor had entered a convent (which would certainly have bound her until her death).[34]

The important point for Simon and Eleanor, however, was to assuage any doubts as to the marriage's validity, so they could live as man and wife unchallenged, and to ensure that no misgivings were ever voiced about the legitimacy of their children. If there was any risk at all that such suspicions would be aired, either now or years into the future, it was worth going to the trouble of obtaining official confirmation of the marriage from the pope. Indeed, Henry III had made efforts, at around the time of his marriage to Eleanor of Provence in 1236, to have a previous contract of marriage (to Joan of Ponthieu) annulled – even though it was clear that his first 'marriage' was never legally valid, and nobody was contesting his marriage to Eleanor of Provence. It was the slenderest of doubts, but for the king it was important to have incontrovertible proof that his marriage was indeed legal.[35] It is not impossible, therefore, that it was Henry who encouraged Simon and Eleanor to seek papal approval for their union.

And so Simon set out for Rome. It was an arduous journey, taking him first across the Channel, then overland through France, across the Alps and into Italy. A large retinue, making this journey at a comfortable pace, travelled at an average of fifteen to twenty miles a day.[36] At this speed it would have taken Simon between seven and ten weeks to reach his destination. But Simon, probably riding with a skeleton retinue, completed the journey in only a month: he set off at the end of March and had already reached the papal court and completed his business by the end of the first week of May.[37] He would have covered an average of about thirty-six miles a day. This pace was hard, but the time of year was in his favour, for by April the snows had cleared and the greatest risk of avalanche in the Alps had subsided. The effort was worthwhile. Completing the journey in such a short time brought not only a quick resolution but also extensive savings when it came to bed and board along the route.[38]

Simon approached the eternal city from the north. This made his probable point of entry the Porta del Popolo, the crumbling Roman gateway in the northern stretch of the Aurelian wall. He would have had to press his way through the threading streets towards the palace of St John Lateran, home of the papal court, lying in the city's south-eastern corner. The complex was built upon the site of Emperor Nero's palace, and the papal home still carried an aura of imperial grandeur: it lay upon higher ground, beyond the alleyed web of the city's centre and surrounded by cultivated fields (whose crops supplied the papal household). Before the palace sprawled the Campus Lateranensis, thronging with lawyers, clerks, cardinals, and petitioners drawn from across the Christian world. Across the campus stood the palace, basilica and its brick-clad baptistery, the last built on the spot where, so legend held, Constantine – the first emperor to have been received into the Christian faith – had been baptized. And it was Constantine himself (or so it was believed) who presided over the campus from atop a

marble platform, cast in bronze riding a gilded horse, his right arm
lifted from the falling folds of his cape to bless those who passed
below his gaze.*

He would be Simon's companion through the days that followed.
Simon and his entourage had to navigate the papal court, for which
they would have needed local help: a lawyer or cardinal who knew
the system and could smooth their path. This was perhaps even
more necessary than it would normally have been, since the archbishop of Canterbury, Edmund of Abingdon, was then also visiting
the papal court and is reported to have given his opinion on the
matter to the pope.[39] But Simon was armed with letters of support
from other authorities: Henry III, of course, but also the Holy
Roman Emperor, Frederick II – for, according to Matthew Paris,
Simon had met with Frederick in the course of the journey in order
to win his support (helped by the fact that Frederick was now
Simon's kinsman, since he was married to Isabella, sister of Eleanor
and Henry).[40] Together, they won the day: by 7 May, perhaps within
days of reaching the Lateran, Simon had secured the necessary
letters from the pope. Gregory IX decreed that, 'diverse things have
been reported to us and our brothers by diverse people, through
which we do not consider to presume against the contracted
marriage'.[41] Simon, his union with Eleanor proven valid, was now
free to return to England.

*

Had Simon managed a similar speed to that of his outward journey,
he would have been home by late June. Yet he did not arrive back
in England until mid-October. What occupied his time during
these months? There is no certain record of his activities, and it is
unlikely that the long summer that Simon was away from Eleanor
was spent entirely in Rome, or in circuitous travel. We can find,

---

* The figure actually depicted is Marcus Aurelius, and the statue survives in the
Capitoline museum today. It was described by writers visiting the campus in
the second half of the twelfth century (P. Borchardt, 'The sculpture in front of the
Lateran as described by Benjamin of Tudela and Magister Gregorius', *Journal of Roman
Studies*, 26 (1936), 68–70).

however, a solitary clue in Matthew Paris's chronicle. In describing Simon's departure for Rome, Matthew noted that Simon 'first served as a soldier for the emperor, so as to please him', in order to obtain the letters asking for the authentication of the marriage.[42]

The chronicler gives no further details, but this report tallies with Frederick's activities. In the spring of 1238 the emperor was beginning a campaign in northern Italy, intent on subduing rebellious subjects. To do so, he was gathering a mighty army and had already sought aid from England – Henry had responded immediately, in early April 1237, sending soldiers under the command of the veteran knight Henry de Trubleville.[43] In such circumstances, Frederick would have been keen to secure further aid, including from his new kinsman, Simon de Montfort. It is unlikely that Simon undertook his service en route to Rome (as Matthew Paris's ambiguous statement seems to imply) – considering the speed with which Simon reached Rome, he can have only broken his journey briefly to meet the emperor en route. But it was perhaps at this point, and perhaps in Turin (where Frederick spent the month of April), that Simon made a pledge to serve on his return from the papal court.[44]

As Simon was reaching Rome, the emperor moved in early May onward to Pavia, then to Lodi and then Cremona, where he held a great assembly to discuss the coming war, before heading to Verona around the end of May, where he would stay throughout June.[45] From here he wrote to Henry in England with news that he was readying to advance 'with a well-equipped army summoned from across Italy, and a mighty force assembled from parts of Germany . . . carrying the conquering battle standards of the conquering imperial eagle, to triumph against our rebels'.[46] Frederick's army was indeed impressive, comprising Tuscans, Sicilians (including some of the island's Muslim inhabitants), Germans, Lombards, Romans, men from Le Marche and from Romagna, from Provence and the kingdom of France, from Greece, the kingdoms of Spain, and England. It was a coalition comparable in its internationalism to an expedition of crusaders heading for the Holy Land. If Simon was to serve in Frederick's army, it would have been to this vast muster at Verona that, with his business in Rome complete, he would have come.

From Verona, on 11 July, the army began a fleet-footed march forty miles westward, skirting Lake Garda's southern shore, towards Brescia – a town that, once captured, would provide a foothold for the emperor's move on Milan.[47] Establishing a base in Brescia's castle, the emperor's army besieged the city. If Simon was indeed part of this force, then this was – as far as we know – his first experience of war as a combatant.

For a young knight such as Simon, there were essential lessons to be learned: the organization of an army (the logistical challenge of moving, feeding and encamping thousands of men) and the operation of a siege. But Frederick's investment of Brescia was not to be the shining example of siege-craft for which a young knight might have hoped. The great weapon of the emperor's army was an engineer, Calamandrinus, who knew how to construct and deploy siege engines most effectively. But he was an unwilling servant, kept in chains, and in August the Brescians launched a sortie and cut him free, offering – in place of the emperor's threats – reward, a house and a wife inside the city, if he would serve the besieged instead. With such expertise now in the hands of the Brescians, the trebuchets of the besieging army were vulnerable to rocks hurled from atop the city walls. The emperor's answer, in September, was to order that captured Brescian nobles be tied to the front of his siege machines, their hands bound behind their backs, to deter their friends inside the city from launching missiles. In return, the Brescians lowered imperial prisoners from the city's walls.[48] The siege dragged on until early October, when Frederick and his army finally withdrew. As a military operation, it was a failure. And from Simon's point of view, it was hardly comparable to his father's impressive example.

By the time that Frederick elected to withdraw, Simon had already departed, presumably having served out the agreed period (forty days was the standard term of military service). He probably left in mid- or late September, as he landed on English shores on 14 October.[49] Disembarking in all likelihood at Dover, he passed through London to receive the kiss of peace from Henry. It was here that he must have been told the news that sent him rushing thence to Kenilworth Castle, his seat in Warwickshire, more than ninety miles north: Eleanor was carrying their child.[50] The baby had probably been conceived in late February, around a month before Simon's departure for Rome. Now, in mid-October, Eleanor was some seven and a half months pregnant, and near her confinement. This was, as far as we know, her first pregnancy: an anxious time. It was probably on 25 or 26 November that Eleanor went into labour. Hearing of this development, the king raced the forty miles from Woodstock to Kenilworth to be at his sister's side.[51] The baby was born safely: a boy. He was given the name Henry.

4

Holy War

Henry de Montfort was born at the beginning of Advent, the most treasured of Christmas gifts. He was baptized within a few days of his birth, as was the custom in an age when infant life was so precarious. The sacrament was celebrated by the bishop of Coventry (who happened to have heard the news of the birth when passing Kenilworth), probably in the chapel of Kenilworth Castle (see plate 9).[1]

The king, having left Kenilworth for Winchester to prepare for the coming Christmas feast, kept the Montfort family in his thoughts. He sent Eleanor a golden robe of patterned silk, trimmed and lined with miniver and, for her comfort as she recovered from childbirth, bedclothes of the greatest luxury: a mattress and a quilt of patterned silk, and a coverlet cut from scarlet cloth and the best grey fur.[2] And Henry was thinking of Simon and Eleanor on Christmas Day. During the festivities, the king turned from his doors the earl of Pembroke, Gilbert Marshal. Gilbert, as the younger brother and heir of Eleanor's late husband William, was due to have paid Eleanor a sum of money for her dower, owed to her as William's widow from the Marshal estates. Gilbert had failed to deliver to Eleanor the £200 that was due by Michaelmas (a sum that Henry, righteously impatient, would pay to her himself in January).[3] Thus on Christmas morning, after Mass, as Henry returned to the palace of Winchester to break his fast, he ordered his doorkeepers to deny Gilbert admittance, and the earl was shooed away in a public show of royal disfavour.[4]

That same day, Henry also gave Simon a most special Christmas gift, one that would secure Simon's status and help him and Eleanor financially: he instructed that Simon was henceforth to receive from the revenues of Leicestershire the third penny, 'as earl of Leicester, as Simon de Montfort late earl of Leicester, father of Simon, was accustomed to take the third penny in his time'.[5] As we have seen, Simon had assumed the title of earl by 1236 – and he clearly bore it with sufficient confidence to tout it at the papal court, for it was as 'the noble man Simon de Montfort, earl of Leicester' that he was addressed in the pope's letters.[6] But Henry's grant of the customary portion of the shire's royal revenues at last made his status official.

A public ceremony would follow later (when Simon was back at court), in which Henry would gird Simon with a sword, signalling to all his elevation. Simon returned to Henry's side by 13 January 1239, but he was made to wait for his girding until a carefully appointed day: the feast of Candlemas, 2 February. The feast's solemnity would add to the lustre of the occasion, and its significance would underscore Simon's attachment to the king – for Candlemas celebrated the churching (or purification – the ceremony that marked the return of a mother into society after the confinement of childbirth) of the Blessed Virgin Mary after giving birth to Christ, an apt choice, given the recent churching of Eleanor, Simon's wife and Henry's sister, after the birth of her child.[7]

It was a relatively small circle of *curiales* who witnessed Simon's transformation (only one other earl, Humphrey de Bohun of Hereford and Essex, was at court), but this was soon put right.[8] It was decided to make a public ratification of Simon's right to the earldom, with regards to the rights of his elder brother, Amaury. Given that Amaury had already quitclaimed his rights in England, and Simon had been living as the holder of the lands for several years, this was a decision moved more by the need to proclaim Simon's status publicly than to give legal assurances. Amaury was invited to England and on 11 April, at Westminster, in the presence of the king and papal legate, he once again declared that the rights to Leicester lay with Simon. Witnessing the act were Richard, earl of Cornwall, John de Lacy, earl of Lincoln and constable of Chester, Humphrey de Bohun, earl of Hereford and Essex, and a number of other *curiales*.[9] The king soon publicized the act further still, at the opening of a parliament, on 17 April, when he confirmed the charter by which Amaury had recorded the transfer of his rights. This provided an even greater audience, including the archbishop of Canterbury, the bishops of Bath, Exeter, Ely, Lincoln, Worcester and Carlisle, and the earls of Lincoln, Surrey, Derby, and Hereford and Essex, amongst others.[10]

His earldom and its full revenues confirmed, Simon was then granted another very public honour. On 17/18 June 1239 the queen gave birth to a son. It was the cause of much rejoicing: an unsettled succession could mean chaos when the king died, and such anxieties were amplified in this instance by fears, however hasty, that Queen Eleanor might be unable to have children.[11] These worries now abated. The boy would be called Edward, the first of that name since the Norman Conquest, in devotion to St Edward the Confessor, the Anglo-Saxon king to whom Henry had recently developed a deep attachment (and whose sword had been carried at the queen's coronation by the earl of Chester).[12]

The selection of godparents was an important means by which the parents could convey favour, and strengthen bonds of friendship. For this reason it had become common practice for the nobility to take a generous approach, naming godparents in great number. This could make for a lot of jostling at the ceremony, with the god-parents crowding around as the baby was anointed, so that each could reach to touch the child and be a party to raising him or her symbolically from the font.[13] Simon was among those named, and was thus clustered at the font with two bishops and a bishop-elect, two other earls, and three other *curiales*, together with several godmothers (presumably, though Matthew Paris, who records the ritual, did not see fit to name them, noting only that the baptism took place 'in the presence of a great many noble ladies').[14] It was a scene of disorderly but good-natured concord.

*

Within two months this happy picture had been blown apart. The cause was Simon's debt. Beginning with the loan he had taken to buy out Amaury's rights in England, he had amassed an eye-watering obligation of 2,800 marks (£1,867): over three times the annual income of the Leicester lands.[15] Initially, Simon owed the money to Peter de Dreux, count of Brittany. Peter was a sworn crusader, and by the spring of 1239 needed the money to mount his forthcoming expedition to the Holy Land. Simon's failure to repay the debt was now imperilling the holiest of causes and, catastrophically, he found himself threatened with excommunication by the pope.[16] In the summer of 1239, Simon found a short-term fix: he persuaded Thomas of Savoy, an uncle of the queen, to pay off Peter to the sum of 2,000 marks (£1,333) and to take on the role of creditor himself. This Simon achieved by promising that the king of England would stand surety for the sum.[17] The problem was that Henry had made no such guarantee.

Simon might not have seen anything underhand or immoral in his actions; acting as surety for a debt was a conventional mark of trust and, given his relationship with Henry, he could reasonably assume that Henry would be willing to take on the role. The problem lay in his failure to ask the king first: it was the presumption that was offensive and, indeed, could be considered an abuse of trust. Simon's misdirection came to light when Thomas visited England soon after the arrangement had been made. The king was furious. Simon and Eleanor had come to London to attend the churching of the queen, which was due to take place on 9 August 1239. Henry, in his anger, barred Simon and Eleanor from taking part in the festivities. Their exclusion would have been shaming, particularly because (unlike the treatment of Gilbert Marshal at the Christmas court of 1238) it was enacted not through doorkeepers but personally by the king. And Henry did it publicly: he showered Simon with abuse, calling him an excommunicate. It was on this occasion, too, that in his rage he accused Simon of having seduced Eleanor before their marriage. The couple retreated hurriedly from Henry's presence, taking a boat from Westminster downriver towards London Bridge, to the palace of the bishop of Winchester, where they were staying. But they would not be protected from Henry's wrath, for their right to these lodgings depended on the king's goodwill (the bishopric of Winchester was currently vacant and Henry, as was his feudal right, was currently in control of all its assets).

Many years later, Simon described what happened next: the king 'ordered that I be seized and taken to the Tower of London, and the community of London was ordered to seize me from my lodgings where I was staying'. At least part of this appalling threat reached the ears of a wider audience, for Matthew Paris knew enough to report that 'the king immediately ordered that they [Simon and Eleanor] be roughly cast out' of the bishop's palace. Thankfully for Simon, he was spared the ignominy of the Tower when Richard of Cornwall interceded, not wishing Simon – or perhaps his sister – to suffer such an indignity.[18]

Simon tried to placate Henry. 'But when I saw his great anger', Simon later recalled, 'and that he did not want to hear reason, I left the country, and put some distance between his anger and myself and the countess.' He and Eleanor, accompanied by a small retinue, clambered into a boat, headed down the Thames and straight out to sea. The urgency of their withdrawal was such that they went with only the possessions they had with them and were forced to leave their infant son behind. Henry was then only eight months old.[19]

For Simon, it was a monumental fall from grace. He had been humiliated, not only by the king's very public fury and threat to lock him in the Tower but also, perhaps, by the pitiable state of his finances that the scandal had uncovered, and the revelation that he had presumed too much upon the king's goodwill.

The place to which he and Eleanor fled is not recorded, but the obvious refuge would have been the Montfort family lands outside Paris. It was perhaps, then, from Montfort-en-Yvelines that Simon wrote to his friend, Robert Grosseteste (who by this point had been elevated to the bishopric of Lincoln). Simon's letter to Robert does not survive, but we have the letter that Robert wrote in reply. 'I have received the letter, dear friend', Robert began, 'in which you make known the weight of your suffering, for which, and rightly, I feel much compassion.' As the bishop notes, Simon had asked Robert to keep him in his prayers, and to comfort the household he had left behind in England. He had also asked Robert to plead his case with Henry, which Robert agreed to do. Meanwhile, Robert offered Simon words of comfort, encouraging him to look upon his present struggles as an opportunity for spiritual reward, a trial of endurance such as the Apostles and Church Fathers had borne before him and survived. 'So', wrote Robert, let the harshness of this world's sufferings not weaken but strengthen you, not cast you down but raise you up . . . For suffering is to the righteous what pruning is to vines, what cultivation is to untilled land, what washing is to dirty garments, what a healing but bitter drink is to those who are ill, what shaping with a hammer is to vessels not yet fully moulded, what proving in fire is to gold. So, the discipline of suffering is – for those who meditate not so much on its present annoyance as on the glory of its future reward – an occasion not for sadness but for joy.

By enduring his present trials, Robert advised him, and contemplating the humility and suffering of Christ, Simon 'may be prepared . . . to endure all suffering with the unshaken and dauntless courage of a resolute mind'.[20]

*

But Simon's trials were not yet over. What made the business still more complicated, and made its resolution of even greater urgency, was that Simon was by now a sworn crusader. He was committed, and eager, to journey to Outremer, and wield his sword in the service of the Cross.

The Christian territories of Outremer were under threat. In 1229, Frederick II had managed to secure the city of Jerusalem by diplomatic means, forging a treaty with the Ayyubid sultan of Egypt, al-Kamil. This was a monumental achievement – since the city of Jerusalem had been lost to Salah al-Din in 1187, two major expeditions had been launched to win it back, and both had failed.[21] But the Christian hold on the Holy City was not assured, for the ten-year truce included in the treaty was due to expire in 1239. In readiness, Pope Gregory IX had issued a call to arms in late 1234.

The message of the summons was a potent one. Those men – knights, warriors – whose swords were needed in the cause should not fear 'to die for the sake of life, to endure hardships and disagreeable things for a time for the sake of Him who, disgraced by ruin, bespattered with spittle, battered by blows, tormented by scourging, crowned with thorns' had handed Himself over for degradation, choosing a cruel and demeaning death on the Cross.

'For this is He', Gregory proclaimed 'who, so that we might seek out higher things, wondrously removed Himself from the throne of His father's glory in Heaven, and descended to the depths of our mortality.'[22] The Christian warrior could find redemption in service of the Lord through emulation of His suffering.

In order to reach as wide an audience as possible, Gregory had enlisted Franciscan and Dominican friars. These Orders had been established in the early decades of the thirteenth century. Their members were committed to service amongst the laity, and accordingly they were educated to a high degree and trained in the art of preaching. The friars bore the papal message across Europe, moving through town and city, as Matthew Paris describes, 'with solemn processions, with banners, burning candles, and with an array of persons clad in feast-day vestments', summoning the faithful to assemble and listen to their words. Christian people should be weeping, they were told, 'by day and night', because 'that land, which the son of God consecrated with His own blood, shed for our sakes, has lost the best part of its excellence and its territory'.[23]

Many knights took these words to heart. Amongst them in England were the earls of Cornwall, Pembroke, Chester, and Salisbury – all of whom Matthew Paris records as taking the vow of the crusader in the summer of 1236. It was perhaps as a member of this group that Simon made his vow, though the fact that Matthew Paris does not include his name suggests that he did so independently, in England or across the Channel. It was the noblemen of France, indeed, who were to answer the call in the greatest numbers. Amongst them was Amaury de Montfort, who took the cross amidst a glittering parade of the great men of France in 1236.[24] Did Simon, perhaps, make his vow as a member of this group, beside his brother?

The sentiment that moved these knights to make their vow was described by one of their number, Thibaut, count of Champagne and king of Navarre, also known as Thibaut le Chansonnier for the songs he wrote of love and faith and chivalry. 'Lords, know this,' wrote Thibaut. 'Whoever will not now go to that land where God died and rose again, and whoever will not take the cross to Outremer will find it hard ever to go to heaven. Whoever has pity and good remembrance in his heart must seek to avenge the Highest Lord and liberate His land and His country.' Thibaut sought to shame those who remained behind, those 'base men who do not love God, goodness or honour or reputation'. They were nothing more than 'snotty-nosed faint-hearts'. They worried about leaving their wives and friends – but these, wrote Thibaut, were 'vain preoccupations, since there is certainly no true friend apart from the one who was placed upon the true cross for us'. Echoing the call to arms issued by the pope, Thibaut set out the need to suffer with Christ and for His sake: 'God allowed himself to suffer pain upon the cross and will say to us on the day when all come together: "You who helped me carry my cross, you will go to where my angels are; and you from whom I had no help will all descend into the depths of hell."' Fighting for His cause was, as Thibaut knew, the path to salvation for warlike men. But it was also a matter of honour and, as Thibaut makes clear, of avoiding shame. 'Whoever does not aid God at least once in his lifetime,' he proclaimed, 'and at so little cost, loses the glory of the world.'[25]

Simon, perhaps moved by the same sentiment, had been preparing for his expedition for some three years in the summer of 1239. Perhaps shortly after taking his vow, at the end of July 1236 he secured from the king a promise that, should he die in England or overseas, the revenue from his lands would be used to pay his debts and fulfil his will for four years.[26] The settling of such business was an integral part of the crusader's preparation: it ensured his spiritual readiness for the campaign, that he would depart free of the stain of sin (for sin would lose him divine favour and with it any hope of victory).

The route that both Simon and his brother Amaury were to take for Outremer suggests that they planned their expedition in concert. Almost the entire force of France would set sail for Acre from Marseille, as would Richard of Cornwall; but a clutch of crusaders took a different path, through the Italian lands of Frederick II, to set sail from the port of Brindisi, on Italy's heel. These were Amaury, his friend Henry, count of Bar, and Simon.[27] In the event, the brothers could not depart together, for Simon's plans and those of the other English crusaders were frustrated. In February 1238, at the request of Henry III, the pope sent orders that they should not leave without papal licence, because they were needed in England to give their aid and counsel to the king, for England (as Gregory explained, probably echoing Henry's words) was 'beset from every side by the plots of enemies'. If the crusaders should disobey, they would lose their indulgences.* Simon was therefore forced to look on frustrated as, in early August 1239, 'almost all the best knights of France' (according to one chronicler), Amaury included, sailed for Acre.[28]

It was while Amaury was travelling to Outremer that Simon endured Henry's rage at Westminster, and fled with Eleanor to France. He must have been eager to depart himself – but he could not do so while his vast debt was still unpaid, and the threat of excommunication hung over his head. Henry knew this too and, despite his fury at being named as a pledge to Simon's debt without his knowledge, decided that the money must be delivered. Simon owed 2,000 marks to Thomas of Savoy: Henry would contribute 500 marks himself, and would loan the rest to Simon – but this loan he would recoup from Simon's lands. This would mean Henry sending his men into the estates of Leicester, with instructions to seize the full amount. According to established procedure, they would take first any precious objects (gold, silver, stones, expensive clothing), then horses and livestock, then grain, and then the contents of the lord's cellar and larder, until the sum was covered.[29] It is possible that the royal agents also turned to another speedy method of raising cash: chopping down trees to sell the timber. The taking of moveable goods was damaging enough, especially plough animals (whose loss would hinder the lord's efforts to farm his crops).[30] But cutting down woodland would severely disrupt the careful stewardship of an estate, ruining the woodland habitat of animals that were to be hunted for their meat and robbing the household of future building material. Henry's stripping of the Leicester lands stirred in Simon profound resentment. So much so

---

* L. Auvray et al. (eds.), *Les registres de Grégoire IX*, 4 vols. (Paris, 1896–1955), II, c. 897. The only significant figure to depart from England at this point was Ralph de Thony, a veteran who had joined the rebellion against King John and returned to Plantagenet allegiance in 1217, and had gone on to lead the army of Henry III against the Welsh. Ralph would die at sea en route to the Holy Land, around Michaelmas (*Matthaei Parisiensis, Monachi Sancti Albani, Chronica Majora*, ed. H. R. Luard, 7 vols. (London, 1872–83) (hereafter *CM*), III, 638); W. Farrer, *Feudal Cambridgeshire* (Cambridge, 1920), 48–9.

that, years later, Simon complained of how 'he levied the 1,500 marks from my land in a harsh manner, and a great damage it did me because of the haste, and because I was signed with the cross and was ready to set out for Outremer.'[31]

As Simon pointed out, the stripping of his property was all the worse for coming at a time when he needed to raise extra money to fund his expedition: 'Thus it was necessary for me because of this great damage to sell my land and my forest, and thus I had, and had again, great loss.'[32] Details of the sale are given by Matthew Paris, who notes that Simon raised around £1,000 by selling the woods of Leicester to the local house of the Knights Hospitaller.[33] Land was a precious resource, a heritable and privileged commodity valued far more highly than cash: selling it meant a permanent diminishment of the family's estates, and would always be the last resort. The loss must have been keenly felt, not least because the Leicester lands were already too small to support his growing family (Eleanor, by the spring of 1240, was readying to give birth to their second child). But it was a personal loss as well, for the Montfort family estates in France had been centred on woodland, its cultivation and the hunting of its animals a major part of family life as Simon grew up, and a core element of family identity: it was as a woodland hunter that the Count had been depicted on his seal, the design that Simon himself had adopted (see plates 11 and 13).[34]

*

In November 1239, something happened that fuelled the urgency of his departure. In France, probably residing on the Montfort family lands outside Paris, he was well placed to hear news of the French expedition, which had embarked for Acre in August. And so Simon would have known, perhaps by the early months of 1240, that Amaury, his brother, was in peril.

The French forces had reached Acre by September 1239. There they had set up camp and debated strategy. By 1 November they had decided on a course of action: first they would head south to Ascalon in order to fortify the city, which stood on the border of the crusader states and Egypt; they would then wheel back to march upon Damascus. But en route south to Ascalon, food became short and the troops began to suffer. The army stopped at Jaffa and set up camp (see map 4).

Peter, count of Brittany, determined to solve the shortage by launching a cattle raid, leading a band of men to lay an ambush for a passing caravan. It was well done: Peter's troop overcame the caravan's armed escort, and led the cattle triumphantly back to the crusader camp. The encounter is told in heroic terms by the author of the Rothelin chronicle, who was writing in the Île-de-France and whose detailed knowledge of the expedition suggests that he was drawing from the testimony of returning crusaders. 'Great was the delight of the rank and file', he writes, when the count of Brittany returned to provide the entire army with a meat dinner. Peter also shared his prize with the other commanders, at which 'some were very pleased', but 'others were scornful and jealous because he had won so much plunder. This led them', the chronicler continued ominously, 'to do things that brought great shame and harm upon Christendom'.[35]

One of the men looking on in jealousy was Amaury de Montfort. He and others 'talked about this together and said that they were just as powerful as the count of Brittany, if not more so, and that it would be a great disgrace, shame and eternal reproach to them if they did not go out too and win booty from the unbelievers.' And so, on the evening of 12 November 1239, Amaury and his comrades mustered on the southern side of Jaffa – a force of 600 knights (the Rothelin chronicler estimates), plus crossbowmen and sergeants. The plan was to head by night to a secluded pasture outside Gaza, the spot (so they had learned) to which a herd had been driven to be hidden from the crusader army.[36]

News of this plan reached the leader of the French forces, Thibaut of Champagne. He and Peter of Brittany, together with the masters of the Templar and Hospitaller orders, rushed to stop Amaury and his band. 'They reproached them vigorously', writes the Rothelin chronicler, 'for intending to ride to war like this, when the whole country was in a state of alarm, the unbelievers had their spies out in all the narrow ways and passes', and when the sultan of Egypt had raised a great army, which was now stationed in Gaza – perilously close to the raiding party's intended destination. But the would-be raiders would not listen. Thibaut reminded them that he was their elected leader and that they had sworn to obey him, and ordered them all to stand down, but they still refused.[37]

And so Amaury and his comrades set out from Jaffa. It was almost forty miles to their intended destination (Beit Hanoun, at the northern end of the Gaza strip). They were venturing far further south than Peter of Brittany had done, and attempting an extraordinarily long night march (although at least they were travelling by road, on a clear and moonlit night). Dawn had already broken when they approached their destination, drawing up in 'a narrow place with hills on both sides and nothing but sand underfoot', close to their target. They decided to wait there until later in the morning, when the livestock they sought would be turned out to pasture. In the meantime, they rested after their long night ride.[38]

Meanwhile, the commander of the Gazan forces, Rukn al-Din, had been tracking their movements. His scouts had detected the departure of the crusader force from Jaffa, so that he knew 'almost before nightfall, that these men were coming to look for plunder, and that they would all be extremely tired, both men and horses, before they got that far'. Rukn al-Din sent up signal fires to alert all able-bodied men nearby, and readied the garrison of Gaza. 'Before the sun was up', continues the Rothelin chronicler, 'he had more men than he needed. His scouts came and went, keeping a constant watch on the valley our men had entered.'[39]

And so the crusaders, resting in their valley, were now roused by 'such a great noise of drums, timbrels, tabors, horns, of men shouting and horses neighing that nothing else could be heard'. Looking above them, they saw upon the hilltops all about Egyptians with bows and arrows, crossbows, javelins and slings. Meanwhile other Egyptian troops were blocking the narrow pass into the valley.

Rukn al-Din had left the pass out of the valley open, inviting the crusaders to opt for flight. This was the option favoured by at least two of the Christian leaders, the count of Jaffa and the duke of Burgundy: the crusaders were 'in a place where both men and horses would be treading up to their knees in sand', they told the others, not to mention that 'for each man of theirs there were fourteen or more attacking'. But Amaury and Henry, count of Bar, refused to flee. They would be lucky to get away, they said, and even if the mounted men escaped 'all those on foot would be killed or taken'. And so the count of Jaffa and the duke of Burgundy flew from the field, and Amaury and Henry prepared to fight.

The Egyptian troops soon closed off the route out of the valley.[40] Amaury and his men, huddled in the valley's basin, unable to fight their way uphill and now surrounded, were in a killing ground. Spears, arrows and slingshots were pouring down upon them from the hilltops ('no storm of rain, no hail could have made the sky darker', writes the Rothelin chronicler). The crusaders fired back, but soon ran out of ammunition.

And so they fought their way towards the narrow route out of the valley. They were successful, managing to take the pass. Here they were protected – the Egyptian arrows could not reach them and they could defend the pass's narrow entrance and exit. But Rukn al-Din, seeing the situation, sent orders to his men to feign retreat. The crusaders, taken in, gave chase, pouring out onto the plain beyond. Behind them, the Egyptian archers swept down the hills to flood the valley they had left.

The crusaders were now exposed out on the open ground, with nowhere to retreat. The Egyptian troops closed in around them. Amaury, together with the count of Bar, readied their men to fight. 'Tenderly, kindly', describes the Rothelin chronicler, they 'urged them to do well and to sell their lives dearly, for there was no question of escape.'

And so the final phase of the battle started, 'arduous, fierce and bloody'. The Egyptians at first kept their distance, raining down volley after volley of arrows in order to inflict as much damage as possible before drawing their swords. Those crusaders still standing began to flee – except Amaury and Henry of Bar, and a few others. 'These did wonders', tells the Rothelin writer, 'and cut great clearings amongst the Saracens surrounding them. No one dared go near them, but they shot and flung at them and hurled lances as if at a target.' But Amaury and his friend were eventually exhausted, and the Egyptians made their final charge.

Amaury was taken prisoner, together with some sixty other knights. They were the last few left alive: only one knight in ten of those who had set out from Jaffa the evening before (not counting the foot soldiers, who were not numbered). The bodies of their hundreds of fallen comrades were decapitated, their heads gathered by Rukn al-Din and taken back to Cairo with the prisoners. There the heads were hung from the city's walls. As for Amaury's companion, Henry, count of Bar, his fate was never discovered – he was not captured, but his body was never found.*

Back in Jaffa, Thibaut and the other leaders soon heard the news – but, fearful that an armed attempt to free their comrades would only provoke the Egyptians to execute the hostages, they let them be led away.[41] Thibaut and his men withdrew from Jaffa, all the way to Acre.

While Thibaut worked to negotiate his comrades' release, Amaury languished in a Cairo gaol.[42] With him there was Philip of Nanteuil, who, like Thibaut, was a *chansonnier*. Philip was permitted – or perhaps encouraged – to compose a poem on their captivity to send to his comrades (it found its way back to France before too long, where it was preserved by the Rothelin chronicler). 'To alleviate my grief', he wrote, 'I want to make my lament over the good and valiant count of Montfort, who used to receive praise and honour, and who came to Syria to wage war.' Philip then addressed his homeland: 'France, sweet country customarily honoured by all, your joy has been utterly and completely transformed to weeping. You will be grieving forever more, such is the misfortune you have suffered! The tragedy is that as soon as you arrived you lost your counts.' The count of Bar, cried Philip, was surely dead: 'How the French will miss you! When they

---

* The heads of the crusaders hung as trophies from the walls of Cairo for some twelve years, until they were wrested back by the king of France as part of a treaty with the Egyptians, so that they could be buried; this is reported by the biographer of Louis IX, John de Joinville, who accompanied the king of France on the expedition during which the treaty was made (John de Joinville, 'The life of Saint Louis', in *Joinville and Villehardouin: Chronicles of the Crusades*, trans. C. Smith (London, 2008), ch. 518. The Rothelin chronicle describes how, after the release of the prisoners, Thibaut's men 'insistently asked and searched [across Egypt] for the count of Bar but could never hear any news of him. Some people said that Bedouins had watched the battle and after witnessing the Christians' defeat had rushed in to gather plunder . . . and that they had taken the count of Bar along with their other booty. Later, when they left the area and made camp, they tethered him to a post, where he was overcome by a flux and diarrhoea, of which he died. So it was said by some, but whatever the facts were, no one ever knew what became of him' ('The Rothelin Continuation', in *Crusader Syria in the Thirteenth Century: The Rothelin Continuation of the History of William of Tyre with part of the Eracles or Acre Text*, trans. J. Shirley (Aldershot, 1999), ch. 35).

hear the news about you they will make a huge lament, when France is deprived of such a valiant knight.' Philip turned his anger on the Hospitallers and Templars who, he felt, ought to have mounted a rescue on first hearing the news. 'A curse on the day', he raged, 'when such brave soldiers are slaves and prisoners!'[43]

Amaury, too, was permitted to send word out of their Cairo gaol. He chose to write to his wife. His letter was laconic, telling her only the bald terms of the situation. 'Know that Damascus is not taken . . . and all have returned to Acre', he wrote, and that 'sixty knights were taken alive' in the battle. He, like Philip, turned his chagrin upon the military orders who, the prisoners felt, could be doing more to pull them from their plight: Amaury had heard that 'the king of France has moved his whole treasury out of the Temple, because neither the Templars nor Hospitallers wished to aid the French in this crisis'.[44] The countess of Montfort sent Amaury's letter onward to England, where it was read by Richard of Cornwall, who passed it to the St Albans chronicler Matthew Paris (it is in his chronicle that the letter is preserved). It is hard to imagine that she did not show it first to Simon.

*

It was not until late May or early June 1240 that Simon at last embarked for Outremer.[45] He set out at the same time as Richard of Cornwall, and it is Richard who swamps the records, for the earl of Cornwall stopped at St Albans en route to Dover, so his visit was described by the house chronicler, Matthew Paris; and Richard later told Matthew all about his journey – how he was received joyfully and generously by townspeople along the route, how he sailed from Marseilles. And one year later, when his sojourn in Outremer was done, Richard wrote a letter to his friends the earl of Devon and the abbot of Beaulieu, providing his own account of his worthy exploits (again, passed on to Matthew Paris for preservation in his chronicle): how he had completed the negotiations begun by Thibaut and secured from the sultan of Egypt the prisoners' release, on 23 April 1241.[46] Simon, in contrast, created no record of his deeds, or at least none that has survived (in this he is more typical than Richard). Our knowledge of his expedition is confined to three fragments of evidence.

The first is a scratchy array of notes, crammed by Matthew Paris into a corner of the page narrating Richard of Cornwall's departure (see plate 14).[47] Clearly, when Matthew had already written up this section of his chronicle, in his fine and regular hand, he obtained further information that he felt should be recorded: the names of the knights who sailed with Richard, and the names of the knights who sailed with Simon, framed by an outline of the course that Simon took to Outremer. In the blank space at the bottom of the parchment sheet, on the left, Matthew has drawn a square inside which, in a quicker hand, he introduced the subject of Richard's knights. From this box a number of green lines splay outwards to the right, like palm leaves, towards a list of names: these are seven of Richard's knights, who sailed with him from Marseilles. To the right of Richard's list, Matthew has added another, longer litany, like its fellow inked around untidily in red. This opens with a note, 'Also in the same passage journeyed with lord Simon de Montfort – who, indeed, kept apart from the household of earl Richard before he withdrew from England' – ten knights, whose names are given here (we shall meet them in a moment). Then, to the right and bottom of this list, in a box shaped like a reversed L squeezed into the very corner of the page, Matthew describes what he learned of Simon's passage. These ten knights, he records, travelled with Simon and his wife, Eleanor, through Lombardy and the kingdom of Apulia, to take ship at Brindisi. There the countess stayed, in a castle well endowed with land that had been given to her – and here the text, faded by centuries of fingers flicking pages, becomes illegible.

Matthew's note is short and lacks the glamour of the elaborate narrative of Richard's journey, but it reveals much concerning Simon's choices. Simon had opted not to attach himself to Richard's expedition: Richard was the king's brother, and one of the richest men in England, but Simon was confident enough in his status to lead his own campaign. It was a confidence encouraged by his closeness to the Holy Roman Emperor, Frederick II, with whom he probably campaigned in northern Italy two years earlier. And, as we have also seen, it was a route probably planned with Amaury. The brothers had been prevented from travelling together, but in their route the cohesion of the Montfort family in waging war – such an important part of Montfort family identity – was kept alive.

Simon could not have travelled through Italy with the speed he achieved en route to Rome in 1238, for this time he had brought his wife with him. It is possible that Eleanor had recently given birth to their second child, in April 1240.[48] The baby was another boy, and had been named Simon (he and the next two Montfort boys would take Montfort family names). His father is unlikely to have been with his family for the birth, for Simon had travelled to England to discuss his financial business with the king, and probably remained there until late May. But the trip at least allowed him to fetch his other son, Henry, who was now about eighteen months and had not seen his parents for the best part of a year. He was brought to France to be reunited with his mother and to meet his baby brother.[49]

It was as a family, then, that the Montforts travelled almost four hundred miles to Brindisi. No doubt the journey was challenging, but they operated as a unit, as Simon had learned, listening to the stories of his parents' exploits in Languedoc. His mother, Alice, had carried him with her to war when he was scarcely more than a babe in arms, and had given birth to another child, Petronilla, during the course of the campaign. Eleanor, unlike Alice, would not be required to take part in the coming expedition. But she now faced the prospect of waiting, and hoping, for her husband's return, under the Apulian sun.

Travelling with Simon and Eleanor to Brindisi, and sailing now with Simon to Outremer, were the ten men whom Matthew Paris names, together with their retinues. Of knightly and, in some cases, minor baronial status, they are the sort of men whose names appear only sporadically in the surviving records. First named are Thomas and Gerard de Furnivall, brothers who held lands in Yorkshire and Northamptonshire respectively.[50] Gerard had at least one son with his wife, Christiana, and three stepchildren, the eldest of whom, Wischard Ledet, joined him now in Simon's following.[51] The two Furnivall brothers also knew another knight of this company, Hugh Wake (they can be found acting together as pledges for a debt).[52] Hugh was of no meagre status, holding lands in Nottinghamshire, Lincolnshire and Yorkshire, the nephew of a great royal lieutenant of the previous reign, William Brewer, and married to Joan, daughter and heir of the great baron Nicholas de Stuteville.[53] Hugh had taken his crusader vow in 1235, and his service was of sufficient value to the cause for the pope, in 1238, to agree that he should receive funding.[54] He and Joan had at least one child, Baldwin, named for Hugh's father and born perhaps a couple of years before Hugh left with Simon.[55] Also of higher status was Amaury of St Amaund, a veteran royal servant (named here by the chronicler as seneschal of the royal court); he was close enough to the king himself to be named, like Simon, as a godfather to Henry's firstborn son.[56] Then remaining were five knights, at least four of whom hailed from Burgundy. These were two brothers, Punchard and William de Dewyme, and Gerard, perhaps also their brother, who came from La Peaume, just south of Lyons. With them came another Burgundian, Peter de Châtenay, and Fulk de Baugé of Anjou.[57]

For the most part we cannot know how this company was raised. It includes none of Simon's own affinity, the men bound to him by homage, tied by neighbourhood, or retained in his service, who from the 1230s formed the core of his companions.[58] Only in the case of two can we infer how they came to join Simon's expedition: William and Gerard of La Peaume were both retainers of the king, in receipt of annual stipends from the royal coffers. They were, in effect, loaned by the king for this campaign – Gerard was even given an advance by Henry in order to allow him to join Simon. Henry also gifted fifty marks (almost £34) to Amaury of St Amaund to help equip him for the expedition.[59] This was, perhaps, Henry's contribution to the holy cause, whose progress he had impeded by stripping Simon's estates.

As to their companions, we can know little about how and why they came to be under Simon's command. Only in the case of one further man, who was not a knight and whose name is not recorded, can we know. He was one of Simon's servants, so one of those lower-status followers who would have accompanied the noblemen in numbers but who so often slip from view in the surviving records. He was to go with Simon to Outremer as penance. His sins had come to the notice of Church authorities in France, so were perhaps committed when in Simon's company in exile after August 1239. During this time an inquisition was underway across the length and breadth of France, led by the Dominican Robert le Bougre, tasked with the rooting out of heretics. Simon's servant had come forward to confess that he had consorted with such people: he had dined and drunk with them, he admitted, and listened to their sermons many times. As a result of his confession, Simon's servant was instructed to take the cross and go on pilgrimage with Simon to Outremer, and also to fast on Fridays for the remainder of his life and to attend the divine office at every opportunity.[60]

Simon had not, of course, been sheltering a heretic (the idea would have been abhorrent to this father's son). The inquisitor, Robert le Bougre, with the support of the king of France, was engaged in an indiscriminate campaign of persecution, accusing innocent as well as guilty and meting out harsh punishment, from public degradation to imprisonment and burnings at the stake, bringing hundreds to a fiery death. In these circumstances some who were concerned that they would fall under suspicion because they had consorted with the guilty came forward to confess their association, hoping to pre-empt any accusation against them: by law this would halt the inquisitor's pursuit and guarantee a moderate penance.[61] That this was the case with Simon's servant is suggested by a letter from the papal court, confirming receipt of the inquisitor's report, acknowledging that Simon's servant had told the inquisitors of his association with heretics 'freely by confession', and noting the penance imposed.[62] The penance was comparatively mild – or at least it could have been much worse. Perhaps it occurred to the inquisitors spontaneously, or perhaps it was suggested by Simon himself.

Several of those who travelled to Outremer with Simon would not return, as revealed in the second piece of evidence for Simon's expedition: the list of the dead given by Matthew Paris. We know almost nothing of how Simon and his comrades spent their time – perhaps a year – in Outremer. The Rothelin chronicle makes no mention of Simon, and speaks little even of Richard of Cornwall (the author by this point had all but given up on the crusaders, and proclaimed that Richard and his men 'did almost nothing in the Holy Land that was of any use').[63] Richard's official account, meanwhile, delivered in his letter to his friends, celebrates his own diplomatic achievements but makes no mention of Simon. And there is no record, here or elsewhere, of any engagement. Yet the list of fallen is grimly long: between Simon's and Richard's cohorts, thirteen named of knightly and baronial rank 'and many other nobles'. Amongst this number were three of Simon's company, Hugh Wake, Wischard Ledet and Wishard's stepfather, Gerard de Furnivall (and it is likely that a fourth, Gerard's brother Thomas, was also killed).[64] The chronicler's choice of words ('fighting for God in the Holy Land ... [they] fled gloriously to Heaven') suggests that these men died in combat, though it is possible that the chronicler was choosing, justifiably, to count losses incurred by other means, such as disease, on equal terms. We cannot know whether the English contingent was battered by sickness or by the enemy, but it is clear that Simon, like Richard, was in command of a company that suffered a serious rate of attrition.

Our third fragment of evidence suggests, however, that Simon came through the trials of command with an enriched reputation. This is a document issued in Acre, dated 7 June 1241 (see plate 15). Written in a clear and regular hand, it is addressed to Frederick II. Frederick was the nominal ruler of Jerusalem, for his first wife had been the heir to the kingdom and had borne him a son, Conrad, before she died. But Conrad was under age (he was then only thirteen), and so king only in name. The barons, knights and citizens of the kingdom – with whom Frederick's relations had been fraught – wanted a regent to govern the kingdom until Conrad's majority. They had chosen Simon.

The document they drew up for this proposal they called a 'form of peace', an agreement between the barons and the emperor for the government of the kingdom. They asked that Frederick give the barons his goodwill, 'and that he will rule over us by the guardian my lord Simon de Montfort, earl of Leicester', until Conrad was old enough to govern. Simon, the barons proposed, 'shall swear to keep and preserve the rights of the emperor, and of his son, King Conrad, and all those who are in the land', both residents of the kingdom and pilgrims, 'and to govern them by the usages and customs, and by the Assizes of the kingdom of Jerusalem. And we the people of the country . . . will swear to keep and maintain him in his office, and to obey him as we would the person of the emperor.'[65]

By the terms of this form of peace, Simon would be regent of Jerusalem. We cannot know the manoeuvring that lay behind this document, though it must have been drawn up with Simon's agreement (it would be something of a gamble to put the request to Frederick without the knowledge of the proposed regent). It is likely that the proposal was constructed with the help of other members of the Montfort family, for one of the barons of Jerusalem who put his name to the document was Simon's cousin, Philip de Montfort, the son of Simon's uncle Gui. Gui had accompanied the Count on an expedition to Outremer in 1204 and decided to remain there, marrying Heloise of Ibelin and raising a family. After his wife's death, Gui had returned to France and joined his brother, the Count, on campaign in Languedoc. He had brought with him his children, including Philip (whom we saw earlier with Alice de Montmorency and her children, Simon included, in the Château Narbonnais in 1218, when Gui was wounded and the Count was killed). Philip was raised in France and had joined his cousin, Amaury, in 1239 on the expedition to Outremer. Following his father's example, he decided to settle in the Holy Land, and in 1240 married Maria, heiress of Toron.[66] He now became a major figure in the politics of Outremer, well placed to propose a candidate for regent in 1241. It is possible that Amaury, too, was now in Acre with Simon and Philip – for he had been released by his Egyptian captors in April. There is a suggestion here of a Montfort family plan to establish Simon in Jerusalem, in a role that would make him one of Christendom's leading potentates. And after his quarrel with the king of England, Simon was, perhaps, putting irons in the fire.

But what the proposal shows, most importantly, is how impressive Simon had been. Even with Philip and Amaury's help, he would only have been selected for such a role by the knights and barons of Jerusalem if he commanded their respect, and to a serious degree. Whether it was his prowess on the battlefield, displayed in some unrecorded fight, his bearing, or his famous name – or some combination of the three – that won him recognition, we cannot know. We are left with the bald fact that Simon, still only in his early thirties, had been invited to govern a kingdom.

*

Nothing came of the request made to the emperor, and the proposal was apparently left to lie, but it marked a success of sorts for the

Montfort family after the trauma of Amaury's experience. Any sense of triumph, though, was not to last – for the war had one more casualty to take. Amaury had been released from captivity, together with Philip of Nanteuil and the other hostages, in April 1241. If Amaury and Simon were together in Acre in June, when the proposal for Simon's regency was issued, it is possible that the brothers set out for home together (only Amaury's journey is recorded, for reasons that will shortly become clear).

Amaury left Outremer in late summer, with the aim of retracing his outward route through the emperor's Italian lands. He landed at Otranto, some fifty miles south of Brindisi, on the tip of Italy's heel, and made it no further. On 28 August, 'the venerable count of Montfort', as one account recalls, 'departed to Christ'.[67] The cause of his death is not recorded. The most likely culprit must be disease or infection, though without knowing the conditions of his imprisonment it is unhelpful to speculate that his experience left him physically or mentally weakened, for disease can be as lethal to a vigorous man in his mid-forties as to any other.

Amaury's body was carried from Otranto to Rome, where he was to be buried in the basilica of St Peter's: a mark of the esteem in which he was held and the status he commanded. There he would lie until his tomb was destroyed by the rebuilding of the basilica in the late sixteenth century. Fortunately, it was visited before its destruction by the Renaissance scholar Rafaello Maffei, who recorded Amaury's epitaph in his encyclopaedia. It is factual and free of sentiment, but tells the reader all they need to know of the deeds that made the man:

Here lies Amaury, count of Montfort, constable of France, who against the Albigensians for the Catholic faith ofttimes fought; afterwards he crossed the sea to the parts of Syria against the Saracens, by whom he was captured in battle, and for a long time held in captivity. Finally, he was liberated by treaty, and while returning to his own land he died at Otranto, in the year of our lord 1241.[68]

While the setting of St Peter's was illustrious, it was also far from home. It was important to Amaury – as it was to those who loved him – that he be reunited with his family in the mausoleum at Haute-Bruyère.[69] The record of the house that describes his parents' tombs also describes the second phase of Amaury's burial. It begins by relating his imprisonment in Cairo, his death at Otranto en route home and his burial in Rome; but Amaury, so the account continues, had 'ordered that his heart be removed, on account of the vast devotion' that bound him and the nuns of Haute-Bruyère, 'whom among all and above all he had always loved'. And so a delegation of the sisters travelled from Haute-Bruyère to Rome, in order to collect Amaury's heart and bring it home. In a ceremony conducted by the bishop of Chartres, 'with hymns and praises', it was buried on the left of the great altar, below a likeness of Amaury's face commissioned by the sisters, hewn in stone.[70]

Amaury now joined the Montfort cohort of the fallen brought together at Haute-Bruyère, their memory to be cherished – and example propounded – to those, like Simon, who survived.

5

An Exemplar of Defeat

After the summer of 1241, Simon disappears from view for the best part of a year. When we meet him again it is in July 1242, in Burgundy, apparently in the company of the duke, a fellow member of the recent expedition to Outremer.[1] It was here that he received a missive from Henry III, requiring his presence in Poitou, some 350 miles to the south-west.

Henry needed Simon's help. In 1224 the English crown had lost swathes of northern Aquitaine (the dukedom inherited from Eleanor of Aquitaine, grandmother of Henry III): the county of Poitou and northern Saintonge, including the port of La Rochelle, were now in the hands of the king of France. Only the duchy's southern lands, with the port of Bordeaux, remained loyal to Henry. It was this region that could, therefore, be used as a base of operations. The truce that held between England and France was soon to expire and so, in 1242, Henry launched a campaign to reconquer his Aquitainian inheritance from the Capetian crown, landing at Royan on 13 May. He opened negotiations with Louis IX – but his object here was not to secure peace but to accuse Louis of violating their treaty, in order to justify the declaration of war that he was to make on 16 June.[2]

Simon arrived, in response to Henry's letter, in early July.[3] He came reluctantly: the king 'wished that I would stay with him', he explained years later, 'and I said to him that I had recently come from Outremer, and it was not convenient for me to stay, because of the many grievances that I had had, most of which came from him'.[4] Whether Henry felt guilty for how he had treated Simon, or whether his pressing need for support in the coming conflict overcame his pride, the king chose to offer recompense. He told the earl that he would return to him the money he had raised from the Leicester estates to pay off Thomas of Savoy, with an additional hundred marks (£67). Simon accepted the offer, though with little grace: 'it cannot be said that this was compensation for the wrong and the loss that he had done me', Simon's later testimony continues, before reprising his account of the stripping of his lands in 1239 while he was preparing to depart for Outremer, and how he had been forced to sell his property. But even an unenthusiastic earl of Leicester would be succour to Henry's cause, for the king was seeking to engage the king of France in battle.

*

The Battle of Taillebourg-Saintes is, today, little more than a footnote in English history: a military embarrassment totted up to Henry's score and, with hindsight, an ineffectual lunge against the expanding power of a vigorous Capetian monarchy. In France, however, the battle is a landmark in the history of national triumph, comparable to the victory of Philip Augustus over King John's forces at Bouvines in 1214, which had ended John's hopes of reclaiming Normandy. In the nineteenth century, at the crest of nationalist fervour, this victory of Louis IX (St Louis, as he was to become shortly after his death) was celebrated in painting, in marble, in song and in poetry. Eugène Delacroix was commissioned to depict the engagement for the Galerie des Batailles at Versailles (see plate 16). His monumental painting shows Louis on a war horse of golden-white, glittering in gilded armour and blue battle-dress patterned with fleurs-de-lis, mace in hand, arm raised to deal a blow. Amidst the tumbling bodies dimly formed around him, Louis gleams. In 1892, for the 650th anniversary of his victory, the people of Taillebourg determined to commemorate the feat, raising subscriptions from the great and the good – from bishops, dukes, counts and countesses, to notaries and pharmacists. In the town, on what was thought to be the land on which the battle was fought, they raised a stela of marble, inscribed in imperious Latin: '*To the most glorious and holy prince, persevering for the liberation of the* patria, *most vigorous champion, Louis IX, who scattered and put to flight the army of the English on the bridge of Taillebourg and under the walls of Saintes'.*

The stela was inaugurated before a teeming crowd. Speeches were made, sonnets were read, an anthem (an old poem of the battle put to music by the renowned composer, the Maître Weckerlin) was sung in chorus.[5]

The praise lavished upon Louis, in his lifetime and in the years that followed, was matched by Henry's humiliation.

*

Louis and his army were stationed in Taillebourg; Henry had pitched camp across the river from the town, intent on calling the enemy to battle. At his side was the man he called his father: Hugh de Lusignan, count of La Marche, married to his mother, Isabella d'Angoulême. Hugh, after recent perceived slights suffered at Louis's hands, wanted to strike a blow.* He had gathered a coalition of southern lords and asked his stepson, the king of England, to join him against the crown of France. Now, at Taillebourg, Henry held Hugh as his chief commander – it had been on Hugh's advice that he had brought his army through the night to Taillebourg.[6]

As the sun rose on 21 July, Henry looked out across the Charente and beheld the army of France, camped around the Oriflamme, the sacred battle-standard of Charlemagne. Now was the time for the battle council, in which Henry and his great lords – including Simon – would consult upon their tactics. But, as Henry turned to Hugh de Lusignan, the ground fell away beneath him.

Hugh's feet had grown cold: he denied that he had ever promised military support to Henry. A furious Richard of Cornwall brandished

---

* He had been Louis's vassal, but then Louis had granted Poitou (within which Hugh's lands lay) to Alphonse, Louis's younger brother. Hugh was now required to accept a lord of lesser rank, a demotion he did not appreciate. Nor did he take kindly to the royal demand that he deliver to Alphonse certain territories that Hugh had been holding from Louis as a pledge. On Christmas Day 1241, Hugh renounced his allegiance to Alphonse. For this defiance the king of France had Hugh tried *in absentia* in a court of his peers, which ordered the confiscation of Hugh's lands. See: J. Le Goff, *Saint Louis*, trans. G. E. Gollrad (Paris, 2009), 102–4.

Hugh's letters at him, letters in which he had written to England with just such a guarantee. But Hugh denied having anything to do with them. According to Matthew Paris, he blamed his wife, Henry's mother, Isabella, for concocting the whole scheme.[7] Henry and his nobles were in shock. Without Hugh's forces, not only did their chance of victory disappear but they risked being overwhelmed by Louis's army. If that happened, Henry would be taken hostage: a disaster – moral and financial – for England.

Richard of Cornwall was sent to negotiate a delay of Louis's attack, because the French held him in high regard for his role in securing the release of Amaury de Montfort and his comrades in Outremer the previous year. Louis, feeling generous, granted the English the rest of the day and also the night to decide what they should do. By the afternoon, Henry had determined to retreat. He ordered his army to strike its camp and head for Saintes, some seven miles to the south.

Louis, seeing the English slipping from his grasp, ordered his forces to cross the river in an attempt to stop Henry's retreat. The accounts of what happened next, on the stone bridge over the Charente, diverge – but it is likely that the mighty battle depicted by Delacroix was in reality little more than a skirmish.[8] The English were able to flee to Saintes.

The episode had been a mighty embarrassment for Henry, deflated by the desertion of a trusted ally and a pell-mell retreat. A tactical and controlled withdrawal would have been nothing shameful, but this was ungainly flight. It was also an uncomfortable reminder of one of the more ignominious actions of Henry's father, King John, who in 1214 had withdrawn for similar reasons in similar fashion in the face of Louis's father at la Roche-aux-Moins. That disorderly disaster had contributed to the loss of the bulk of John's possessions on the Continent and had sealed his reputation for military incompetence and cowardice.[9]

But for Henry worse was yet to come. Two days later, with the king of England and his forces ensconced behind the walls of Saintes, Hugh de Lusignan decided to redeem himself. The French army, led by Louis, was coming in pursuit and a detachment had ventured close to the town walls. Hugh – without consulting

Henry or anybody else – launched an attack. Henry and his commanders were compelled to follow him. It was now that Louis's main force arrived. The English were drawn, jumbled, into battle on the narrow roads running between the vineyards past the town. In the chaos, the king of England fled back into Saintes, and his soldiers scattered.

Amidst this degrading mess, a number of English nobles acquitted themselves finely: Matthew Paris names Simon first amongst the number who earned 'ever-lasting praise; this declared even by their rivals'.[10] Hostages were taken on both sides, at least one of them by Simon. We know this because he was permitted to keep the ransom of one hundred marks (customarily the ransom of a hostage taken in the royal presence would go to the king).[11] He must have felt that this was the least Henry could do for him.

With Henry and his men secure, for the time being, inside the town, out poured the recriminations. Henry (even within hearing of the French hostages, from whose report his next words are drawn) turned in fury upon Hugh de Lusignan. He was to blame for the disaster, the king of England screamed, because he had entreated Henry to cross the Channel and had assured him 'that he would find plenty of support in France'.[12]

But, to Simon, it was clear that Henry should take the greater share of blame. Turning to the king, he said: 'It would be a good thing if you were taken and shut away, as was done to Charles the Simple. There are houses with iron bars at Windsor that would be good for imprisoning you securely inside.'[13] (See plate 17.)

Simon's words could not have been harsher. He was shaming the king for his defeat (Charles the Simple, the Carolingian king, had been imprisoned after his defeat at Soissons in 922), but also cutting at Henry's character. Henry was coming to earn for himself, amongst the prelates and magnates of England, an epithet: *simplex*.[14] While the word could mean 'straightforward', it could also mean merely simple-minded and even foolish (like Charles 'l'Assoté', the fool, as Simon called him here). The insult was barely veiled: Simon was calling Henry stupid.

Worse still, Simon was issuing a threat. Charles the Simple had been shut in gaol by his own men, when they had had their fill of his incompetence. Now Simon was telling Henry that he was poised to follow their example (having already, it seems, appraised Windsor Castle as the place for the king's captivity).

Simon's words show not only his acuity – an ability to summon cutting words in the moment's heat – but also his willingness to humiliate, to degrade those he deemed to be weak, and to do so with no regard for royal status. It was a dangerous trait, which concerned those who knew him. A few years after this episode, Simon's close friend, the Franciscan friar Adam Marsh, would write to Simon, advising him to be more circumspect:

> Although it belongs to your generous nature to speak openly, freely, and boldly the thoughts in the heart, without distinction of persons, yet it is always advantageous for a generous man to use his heart to govern the utterance of his tongue, lest, while it is pleasant to speak more freely, lack of restraint causes offence and may hinder fine works of generosity and virtue . . . I think we should not be slow to notice that in both sacred and humane letters, amongst the excellent virtues circumspection in speech is a precept that is closely commended; for it is acknowledged from the evidence of wisdom that thoughtlessness in speaking is the downfall of both holy religion and human need.[15]

*

The campaign had been an utter failure. The English withdrew almost immediately from Saintes, heading first to Blaye – a fifty-mile retreat conducted so chaotically that the English foot soldiers, left by Henry to trail behind without provisions, began to perish from hunger. The army eventually reached the safety of Bordeaux.[16] Hugh de Lusignan, meanwhile, was forced to throw himself at the mercy of the king of France, a humiliation that gave much satisfaction to his enemies amongst the French, with whom, on account of his inconstancy, he had never been popular.*

---

* Louis's biography (written by one of his men, John de Joinville) recounts how one knight, Geoffrey of Rancogne, had sworn that he would not cut his hair again 'in the style of a knight' until he was avenged on Hugh for the wrongs that he had done

Louis, mindful of the coming winter and with his army weakened by sickness, had granted the English a truce.* This allowed Henry to linger in Bordeaux until October the following year. Simon was one of the few earls to remain with him.[17] The decision to stay was an onerous one, for Simon would have had to maintain his household overseas at great personal expense. The time was trying in particular for Simon for another reason: the nobles of southern France bore an innate animosity towards him, on account of his father – who had fought against them in Languedoc and, famously, defeated them at the Battle of Muret in 1213.† Both the king of Aragon, James I, and Raymond, count of Toulouse, were now using their influence with Henry to satisfy their hatred of the Montforts, and,

---

him. Without the opportunity, he had been forced to wear his hair long, parted in womanly fashion. But, on seeing Hugh kneeling at Louis's feet after the Saintes debacle, begging for forgiveness, Geoffrey called for a stool and there, before Louis and the pleading rebel, had his long locks cut (John de Joinville, 'The life of Saint Louis', in *Joinville and Villehardouin: Chronicles of the Crusades*, trans. C. Smith (London, 2008), ch. 104).

* Which he was to renew on 23 April the following year, 1243. By the terms of the pact, Louis was to keep what he had conquered, and Henry was to pay him £5,000 (£1,000 for each year that the truce lasted).

† The king of Aragon, James I, hated Simon for the memory of his father, the Count, for James's father, Pedro II of Aragon, had been killed at Muret. The killing was an accident, because Pedro – in an attempt to avoid being taken hostage – had been wearing borrowed armour (it would have been imprudent in the extreme for the crusaders to kill him knowingly, for he was the famous victor of Las Navas de Tolosa). James did admit, however, in his autobiography, that his father might have been partially responsible for the defeat at Muret: he had exhausted himself with a woman, so much so that during Mass before the battle he could not stand for the reading of the Gospel and had to sit down. James, only five years old at his father's death, was taken hostage by the Count. His freedom was secured only when he was rescued by a papal legate, and placed into the care of the Templars in Aragon (*The Book of Deeds of James I of Aragon: A Translation of the Medieval Catalan Llibre dels Fets*, trans. D. Smith and H. Buffery (Farnham, 2010), chs. 9, 10). One of the other mighty magnates of the region was Raymond VI, Count of Toulouse. Raymond's father, Raymond V, had been the foremost enemy of Simon's father, leading the Toulousains against the crusading forces in Toulouse in 1218, when the Count was killed. Raymond VI's mother was Joan, sister of King John (fifth wife of Raymond V), making the current count of Toulouse Henry III's cousin. He had joined with Henry in the alliance of southern nobles mustered by Hugh de Lusignan in 1241 to resist the advance of Capetian power into the south.

as Matthew Paris records, 'attempted to sow discord' between the king and Simon.[18]

Yet Simon's decision to remain with Henry, and to go with him back to England in October 1243, suggests that relations between the two remained at least amicable – and, that winter, Simon resumed his position at court. His return coincided with a grand occasion: the marriage of Richard of Cornwall, the king's brother, to Sanchia of Provence, younger sister of both the queen of England and the queen of France. Simon is likely to have been one of the many nobles who gathered at Dover to greet Sanchia and her mother, Beatrice, countess of Provence, and he certainly attended the wedding on 23 November 1243.[19] He stayed with the royal party for Christmas Day, celebrated at Reading and Wallingford, and moved with the court back to Westminster on 26 December.[20] Making the most of this opportunity, Simon set out to secure the goodwill of Beatrice of Provence. He and Eleanor hoped that the king's mother-in-law would intercede with Henry and persuade him at last to provide Eleanor's *maritagium*, the settlement of land or money customarily granted to a couple and their heirs by the bride's family.[21] The couple had been married more than five years and were also, perhaps, suffering a strain on their purse after their prolonged stay in Gascony. To add to their financial struggles, they now had three sons for whom to provide, for Eleanor had given birth at some point between the spring of 1242 and the spring of 1243. Little Henry and Simon now had a brother, Amaury.[22]

Beatrice's support brought a transformation in the Montforts' fortunes. Henry not only granted the couple 500 marks (£333) cash per annum (to be translated into land at the first opportunity), but also pardoned debts amounting to almost £2,000. The couple's annual income now totalled around £1,950.[23] A large part of this sum was secured only for their lifetimes, and so could not be passed on to their growing brood of children (a fourth son, Gui, was born in around 1244).[24] But now, at least, Simon could be numbered amongst the middling ranks of England's earls.

In the eighteen months following the Christmas festivities of 1243–4, Simon was only sporadically at court. When he was there his visits were short, except when he was attending parliament (as in early November 1244).* He seemingly spent the greater part of this period at Kenilworth and on his and Eleanor's southern estates.[25] These included the castle of Odiham in northern Hampshire (granted to Eleanor by Henry in October 1236, when she turned twenty-one), which Simon and Eleanor now began to rebuild. They added a strong new keep: a gleaming eight-faced tower, its mortared flint walls standing ten feet thick and rising to almost seventy in height, encased in the rich and creamy stone of Caen (see plate 18).[26]

Just ten miles south-east of Odiham stood Waverley Abbey, a Cistercian house to which Eleanor was particularly attached (see plate 19). In 1245 Simon accompanied her on a visit there, taking with them their two elder sons Henry, then six, and Simon, who was about four, to mark the feast of Palm Sunday on 1 April. It was Eleanor, rather than Simon, who was the abbey's patron, but her choice converged with the Montforts' strong attachment to the Cistercians.†

The chronicler of Waverley describes the scene, offering us the

---

* When he was asked by the king to work with Richard of Cornwall and others in securing a new tax from magnates and prelates – in which the committee was unsuccessful (*The Royal Charter Witness Lists of Henry III (1226–1272) from the Charter Rolls in the Public Record Office*, ed. M. Morris, 2 vols. (Chippenham, 2001) (hereafter *RCWL*), II, 3; J. R. Maddicott, *The Origins of the English Parliament, 924–1327* (Oxford, 2010), 461).

† The Waverley chronicler names her proudly as a 'most sincere lover of our house', and describes how she had obtained a dispensation from the pope to visit the abbey (women were not usually permitted to enter Cistercian monasteries). The chronicler also notes how, after the Montforts' visit in 1245, she had granted the abbey 50 marks and contributed another 18 marks for building works, as well as helping the monks to secure a piece of land at nearby Neatham (H. R. Luard (ed.), *Annales Monastici*, 5 vols. (London, 1864–9), II, 336). The Cistercians were popular amongst the nobility of the early thirteenth century. As we have seen, the Montforts had been the principal patrons of the Cistercian abbey of les Vaux-de-Cernay; and the Cistercians had been integral to the Count's crusading mission in Languedoc, their twenty-eight houses in the region bastions of orthodox power and their personnel (abbot Gui des Vaux-de-Cernay included) leading the Church's preaching mission, as well as acting as the Count's counsellors. See: B. M. Kienzle, *Cistercians, Heresy and Crusade in Occitania 1145–1229: Preaching in the Lord's Vineyard* (York, 2001), 135–73; B. Wildhaber, 'Catalogue des établissements cisterciens de Languedoc aux XIIIe et XIVe siècles', *Cahiers de Fanjeaux*, 21 (1986), 21–44 and other articles in this volume of *Cahiers de Fanjeaux*.

rarest of glimpses into Simon and Eleanor's family life, and their devotions. The couple, with young Henry and Simon and three maids, arrived at Waverley during a morning Mass (probably at around 9 a.m.), which the monks were celebrating in honour of the Blessed Virgin. The family crossed the threshold of the church at the very moment of the elevation of the Host, the mystical climax of the Mass that would have been accompanied by the ringing of bells (that the Montforts arrived at this most sacred moment was uncanny, as the chronicler noted, and suggested divine arrangement). Eleanor made an offering of precious cloths, which she wished to be used to cover the church's altar on those days when the abbey's relics were placed upon it for veneration. Eleanor was then allowed (and we can presume that Simon and the boys were too) to view the relics, including a portion of the True Cross, which she reverenced with a kiss.

There was a particular reason that the Montforts had chosen Palm Sunday for their visit. Every year on this feast day houses of the Cistercian Order held grand processions for lay friends and patrons, a solemn ritual that recalled the triumphant entry of Christ into the Holy City at the beginning of Holy Week.* This annual event had been planned by the Order's original leading member, St Bernard of Clairvaux, who had even written a sermon for the occasion. Titled 'On the Procession and the Passion', it unpicks the symbolic significance of each element of the Palm Sunday ritual. Simon, Eleanor and their boys would have listened to this sermon being read out in the Chapter House of Waverley that morning.[27] It opens with a warning to those lay members of the congregation who, like the Montforts, enjoyed the fleeting pleasure of earthly glory:

> Who then should now trust in the doubtful glory of this world, seeing that, even after such exaltation, such humiliation came upon the one who is Creator of time and Maker of the universe, who

---

* This was one of only two days during the year when lay friends and guests of a Cistercian house were allowed to enter into the most sacrosanct of spaces, the choir – the other being the feast of the Purification, 2 February (M. Sternberg, *Cistercian Architecture and Medieval Society* (Leiden, 2013), 179).

committed no sin? In the same city, by the same people, and at the same time, He was one moment honoured by the glory of a procession and divine praises, and the next examined with insults and abuse . . . This is the end of transitory joy: this is the result of temporal glory.[28]

It was a lesson that the Montforts – barely returned to royal favour after their ignominious expulsion of 1239 – could understand. Suitably prepared, they now took their place for the procession, moving out of the Chapter House and into the church.[29] There, together with the monks, the Montforts would have been handed palms blessed on the occasion, as the monks chanted the verse 'Pueri hebreorum': 'The children of the Hebrews, carrying olive branches, met the Lord, crying out and saying "Hosanna in the highest!"' Then, with the monks' song heralding their journey and the processional crucifix held aloft, the congregation would have left the church to begin its passage around the Waverley cloister. The procession paused at three stations, each with its own song to recall an element of Christ's experience. At the third, in front of the church, the congregation heard a passage of Matthew's Gospel, telling how Christ had come to the Mount of Olives and had sent two disciples off to fetch a donkey, and how He had ridden the animal into Jerusalem, the king making himself meek, as 'a very great multitude spread their garments in the way: and others cut boughs from the trees, and strewed them in the way: And the multitudes that came before and that followed, cried, saying: "Hosanna to the Son of David: Blessed is he that cometh in the name of the Lord."'[30] The procession then entered into the abbey church for the celebration of High Mass, the re-enactment of the sacrifice that Christ was to make a few short days after his triumphal entry into Jerusalem.

The two eldest Montfort boys were just old enough to appreciate the drama of the procession (and to respond to instructions to behave), and it was not long before Simon and Eleanor turned their attention to the children's education. In 1248 they entrusted their eldest, Henry, to the care of Robert Grosseteste for his schooling, and by 1249 or early 1250 Amaury had joined his brother.[31] There was nobody better qualified to educate the boys. Robert's interests were wide (the liberal arts, medicine, mathematics, astronomy, theology), and he was one of the greatest scholars of the age – indeed, of any age. In his early career his research on optics led him to develop a theory on the beginnings of the universe that has been hailed, today, as a precursor of the Big Bang Theory, and in his sixties he learned Greek, in order to translate Aristotle's *Nicomachean Ethics* for a Latin-reading audience.[32] The placement of the boys in Robert's household was a recognition of both the bishop's distinction and of his continued closeness to the Montforts. During this time their mutual friend, Adam Marsh, wrote regularly to Simon and to Eleanor, always sure to let them know that their children were happy and well in Robert's charge.[*]

*

Simon might have spent the greater part of the year and a half that followed his return from Bordeaux with his family, but he was soon pulled back into Henry's orbit. In the summer of 1245 the king was mounting a campaign against the Welsh. As king of England, Henry was overlord of Wales, and had taken the homage of Dafydd, ruler of Gwynedd, in 1240. A year later, Dafydd had rebelled and been forced into submission, handing over his half-brother, Gruffudd, to the English king as hostage for his good behaviour. Gruffudd was shut away in the Tower of London but, in March 1244, had attempted to escape – pulling down the tapestries that adorned the walls of his room and knotting them to his bedsheets and tablecloths to form a rope, down which he clambered from his tower. But Gruffudd was a big man: the makeshift rope tore under his weight and he plunged to the ground.

---

* Adam's letters to Simon did not always concern such serious matters: his correspondence with Simon, Eleanor and Robert encompasses not only the saving of souls and matters of conscience, politics and Simon's troubles with the king, but also domestic arrangements. One letter from Adam to Robert records how Eleanor had loaned to Robert her cook – Robert had then wanted to keep him on, and so Adam had checked with Eleanor whether this was acceptable. Adam wrote back to Robert with Eleanor's reply: the countess had said that 'if she had the best of servants however indispensable they might be to her, she would joyfully and promptly grant them to you to minister to your lordship' (C. H. Lawrence (ed. and trans.), *The Letters of Adam Marsh*, 2 vols. (Oxford, 2006–10), I, 159).

His body, according to Matthew Paris, 'provided a miserable spectacle to those who saw it. Indeed his head, with almost his whole neck, was buried in his chest between his shoulders'. Dafydd, now with no one to lose, declared himself prince of Wales, sought the support of the pope and mustered the chieftains of Wales in resistance to English rule.[33]

And so, on 13 August 1245, Henry arrived at Chester. There, over the course of the following week, his mighty army gathered, at its head Simon and the earls of Cornwall, Winchester, Albermarle and Oxford. The force set out on 21 August, moving westward in stages of between five and twelve miles per day along the Welsh coastline. Henry brought them to a halt at Deganwy, on the eastern shore of the Conwy estuary, on 26 August. There he decided to build a castle upon the ruins of a Welsh fortress.[34]

Deganwy stood on high ground – an optimal choice for a castle site, perhaps, except that it was far too high for supplies to be delivered directly from the river, and also too far from the coast to be supplied by sea.[35] The Welsh, who read the terrain far better than Henry, saw their advantage. From their base on Snowdon, immediately to the south-west, they sortied at will, attacking the English supply lines. Henry's army soon started to get hungry. The situation worsened at the beginning of September, when the earl of Gloucester (who, along with Richard of Cornwall, was one of the two mightiest earls of the kingdom) arrived with his contingent, swelling the ranks of soldiers needing to be fed.[36] The men began to starve.

We know of their desperation because, at the end of September 1245, one of the knights of the army wrote a letter describing those nightmarish weeks (this letter made its way to Matthew Paris at St Albans, who copied it into his chronicle).[37] It is a wretched tale: 'such a want of provisions came about', wrote the knight, 'that we met with an irreparable loss of men as well as horses'. Not only foot soldiers but nobles too were suffering, for 'there was no wine in the king's household, nor indeed amongst the army, except just one cask' (wine was no luxury: here in a castle with no access to fresh water except rain, it was vital). Simon and his fellow nobles were at least safe from starvation for, as always in such situations, a free market operated ruthlessly. The price of corn rose to twenty shillings, that of an ox to three or four marks, and that of a hen to eightpence. The latter was about eight days' wage for an unskilled labourer (the sort of man who made up a large part of the feudal host), and was a sum high enough to bring a wince even to the knight making the report. Living conditions, though, were as trying for Simon and his fellow knights as for the men. Because the castle was under construction, the troops had to spend the whole two months living under canvas. On an exposed site, with only meagre shelter, and without winter clothing as the weather turned, the cold began to bite.

Famished and desperate, armed foraging parties were sent out into the wild Welsh-infested landscape. Every sortie was a highly dangerous operation. 'We have been exposing ourselves to many dangers', wrote the knight, 'in order to obtain necessities, sustaining many ambushes and assaults from the Welsh, enduring losses.' The English fought hard: the letter writer could report with pride that 'we inflicted losses upon the enemy often'. The encounters were brutal. 'After one fight,' he continued, 'returning in triumph to the castle we brought back almost a hundred heads of those we had decapitated.'* Presumably the trophies were taken to be displayed upon the palisades of the Deganwy camp – within sight of the Welshmen who controlled the western bank of the estuary below. This savagery was a mark of how things were done differently in Wales, a land ungoverned by the chivalric values that prevailed across most of Europe.[38]

One particularly vicious encounter occurred on 25 September. A ship dispatched from Henry's lands in Ireland made its way into the estuary and drew up beneath the English camp, attempting a resupply. But the crew made a mess of anchoring their ship and, as the tide went out, she was left grounded on the Welsh side of

---

* Headhunting was a characteristic of warfare between the Welsh and English. Prior to 1245, the English are recorded as headhunting as recently as 1233, when Henry III rewarded a marcher lord who presented him with the heads of fifty-seven Welshmen who had been raiding into English territory, bestowing a shilling for each head (F. Suppe, 'The cultural significance of decapitation in high medieval Wales and the Marches', *Bulletin of the Board of Celtic Studies*, 36 (1989), 147– 60, at 147).

the estuary. From the fortress above, the English command dispatched 300 soldiers in boats across the water, led by a cadre of knights from Richard of Cornwall's retinue, accompanied by crossbowmen to provide fire support. The detachment was able to chase away the Welsh who had descended upon the ship – but instead of securing the provisions they pursued the fleeing enemy, chasing them as far as six miles. When Richard's men finally returned, they did not head straight for the safety of the English camp, but piled into the local abbey, Aberconwy, which stood across the estuary.* This was a sacred site, a Cistercian house (like Waverley) and the English ought to have respected its grounds as they would those of any other church. But, still coursing with the dark thrill of the fight, they sacked the monastery, pillaging its precious objects and setting fire to the workshops within the precinct.

It was an egregious crime, and it horrified the knightly letter-writer. It invited, he thought, divine retribution. His concerns were justified by what happened next. For, while the English band were ravaging the abbey, the enemy had been regrouping. A great throng of angry Welshmen had been mustered, and they now entered the abbey to set upon the pillagers. The English fled. Some pelted for the supply ship, hoping to find refuge behind its wooden walls, while others threw themselves into the river and tried to swim to the far shore. Some hundred men were cut down as they ran, not counting those who drowned.

Four knights were taken alive.† At first the Welsh considered imprisoning them, for the knights would have been a powerful bargaining counter, but then realized that amongst the many Welsh felled in the pursuit were several native nobles, amongst them a

---

* The site of Aberconwy Abbey is where Conwy Castle now stands: Edward I ordered its monks to move, and levelled the abbey in order to build the castle – an imposing statement of his lordship, given that it was the burial place of both Llywelyn the Great and his son, Gruffudd, Dafydd's brother, whose body had been fetched from London by the monks after his fatal escape attempt from the Tower the previous year. For the building of Conwy, see: M. Morris, *Castle: A History of the Buildings that Shaped Medieval Britain* (London, 2003), 111–18.

† Alan Buscel, Adam de Moia, Geoffrey Sturmy, and Raymond, a Gascon whom, we are told, the king liked to josh (*Matthaei Parisiensis, Monachi Sancti Albani, Chronica Majora*, ed. H. R. Luard, 7 vols. (London, 1872–83), IV, 483).

young, handsome and vigorous man, Naveth ap Odo, whose loss was felt particularly hard.

And so the Welsh, in their fury, hanged the captive English knights. It must have been done on the western bank of the Conwy estuary, in full view of the English army at Deganwy, for the letter-writer to recognize the men and know how they were killed. The English commanders could only stand and watch the killing, and then what followed. The Welsh took down the bodies and, 'cutting off their heads and tearing them to pieces, finally threw their miserable corpses limb by limb into the river'.

The Welsh campaign had been a wretched thing. Many had died, and for nothing. Henry, upon his return to England, arranged for a Mass to be celebrated for their souls at Oseney Abbey, and for 400 poor people to be fed with 400 loaves, 'for the souls of the same persons' – the number probably determined by the number of the slain.[39]

For Simon – who had now campaigned in Italy, Syria and France – the disaster must have merited the sort of scorn he had poured upon the king at Saintes.

6

Ruler of Gascony

Although Simon remained reliant on his king to some extent, he
had shown his calibre on a global stage, building his reputation
independently. The shifting dynamic between the two had been
revealed in their quarrels across the past six years and it was this
tension – in which contested notions of status, reputation, honour
and proper treatment cut across each other – that was to mark the
next phase of Simon's career.

The two years that followed the disaster at Deganwy were
remarkably uneventful for Simon and in the autumn of 1247 he
once again took the crusader's vow.[1] The Christian territories in
Outremer were in a newly perilous state. The city of Jerusalem,
won back by the Christians through diplomatic means in the 1220s,
had been lost again in 1244, in battle. The turn in fortunes moved
many to take the cross, most notably the king of France, his brothers
and many French noblemen. Louis made his vow in 1244 and spent
the next four years preparing for his departure – financially, militarily
and spiritually – until, in the spring of 1248, he was ready to lead
15,000 men to Damietta, on the Egyptian coast.[2] There are hints
that Simon coordinated his new expedition with Louis (he can be
found later discussing his plans with the chaplain of Alphonse of
Poitiers, one of Louis's brothers).[3] But he was certainly helped by
two of his closest friends, Robert Grosseteste, bishop of Lincoln,
and Walter de Cantilupe, bishop of Worcester, who secured for him
a papal subsidy of 4,000 marks (£2,667). This was awarded to Simon
in recognition (so the papal letter runs) of 'the merits of his probity
and zeal for the Christian faith' and his 'fervour to imitate his

ancestors' in fighting for the Church.[4] The sum awarded was substantial (considerably more than his annual income), and was intended to support Simon's costs in mounting a significant campaign.

Simon's plans were disrupted, though, in the spring of 1248, by a request from the king: Henry wanted Simon to take up the governorship of Gascony. This would be a major undertaking. Gascony, although under the authority of England's kings, was something like the Wild West of Europe, its towns riven by feud, its lords unheeding of Henry's authority. Indeed the Gascons' loyalty was negotiable, lured as they periodically were to the allegiance of one or other of the neighbouring rulers who cherished designs upon the region, including the king of Navarre (Thibaut of Champagne, the leader of the 1239 crusade) and the king of France (whose truce with England, negotiated in the months after the English rout at Saintes, was shortly to expire).

The challenge of the task, and the inevitable delay it would entail in the fulfilment of Simon's crusader vow, required careful thought. He discussed the proposal with those he trusted, sieving through potential trials and hazards. Later, when he was in the midst of struggling with the task he had undertaken, his good friend Adam Marsh wrote to him recalling those conversations. 'If you are receiving the responses of a broken treaty and feigned affection', Adam asked, 'are you enduring anything other than what you had expected? . . . With your clear-sighted wisdom', he continued, in his typically elaborate style, 'you recall the frequent anxious conversations in which we afflicted each other's ears with tales of the detestable treachery and cunning which we now see with our eyes.'[5]

Despite such misgivings, Simon decided to accept the commission. He explained his reasoning a few years later: knowing that 'the land of Gascony was at the time in an evil and dangerous state, and in great fear of being lost by the king and his heirs', he had heeded the entreaties of the king and his counsellors, as well as the queen, for 'he did not wish at all that the king, his lord, should have shame or loss for want of something that he was able to do'.[6] And so it was that Simon (as Adam Marsh later recalled) 'not in the least feared to incur the uncertain risk of a large-scale undertaking, despite insistent suspicion of amazing bad faith'.[7]

There is no reason to doubt this presentation of Simon's motives, given by the earl himself and by his friend. But perhaps he was also persuaded by the recognition of his reputation that Henry's request embodied. Like the proposal for his regency of Jerusalem, it was an invitation to rule, on a scale far beyond an earldom and with quasi-royal power. And, what was more, this governorship of Gascony formed a pleasing parallel with the rule of Simon's father – for the Count, now as ever, stood as Simon's exemplar.

The association with his father was one that Simon had long cultivated and proclaimed. When he had first come to England, and had been seeking to establish himself, it was to his father's authority that he had turned: in two of his surviving early charters, he styles himself 'Simon de Montfort, son of count Simon de Montfort'.[8] At a time when he was seeking to set out his credentials and before he could claim an imposing title (he was not an earl at this point but only 'lord of Leicester'), the greatest boost to his authority was to declare his closeness to the Count, marking himself as the heir to the great crusading hero.

Simon would go further still. After his marriage to Eleanor brought a major elevation to his status, he ordered the making of a new seal matrix (the metal mould into which wax would be poured to produce the seal that would authenticate his documents). For it, Simon appropriated his father's image (see plates 10–13 for all the seals that follow). The Count's seal had been acutely distinctive. By the thirteenth century the most common image for noblemen's seals was a knight riding on horseback into battle, his heraldic device upon his shield and his horse's battledress, often with the counterseal used to display the device in fine detail. The Count, in his first seal, which he used from the 1190s, had adapted this familiar image: he wears a helm, and his shield bears the roaring lion of the Montforts, but in place of a sword he holds a hunting horn, raised to his lips, while at his horse's feet run hunting hounds, amidst a field of foliage.[9] This image spoke of his family's hereditary office, the keepership of the royal forest of Yveline (the forest that ran alongside the Montfort seat outside Paris). The role entailed supervision of the royal hunt, and thus brought an enviable closeness to the kings of France, a point worth emphasizing. Around 1200, though, he ordered the design remade, in imitation of the seal of his grandfather, Simon, count of Évreux and lord of Montfort. To this end (and perhaps surprisingly for this most warlike knight), he had all vestiges of the standard knightly design removed. In the image set upon his second seal, the Count wears no armour and carries no shield: he is bare-headed, his robes draping elegantly, his hunting horn prominent, a single collared hound at his stallion's feet.

This was the image Simon used for his own seal. The variations between his own and his father's design are barely noticeable (only in the plume of the background foliage and the lift of the head of Simon's hound'). That Simon made this choice was not inevitable. His eldest brother, Amaury, had opted for a conventional depiction: he is shown helmed, with sword and shield, his horse like its rider dressed for battle with the Montfort lion loudly displayed. But Simon was shown literally in his father's image. The seal was a very public portrayal of authority, appended to charters and letters, the instruments of rulership, the face the lord chose to show to the world. Simon had bound himself to his father in the most demonstrative manner possible.

The governorship of Gascony was, therefore, another opportunity to follow in his father's footsteps as a ruler of a major region – his very footsteps, in fact, for although Simon was operating in the south-west, while his father had operated in the south-east, there was considerable overlap around the region of Toulouse. But this association with the Count, as much as it offered Simon inspiration and authority, was also dangerous – because, for the people of the region, the Count was not a glittering hero but the bringer of war and terror. In this context, for Simon to be showing himself as the Count's successor, sealing the legal instruments of his rule with an image near-identical to that with which his father, at Pamiers, had sought to exorcize the customs of Languedoc and impose foreign power, was incendiary. So much is revealed by one Gascon, who announced that he would not trust Simon as

---

* The animal on the Count's seal is a scent hound, so has its nose to the ground (a point I owe to Nicholas Vincent).

governor, 'since he had heard tell of the evil reputation of the family of Montfort'.[10]

*

When Simon set out for Gascony at the end of summer 1248, he expected to rule the region for seven years. Simon wanted to ensure the best possible chance of completing his mission, and so had apparently dictated the terms of his appointment. These are set out in his commission (the original of which survives, kept carefully in the Montfort family archive). 'Know', Henry proclaimed, 'that we have committed to our dear brother-in-law and faithful man Simon de Montfort, earl of Leicester, the custody of our whole land of Gascony, from Easter in the thirty-second year of our reign [1248] until the end of the following full seven years, entirely.' For the whole term, Simon was to have at his disposal all Henry's Gascon income, so that he could 'sustain throughout the aforesaid seven years all wars [guerras] in progress or to be begun in the aforesaid land against all people', unless the opponent happened to be one of the neighbouring kings, who would present a challenge of such financial and military magnitude that extra resources would have to be supplied by Henry in support of Simon's efforts. Simon also secured from Henry the service of a small army – fifty knights – and the promise of 2,000 marks (£1,333). 'And, moreover', continued Henry's proclamation, 'Simon himself will revive our laws, liberties and goods dispersed and alienated in that land for the sake of his power', and have control of the king's castles.[11] Simon, then, was endowed with significant authority. As he later pointed out, he undertook the appointment 'in this manner, not in any way as a guardian to be removed at the will of his lord, but in place of his lord in all things until the end of the seven-year term'.[12]

Simon's remit is revealed in the commission, too. It stipulates that he was to sustain 'all wars . . . against all people' present and future during his term of office. This was not a governorship in the sense that we might otherwise conceive of it – the normal rule of a subsidiary territory by a deputy – but rather the subduing of a recalcitrant people by military and judicial means. And this is certainly how Simon understood his role. The chronicler Matthew

Paris, in recounting a later argument between Simon and Henry (about which we will hear more later in the chapter), notes Simon's pointed reminder to Henry that 'when he was going to Gascony ... the king had persuaded him compellingly that he should suppress the traitors'.[13]

Simon's mission, then, was dangerous. Letters written by his friend Adam Marsh give a precious window into Simon's inner world as he waged war on the Gascon rebels. Simon, it seems, wrote frequently to his friend back in England, seeking counsel and comfort, and Adam's responses (although they can be dated only roughly) make the mood of their discussions clear.* One letter is particularly striking. In want of recent news of Simon's state, Adam had become anxious. 'I have had varying reports', he fretted, 'now with news of your safety, now of your being in danger, which cause me to vacillate between anxiety and fear for you and relief, hope and joy'. But he had comforted himself, he told Simon (in words now turned into succour for the earl), by thinking on God's proclamation in the book of Exodus: that, to those who held true to Him, God had promised to 'be an enemy to thy enemies, and afflict them that afflict thee ... I will send my fear before thee, and I will make all thine enemies turn their backs unto thee'.[14] Adam continued with a passage from Deuteronomy. He quoted it at length, for its relevance to Simon:

> if thou say in thy heart: these nations are more than I. How shall I be able to destroy them? Fear not ... because the lord thy God is in the midst of thee, a God mighty and terrible. He will consume these nations ... and shall slay them until they be utterly destroyed.

---

* Adam told Simon of his 'sure hope that in the midst of conflict and danger, the contrivances of treachery and the uncertainties of a shifting world, your anxious and devout soul will be preserved' by the Lord, and comforted him with the example of the prophet Elisha: 'because he did not abandon his fear of God, heaven delivered him from the fear of men when an armed conspiracy had risen against him, unarmed as he was, and repeatedly sent him fiery reinforcements' (C. H. Lawrence (ed. and trans.), *The Letters of Adam Marsh*, 2 vols. (Oxford, 2006–10), II, 325). Again, Adam reminded him that 'the warfare of the saints has this saving dispensation, that when confidence in worldly assistance is gone, the triumphant courage of the warriors becomes entirely dependent upon the invincible strength and protection of heaven' (ibid., 335).

And he shall deliver their kings into thy hands, and thou shalt destroy their names from under heaven. No man shall be able to resist thee, until thou destroy them.[15]

Adam knew that God was on Simon's side. He advised the earl that – so long as he continued as a faithful Christian, a good lord, generous to his men and protective of the weak, a keeper of his word and prudent in his action,

then even amidst the dreadful clamour of trumpets, the fearful shouts and the grim screeching of arms, the pressing concourse of combatants, the sudden death of those who fall, even amidst the blood streaming from the wounded and the piteous cries of the dying, that judgement of God shall assuredly be fulfilled upon your adversaries: 'the wicked man fleeth, when no man pursueth' and regarding you, 'the just, bold as a lion, shall be without dread'. But if the great-hearted captain should happen to lose his life to save his men, what will ever be judged more glorious or more seemly or salvific than to end one's life for the sake of the living?[16]

*

Simon's time in Gascony (as one might expect from Adam's tone) was one of conflict. It was a conflict that arose from contending interpretations of his role, in terms of what he symbolized as ruler – his self-presentation as the Count's successor was ill matched with Gascon perceptions of the Montfort name – and in his objectives, as Simon sought to impose English authority and the Gascons to avoid it. These competing energies clashed and swirled for four years and, in 1252, erupted in an episode that would change everything. The Gascons, seeking to overthrow Simon, turned to the king of England. Henry heard them out, and in response to their complaints rescinded Simon's authority.

The king also subjected Simon's rule to an inquiry, and one which was highly unusual. The records of this inquiry form the bulk of our evidence of Simon's time in Gascony. They are in some cases very detailed, appearing to offer a sharp insight into the goings on of these four years. But they are not all that they seem. The first difficulty is that the versions of the story they present diverge dramatically, with first the Gascons and then Simon giving their account of the same events. But the challenge runs deeper than this, for these testimonies were produced in an extremely irregular manner. This was not a trial, in which (in the thirteenth century as today) there would be an effort to discover 'the truth', or at least the most reliable version of the truth available. Indeed, it was not clear at all what this inquiry was supposed to establish. As a result, those involved had no hope of establishing 'the facts', any more than we do now.

In tracing the course of Simon's career, the strangeness of the Gascony inquiry is important. For it was the process of the inquiry, more than what actually happened during the four years of Simon's rule, that impacted on so much that followed. It transformed Simon's relationship with Henry, for Simon, objecting to it in the strongest terms, felt that Henry had done him a profound wrong. Moreover, it provided an example of how not to rule, one that he would call upon in the next, transformative stage of his career, when he and his confederates would decide that Henry was not fit to wield power, and that they could do a better job themselves.

The inquiry lasted around a month, through May and June 1252, and was held in Westminster Abbey, in the monks' refectory.[17] This long hall, spanning the length of the south cloister, was ordinarily used to seat the monks at mealtimes. Their refectory tables, flanked by benches, ran end to end the length of the long space, either side of a central gangway that allowed passage up and down the hall. Assemblies (or, as they were now called, parliaments) were sometimes held here, with the king taking his seat at the far eastern end upon the raised platform normally reserved for the abbot. (This configuration, necessitated by the use of the monks' dining hall for great assemblies, would endure throughout the Middle Ages and, ultimately, form the seating plan for the modern House of Commons).[18] Onto the benches now crammed perhaps hundreds of Gascons and *curiales*.

From the documents produced for the inquiry we can infer something of the procedure that was followed. The Gascon delegations, each representing individuals or towns, were required to draw up a schedule outlining their complaint (some were provided with a royal scribe, others brought their own). Each delegation apparently had total freedom, in both the content of the schedule and in its structure.[19]

There were several anomalies in this procedure. The first was the freewheeling nature of the complaints that it permitted. Royal officers were used to conducting inquiries, but they would usually do so within a framework provided by the king. For instance, the king's justices in eyre, who travelled around the kingdom at regular intervals, were provided with 'articles of the eyre': questions to put to panels of local jurors designed to uncover the crimes that were of interest to the crown, as well as any misdeeds committed by royal officials. (Had anyone been imprisoned arbitrarily by bailiffs, without reasonable cause? Had any prisoners been freed without warrant? Had any thieves been allowed to escape?) But in this case the Gascons could make any complaint they chose. Indeed, the openness of the procedure encouraged them to range widely in their accusations, sometimes alleging what might be called crimes and sometimes pointing to acts that were licit but (according to the Gascons' estimation) morally objectionable. At other points they attributed to Simon incidents that could be connected to his actions only in the loosest terms.

The second irregularity was that accusations were not subject to proof. In a trial, anyone making an accusation would be required to swear to it on oath, meaning that he or she would either have to tell the truth or risk their souls for the sake of their perjury. They might also be required to muster others who were willing to swear similarly to support their story and, if that were not sufficient, ultimately to stake their lives in trial by combat, calling upon God to pronounce judgement.[20] These measures served to deter vexatious or scurrilous accusations, because anyone making an allegation had to be prepared to back it up, even with life or limb. They also provided a means by which a jury could determine the truth of what had happened. But here the complainants were free to make their claims without repercussion.

Adam Marsh, Simon's friend, had come to Westminster to offer his support, and wrote a detailed account of what happened for Robert Grosseteste; in it he describes how, as the hearing went on, Simon's party called for some standard of proof to be imposed. The earl and his men 'offered to underpin their statements at all points either by bodily duel with any number of persons or in any other way that the court decided', and put pressure upon the king to impose 'a necessary requirement . . . that anyone bringing a charge or defending himself should obey the law, should receive judgements given for him and accept judgements against himself', either in the king's court in England or in a trial held in Gascony. But 'the party opposing the earl . . . was unable or unwilling to do any of these things; shameless in their evasion and dismal folly, they utterly refused to undertake the burden of proving their declarations, or to submit to the law in any prosecutions or defensive actions', in either Gascony or England.'

The third irregularity was that, at least initially, there was no provision made for Simon's response. The right of the defendant to reply to an accusation was a standard part of legal procedure. But Simon was clearly not to be given this opportunity. So much is obvious from the report of Adam Marsh, who complains that it was only eventually, following the lengthy hearing given to the Gascons, that 'after laborious perseverance it was only just possible to extract a concession allowing the earl of Leicester to be heard, as reason dictated', and present witnesses in his defence. Adam then describes how Simon's men spoke in support of him and produced several written proofs, including a statement from a faction of the townspeople of Bordeaux and various written instruments of Simon's rule.[21]

The fourth irregularity was that no one had been appointed to act as judge. Any person in England of free status was entitled to be judged by a panel of his peers – so much was guaranteed in Magna Carta (Chapter 29 of the 1225 version). In the case of a tenant-in-chief of the crown (as Simon was) this panel would comprise an assembly of bishops, earls and barons, meeting under the king's supervision. There were precedents for such trials, including one held by Henry's father, King John.[22] For the 1252

* *Letters of Adam Marsh*, I, 83, 85. As Simon recalled, the Gascons 'did not wish to make a guarantee to declare that what they said was the truth', and the king 'either through his will or through another's counsel' would not compel them to (C. Bémont, *Simon de Montfort* (Paris, 1884), 337).

inquiry, various senior figures were in attendance, including several bishops (Walter de Cantilupe of Worcester, and the bishops of Ely, Norwich, Salisbury, and Bath and Wells) and a number of earls (Cornwall, Gloucester, Norfolk, and Hereford).[23] Also present were Peter de Montfort (no relation of the earl but a close friend, a major baron and Walter de Cantilupe's nephew), and Peter of Savoy, the queen's uncle – as well, of course, as Adam Marsh. But none of these men was summoned to appear in any formal capacity. We know from Matthew Paris that the earls of Cornwall, Gloucester and Hereford were there because Simon had asked them to attend (presumably Walter de Cantilupe, Adam Marsh and Peter de Montfort, as close friends of the earl, did not need to be asked).[24] Simon's objective here was presumably – in the absence of a legal panel – to ensure that voices of authority would be there at least to speak in his support.

What, then, was the reason for this irregular format? The closest parallel – and possible precedent – was the set of inquiries (*enquêtes*) established by the king of France, Louis IX, in 1247. Louis had empowered his *enquêteurs* 'to hear and to write and to inquire simply and *de plano* about injuries and exactions, services received but not due and other burdens, if such things have been done to anyone anywhere by our bailiffs, reeves, foresters, servants, or their households'.[25] Louis, whose conscience was acute, felt that he was ultimately responsible for any misdeeds committed by his officers; the objective of the *enquêtes* was thus to cleanse the king from any sins he had committed through the persons of those officers, allowing him to depart on crusade in a state of grace, worthy of God's support.[26] These *enquêtes*, then, were concerned with uncovering not only illegal actions but also immoral ones. For this reason Louis chose Franciscan and Dominican friars (experts in hearing confessions and assigning penance) as his *enquêteurs*. They were responsible for hearing the complaints and assigning monetary compensation as they judged appropriate.

The 1252 Westminster inquiry has much in common with Louis's *enquêtes*, in both inspiration (inviting subjects to come forward with complaints about a royal officer) and procedure (in the initial process of taking depositions from the complainants, which is why the schedules of complaint drawn up in 1252 look similar to their

French counterparts).[27] But there were crucial differences. The *enquêtes* were conceived with far greater rigour of procedure. For instance, Louis's *enquêteurs* were furnished with a set of 'articles' that guided their lines of inquiry; accusations were subject to proof (both sides had to provide oaths that they would proceed in good faith, and the *enquêteurs* established the veracity of a complaint by gathering multiple witnesses to an alleged crime and questioning them); defendants were summoned to offer a response to allegations; and the *enquêteurs* were tasked with giving judgement, with the clear goal of assigning compensation accordingly.*

The Gascony inquiry seems to have been, then, a haphazard transplantation of this new French procedure into an English court context. Both Henry and the Gascons would have known of Louis's inquiries: in 1247–8 they had operated on the very borders of Gascony, in Saintonge to the north and in Béziers and Carcassonne in Languedoc.[28] Whether the impetus came from the Gascons (whose expectation of Henry's lordship had been altered by Louis's example) or from Henry himself (in an effort to equal the benchmark for good lordship set by Louis) we cannot know. The result, however, is clear. This choice of procedure sat uneasily within the context of the English court, whose members possessed a strong sense of their judicial rights. And the problem was worsened by the ungainly and less than rigorous way in which the inquiry was conducted.

*

* The existence of articles is suggested by Louis IX's letter of 1247 setting out the powers of the investigators 'to hear and to render in writing and to inquire according to the form delivered to them by us concerning complaints' (M. Bouquet, *Recueil des historiens des Gaules et de la France*, 24 vols. (new edn., 1869–1904), XXIV, 4; M. Dejoux, *Les enquêtes de Saint Louis: Gouverner et sauver son âme* (Paris, 2014), 77–8, 79–80, 84–5). For the *enquêtes*' procedure of establishing the veracity of a complaint by gathering multiple witnesses to an alleged crime, and questioning those witnesses, see: Dejoux, ibid., 79–80, 84–5. Adam Marsh lays great stress upon the documents produced on Simon's behalf, suggesting that he regarded these as vigorous proofs, even if it was generally considered that written proofs were not as strong as oral testimony (as was the case in the French *enquêtes*). It also fell to Simon's party to demonstrate that the complaints were vexatious, a determination that in France fell to the *enquêteurs* as part of their questioning of the complainant (*Letters of Adam Marsh*, I, 80–3; Dejoux, *Les enquêtes de Saint Louis*, 82–4).

As we listen, then, like the *curiales* gathered in the Westminster refectory, to the complaints of the Gascons and to Simon's replies, we must bear these conditions in mind. For whatever decision we come to – the truth of 'what really happened', as far as it exists beyond the subjective perspectives of those involved, the rights and wrongs, legal or moral, of Simon's rule in Gascony – will depend upon whose version of events we choose to believe, in circumstances in which it is harder than ever to trust in the scrupulousness and accuracy of the accounts.

One of the principal complainants was Gaston de Béarn, a leading noble of the region, who sent a proctor to present his case. Gaston had been Simon's chief target in Gascony, one of the 'traitors' whom 'he should suppress'.* That Simon was successful in circumscribing Gaston's power is made clear by his complaint, which describes the manifold ways that Simon usurped his rights as lord.[29] Gaston, for instance, had customarily exacted tolls in the lands of le Marsan and le Gavardan in the region of Landes, but Simon had diverted travellers into the king's lands of Armagnac, where he exacted tolls from them himself, thus defrauding Gaston. Simon's reply was contemptuous. He 'never compelled anyone to go through the lands or roads of the king . . . but merchants and all others are able to go and return through whichever paths or lands they wish, and if it is more pleasing to merchants and others to go through the land under the power of the earl than through that of my lord Gaston, then the earl has done no wrong in this matter to anyone'.[30]

---

* Simon made serious progress towards the goal of containing Gaston, encircling his lands, firstly by seizing the neighbouring lordships of Soule (based at Mauléon) and Gramont (whose lords were accused, probably rightly, of banditry and summarily imprisoned) and secondly by securing custody of the county of Bigorre. The county was held by the countess Peirone, who had been married five times: her third husband had been Gui de Montfort (Simon's elder brother who was killed at Castelnaudary in 1220), her fifth Boso de Matha, lord of Cognac, Gaston's father-in-law. Gaston was therefore staking his claim as heir to Bigorre on behalf of his wife, a prospect that would have made him unbearably powerful in the region. Simon persuaded Peirone to grant him custody of the county, in return for an annual rent, and to designate as heir a grandson sprung from her marriage to Gui. For the Bigorre affair, see: J. R. Maddicott, *Simon de Montfort* (Cambridge, 1994), 134.

Gaston also alleged Simon's disregard for the cherished principle of 'judgement by court' and his preference for violence over reason. In one instance, Gaston claimed, Simon's men had assaulted and killed a certain Bidot de Saubonaes: they had seized him, so Gaston said, together with his horse and 1,000 Gascon shillings, and then tied Bidot to the tail of the horse and had him dragged, before hanging him.[31] Simon responded that he was not involved in Bidot's case. He 'heard it clearly said by the community of the country that this Bidot was a robber and was breaking the law on the king's roads, and had done much in the way of evil in the lands of the king, and specifically to the bishop of Bazas', but Simon had not ordered the execution, and had only heard a report of it later (he 'clearly heard it said that he [Bidot] was taken and hanged at Bazas, just as the *prudhommes* of Bazas know well').[32]

As Gaston's complaints continued, Simon's answers began to betray his waning patience. Gaston alleged that Simon had sent his provost into Le Marsan, a land of Gaston's lordship 'by right and custom'. Simon replied that 'into his [Gaston's] land he sent no provost, but he did send a provost into the land of the king, just as he was always accustomed to do, just as he does in the whole country, and concerning this he has not done any wrong to my lord Gaston'.[33] Gaston complained that Simon had deprived him of the castle of Ideu, in Le Marsan. Simon replied that he 'does not know anything of this castle, nor has he ever spoken or heard of it, nor does he even know where it is'.[34]

If Gaston's complaints had been all that stood against Simon's conduct then the earl's defence would perhaps have been straightforward. But complaints were brought in numbers by the people of Saint-Séverin, Sault-de-Navailles, Bayonne, Saint-Laurent-de-Gosse, Orx and Dax, all of whom drew up schedules of grievance and sent proctors to Westminster. They were led by the greatest of the Gascon towns, Bordeaux.

Bordeaux's economic and political importance as a major trading post and chief port of entry into Gascony for England's kings had made its governance a priority for Simon, and meant that the complaints of its people now against the manner of his governance would weigh heavily. The case was presented here by Gaillard del Soler, a member of one of two rival factions whose enmity cleaved the city. This schedule is the most extensive, and the most elegant in its rhetoric – it is not, like the others, a cluster of complaints dictated more or less in random order but has been carefully composed.[35] Here the protests of the del Solers were set within a measured narrative of scheming and betrayal.

Before Simon's arrival in Gascony, Gaillard reported, the region had enjoyed 'a prosperous and tranquil state', and Simon had been welcomed in Bordeaux 'with greatest honour and praise' by Rostand del Soler, Gaillard's father and head of the del Soler clan, and his friends. But, within days, Simon was showing partiality to their adversaries, the Coloms, taking them as his counsellors. At this point Rostand had been warned by his friends to beware, for the earl would surely ally himself with Rostand's enemies. But Rostand did not want to believe it, saying that he would continue to serve the king faithfully and would not beware of his governor, Simon, 'who was the brother-in-law of the lord king, and was reputed to be an honest and faithful man, nor could he believe at all that such a law-worthy man would grieve him or his friends in any way'. Simon had then 'promised him [Rostand] that he would be to him and his friends a law-worthy lord and a good friend, and would defend him and his friends from all violence'.

But this promise would prove to be false. Around a year later, on 28 June 1249, Rostand had been laid up sick in his house in Bordeaux when he was told that the earl had indeed allied himself with Rostand's enemies, who were now rallying against him. Again, Rostand did not want to believe it. But the mayor (a del Soler ally), hearing that men were arming themselves in the city, raised the militia, a force of 300. He led his posse to the marketplace with the aim of suppressing the Coloms. When the militiamen arrived, they were set upon by the Coloms, who poured out of the surrounding houses, weapons raised. Three of the mayor's men were killed, and so he ordered a retreat.

At this point, Simon arrived on the scene with his men, in warlike fashion, mounted in arms with banners raised, and joined the Coloms. They rode against the mayor's militia 'and threw themselves upon those who did not wish to defend themselves, although they were able to, on account of their deference to lord Simon'. They killed two men (one of whom, Bernard Monent, it was pointed out, 'was a wise and peaceful man'), and wounded many others.

Simon then sent two of his knights to fetch Rostand, who came even though he was sick. Simon said that he wished to see Rostand receive justice for the various damages he and his friends had suffered. Would Rostand, Simon asked, place himself in Simon's hands, and allow Simon to see him right? Rostand wanted to consult his friends, but Simon assured him that this was not necessary, because he would look after him. Then, publicly, in view of many, he declared to Rostand that he was his 'good and law-worthy lord' and gave him the kiss of peace.

Simon then asked Rostand to meet him at the king's castle, together with fifteen of his party; Simon would bring the same number of Coloms, and arrange a peace between them. Afterwards, Simon promised, they would enjoy a meal together (the customary way of sealing a peace). When the parties duly arrived, Simon asked that both deliver themselves and three of their houses into his hands as security, promising to restore everything fully when the peace was settled. But, when this had been done, Simon released the Coloms and put the del Solers in chains. With their adversaries locked up, the Coloms ran amok through the town, raiding the houses of the del Solers and killing many, even cutting down men on holy ground, in the city's churches. Those del Solers who were not in Simon's custody fled the city, and their property was seized by the Coloms.

Simon was told of what had happened, but 'dissembling, he let these things pass entirely unpunished, and did no justice whatsoever concerning them'. Instead, he had announcements made throughout the city that those who had fled could return in safety. But, when they did so, many were killed or taken prisoner by the Coloms, and 'the earl did not care to do justice concerning these things'. What was more, Simon refused to return Rostand's house, which he had taken as security. Instead, he stripped it of its valuables and ordered its destruction. He then cast from the city 'a great many good men' and seized their property – which he held to ransom, along with their owners' right to abide within Bordeaux.

Rostand, distressed by the news of the injuries done to his people, and of the earl's unwillingness to compensate them, fell gravely ill.

1. Perched in the hills north of Carcassonne, Cabaret (its towers known collectively today as Lastours) was described by Peter of les Vaux-de-Cernay as 'a veritable fount of heresy' and 'almost impregnable'. Simon de Montfort, the Count, secured Cabaret by negotiation in 1210 – one of the many fortresses he took during the course of the Albigensian Crusade. It was amidst the dramatic landscape of Languedoc that Simon spent the early years of his life.

2. & 3. Fragments of the vestments and crozier of Walter de Cantilupe, bishop of Worcester and one of Simon's oldest and closest friends, found when his tomb was excavated in 1861. The vestments (left) were made, in the second quarter of the thirteenth century, of imported silk woven with silver-gilt thread, depicting seated kings and lions amidst foliage. Gilt foliage set upon a red ground was a popular design of the period (see image 28).

4. One of the most celebrated moments of the Count's career as leader of the Albigensian expedition was the issuing of the Statute of Pamiers in 1212. Although several exemplars of the Statute were probably produced and distributed, only one now survives, in Paris. To it were appended the seals of the Count (far left) and seven bishops (although only five of these now survive), proclaiming the Count's partnership with the Church.

5. The Count was killed at the siege of Toulouse in 1218, and he was buried in the great church of St Nazaire in Carcassonne. A fragment of his tomb is preserved there, depicting the events of the siege.

6. Popular antipathy towards Europe's Jewish population had been widespread for generations, but it was only during the thirteenth century that such attitudes came to be institutionalized. A royal scribe has doodled this elaborate cartoon on a roll of Jewish tallages from 1232–3. It depicts Isaac of Norwich, a patron of Jewish learning and wealthy moneylender, as having three heads and a crown. The other figures represent other Jewish people and demons.

7. Matthew Paris, a Benedictine of St Albans Abbey, provides one of the most extensive and lively accounts of Henry III's reign up to 1259 in his *Chronica Majora*. As well as composing and writing the text he provided numerous illustrations, including these depictions of Queen Eleanor's coronation in 1236. These include the earl of Chester bearing the legendary sword of Edward the Confessor – Curtein – as part of the procession. The constable of Chester and the earl of Pembroke carried staffs to keep the crowds from pressing the wedding party.

8. Simon's hereditary title of Steward of England did not entitle him to a role in the coronation ceremony itself, but rather in the festivities that followed, during which Simon was responsible for washing the king's hands before the banquet, using an aquamanile. A fine example of this type of vessel, made in England in the final quarter of the thirteenth century, depicts a knight in armour and surcoat couching his lance.

9. Kenilworth Castle in Warwickshire was held by the Montforts, granted to Simon and Eleanor jointly for life in 1255. It was where their first child, Henry de Montfort, was born in November 1238.

10–13. The seal, used to authenticate legal documents, was the ideal vehicle
for proclaiming the identity of its owner. Most knightly seals showed their owners
riding into battle, but the Count's first seal (image 10, top left) shows him hunting – a
reference to his family's hereditary keepership of the royal forest of Yveline. When he had a
new version made around 1200, he emphasized the sylvan nature of the scene by stripping
away the knightly accoutrements (image 11, top right). It was this design that Simon copied
(image 13, bottom right). This made their designs highly distinctive. In contrast, Simon's eldest
brother, Amaury, opted for the more common equestrian form, with the
Montfort lion proudly displayed (image 12, bottom left).

14. This page from Matthew Paris's *Chronica Majora* describes the expedition to Outremer by English contingents in 1240. After writing his account, Matthew received information about the names of the knights led by Simon and Richard of Cornwall, as well as Simon's route, which he added at the bottom of the page.

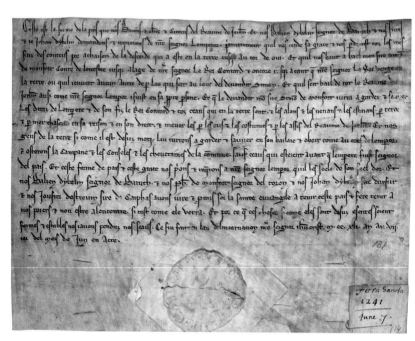

15. In this letter, issued at Acre in June 1241, the barons of Jerusalem proposed that Simon be made their regent while their king, Conrad, was underage. Simon's candidacy was perhaps supported by his cousin, Philip de Montfort (whose name is given on the fifth line from the bottom), now lord of Tyron.

(He had recovered from his earlier sickness, the complainant was careful to point out, implying that this new affliction was definitely Simon's fault.) Rostand asked Simon for bail in order to leave the royal castle and recuperate on one of his own manors. But Simon refused, and Rostand died in gaol. Simon then seized all Rostand's land, depriving his heirs and dependants – until his eldest son, the complainant Gaillard del Soler, now leader of the del Soler faction, and his friends promised Simon a payment of 3,000 marks. On top of this, Simon asked Gaillard and his friends to meet him outside the city, where he demanded that they issue a charter to his benefit. In fear of their lives, they obeyed. The charter described how they had sworn not to cause Simon or his friends any trouble, nor to reveal Simon's deeds to the king, and that they would stay or move from place to place according to his will.

Following these events, Gaillard and his friends determined to put their grievances to the king of England. Henry (Gaillard recalled) had ordered Simon to restore what he had seized and make restitution, 'but the earl, slighting the order of the lord king, did nothing, but rather heaped troubles upon troubles'. Meanwhile, several of the men imprisoned on Simon's orders were languishing in prison, where some had fallen ill and died. Gaillard estimated the damage done at Simon's hands to the people of Bordeaux to be 15,000 marks.

Simon responded to these allegations, point by point. His account stands in complete contradiction to that of Gaillard del Soler. 'When he first came into the land [of Gascony]', his response begins, there was no 'good peace between the barons, as they falsely say'. His account describes the various wars active in the region at the time of his arrival, and points out that he 'put a stop to these wars'. 'Nor was there peace among the citizens of Bordeaux, as he says', Simon continued, for the del Soler faction held others under their power. Simon had not favoured the Coloms from the beginning; indeed, he had taken Rostand and another del Soler, the prior of Le Mas, into his circle of counsellors along with certain Coloms.

As to the disturbance on 28 June 1249, 'it did not happen as they say, but entirely otherwise'. Simon had been in bed when two of his knights had arrived and told him that the Coloms had armed themselves and that 'already there was a great mêlée'. Hearing this,

Simon at once ordered everyone concerned 'by the fealty that they had for the lord king and for him, to lay down their arms and hold themselves in peace', assuring them that, if there had been any wrongdoing, he himself would have it put right. But his words had no effect, 'and they fought each other fiercely through the streets and through the squares of the city'.

Then Simon heard that a prominent Colom, William Gondomer, had been mortally wounded, and his son killed. And so he armed himself, and ordered his men to do the same. He hastened to the fray – although he only brought with him eight or nine knights (he had some fifty in the city), as he still hoped to calm the quarrel. It seems that Simon ordered both parties to come to him and lay down their arms. The Coloms did so immediately, but the del Solers 'did not wish to do it at all but rather, lacking all respect for the earl and for his people', continued fighting throughout the city, fiercely hurling arrows and lances and stones. They killed two of Simon's knights and another of his men, wounded several others and killed and wounded a number of their horses. Amidst the fighting, the Coloms managed to seize some of the del Solers, while another surrendered to Simon.

One of Simon's men, Peter de Montfort, then went to Rostand's house. He found Rostand armed and surrounded by his men. Peter chastised Rostand, telling him 'that he had wickedly and foolishly held himself against our lord the king and the earl, and that he had gone against his oath'. Rostand replied 'that he wished very much to speak with the earl, provided that he could go and return safely'. And so, in order to assure him of this, Peter remained in the house as hostage while Rostand left to meet with Simon.

'When Rostand came before the earl', Simon's response continued, 'the earl said to him that he had behaved wickedly towards the king and towards him, and that he was amazed, for he could hardly believe that he had done such things.' And so Simon asked Rostand if he was willing to stand to right concerning these matters. Rostand answered, 'I will not plead now, but I put myself at your will concerning everything.' Rostand sent word back to his people that they should release Peter de Montfort, because Rostand had placed himself at the earl's mercy. Upon Peter's arrival, 'in the presence of all, he [Rostand] explicitly quitted my lord Peter of the promise he had made' concerning Rostand's safe conduct to return home.

Then Rostand and a companion went with Simon to the royal castle 'of their own will, without any force at all'. Simon immediately sent for the leading Coloms, 'in order to better quell the argument, and to hold the peace'. He also sent for the prisoners whom the Coloms had taken in the mêlée, men who had been responsible for killing several leading Coloms. Simon was in a great hurry to get hold of the prisoners, 'for he feared that, when Gaillard Colom and his party should learn that their friends had been killed, they would have them [the captured del Solers] killed, for they did not know yet at this point that their friends were dead'.

The following day, the earl summoned the leaders of both parties. He said to Rostand, 'Yesterday you placed yourself at my will: do not say that I have captured you, for you are very much responsible for this affair. Go to your house if you wish . . . for I am ready to conduct you to your house freely and safely, if you do not wish to stay gladly at my will, as you said to me yesterday.' Rostand gave assurances that he had not changed his mind, and was prepared to place himself at Simon's will, 'for the emending of trespasses, the making of peace, and following the decree of the earl'. Simon, having taken counsel with his men, then asked both parties to provide an oath, 'and they swore that whatever the earl should decree for the trespasses and for the peace of the vill they would observe without violation, and that they would offer hostages'.

And so Simon had asked for twenty hostages and three houses from both parties, though he was able to obtain only nineteen hostages from the Coloms and thirteen from the del Solers. But 'when this was done, the earl saw that Rostand and his supporters had greatly wronged our lord the king and the earl, for the mêlée was begun by their party, not by the order of the earl'. And they had refused to withdraw when he instructed them to do so, 'but rather they had damaged him as much as they could'. 'It was very clear', Simon now knew (from a report, or upon reflection, he does not say), 'that concerning this Rostand was culpable', for his house had been the centre of the disturbances: one of Simon's knights had been seized outside the house, 'and dragged into another house, and there was mortally wounded by sixteen wounds or more, and was disarmed and cast into the middle of the street'.

In contrast, Simon now saw, the Coloms were not culpable at all, because they had withdrawn when instructed and obeyed all his orders. And so Simon had allowed the hostages he had from the Coloms to be swapped for others of lesser status: sons, nephews and cousins of the senior men. The del Solers, the guilty ones, 'he had guarded safely and honestly; specifically, he had Rostand guarded in a well-appointed chamber honestly and honourably, where his people could serve him if he wished, free from any bodily restraint'. When Rostand then complained that the Coloms had been released, Simon had him told that he would recall the original Colom hostages 'provided that he [Rostand] and his party and the party of the Coloms would deliver themselves to judgement'. But Rostand and his party refused, saying 'that they wished more for mercy than for judgement'.

Simon then explains why he had announcements made throughout the town encouraging those del Solers who had fled to return. This was done 'not at all on account of a grievance towards anyone, but because he wished to act according to the law, to bring them back to peace and to the faith of the lord king'. While some had returned and agreed to stand to right, 'several did not wish to come'. For this default (a refusal to obey a summons issued in the name of their lord and to submit to justice), Simon had seized their goods. As to what the del Solers were claiming – that the earl had ignored the plight of those who had returned only to face death, capture, and despoliation at the hands of their Colom enemies – 'this is not true'. The earl had listened to their complaints, and initiated an inquiry, 'but he was never able to find anything that had not been emended, and those people who had made the complaints were not in any way able to prove them'. It was true that two men had been killed, but 'they were killed before the mêlée was pacified and the hostages were handed over' (not, then, in the second wave of violence after Simon had invited the fleeing del Solers to return). Nor was Simon culpable for the other deaths, as the del Solers were claiming, and indeed he had meted out punishment for these. It was true that those men deputed as night watchmen in the city after the mêlée had taken the opportunity to break into houses and make off with goods, but the mayor (a new one, a Colom man) had ensured that amends were made, and that restitution was offered by the guilty parties.

As to the complaint that Simon had refused to restore custody of Rostand's house as he had promised, but instead had ordered its destruction, the earl insisted that he had made no such promise. He had caused the house to be knocked down 'because the *prudhommes* of the vill said that Rostand had raised it to a height greater than he ought, against the prohibition of my lord the king and against the law codes of the city' (in other words, because the house had contravened building regulations), and also because, as Simon had pointed out earlier, it had been in this house that Rostand and his party had plotted against Simon, and it was this house on which the action had centred that led to the wounding and killing of his men.

Case by case, then, Simon refuted the blame cast upon him for the deaths of various prisoners. As to the allegations that Simon was responsible for Rostand's death in prison, Simon denied the charge utterly. While he had kept Rostand in a castle, he had never kept the man in irons, or in any sort of restraint. It was true that Rostand had asked to be bailed in order to recuperate from his illness, but it was not the case that Simon had simply refused. What happened was this: Rostand had offered his son, Gaillard, as hostage in his place; but Gaillard, instead of delivering himself to Simon, had gone to Fronsac (some twenty miles eastward), joined with his brother and friends, and proceeded to seize the castle there 'against the king, with the enemies of the king'. While Gaillard was thus treacherously occupied, his father had died, 'and his death is to be blamed more on his son', went Simon's response, 'because he did not wish to be a hostage, than on other new causes'.

Following Rostand's death, Simon had seized the property of Gaillard and his friends, because of their actions against the king at Fronsac. As to Gaillard's claim that Simon would not allow him his inheritance without a payment of 3,000 marks, Simon replied that the confiscation had been enacted on account of the del Solers' wrongdoing, 'and he clearly made them the offer that, if they wished to submit themselves to judgement, then he would willingly deliver to them all their goods, and they did not wish to do so'.

As to the claim that Simon had forced Gaillard and his friends to issue a charter promising not to cause Simon any trouble, 'they do not speak the truth at all'. The agreed peace had required them to provide an oath and charter, and to find pledges that they would hold the peace, and be faithful and loyal to the king and to the earl, and would stay during the term of the peace outside Bordeaux in the king's lands. But 'concerning this matter they are lying', for they never made any charter for the earl himself.

So ran the statements of both parties in the case of the Bordelais. The complaints of the other towns, and Simon's responses, were piled up one against the other in a similar way, though there had been no events outside Bordeaux of comparable drama. The other complaints implied, however, that what happened in Bordeaux had coloured Simon's relationship with the other towns. One schedule of complaint described how two men of the town of Bazas had heard that the earl wanted to take hostages from the townspeople. They were so fearful that they 'fled to a church and remained within for as long as the earl was in the town; so that, shamefully, it was necessary for them to answer the call of nature inside the church itself'.[36]

*

The Gascons laid out their complaints, both in the public forum of the refectory meeting and in private audience with the king – as Adam Marsh reports, they 'furiously assailed the earl with a pack of malicious lies'. During the inquiry, Adam continues, Simon 'frequently suffered reproaches and vociferous abuse from the lord king in front of many great persons'. The king, in other words, had decided to believe the Gascons' version of events – and, to make his treatment of Simon all the worse, was shaming him publicly. But Simon suffered these attacks, reports Adam, 'while himself maintaining self-restraint and meekness and a mature magnanimity towards both his lord and his adversaries'.[37]

Adam was Simon's friend and was bound to present him in a way that emphasized his position as the wronged party – but Matthew Paris agreed, and was similarly scathing about the king's treatment of the earl. In Matthew's version, though, Simon did not meekly accept the 'reproaches' and 'abuse' heaped upon him by the king. Instead, Matthew tells how 'by equivocal exchange of words, each provoked the other to angry disputes and rages'. And as their row continued, 'they recalled those things that had been over and done with some time since'. Simon reminded Henry how he had saved him 'from the snares of the French' at Saintes, and how Henry had offered to support him completely in his governorship of Gascony in order that 'he should suppress the traitors'. He chastised Henry, telling him that his 'words should be held to be steadfast and certain', urging him to preserve the guarantees set out in the 1248 commission – or else to repay Simon the expenses he had incurred in royal service, since 'it is accepted that I have impoverished my earldom irreparably for the sake of your honour'.

To this Henry replied ('far too quickly and thoughtlessly', Matthew judges) that he would not observe the terms of the commission towards Simon, such an 'undeserving supplanter and traitor, for one may recoil from pacts made with those who go back on their own agreements, and rage publicly against the wicked'.

On hearing this, Simon 'flew furiously into a rage and, standing up, openly declared that in this word ["traitor"] the king manifestly lied; and were it not for the fact that he is set apart by the delusive name [of king] and royal dignity, it would be a bad hour when he hurled such a word from his jaws'.

Henry, 'hardly able to contain himself on account of his anger', ordered his men to seize the earl, but the other nobles would not allow it.

The argument had plunged into such animosity that Simon now turned on Henry in the most personal and piercing manner possible: he questioned Henry's credentials as a man of faith and piety.

'Who could believe that you are a Christian?' Simon exclaimed. 'Have you not ever confessed?'

'Indeed,' Henry replied.

'What is the value of confession', Simon returned, 'without repentance and atonement?'

Henry was a ruler renowned for his devotion (he was, at this time, rebuilding the very abbey in which the inquiry was being held for the honour of God and St Edward). Simon's implication was that Henry was in fact only concerned with outward shows of piety, unready to examine his conscience – for, with his conscience searched, how could Henry possibly still justify his actions in withdrawing from his guarantee to Simon and branding him a traitor?

Henry, 'glowing with anger', played upon the words of Simon's taunt, telling the earl, 'Never yet have I repented any act, so much as I repent now that I ever allowed you to enter England, and to hold an honour or anything in this land.' At this point their friends stepped in to separate them.*

It was Simon's friends, indeed, who rescued him from the ignominy of the Gascons' allegations and the royal wrath. Although, as we know, this was not a trial, and so Simon's fellow potentates could have no legal role in proceedings, it would always be hard for the king to proceed against the wishes of his greatest subjects – which is why Simon had brought along or asked as many as he could muster. Nor was his belief in their support misplaced. As Adam Marsh reports, Walter de Cantilupe and Peter de Montfort 'offered the earl loyal protection in the midst of so much obloquy and danger', as did Peter of Savoy. And before long many others, including the earl of Cornwall, were rallying to Simon's side. They 'declared and extolled the splendid virtues of the earl of Leicester', Adam proclaims, 'his fearless loyalty, his victorious energy, and the justice of his purpose'. Adam himself then spoke in Simon's defence, which must have made a powerful impression, for Adam was not only a respected man of God and a renowned scholar but also a skilled rhetorician. Soon the *curiales* 'did not hesitate to promise help and advice to protect the earl from danger, loss, or disgrace. Really,' reflects Adam, 'in such constant expressions of goodwill he experienced very rare and genuine friendship.'[38]

---

* Henry rounded off the outburst by referring to Simon as 'the fattened one' who was now kicking out, a reference to a verse from Deuteronomy: 'The beloved grew fat, and kicked: he grew fat, and thick and gross, he forsook God who made him, and departed from God his saviour,' Deuteronomy 32: 15 – a succinct summary of the turn their relationship had taken (*Matthaei Parisiensis, Monachi Sancti Albani, Chronica Majora*, ed. H. R. Luard, 7 vols. (London, 1872–83), V, 289–91).

The bishops, earls and barons, then, whether officially or not, had made their judgement as to who was in the right. Their support for Simon was probably moved to some extent by their approval of his methods, especially given their shared experience of Gascon treachery in the war of 1242, and their trust in his replies to the complaints. But they must also have been disturbed by the nature of the proceedings against Simon. The grounds for the inquiry were themselves unsteady, given Henry's promise in 1248 to provide Simon with unqualified support. Henry's refusal to adhere to his promises must have won Simon some sympathy. But more than anything they would have been troubled by the way in which Simon had been exposed to 'so much obloquy and danger' in a haphazard inquiry without the protection of formal judicial process. The meting out of such treatment to an earl, the denial of customary justice to a leading subject, was a precedent that they could not allow.

Henry, then, was forced to back down. His decision must have come by 7 June, for this is when Simon's name reappears in the witness lists to royal charters.[39] According to Adam Marsh, Henry 'made a public pronouncement confessing that manifest truth compelled him to find for the earl and his supporters'. Given the bile of Henry's recent row with Simon, the decision was probably reluctant, though Adam – moved by indignation on his friend's behalf – reported differently: Henry said 'that without a shadow of doubt the reasonable case they [Simon's party] had set out had vanquished the fallacious and fraudulent lies of their adversaries, declaring that the former deserved to be believed and that the latter did not.' This pronouncement was 'unanimously acclaimed', Adam declares, by all the prelates and nobles present. Simon had won.

7

A New Enemy

It was a short-lived victory – indeed, Simon had only one night to savour the satisfaction of seeing Henry pronounce in his favour. The next day, reports Adam Marsh, 'the bonds of equity and justice were broken, the king's wrath boils over, and we return to savage threats against the earl of Leicester . . . and malicious people whispering fraudulent accusations'.[1] With the case against his Gascon rule exhausted, it is unclear what new accusations could be found to throw at Simon, nor what threats were shot at him in consequence. And whether this was simply the caprice of a king resentful of the ruling forced upon him, or whether Adam's account conceals something improper on Simon's part, we cannot know. But the result was that Simon faced a new assault on his position.

And so he approached Henry with a proposal (his forthright manner can be inferred from Adam's purposely discreet account: 'the earl, as vigorous as ever, assiduously urged the lord king in ways thought appropriate'). The proposal was that Henry should send Simon back to Gascony. Simon would first be reconciled to the various Gascon parties, he suggested, and then would govern the land with 'mercy and compassion'. But, if this were not possible, then he would raise a mighty army to subdue the Gascons.

The first scenario was, of course, unlikely. What Simon was seeking was licence to continue as he had begun. But he also put forward an alternative: he would resign his commission, as long as Henry would guarantee three things. First, that Simon would not be left out of pocket. Second, and 'more important', notes Adam, 'that he would not incur the stigma of infamy or disgrace', and third, 'and above all', that his men and supporters in Gascony would not be subject to recriminations in persons or property. Simon perhaps feared that Henry would tolerate reprisals, or that his men would be subject to the sort of inquiry that he had been made to endure.

If the first offer could not be countenanced, then its alternative might have seemed a tolerable compromise. But Henry would have none of it. Instead, he ordered the drawing up of a new ordinance for the governing of Gascony. According to its terms, the current truce between Simon and his adversaries would hold until the coming Candlemas (2 February 1253). At that point, either Henry or his first-born son, Edward, would set out to take control of the land (Gascony had been granted to Edward, who at the appointed time would be approaching his fourteenth birthday, and so ready to begin gaining experience in the field). Meanwhile, Henry would send out an officer who would be charged with countermanding all decisions, more or less, that Simon had made as governor.[2]

*

Simon wasted no time in his response, and left England. Adam Marsh states that he did so 'having been dismissed with a permit that was unclear'. The ambiguity of the terms on which Simon and Henry parted is important, for some were given to believe that Henry had ordered Simon back to Gascony. Matthew Paris certainly thought as much. 'Return to Gascony', he has Henry telling Simon, 'so that you, who are a stirrer and lover of wars, may find wars enough, bringing back from thence the worthy reward, as your father did.' Simon, 'fearless and with alacrity' (and ignoring Henry's invitation to follow the Count in having himself killed in battle) replied, 'I will freely go there. Nor, as I believe, shall I return – until I subjugate the rebels to you, though you are an ingrate.'[3] If Matthew Paris's report is anywhere near accurate, then perhaps Simon – with wondrous audacity – seized these careless words as licence to return and impose his might on Gascony. And so he set sail, on 13 June.[4]

What precisely was Simon's purpose? In his later account of the episode, he says that he was responding to recent news that the

Gascons were once again in rebellion against the king, laying siege to La Réole (as Simon had told Henry, his purpose in Gascony had always been to 'suppress traitors'). But he was also 'blazing', as Matthew Paris describes him, 'and entirely inflamed to the purpose of revenging his defamation'.[5]

He took with him Eleanor, together with their eldest son, Henry, who was now thirteen years old. Young Simon (eleven years old), Amaury (now nine or ten) and Gui (about eight) were left in England, together with their infant brother, Richard. Eleanor had spent the first three years or so of Simon's rule at his side, but she had returned from Gascony for her confinement. The new baby had probably arrived not long after 9 October 1251, for on that date Eleanor had thought that she was going into labour, as Adam Marsh informed Simon in a letter, also recording that it had been a false alarm.[6] The baby made his appearance soon after and now, in mid-June 1252, he was about eight months old and could be left in the care of his nurse, perhaps at Kenilworth with young Simon and Gui, while Amaury remained in Robert Grosseteste's household.

In whatever was to come, then, Simon, Eleanor and their eldest son would operate as a unit. Simon and Eleanor had worked together in Gascony before the countess had returned to England, and we can see glimpses of their partnership. A letter from the chaplain of Alphonse, count of Poitiers, for instance, describes how he was invited by the couple to visit them at La Réole, and how he stayed there for a night in happy company.[7] The chaplain's master, Alphonse, was a neighbour of great importance, the brother of the king of France, at that time with Louis on expedition in Egypt. Courting such persons was an important duty, which Simon and Eleanor shared. The letters of Adam Marsh are revealing on this point, making it plain that Adam saw the two very much as a team. Writing in 1249 or 1250, concerned for Simon, Adam reminded Eleanor of her duty to advise her husband on the policies he should pursue towards the Gascons.[8] Now, on their return to Gascony, the couple would have the support of their eldest son as well. Thirteen was a ready age to start practising his knightly trade – indeed, he was of a similar age to his late uncles, Amaury and Gui, when they had begun to take a part in their parents' expedition. Simon's new campaign in Gascony, like the war prosecuted by the Count in neighbouring Languedoc, would be a Montfort family enterprise.

Simon first looked to the kingdom of France, in order to seek the help of relatives and friends in gathering an army ('for the safety of the land', as he later claimed). It was fortunate that he was able to call upon his friends in France for their support, for he had little cash to lure potential troops (he apparently promised his mercenaries that they would be paid from the spoils of war).[9]

Once he had amassed sufficient men, Simon led his army into Gascony. He soon saw action, as we know from Matthew Paris. His account describes how Simon sent a detachment to set an ambush at a by-way; the cohort sprang upon a Gascon band, but in the bloody skirmish that followed Simon's lieutenant was captured – a knight who (as Paris tells us) was *strenuissimus*, the strongest and most vigorous of men.[10] With his soldiers scattered, the knight was led away in chains.

Simon had stationed himself at a nearby spot where he might have vantage of the expected action. He was on the lookout when one of the soldiers, fleeing from the fight, 'moving swiftly on the fastest of horses, so that he could bring news to his lord', arrived before him. The man, 'wounded, bleeding, and torn to pieces, with panting breath gave his report of what had happened'. He then added that Simon's lieutenant – his *carissimus*, most beloved – had been taken captive.

Upon hearing the news, Simon, 'astounded and as if awaking from a deep slumber', said, "'We delay too long. Is the enemy very far from us?"'

"'No indeed,"' replied the soldier. "'They are threatening close at hand, and pressing on so that without delay they may meet you in warlike fashion for a fight."' The Gascons were in jubilant mood, the man told Simon, "'since, with our men scattered, they have found Mars favourably inclined to them".

'Hardly had the man finished these words', Matthew continues, but 'the earl, eager to free the aforesaid knight, hardly waiting for his troops, flying faster than a rapid whirlwind, with the messenger as guide, did not spare the sides of his horse. And reaching the enemy all the quicker, he drenched his lightning sword with the blood of many men.'

He freed the prisoners, 'cutting their chains and breaking them to pieces'. The liberated men flung themselves into the fray and 'charged furiously against the enemy'. But the contest was bloody, and victory far from certain, for the Gascons now focused their attack on Simon, 'whom they were craving thirstily to capture or destroy, and the weight of the battle was thrown against him. And since they had thrown themselves savagely upon him in ever greater numbers, he was struck from his horse and in peril of his life.'

But then the knight – the one whom Simon had just freed – beheld his plight. Determined to save the *strenuissimus* earl in turn, he forced his way through the enemy's battle-line, 'wounding several of the enemy irredeemably, or knocking them down to be trampled underfoot'.

The fighting thundered on, writes Matthew Paris, for almost half a day. Eventually Simon's side won out, scattering the Gascons. Several were seized as prisoners, including five of the most important men of Gascony. 'And the earl triumphed gloriously on that day,' so much more so for the dreadful peril evaded. Thenceforth, Matthew concludes, 'his enemies no longer dare to murmur against him'.

This narrative might well be accurate in essence, for it is rich in detail, and the manner of courage it describes was that expected of the best commanders. The same willingness to risk his life to save his men was a trait for which Simon's father, the Count, had been much admired. In one celebrated episode, when the crusaders were besieging Carcassonne in 1209, the Count and his men had been forced by a ferocious bombardment of stones to retreat from a ditch they had been occupying. But the Count, looking back, had seen one of his knights left lying there, defenceless, with a broken leg. And so this 'man of consummate probity' (recounts Peter of les Vaux-de-Cernay), returned amidst the hail of rock and 'threw himself into the ditch . . . not without great risk to his own life'. He was the only one to do so, apart from the squire whom he took to help him drag the man to safety.[11] Again, in 1211, outside the gates of Castelnaudary, the Count had sighted a detachment of his men assailed by the enemy as they were riding in; while some of his knights urged caution, the Count declared, with tears of passion, 'Heaven forbid that my knights should die gloriously in battle and that I should escape alive and in shame. I will either conquer with my friends or fall with them.' 'Who', asks Peter of les Vaux-de-Cernay, 'hearing these words could hold back the tears? ... At once he set off to help his comrades.'[12] Such acts of physical courage, especially when done for the sake of one's men, embodied the highest of knightly values. In their distinction, they were necessarily rare. They were what made a reputation, and fed admiring tales.

Indeed, the telling of Simon's exploits in 1252, in the chronicle of Matthew Paris, unfolds with such heroic flare that it might have been sung as a *chanson de geste* in a lordly feasting hall. The points of emphasis are those that feature typically in epic songs of deeds: the chivalric epithets, the love between knights, the hero's eagerness for battle proved by the spurring of his horse, the revelling in images of bloodshed. In neither content nor rhythm is this narrative typical of Matthew Paris; it seems likely that the chronicler is reporting a tale brought home by Simon's party and passed from knight to knight in admiration, embellished in the telling, gilded with the motifs in which the knightly kind delighted.

Not long after this episode, Simon moved to Saint-Émilion. There, in August 1252, he secured from the mayor and citizens formal recognition of his rights as governor, based upon his 1248 commission, and a renewal of their oath of obedience to him.[13] Simon then moved on to La Réole. The castle (as he later reported) was indeed under threat, just as he had heard it to be. While he was there, in late August or early September, he received messengers from the king. They bore letters ordering him to honour the peace treaty that had been made with the Gascons before his departure from England. To this mandate Simon gave no ground, replying that 'he was not, at the present time, able to maintain the treaty, nor ought he to do so, when they were making war on him; and if damages had been sustained – in the cutting down of vines or in other things – this was done by the wrongdoing of those who had broken the treaty, not in the least by the wrongdoing of the earl'. The messengers then informed Simon that the king had removed him from the governorship of Gascony, and issued instructions to the people of the land not to obey the earl. But Simon was unperturbed. The king's orders were to be disregarded, he declared, 'because these letters were made more by the will of the king than through reason', since Simon had been guaranteed the governorship for seven years.[14]

Our knowledge of further manoeuvres is confined to the rumour of a single episode, which by mid-October had flown to England to reach the noblemen and bishops gathered for a parliament. The incident was not so glorious as Simon's earlier fight, however. The earl had withdrawn to the castle of Montauban in order to regroup, choosing the site because it seemed impregnable. But, when he arrived, he realized that it lacked provisions, and that there were not enough men to defend it. But before he could make any remedy, the Gascons arrived and laid siege to the fortress, encircling him and trapping him inside. He was saved by some of his faithful men, who arrived in time to negotiate his release in return for the freeing of some of Simon's Gascon prisoners.[15]

Perhaps it was the prospect of the peril and expense of sustaining operations in Gascony without royal backing that finally moved Simon to concede. He was in a strong position to negotiate, for he still had the strength to cause more trouble and he enjoyed the support of his fellow potentates in England. In the October parliament, moved by the rumours of Simon's predicament at Montauban, they had told Henry that 'if the earl of Leicester is striving to conquer those rebelling against the king, that is not something to be wondered at, nor to be sorry for', for the Gascons were notorious traitors and brigands.[16] Henry was forced to relent. He spoke to Simon's friends in England, letting it be known that he would offer the earl a generous settlement: Simon would deliver Gascony to Edward – in return for a payment of 7,000 marks (£4,667).

According to Simon's own account of these events, given later, he accepted with the air of one doing the king a favour: 'when the earl saw that the king, his lord, was resolute in this will, he did not wish to oppose it by resisting the terms that his lord willed, and took the 7,000 marks'.[17] This was an impressive sum, far more than double his annual income, and must have made much headway against the debts he had incurred in royal service. By the end of the year, an agreement had been made in writing, and in addition Simon had secured a promise that Henry would pay to him the ransoms of those prisoners taken in Gascony (and the earl was sure to have it noted in the treaty that he was not to be held responsible for any sickness the captives might be suffering, having learned from the accusations thrown by the Gascons in the Westminster inquiry).[18]

It was a success, of sorts: Simon had not crushed the Gascons, but he had at least escaped 'the stigma of infamy or disgrace'. Indeed, by the following spring he had been vindicated in his approach to Gascon rule. For now the king of Castile was laying claim to Gascony, and winning the allegiance of many of its nobles, who took up arms against the king of England. And so Henry (as Simon's later testimony relates) 'found those on whose account he had been enraged against the earl all against him'.[19]

The Gascons were once more in rebellion, and this time Simon could not be blamed – for, one year on from the Westminster inquiry, it could not be Simon's rule they were protesting. Indeed, if Simon had still been governor, then the king of Castile would not have dared to form designs on Gascony – at least, this was the perception in England (given voice by Matthew Paris): Simon was a *vir Martius*, a man born under the star of the god of war.[20] What was more, if Henry had only trusted Simon's judgement as governor and supported his strategies then the new rebellion might not have taken root – for who was now leading the rebellion but Gaston de Béarn. Simon recalled how, 'because he did not wish to consider his own advantage as much as he wished for the honour of his lord the king', he had in December 1249 sent Gaston as a prisoner to England to receive judgement from Henry for his many crimes, and how Henry had been oh-so-generous in lavishing forgiveness upon him – a liberality that 'the king must rightly have repented, when he found him [Gaston] at La Réole, holding his vill against him, and found that he had done homage to the king of Castile', and indeed continued to do everything in his power to draw Henry's subjects from their fealty.[21] Simon was not alone in casting the current situation in this light: Matthew Paris presents a very similar assessment, and was surely reflecting the view of the political community.[22] For Henry, this must have been a most shaming rebuke.

*

The king was forced to set out for Gascony himself, in early August 1253.[23] He summoned Simon too to come in arms, but had no response. Anticipating Henry's demand, and adamant that it would not move him, Simon had decamped to France.[24]

Henry, even without the aid of the *vir Martius*, enjoyed some success, but he was unable to take La Réole or Benauges.[25] And so he wrote again to Simon, in early October, this time in placatory tone, 'asking that you come to us in Gascony to speak with us; and when you come to us we will set out our will to you; if you consider that – to our advantage and honour and equally to yours – you are not able to stay with us, we will and grant that without our indignation and ill will you shall be able to return as soon as you wish'.[26]

Simon still might not have answered – for, by this time, he had been made another offer: the nobles of France had asked him to be their regent. King Louis was on crusade in Outremer and his mother, Blanche of Castile, who had been ruling in his stead, had died in the autumn of 1252. And so, in the weeks leading up to Easter 1253, while Simon remained in his ancestral homeland ignoring Henry's summons, the French had entreated him 'to be sole guardian of the crown and realm of France'. They did this 'seeing his fidelity and greatness', Matthew Paris reports, and how 'he strove to be like his father in all things', setting out to him in letters their eagerness to have him rule them, for he 'held of old a deep-seated love for the kingdom of France, just like his father, who fought for the Church against the Albigensians, and nor was he by blood a foreigner to the French'.[27] Their intent was strong: when Simon refused their first request they would not be deterred and renewed their entreaties, only to be turned away again.*

That the nobles of this most mighty and celebrated kingdom wanted Simon for their regent, 'sole guardian of the crown and realm of France', proclaims the height of the esteem in which the earl was held by his fellow potentates, his fellow knights. The regency council, which had advised Blanche but which now took full responsibility for France's government, consisted only of bishops,

---

* Simon's first refusal would not necessarily have been taken at face value by the

and it was felt that this body was representing only the interests of
the Church and not the lay nobility. The first choice for the role
of regent might have been one of Louis's brothers, Charles of Anjou
or Alphonse of Poitiers, but they were both preoccupied.[28] That
Simon was a ready alternative to two of the greatest potentates of
Europe, brothers of the king of France, speaks of the pre-eminence
of his reputation. In this the French request follows – and indeed
surpasses – that of the barons of Jerusalem in 1241, who had also
wanted Simon as their governor.

The request from France declared, moreover, the standing the
earl enjoyed in that kingdom. This had not always been the case.
In the 1230s, his plans for marriage to the great continental heiress
Joanna of Flanders had been obstructed by Blanche of Castile,
according to one report, because he had made himself an outsider
by offering his fealty to the king of England, so that 'he was
suspect in the court of France'.[29] His popularity now amongst the
French nobility perhaps owed something to his late brother,
Amaury. After relinquishing his rights in Languedoc in 1229,
Amaury had bound himself wholeheartedly to the French crown,
and had become close to both the French king and the queen
mother. It was Louis and Blanche who had funded his expedition
to Outremer in 1239, in effect making Amaury their representative
on the expedition. Blanche's household accounts (a rare survival)
catch her response to Amaury's fate: she gave the sum of 8 livres
to Amaury's servant when he carried to her news of the captives,
and upon his death she offered his daughter condolence with the
gift of a golden belt.[30] That Louis had an interest in Amaury's
plight is also clear. As Amaury himself had noted from his Cairo
gaol, the French king had removed the crown's treasure from the
Templars' keeping in anger at their failure to help the prisoners
taken at Gaza; and, in his negotiations with the Egyptians in 1252,
Louis had insisted that the heads of the Christians killed at Gaza,

French nobles. By convention, whether in Church or lay government, candidates for
high office were expected to show reluctance to accept their elevation, and even to
refuse when first invited – in part because eagerness for power did not encourage trust
in a candidate's moral fortitude (B. Weiler, 'The *rex renitens* and the medieval idea of
kingship, *c.*900–1250', *Viator* 31 (2000), 1–42).

seized from the battlefield and strung ever since from the walls of Cairo's fortress, be returned, so that he could bury them in consecrated ground.[31] That Simon was bound to Amaury in this expedition – the brothers having seemingly planned it as a joint campaign – perhaps served to demonstrate to the French that Simon's family identity had not been forgotten in his allegiance to the English crown.

Simon's rule as governor of Gascony encouraged this perception. The French barons – as they told Simon in their request of 1253 – had seen how, in Gascony, Simon sought to emulate the Count, his father, warring relentlessly against the rebellious and unfaithful southern lords. The remark also voiced implicit approval of Simon's style of rule. Like the earls and barons of England, who had expressed support for his strategies to Henry in the parliament of the previous October, the noblemen of France had observed Simon's government of Gascony and deemed it proper. Indeed, they had looked on in admiration. So much had been clear already during Simon's time as governor: early in 1250 the chaplain of Alphonse of Poitiers, observing the earl's government at first hand, had written to his master to report that Simon 'holds Gascony in good state, and all obey him, and have no courage to undertake a thing against him'.[32] Simon, like the Count, was mighty and feared (the Gascons, Matthew Paris says, 'dreaded him like bolts of lightning').[33] By the measures of his kind, Simon was seen – just like the Count – to be the best of rulers in the worst of times.

Why, then, did he turn down the invitation? According to Matthew Paris, Simon did not want to appear disloyal, by serving the king and kingdom of France when he was sworn to the king of England.[34] Henry and Louis were periodically in conflict and Henry still maintained his ancestral claim to Normandy, in the wake of the conquest led by Louis's father. A state of war between them was staved off only by the truce made after the battle of Taillebourg-Saintes in 1242 (extended by Simon's own efforts in November 1248).[35] No man could serve two masters, Simon knew, especially when those masters clashed.

This did not have to mean, of course, that Simon would answer his lord's demand – now turned into a polite request – to lend military support in Gascony and help to clean up the mess that Henry had created. But Simon's mind was eventually swayed not by the efforts of the king, but by the urging of Robert Grosseteste. The bishop of Lincoln, so Matthew Paris records, advised Simon 'to repay good for evil', and recalled for him the many kindnesses that Henry had done him in the past: how he had given Simon his sister in marriage, how he had granted him the earldom of Leicester and then a valuable wardship. 'To this counsel', Matthew reports, Simon 'inclined his heart obediently'.[36]

It is little wonder why. Robert was one of Simon's oldest and closest friends. He was also dying. Now in his mid-eighties, he had still been going strong in the first half of the year, but as summer turned to autumn his health had begun to fail. Stricken by infirmity, he rested at his manor of Buckden in Huntingdonshire. Robert knew his day was drawing in and looked to settle his affairs. He made one last push for the fulfilment of his pastoral and political duties, and then sent for a certain Master John de St Giles, a Dominican friar and an expert medic and theologian, who was equipped to console him in body and in mind. On 9 October, Robert departed this world. It was reported that, during the night, in nearby places, the sweet melody of celestial bells was heard to carry upon the air, singing the passage of Robert's soul to heaven.[37]

It is not clear whether Simon returned to England to be at Robert's side, or whether he received the advice by letter. But, within a few days of Robert's death, he had gathered his force and headed to Gascony, reaching the king by 22 October.[38] He found Henry at Benauges, some twenty-five miles east of Bordeaux. Although Simon was ready to be reconciled, this could not be done until he had seen some serious concessions. There were two matters in need of resolution: first, the losses Simon had sustained in mounting his campaign 'in the service of the king' the previous year; second was Eleanor's marriage portion. In 1244 Henry had granted to the couple an annual sum of 500 marks (£333), to which was added later the valuable wardship of the Umfraville lands (allowing Simon and Eleanor to take the profits of the estate until its heir came of age). But neither was a hereditary endowment – for 200 of the 500 marks were for life alone, meaning that they could not pass to the couple's children (and, in any case, it was far preferable to have that sum in land and not in cash). Now, in an agreement struck on 9 November 1253 at Saint-Macaire (almost thirty miles south-east of Bordeaux), Henry was willing to be liberal in order to secure Simon's aid. First, he granted Simon a lump sum of £500 in recompense for his Gascon expenses of 1252.[39] Second, he poured funds into Eleanor's marriage portion: an additional £400, to be translated into land when possible, with the entire sum now heritable.

Although this was a generous grant, boosting his income by some 20 per cent, it was not yet enough and Simon went further still in the extraction of concessions. Having little faith in Henry's ability to keep to the annual payments, he insisted that he be allowed to take the money directly from the sheriffs of various shires. The standard procedure was for sheriffs to carry royal income raised from their bailiwicks (revenues from royal estates, the profits of justice, and so on) to the exchequer at Westminster to render their accounts, after which money could be disbursed by royal order. According to the terms of this agreement, though, the sheriffs of six shires would have to bring the sum allotted for Simon and Eleanor's grant directly to the Montfort lands twice yearly. Simon was also permitted to demand oaths from these sheriffs guaranteeing that they would uphold this obligation, and to distrain upon their property if they failed to do so. He was even granted the right to block the appointment of any candidates to these sheriffdoms, allowing him to exclude those he thought unready to support his interests – a concession that, setting aside the payment of the fee, promised Simon enormous influence in the shires concerned, including his Midland homelands of Leicestershire and Warwickshire. It was an extraordinary subversion of procedure, and one that testified to Henry's eagerness to secure Simon's aid, as well as the supreme bargaining power that Simon's military prowess placed at his disposal.*

---

* Simon appears to have been exploiting the situation to his own advantage, pushing the king to go against royal interest in the long term by eroding government power in the shires. It is worth noting, however, that the agreement was drawn up with the approval not only of other magnates, but also of the king's counsellors and intimates: its witness list names the bishop of Hereford (a close adviser of the king), the earls

Simon remained with Henry in Gascony for the next few weeks, perhaps until early February 1254. He stayed despite the fact that 'it soon caused him much trouble' (as he later testified, though he was quick to point out that 'throughout the whole stay and during the whole time that he remained there, not once did he complain that he wanted to withdraw from him'). Certainly by May 1254 Simon was back in England, though still dealing with Henry's Gascon business. At Christmas Henry had written an open letter to his subjects, warning them that the king of Castile was planning to invade Gascony 'with a vast army of Christians and Saracens', with the intention of using the land as a base from which to launch an invasion of England and Ireland.[40] Queen Eleanor, governing England in his absence, had called an assembly to meet in January to raise a subsidy to fund Henry's continued campaign in Gascony, but the request was refused. And so another assembly was called, to open in late April. Simon returned, in May, in time to intervene – but not for Henry's benefit. Judging the subsidy unnecessary and its justification spurious, he 'announced the truth' to those assembled, as Matthew Paris records.[41] In the event Simon was proved right, for by August the king of Castile had come to terms and peace had been declared in Gascony. The price was the marriage of Henry's heir, Edward, to Eleanor of Castile, the king of Castile's half-sister – though only if Henry would endow his son with lands worth a vast £10,000 a year.[42]

The resulting grant ceded to Edward the mightiest of estates: the Channel Islands, almost 'the whole land of Ireland', a slew of Welsh and marcher castles and their lands, the city of Bristol, the

---

of Norfolk and Hereford, two of the king's Poitevin half-brothers, as well as Peter of Savoy (the queen's uncle), all of whom to some extent were obliged to prize Henry's interest. So also were two more whose authority supported the agreement, though, unlike the others, these men were also Simon's friends: Peter de Montfort and Peter's uncle, Walter de Cantilupe. Walter oversaw the process put in place for drawing up and sealing multiple exemplars of the grant (an understandably rigorous process, given the grant's irregularity, carefully noted by a royal clerk in the Patent Rolls). Walter was also a member of the royal council; with loyalties on both sides, he was well placed to broker an agreement that advanced, in one way or another, the interest of both parties (*Calendar of Patent Rolls, 1232–72*, 4 vols. (London, 1906–13), *1247–58*, 249; J. R. Maddicott, *Simon de Montfort* (Cambridge, 1994), 122–3).

earldom of Chester (once held by Simon's mentor, Ranulf, earl of Chester) and the honour of the Peak in Derbyshire. He was also set in charge of Gascony, the grant of which was now renewed.[43] Just one year earlier, as the royal ships had prepared to depart for Bordeaux, Matthew Paris had told how Edward's father had 'wept [over him] with many hugs and kisses', and Edward, as he watched his father's ships set out, 'standing on the seashore crying and hiccupping with sobs, did not want to leave while he could still see the bending sails of the ships'.[44] Now, in November 1254, the heir to the throne was fifteen years old; he was a knight (having been girded with the sword by the king of Castile), he was married – and to a member of one of the major European houses – and he was the greatest of English landholders.[45] He was ready to take to the political and military stage, alongside his father and his uncle, Simon.

*

It was, however, Henry's plans for his second son, advanced at the same time, that were to propel the next tempestuous phase of Simon's relations with the king. Edmund, born in 1245, was nine years old in February 1254, and, like his brother, in need of his own lands. In December of the previous year, in Gascony, Henry had been approached by a papal envoy, who offered him the chance to extend Plantagenet territory southward into the Mediterranean by taking the kingdom of Sicily. This kingdom, encompassing not only the island of Sicily but also the southern half of Italy, had been held by the Holy Roman Emperor, Frederick II. But in 1245 Pope Innocent IV had denounced Frederick as a tyrant and deposed him, and had begun to look for ways to expel the erstwhile emperor from his Italian lands. Frederick had died in 1250, but his sons still maintained the power of their Hohenstaufen house. And so the pope now proposed to Henry that he should lead or send an army into Sicily to oust the Hohenstaufen and place Edmund upon the throne. In 1255 Innocent's successor, Alexander IV, stipulated that, for licence to take this course, the king of England must compensate the papacy with £90,000 for the funds already spent dealing with the Hohenstaufen. Henry agreed.[46]

The extension of Plantagenet power into Italy was a glamorous prospect, but Henry's subjects did not consider it to be a sensible one. The cost of raising such an army and the logistical challenges of such a campaign were too great. As a council of churchmen instructed the king in 1256,

> the whole kingdom of England would not suffice for such a burden, even if earth would be made into gold, especially since the kingdom of Sicily is unconquerable and as good as inaccessible to an army of our men. And if we had mercenary knights and paid soldiers from that land, the value of their loyalty would be in doubt, because of their long familiarity with Frederick and his men.

The sending of an English army to Italy would also leave the kingdom vulnerable to attack from the Welsh. It was obvious, Henry was told, that 'such a sum of money is spent uselessly and clearly wasted, just as obviously apparent and well known'.[47]

If Henry's greater subjects had been given the opportunity to point this out before the deal with the pope was made, they would surely have done just that. But Henry had never sought advice about the scheme, at least not beyond his inner circle. The conquest of Sicily was an enormous undertaking that required the cooperation of England's bishops, barons and knights, and impacted upon them in all sorts of ways; according to custom the king should have sought their counsel. No subsequent attempt to make the case could remedy this failing (even, as Henry did in 1255, parading young Edmund in traditional Sicilian costume before a parliament and proclaiming his son's God-given right to rule).[48] For a king to act in such a manner was a profound violation of the values that underpinned his office.

Henry's resolution to take Sicily seemed all the more reckless given the profound level of debt in which the crown was mired. The preservation of Henry's Gascon territory throughout Simon's governorship and his own campaign had cost him £44,000 or more. This was at a time when annual royal income was around £30,000, far from sufficient to sustain such spending.[49] The shortfall might have been satisfied by general taxation, but successive parliaments had refused to grant any subsidy.[50] Now, Henry was promising to pay the pope an eye-watering sum merely for permission to launch another, enormously expensive campaign.

Henry did have a solution, though, which he pursued with papal endorsement: the Sicilian agreement would be financed by the English Church. This scheme faced ferocious opposition. In 1253, only a year before the Sicilian plans were launched, Henry had been planning to lead an expedition to Outremer, and so England's prelates had granted him a tenth of their income by way of finance. But then, two years later, it was decreed that these funds would now be turned towards the Sicilian business – and that the clergy would be paying this tax for five years instead of the original three. Enraged, the prelates refused the king's demand. They would not, they insisted, give further funds willingly, 'since the reason for the payment, which seemed pious at first sight, now is not pious, as it seems to them, since it has been changed'.[51] When a papal envoy demanded their cooperation, Walter de Cantilupe and the bishop of London led the prelates in declaring themselves willing to follow the path of St Thomas Becket (who, they recalled, had allowed his head to be caved in for the cause of ecclesiastical liberty) before they would allow the subjection of the Church to such oppression.[52] The prelates struggled for several years against the combined demands of pope and king. But eventually, in 1257, backed into a corner and without the legal wherewithal to offer more resistance, they offered to pay 52,000 marks (almost £35,000), on condition that they would be obliged to pay nothing more.[53]

For the prelates of the English Church and for other greater subjects, Henry's uncounselled actions and failure to recognize his fiscal responsibility were deeply frustrating. But for some, Simon included, Henry's actions were to be seen in a more sinister light – for new strains of thought had begun to seep into political discourse in England. Their progenitor was Robert Grosseteste. In his later years, the bishop of Lincoln had translated Aristotle's *Nicomachean Ethics* and its ancient commentaries, and had even supplied a commentary for Book VIII when he had found the original missing.[54] The subject of Book VIII, and so of Robert's commentary, was kingship.

According to Aristotle (as Robert explained) there are three types of polity: monarchy, aristocracy and timocracy (where the ruling class is determined by property qualifications). Of these three, kingship is the best, for the community is a single body and thus should have a single head. The worst sort of rule is therefore the corruption of royal power, tyranny – when the ruler strives for his own advantage rather than the advantage of his people. It is true, wrote Robert, that many kings would appear to fit this description, for they seize the property of their subjects because their own is insufficient to sustain the majesty of royal rule. But here is a crucial distinction, he explained: a true king – one fit to bear the title – commands vast personal resources and so never needs to claim the resources of his subjects.

A superabundance of wealth was, therefore, essential to the definition of kingship as an office. Accordingly, a monarch who did not have the funds to finance his own rule without imposing upon his subjects was not truly a king at all: he was a *clerotes* (Aristotle's term, which Robert understood to mean a man drawn by lot to act as a ruler, as if he held the office of king only by chance). An impecunious ruler, a *clerotes*, would inevitably be driven to oppress his subjects financially in order to sustain his rule. He would thus, in contravening their interests for his benefit, become a tyrant.[55]

These definitions of kingship and tyranny and the distinction between them differed from established thought. Traditionally, a tyrant was defined as someone who ruled arbitrarily, according to his own whim, rather than according to the law. This understanding was bolstered by the contemporary belief in the importance of government by counsel: a decision was lawful if it was made by the counsel or judgement of the ruler's court. The word court had two overlapping senses, both relevant in this context: the group of magnates and prelates surrounding the king could both provide him with counsel about decisions to be made in governing the kingdom and could also form a judicial panel to pronounce judgement on one of its members, in the baronial version of trial by peers.*
According to contemporary thinking in the early thirteenth century,

---

* The barons who had rebelled against King John in 1215 had demanded that the king should *only* take punitive measures against a free subject of any status via this process or its equivalent, hence Magna Carta's guarantee that the king could not act arbitrarily

then, a tyrant was someone who habitually acted without consulting his greater subjects and without regard for judicial process; in other words, someone like King John. Robert Grosseteste's definitions of kingship and tyranny were quite different. Royal wealth and the ruler's obligation to his subjects were paramount, rather than the willingness to rule by law. Here Robert conceived of a new type of tyrant, someone who was not necessarily a malevolent person (as John had been) but someone who might well have been a good man had he not found himself lacking resources, and was thus driven to rule tyrannically by burdening his subjects.[56]

Robert discussed these ideas with his circle of learned friends. At some point in the first half of 1249, he sent his translation of the *Ethics* and its commentaries to Adam Marsh, and a summary of his new definition of kingship to Simon (we know this because Adam, in a letter to Robert, noted that he was returning Robert's summary sealed with Simon's seal, and commended Robert for his work on the *Ethics*).[57] Other evidence allows us to expand the group amongst whom these ideas circulated. Two others, close to Robert and members of his diocesan administration, were chosen to accompany him to the papal court in 1250 to help him make a case based on Aristotle's definitions. John of Crakehall was Robert's steward, in charge of managing the diocese of Lincoln's vast estates. He was, therefore, familiar both in principle and in practice with the ruler's moral responsibility to set his government on a sound financial footing for the benefit of his subjects (we shall meet John again, in the next chapter). Richard Gravesend was archdeacon of Oxford, and thus one of Robert's trusted lieutenants. He had been in charge of drawing up a memorandum of the case made by Robert at the papal court, so that it could be sent back to the

---

against any free subject – by arresting or imprisoning them, seizing their property, outlawing or exiling them, or worse – and all free people were entitled to be tried by their peers or by the law of the land. The 'law of the land' meant judicial processes other than trial by peers that could determine guilt or innocence, such as trial by ordeal or trial by combat. As it happened, trial by ordeal was in effect banned by Pope Innocent III at the Fourth Lateran Council in 1215, on the basis that it did not work, and that mortals could not demand God's intervention (F. McAuley, 'Canon law and the end of the ordeal', *Oxford Journal of Legal Studies*, 26 (2006), 473–513). Trial by combat continued throughout the Middle Ages.

cardinals to keep the arguments fresh in their minds. It was from this memorandum that the summary on kingship was taken, and sent to Simon. Both John of Crakehall and Richard Gravesend, as intimates of Robert, were known to the earl. Indeed, Richard was Simon's friend, for he is described in one of Adam Marsh's letters to Simon as 'your lordship's faithful spiritual servant', and Simon made him an adviser to the executors of his will a few years later.[58] This suggests that Simon and his circle were beginning to consider kingship in terms of Aristotle's definition, precisely at the time that England's king was failing to steward his resources and – consequently lacking the wealth to run his kingdom and pursue his foreign schemes – was bearing down financially on his subjects.

The English Church bore the burden of this failing, but so too did the poor and the gentry of the shires. Henry sought to extract money from the latter group in two ways. The first was through the eyre. This comprised panels of judges, sent at the king's behest every few years to tour the shires of England, hearing both criminal and civil cases.* While the eyre improved access to royal justice for many of the king's subjects, it had become principally a way of making money for the king, for it provided various opportunities to penalize local people for failure to cooperate adequately with the machinery of justice, in failing to report a crime, for instance, or reporting it inaccurately.

During the eyre of 1245–9 the judges – presumably under direction from the cash-strapped king – had invented a series of new penalties

---

* This was in addition to the shire courts (operated by the sheriff) and the central courts of the King's Bench and Common Pleas. Any free person could bring a case to the shire court or, as became the norm and an increasingly popular practice in the thirteenth century, have a case transferred to the central courts or the eyre or heard at a specially commissioned assize. They could do so by obtaining either a writ *de cursu* (issued by the chancery for a standard administrative fee of sixpence), or *de gratia*, the cost of which could be set quite high, for instance at half a mark, for those who could afford it, but it could be waived for favoured subjects or, like the *de cursu* writ, for those who were too poor to afford justice otherwise (T. K. Moore, 'The Fine Rolls as evidence for the expansion of royal justice during the reign of Henry III', in *The Growth of Royal Government Under Henry III*, ed. D. Crook and L. J. Wilkinson (Woodbridge, 2015), 55–71, at 61, 63–4, 68–71).

and applied them determinedly.[59] One of these, deemed the most unfair, was the extension of the *murdrum* fine to cases of accidental death. *Murdrum* was a penalty devised after 1066 by William the Conqueror in an effort to stop the native English ambushing and killing his Norman men: the inhabitants of the settlement in which a homicide took place would either have to produce the culprit or prove that the victim was English to avoid facing a substantial monetary penalty (although, by the thirteenth century, proving 'Englishry' simply meant proving the victim was not freeborn). The prime objective of the *murdrum* fine was, in the absence of a standing police force, to incentivize communities to detect murderers and either arrest them or force them into exile. Accordingly (and as legal authorities were clear), the imposition of the *murdrum* fine in cases of accidental death was an abuse. Nevertheless, the royal judges now began to do just that in order to raise money.[60]

The extent to which the eyre bore down with mounting severity on the ordinary people of England can be seen in the rising levels of amercements, or monetary penalties, demanded: £10,153 was levied from the eyre of 1234–6, rising to £18,698 for the eyre of 1245–9 (in which the new penalties were introduced), and a similar figure of £17,859 for the eyre of 1252–8.[61] In total, the eyre of 1245–9 had netted the king some £22,000, a massive sum not far off the level of the crown's ordinary annual income.[62] The fact that around 85 per cent of this considerable total was gathered through amercements levied on the poorer of his subjects, in ways that went against legal custom and carried little or no legal rationale, testifies to the extraordinary burden Henry was placing upon his people in order to supplement his resources.

The second way in which Henry sought to levy money from his subjects, particularly those who were not members of the nobility, was perhaps more troubling still: he put increasing pressure upon sheriffs to raise more cash from their shires. Every year, each sheriff had to account for his shire's 'farm' (the customary sum made up of revenues from royal manors, local courts and other long-standing sources of income), as well as 'increments', a sum demanded on top of the farm to bring the total up to whatever the king thought to be a good return. The increments were set at the king's discretion, and throughout the 1240s and 1250s the sums demanded rose in staggering fashion: in Norfolk–Suffolk, for instance, from 90 to 200, to 300, to 400 marks between 1229 and 1257.[63]

There was simply no way that sheriffs could produce this sort of money – for which they were personally liable – in the customary ways. They therefore turned to drastic and deeply unpopular measures. The sheriff of Cambridgeshire, like the judges of the eyre, devised new ways of levying amercements, through his shrieval court (it was either that or mortgage or sell his own lands, he later complained).[64] Other sheriffs started to hold their courts (known as 'tourns') more frequently than the twice a year decreed by custom and guaranteed by Magna Carta, in order to amerce people for failing to attend or for various infringements during the session. The inhabitants of Lincolnshire were spared such oppressions only because their bishop, Robert Grosseteste, strode in to protect his people, preventing the sheriff from holding uncustomary sessions.[65]

The tourn was the least of people's worries with regard to the sheriffs' activities, however. The most dangerous aspect of the increments system was that sheriffs did not have to account for how they obtained the money. The result was a myriad of methods devised to extort cash from vulnerable subjects. One of the most popular strategies employed by sheriffs was arresting people at random so as to extort a bribe for not consigning them to prison – or else to consign them to prison in order to extort a bribe for their release. Some sheriffs even forced people, by means of unjust imprisonment and even torture, to make false accusations against others.[66] Of the many offenders, the most notorious was William Heron, sheriff of Northumberland, to whom Matthew Paris awarded the epithet 'the hammer of the poor'. His crimes ranged from imprisoning one man just 'for giving a cheeky answer' to forcing merchants to sell him wine at a reduced rate and selling it at profit, and taking bribes from those wishing to avoid jury duty.[67] Heron's conduct was made even more dismal than it first appears by the fact that, like several others, he was corrupt; large quantities of money taken in this fashion never made it to the treasury.[68] Henry's shrieval administration was, therefore, not only inordinately oppressive but also inefficient. It was his people who suffered in consequence. Their grief was widespread, as we know from the testimonies of the many local people who came forward to complain.[69] But no action was taken, and their plight continued.

That these two groups – the Church and the people of the shires – bore the weight of Henry's money-making ventures was a product of the Magna Carta age. When the king found himself in want of money, the obvious way to obtain funding was through taxation. But, according to the principles embodied in the Charter, this could be procured only by the consent of a parliament.* Between 1237 and 1258, Henry set out such requests ten times, and was refused on eight of those occasions.[70] He was thus forced to look for other sources of cash. This is why Henry identified the English Church as a source of funds: he could not tax the baronies of great churchmen without parliamentary consent, but he could tax their ecclesiastical income (that is, lands donated to the Church), because it was not covered by Magna Carta. It was covered by Church law, which decreed that Church lands could not be taxed by a lay ruler without the consent of their prelates – but in this case the bishops could not easily refuse, because they had already been ordered by the pope to support the conquest of Sicily.[71] The peasantry and gentry suffered on the same account: the creative levying of amercements at the eyre and the increasing shire increments were not regulated by Magna Carta.

Amidst all this, Simon and his fellow nobles did not suffer. The protection of Magna Carta they enjoyed insulated them from Henry's quest for cash: unlike their forebears under King John, they could not be charged for the use of royal justice, nor could they be charged a sum above the now-standard £100 in relief (inheritance tax), nor could the widowed women amongst them be charged for the right to stay single. And, importantly, they could simply refuse a request for taxation in parliament and walk away.

Nor were the nobles threatened by the sheriffs. In previous times,

---

* Such was set out in chapters 12 and 14 of the 1215 Charter; these clauses were omitted in later issues but this made little difference, since the magnates insisted that the custom still held 'according to the tenor of Magna Carta' (S. T. Ambler, *Bishops in the Political Community of England, 1213–1272* (Oxford, 2017), 84; J. R. Maddicott, *The Origins of the English Parliament 924–1327* (Oxford, 2010), 198–9).

the sheriffs had been *curiales*, great men who were sold or awarded the office as a form of patronage. In the mid-1230s, however, the king had decided to replace such office-holders with lesser men upon whom he could exert pressure to produce more money.[72] These men lacked the clout to confront the earls and great barons of the kingdom. Indeed, several potentates – including Simon – reportedly prevented sheriffs from entering their lands to carry out their duties.[73] Simon's power over local sheriffs was even boosted, as we have seen, in 1253, when Henry awarded him the right to veto the appointment of the sheriffs of six counties and to exact oaths from the office-holders.

Nor did the magnates, unlike their forebears under King John, expect the king to call in the money they owed to the crown. Indeed, the king often stepped in to prevent the exchequer chasing up their debts. Simon was amongst those who benefited in this respect, being excused payment of aids in 1245 and 1253.[74] It was a reversal of the pervasive situation in John's reign: now, the grievance of a major baron such as Simon de Montfort did not stem from his being forced to pay vast sums to the crown but, instead, from the debts that the king owed to him. From Simon's perspective, this was a serious issue. But, taking a longer view, he and his fellows enjoyed a far easier existence in relation to the king than almost any of their predecessors since the Conquest.

Still, there was a feeling – which under Robert Grosseteste's influence, as we have seen, began to spread through Simon's circle from the early 1250s – that Henry's behaviour was unacceptable. It did not matter whether Simon and other potentates suffered personally or not. They now saw that a monarch who lacked sufficient resources to enact his rule, especially if by his own fault, and who consequently demanded money from his subjects, was violating the tenets of his office in the most fundamental way. The best sort of government, they knew, was that which disregarded the personal interests of the powerful and ruled with the wellbeing of its subjects close to heart.

*

Henry's debts to Simon, the Gascony affair and the way in which Henry ruled his kingdom were not the only grievances Simon nursed at this time.* He had made a new enemy, and his name was William de Valence.

William was one of the brood of Henry's half-brothers, sons of Isabella d'Angoulême (widow of King John and former queen of England) by her second husband, Hugh de Lusignan, count of La Marche. The brothers were known interchangeably by their names of Lusignan and Valence or – with venom and contempt – merely as 'the Poitevins'. The king, looking to garner their support in the regions around Gascony, had invited them to join his court. In 1247, William de Valence and his brother Aymer had accepted Henry's invitation and settled in England. They were rewarded lavishly: William with marriage to a substantial heiress, Aymer with the rich bishopric of Winchester (although Aymer was too young to take up office, and thus remained bishop-elect). Two elder brothers, meanwhile, Gui and Geoffrey, remained in Poitou but visited the English court regularly and were granted money fees.

The first problem, from Simon's point of view, was that Henry's generosity to William and his brothers was interfering with the king's ability to discharge his debts to Simon.[75] At this time the king owed the earl a significant sum, 1,000 marks of Gascon debt that Henry had been compelled to take on.[76] For this Simon could rightfully blame the Lusignans, first because Henry had granted William de Valence an annual stipend of some £833, and second because William had married one of the heirs to the great Marshal inheritance and thus owed Eleanor dower from the Marshal lands – the king was forced to take on the payments himself, and recoup the money from William.[77]

But the Lusignans' conduct also contributed to the enmity. They soon gained an evil reputation for themselves, for they were disrespectful of their fellow magnates and disregarding of the law.

* After leaving Gascony in the spring of 1254, Simon stayed away from court and was hardly seen at Henry's side again until the last days of 1256. Part of his time away was spent on diplomatic service (he was sent to the king of France in the spring of 1255 and again in late February of 1257) but, for the most part, he must have been with Eleanor and the children on their English manors or in France. In the latter half of March 1257 he attended a parliament at Westminster, summoned by the king to consider the Sicilian Business.

Rightfully trusting in Henry's willingness to shield them from recrimination, they acted as they wished. Matthew Paris, who was revolted by their impropriety and arrogance, details their behaviour. In one infamous episode, Aymer de Valence (see plate 20) had escalated a dispute with his superior, Boniface of Savoy, archbishop of Canterbury. One of Aymer's priests had infringed the rights of an archiepiscopal official and resisted all reprimands, and so the archbishop's official had the priest arrested and detained. Aymer's response was to raise a posse, with the help of his brother William. The gang made roughshod searches of the archbishop's manors, first Southwark and then Maidstone, before heading for the archbishop's palace at Lambeth. Aymer's men broke down the doors and stormed the building. Inside they helped themselves to seventy shillings in cash, as well as silver plate and jewellery, before seizing the archbishop's official together with various servants. They carried their prisoners off to Aymer's castle at Farnham, where they consigned them to gaol. They kept some of them imprisoned for as long as fifteen days. Eventually, Aymer's men released the archbishop's official, but they simply turned him out onto the street, without bothering to supply him with a horse or another means of transport. Elderly as he was, he was forced to make his escape on foot. 'Not daring to look behind him' (as Matthew Paris recounts), he trudged three miles to the Cistercian house of Waverley, where the monks gave him refuge.[78] For this assault on the servants and property of the archbishop of Canterbury (not only Aymer's fellow potentate but also his superior) Aymer got off scot-free.*

William de Valence, having assisted his brother in mounting this attack, was also guilty of his own offences. The accusations against him were of a particular shade: he not only broke the law, but he also broke the unwritten rules that governed noble society. He was uncourtly, and uncouth. On one occasion, in 1252, he had entered the lands of the bishop of Ely and hunted there without permission, before breaking into the bishop's manor house in search of something

---

* Archbishop Boniface managed to recover his valuables (though not his money), but this was by his own efforts (A. Hershey (ed.), *The 1258–9 Special Eyre of Surrey and Kent* (Woking, 2004), no. 163).

to slake his thirst. After his initial search turned up only beer, he broke down the doors of the bishop's wine cellar. According to Matthew Paris (who seems well informed about the episode), he did so 'shamefully and roughly, swearing, and cursing beer and all those who first made it'. After serving himself, William had the best of the cellar's offerings distributed amongst his men, who promptly drank themselves to the point of vomiting. When they eventually left, they did not even bother to replace the corks in the casks, allowing the valuable contents to flow freely onto the floor. The poor servant who had charge of the cellar, returning to see the doors broken down 'as if it had been done by an enemy in times of war', was left to wade through the spillage and hurriedly secure what was left. When the bishop was told of these goings on, he bore it stoically, but wondered why William and his men had felt the need to pillage that which the bishop would have given to them 'freely and civilly' if they had only asked. Such conduct, as Matthew Paris noted, 'contravened the law of the land as well as the honour of the proper conduct of knightly society'.[79]

The bishop of Ely was, perhaps, a soft target for William's brutishness, but the Poitevin was not fearful of going after his fellow magnates, too. Early in 1257 he broke into one of Simon's manors, and made off with some booty. When Simon's seneschal recovered the stolen goods, William had burst into a rage, and heaped insults upon the earl. None of this could be tolerated. Simon did what was expected of a tenant-in-chief of the crown in such a situation, and brought the dispute before the king. This he did in May 1257, when the court was in London.[80] It was a tense time, for the exchequer had been busy tallying up Henry's debts to Simon. Now the earl was forced to confront an injustice thrown upon him by one of the very men responsible for obstructing his payments.

The king, meanwhile, was in little state to deal with the quarrel. He had returned to London on 14 May, after a period spent at Merton, to attend to a tragic task: the burial of his youngest daughter, Katherine. She was only three years old, and had suffered in her short life, seemingly born deaf and victim to a serious illness the previous year. The queen was overcome with grief, languishing, inconsolable, in her bed at Windsor.[81] It was left to Henry to lead the mourning at Katherine's funeral, in Westminster Abbey, on 16 May. He paid for the feeding of 10,000 paupers, an extravagant act of charity of a magnitude to match his grief.[82] It was a grief that Simon and Eleanor knew, too, for they had lost a daughter (her name is not known to us) at some point between 1248 and 1251, when the couple were in Gascony. She had been buried in the chapel of St Peter the Apostle in the Dominican church of Bordeaux.[83]

No ruler had the right, however, to submit to grief, so it was in this state that Henry listened as Simon and William de Valence laid their enmity before him. William (in Matthew Paris's account) was characteristically bad mannered, 'raving openly' before the court, and 'irreverently imposing upon him [Simon] the brand of traitor, which is a great insult to knights'. Perhaps William had a certain allegation in mind, or perhaps he had simply judged this insult to be the most effective at provoking Simon's temper. If so, he judged correctly, for Simon 'was roused vehemently'. Here Matthew Paris turned to a quotation from Horace, 'anger is a brief mad fury': an allusion to *furor*, the name the Romans had given to battle-fury, the red mist that descends upon a man in the face of the enemy and drives all rational thought from his mind. This was the fury that took Simon now: he wanted 'to rush upon' William (*irruere*, to charge, a verb otherwise reserved for descriptions of battle). Simon would have killed him, we are told. He was stopped only by the king himself, who leapt forward and forced himself bodily between the two men.[84]

Simon remained at court for the rest of May and early June, part of that time spent in the seething company of William de Valence. He at least managed to secure a promise from Henry to repay some of the money owed him – with the right to distrain upon the king's lands in the event of his default. The practice of distraint (the confiscation of lands or property for the purpose of coercion) was customarily exercised by lords upon their tenants, and the king's surrendering of this right to one of his subjects speaks again to Simon's bargaining power. Perhaps it was Simon who also insisted that various *curiales* step forward to act as guarantors for the debt. These men even had to be willing to subject themselves to excommunication at the hands of Simon's friend, Walter, bishop of

Worcester.[85] The extent to which this new agreement helped to assuage the situation is not clear, but when the exchequer drew up a reckoning in December 1257 it found that the king owed Simon precisely £1,198 14s 10½d.[86] This was just under half Simon's annual income at this time – a substantial sum. Henry took steps almost immediately to alleviate the burden, pardoning Simon some £73 10s od in miscellaneous petty debts.[87] But this was a drop in the ocean and, meanwhile, Simon was still waiting for his annual stipend to be converted into land.

Yet, despite the weight of debt owed him by the king, Simon was making efforts to fulfil his duties to his lord. In June 1257 he agreed to undertake a diplomatic mission to Louis IX, and there was even a suggestion that Simon would then go on, with others, to the papal court to haggle over the terms of the Sicilian business (although the latter embassy never took place). He was also part of a team that went again to France, around Michaelmas 1257, with the optimistic goal of persuading Louis to return the territories he and his father had conquered from Henry's house. But he returned, or was recalled, to the king's side by the last week of October, leaving the rest of his colleagues to pursue the embassy over the Christmas period.[88]

In the early months of 1258, Simon was only sporadically at court, presumably attending to business on his estates and spending time with his family. But as the early months of the new year passed, he found himself contending with a mounting crisis, one far greater than his bickering with the Lusignans, greater even than his concern to recoup the money owed him by the king. It was a catastrophe that reached across the kingdom and its people: famine.

8

The Seizure of Power

In the spring of 1257, on the island of Lombok, in Indonesia, the Samalas volcano erupted. It spewed a mighty cloud of ash into the atmosphere, dimming the skies, cooling the earth, and bringing incessant rain.[*] From early February until the end of March 1258 (writes Matthew Paris), 'the north wind blew without intermission, constant frost, snow and cold afflicted the poor and suspended cultivation, and killed . . . ewes and lambs'.[1] These conditions were all the harder because they followed two years of atrocious weather: 1256 and 1257 had seen deluge and flood, leading to two years of bad harvests.[2] As stores of food began to dwindle, the price of crops began to rise (in London, a measure of corn was now worth nine shillings). Proclamations were issued, forbidding wealthier citizens from stockpiling supplies for profit. Some meagre respite was provided by three ships sent by the king's brother, Richard of

---

[*] The nature and impact of the Samalas eruption is the subject of current scientific and historical research. It had been claimed that the episode was comparable to the eruption of Mount Tambora in Indonesia, in 1815, which led to 'the year without a summer', famously depicted by Turner and described by Lord Byron in his poem 'Darkness'. Recent research has suggested that the darkening and cooling effects of the 1257 eruption were, in fact, partially offset by solar forcing. It has also been argued recently, contrary to claims that the eruption was the direct cause of the 1258 famine, that the famine followed the poor weather and failed harvests of 1256 and 1257, but that the effects of the 1257 eruption exacerbated the climatic problems and delayed the harvest of 1258 (B. M . Campbell, 'Global climates, the 1257 mega-eruption of the Samalas volcano, Indonesia, and the English food crisis of 1258', *Transactions of the Royal Historical Society*, 27 (2017), 87–121, at 114–18).

Cornwall, from Germany (where he was currently pursuing his career) bearing corn, wheat and bread. But still, through April, May and June, 'the north wind blew', and no plants would bud.[3]

People began to die. In larger settlements, where the dying gathered in greater numbers in search of sustenance, the townspeople turned to digging single capacious holes to house the multiplying bodies: mass graves. But there were soon too many, so that (as Matthew Paris tells) 'their livid and swollen corpses were found everywhere, in fives or sixes amongst the pigs, on middens and on the muddy streets, the flesh of the bodies wretchedly melting into each other'.[4]

Adding to the problem was the law: all untimely deaths were supposed to be reported to the coroner before burial, so that he could view the body in the company of local men to determine the cause of death. Communities were fearful of failing in their legal duty, lest they be subject to amercements that now, more than ever, they could not afford to pay – and so they dared not bury the bodies before the coroner had arrived on the scene. The coroners, in turn, could simply not keep up with the number of deaths being reported. And so the bodies piled higher. In April, the king had to make special provisions in Lincolnshire, Norfolk, Suffolk and Essex, ordering the local sheriffs to empower local law-worthy men to view bodies in the coroners' stead – if there was no sign of foul play, the bodies could be buried immediately.[5]

The ghastly tableaux of corpses piled high marked the route to Westminster, as Simon and his fellow nobles made their way to parliament in early April 1258. They were gathering to discuss the Sicilian Business, a project that must have seemed now, more than ever, an expensive extravagance. A year before, in the spring of 1257, the bishops and clergy had laid out their reasons for opposing the scheme, and had made the point that they were obliged, as stewards of Church property, to channel income towards pious causes, specifically the support of the poor, and that diverting funds towards the present project – a war against fellow Christians, that brought no benefit to the king's subjects – would thus be illegal and immoral.[6] For the king to be extracting tens of thousands of pounds from Church resources, at a time when the abbeys and churches of

England needed to feed the starving, cannot have been viewed as a pious or sensible move.

*

As the magnates and prelates headed to Westminster in the first week of April, a new cause of discord erupted. It involved the Lusignans. At Shere, in Surrey, the great curial baron John fitz Geoffrey had installed a priest to a living in the local church; Aymer de Valence, bishop-elect of Winchester, disputed John's right to do so, claiming the right of patronage in Shere as his own (see plate 21). The proper response would have been to obtain a judicial writ and have the case heard in court. Instead, Aymer sent a posse to attack the church and manor. His men beat up John's servants and carried them off to Farnham Castle. It seemed to be an iteration of the raid perpetrated against the archbishop of Canterbury's people at Lambeth in 1252 – except that this time one of the victims, a man named Philip Carpenter, was killed.[7]

So, when the parliament opened, John approached the king and made his complaint against Aymer. But Henry (as John later told it) 'did not wish to hear him and wholly denied him justice'.[8] Matthew Paris provides a more detailed account of the king's response: Henry made excuses for Aymer, and asked John not to take such grievous accusations further or set in train judicial proceedings, lest it cause a scandal.[9] Whatever Henry's motives, or the tone of his response, the result was the same: a lord denying justice to his vassal.

It was clear that the Lusignans were entirely free to behave as they wished, to attack the property and people of such mighty men as the archbishop of Canterbury, the bishop of Ely, Simon de Montfort and John fitz Geoffrey without fear of punishment. If Simon and the other *curiales* had not seen this before, then Henry's refusal to act now – when a man had been killed – certainly brought them to the realization. And, as they would have recognized, the Lusignans knew it too, and in this knowledge would probably go on to commit further crimes against all or any of their number. What was to be done? If the king, they reasoned, was not going to defend them against such criminalities, then they would have to defend themselves.

And so, on 12 April, three days after the parliament had opened with John's complaint, seven of the magnates met in secret: Richard de Clare, earl of Gloucester (the greatest landholder of the kingdom outside the royal family), Roger Bigod, earl of Norfolk and marshal of England, his brother Hugh Bigod, Peter of Savoy (brother of archbishop Boniface, and so too the queen's uncle), John fitz Geoffrey, Simon's close friend Peter de Montfort and Simon himself. They agreed on a strategy: they would stand together against the Lusignans, one for all and all for one. They had a document drawn up recording their agreement, all appending their seals to imbue the pact with legal authority (see plate 22). In this document, the seven named men proclaimed 'to all people' that 'we have sworn on the Holy Gospels, and are held together by this oath, promising in good faith that each of us and all together will aid each other, both we ourselves and our followers, against all people . . . saving the faith to our lord the king of England and to the crown'.[10] The oath bound the seven to act as one, 'against all people' (the customary formula in pacts of mutual aid), but in reality this meant the Lusignans.[11] The implication was that if called upon they would fulfil the oath by force.

Their solidarity was tried almost immediately. A week later, on 19 April, England's truce with the Welsh expired. In readiness, the king had on 14 March issued orders for an expedition to Wales, planned for July.[12] But Welsh incursions had followed immediately upon the expiration of the truce, as – according to Matthew Paris – the Welsh set themselves to 'robberies, murders, and conflagrations', attacking the people of Pembroke in the Marches, where they had 'killed very many of them in savage manner'.[13] The timing and ferocity of the attacks seems to have caught those gathered at Westminster by surprise.

The lord of Pembroke was William de Valence. When news of the attacks reached parliament, William complained to the king about the assaults on his lands. Henry's response, couched though it was in gentle terms, was to suggest that William use his ample wealth to defend his lands himself. This, indeed, was precisely what was expected of every marcher lord, for they were the principal line of defence against the Welsh and held quasi-royal powers in the region for this purpose. But William was not to be directed. Instead, 'heaping threats upon threats, and adding insults to abuses, he asserted that all these things had proceeded deceitfully by the consent and favour of English traitors'. William went on to lay specific charges against 'many nobles'. Matthew Paris does not repeat the precise allegations but we can imagine what they comprised. For, as William's tirade continued, it was Simon he singled out. The implication, perhaps, was that Simon had encouraged the Welsh to target the Pembroke lands as a means of pursuing his feud with William.

Upon hearing William's charges, Simon's newfound confederate, the earl of Gloucester, joined with him in anger, but it was Simon who went toe to toe with his accuser. William, 'multiplying reproaches further against the earl of Leicester', describes Matthew Paris, 'dared openly to assert in insolent manner before the king and many magnates that he was a longstanding traitor and had lied'. Simon, 'inflamed by anger and boiling with rage', responded, 'No, No, William, I am neither traitor nor son of a traitor; our fathers were unalike.'

The comparison, of course, was between the Count, Simon's beloved father, and William's father, Hugh de Lusignan, count of La Marche, the same feckless ally who had abandoned the English king at Taillebourg in 1242. Hugh's refusal to fight had left Henry open to defeat and capture by the French, when Henry's cause as well as his person had been saved only by the fearsome rearguard action of Simon and his fellows. It was a characteristically incisive statement, combining Simon's speed of thought with his ability to identify the weak points of his adversaries, and his willingness to exploit them in order to cause maximum offence. But, for Simon, insulting words were not enough to satisfy his fury. And so 'wishing to exact vengeance for so great an insult', Simon rushed upon William (as in their row of the previous year, the word used by the chronicler is *irruere*, to attack, to charge as if in battle). Again, an outright brawl was prevented only by the king forcing himself bodily between them.[14]

A week went by, with discussions continuing between bishops, earls and barons on the Sicilian Business and the problem of the Welsh – and, we may assume, with antipathy continuing to seethe between the seven confederates on the one side and the Lusignans on the other. By 28 April the king had decided to press on with his plans for Sicily. The 52,000 marks offered unwillingly by the Church in the spring of the previous year to support the Sicilian business (and still in the process of collection) was not sufficient. Already, early in 1258, the pope had grown angry at Henry's lack of progress, and the king had been forced to put down a deposit of £5,000.[15] What Henry needed now was for his magnates and prelates to grant him a tax. If extracting a concession from bishops and abbots for a tax on Church lands had been an extraordinary challenge, then obtaining a general tax from the bishops and barons on their lay landholdings would be far harder. They were under no obligation to agree and, indeed, had refused Henry's requests for taxation eight out of ten times over the previous decades.[16] The earls and barons, of course, shared with the bishops and abbots profound misgivings about the Sicilian venture, and the same complaint that the scheme had been advanced without their counsel. All Henry could do was ask, and hope.

What happened next happened in secret, or at least was kept from the wider public beyond the court. Not even Matthew Paris, usually so well informed of events, realized what was going on – or, if he did, he did not want to reveal it.[17] We know of what followed because a monk of Tewkesbury Abbey, then in the earl of Gloucester's retinue, was a witness, and sent a report back to Tewkesbury that was copied into the abbey's annals.[18] The witness describes how the nobles, upon hearing the king's request for taxation, replied that they would consider the matter and respond within three days. We may assume that the earls and barons had no real intention of granting the tax, but that some – particularly the seven confederates – wanted time to decide upon their move. At this point the bishops withdrew from parliament, 'lest they incur the anger of the king'. This they would have done at the command of the archbishop of Canterbury, Boniface of Savoy. Perhaps Boniface sensed, in the simmering atmosphere, an imminent eruption and wished to remove his bishops from the site of any trouble (even though to do so would have been to contravene the expectations of his office: in similar situations in earlier times, his predecessors had stepped in to try to quell unrest between king and barons). More likely, Boniface acted in consultation with his brother, Peter, one of the seven confederates. The archbishop would step back and allow the seven to execute their plan without impediment.[19]

Their plan was revealed three days after Henry's request for a tax, on the day appointed for the magnates' response. On this morning the confederates dressed carefully, in attire fit for war, donning suits of mail and tabards emblazoned with their emblems, and strapping on their swords (see plate 23). Then, 'as the third hour approached' (a little before 9 a.m.), they marched on Westminster Hall. Here, they knew, they would find the king.

The effect, as intended, was fearsome: these were 'noble and strenuous men', as the eye-witness recognized, hardened fighting knights. As they crossed the threshold of the hall, they made a point of unbuckling their blades and placing them in the entranceway – let it not be said that, in what followed, they had held the king at the point of their swords – but it was clear that their weapons remained within reach. They strode across the hall and stood before the king. They greeted him 'devotedly and with the honour due'. But their greeting did not diminish their martial demeanour, nor was it meant to. Henry was 'immediately shaken in spirit, uncertain as to why they had approached thus armed'.

'What is this, my lords?' he said. 'Truly, have I, poor wretch, been captured by you?' He spoke as if the hall were a battlefield, and enemy knights were seizing him for ransom.

It was the earl of Norfolk who replied. 'No, my lord king, no. But let the wretched and intolerable Poitevins and all aliens flee from your face and from ours, as from the face of a lion, and there will be glory to God in the highest and in your land peace to people of good will.'

The earl of Norfolk's words were carefully chosen, and again calculated to proclaim the martial intent of the seven. The call for the Poitevins to flee from the faces of king and confederates took up the words of the sixty-seventh Psalm: 'Let God arise, and let His enemies be scattered: and let them that hate Him flee from before His face.'[20] This was an entreaty against enemies, and one employed time and again in the thirteenth century in prayers sung during Mass for the success of the crusades, a call for divine wrath to be visited upon the enemies of the righteous and a plea to God to strengthen the sword arms of the *crucesignati*.[21] The earl of Norfolk's next words played upon another familiar verse: 'Glory to God in the highest; and on earth peace to men of good will.' Taken from the angels' proclamation of Christ's birth to the shepherds in the Gospel of Luke, this verse formed the opening of the Gloria sung at Mass, and was thus one of the most familiar of biblical verses. But here the earl added one word that altered its meaning: he changed *in terra pax*, 'peace on earth', to *in terra vestra pax*, 'peace in your land'.[22] This was a warning to Henry that, if he failed to scatter the Poitevins, there would be no peace in his kingdom. It was a threat of war.

And the earl of Norfolk continued. 'This truly is our secret (*secretum*), which we – all of us here – reveal to you for the sake of the dignity, honour and success of your power and that of your whole kingdom. If you will only swear and assert that you will adhere to our counsels, observing them entirely, the best remedy and solace will come about for you.'

'And what is it you mean', the king replied, 'that I must obey your counsels?'

The barons, together now, explained to him: 'Providing and touching the Holy Gospels, you – together with your son and heir, Edward – shall provide an oath, that without the counsel of twenty-four prudent men of England, namely bishops, earls, barons and those chosen, you will in no way presume to impose any financial burden or unaccustomed yoke, and you shall not delay in handing over your royal seal, by the counsel of the aforesaid men, to a discreet man whom they will provide.'

This, then – this secret plan, devised by the confederates over the course of the past few days – comprised far more than the expulsion of the Lusignans. It was a demand for a new order. Not only must the king now rectify his bad decisions, banishing the Lusignans, but he must also empower leading members of the political community to ensure that he made no such mistakes in future. Major decisions would henceforth be decided by a council of twenty-four leading subjects.

The confederates had referred explicitly to the imposition of taxation. Their objective here was to prevent Henry from advancing expensive and unrealistic policies, such as the Sicilian Business, which required massive financial subsidies from the king's subjects. If the king could not be trusted to consult his potentates before making such commitments, he must be compelled to do so. Importantly, this council of bishops and barons would have the right not only of counsel (that is, to advise the king on such matters) but also of consent, meaning the power to veto any proposal.

The insistence that a man appointed by this council have charge of the royal seal was also essential to this secret plan. The office of chancellor provided a critical oversight to the issuing of royal grants and orders, for the chancellor had direct control of the royal seal and thus could refuse to authenticate any royal act that was unjust or irresponsible. But the office of chancellor had effectively been in abeyance since 1238, with the royal seal kept by minor household officials, who would naturally do whatever the king commanded. Before 1238, for twelve years or so, the office had been held by Ralph de Neville, bishop of Chichester. It had been Ralph's refusal to put the seal to documents he thought irregular or improper that had caused the king to take the seal from him, so that the issuing of royal charters and orders would come directly under the king's control.[23] By recovering the seal, then, Henry had removed one of the most important checks and balances on the exercise of royal power. It was this that the confederates were seeking to reinstate.

It was not only the reinstatement of the office that was demanded now, but also the power of the new council to choose the office-holder. This was partly a matter of ensuring that the candidate was suitable, possessing the integrity and the strength of will to stand firm in the face of royal pressure (someone just like Ralph de Neville). But the demand also ran deeper, for a sense had been building that it was actually the right of the kingdom's greater subjects to make such appointments. This idea had emerged during Henry III's minority (1216–27), when all major decisions (including the appointment of Ralph de Neville) were made by a council of leading subjects on behalf of the underage king. Even after Henry came of age, his potentates clung to the idea that it was their authority – not the king's – that mattered here. Henry, for instance, had first attempted to take the seal from Ralph de Neville in 1236, but Ralph had refused to relinquish it, because 'he had received it by the common counsel of the kingdom, and therefore could not resign it to anyone without the common assent of the kingdom'.[24] When bishops and barons demanded the restoration of the chancellorship in 1244, 1248 and 1255, they did so with the proviso that they would have the right to choose the office holder.[25] On those occasions, their demand had been refused. Now, the confederates decided, they would not allow the king the chance to refuse once more.

The confederates, then, had decided that England's government should revert to conciliar rule, with the king holding no more power now, at the age of fifty, than he had as a nine-year-old boy. Government by council during a minority was well established and uncontroversial: there were recent examples not only in England (during Henry III's minority) but also in Aragon (established in 1213 for James I) and Scotland (set up in 1249 for Alexander III). But never before had conciliar rule been imposed upon a mature king. Of course, all kings were expected to rule by *counsel* – taking the advice of their leading subjects before making important decisions – but this was something very different. A king was expected to take counsel but he was not obliged to follow the advice he received: he might weigh the matter up and decide upon a different path. It was the king, not his counsellors, who actually made the decision. There was a strong line of thinking, in fact, that vassals were actually obliged to follow all decisions made by their ruler in this way, whether they agreed with the decision or not (because the taking of counsel, like the judgement of peers in a court case, made the decision legal).[26] The confederates, in 1258, were removing all decision-making power from the king entirely. This amounted to a transformation in the very form of government. It was revolutionary.

There was no precedent, and no political theory, that justified such a course of action. Indeed, the theories of power with which Simon was probably familiar argued against it. The rights and wrongs of subjects seizing power from their monarch had been discussed by his great friend Robert Grosseteste. Robert was moved to set out his arguments when the canons of Lincoln cathedral attempted to usurp some of his powers as bishop. Robert, as the single ruler of his dominion, recognized himself as a 'monarch' in the abstract sense, just as an archbishop or the pope, or an earl or the king, would be. The point was that monarchy – the wielding of power by a single ruler – was underpinned by properties that precluded subjects from seizing power for themselves. The monarch was the source of all power enjoyed by his subordinates, like the spring that gives life to a stream. To cut off the source would therefore mean that there was no power from which the subordinates could draw: 'Once the bubbling spring of a source has been reduced in size or drained dry, it follows that the stream, too, must suffer the same fate,' wrote Robert.[27]

Robert's drawing of his example from the natural world was intended to show that for subordinates to seize powers from their ruler went against the laws of nature. He continued by explaining that the monarch was like the sun, and his power like its rays: because the sun can only illuminate half the world at once, it uses the moon and stars to reflect its light onto the dark side of the Earth (in other words, the monarch cannot do everything necessary to govern his kingdom at once, and so devolves some of his power to subordinates to help in the running of his kingdom). 'It would be astonishing and utterly detrimental', wrote Robert, 'if, at the sun's rising over the earth, the moon and stars were to attempt to obstruct its rays. Suppose', he continued, they 'were to say of their obstruction: "Because we have light to illuminate the earth, the task is no longer yours." Would they not be taking . . . the power of growth from the earth's plants, life from animals, and the full development of perfection from both?'[28] This was not an analogy – it was a scientific proof. Robert's scientific specialism was optics, the study of the movement of physical light. Light, Robert understood, was one manifestation of *lux*, the primary generative force by which God had created the universe, which from the beginning of time had spread out from a central point carrying matter with it to create the physical world (it is this theory that has seen him hailed as the founder of the Big Bang Theory).[29] Temporal power – the power of monarchs, whether kings or popes, earls or bishops – was, like physical light, a manifestation of *lux*.

As such it was divine in origin but also demonstrable by scientific reason and experiment. And, importantly, it had the same physical properties and was similarly bound by the laws of nature. Power, like a beam of light, travelled in one direction from a single source.

When Simon, then, marched on Westminster Hall, he was participating in a revolution that, according to his great friend and mentor, contravened the laws of nature and thus also divine will. If Robert had lived five more years, what would he have said to Simon? We can certainly know what course of action he would have thought appropriate when faced with the failings of Henry's rule. That was, in the first instance, to reprimand the ruler. Robert himself was not shy of doing so, and indeed held a deep conviction that this was his duty. He had said as much to the pope, who had once issued an order that Robert considered destructive. Innocent IV wanted his nephew to be provided with a parish living, and had asked Robert to oblige – but, since the nephew would not be in residence and would only draw the income from the parish, and would thus be unable to minister to the souls of his parishioners, Robert felt the demand to be unethical, and so believed it his duty to refuse: 'Because of my obligation to be obedient and loyal', he told the pope, 'I disobey, I oppose, I rebel . . . you can take no harsh measures against me because of my stand, for my every word and deed in this matter is neither opposition nor rebellion, but rather a demonstration of the filial respect due by God's command to one's father and mother.'[30] It was the duty of a faithful subject, then, to point out a command from his monarch was flawed, and to refuse to execute that command.

When it came to the king of England, it was the particular duty of Robert and his fellow bishops to follow such a course of action. In England there was a long and well-established role played by bishops in the political community: if the king erred from the path of lawful or moral rule, it was their duty to reprimand him and set him back on the righteous path. This role was ultimately based upon God's plan for humanity, as set out in the Bible. For the Bible made clear that all kings, inevitably, would fall to sin, for God had never intended men to wield such awesome powers, and they did not have the moral strength to do so without it corrupting them. In the Old Testament, one king after another – from the first, Saul, to David, Solomon, and their successors – fell to warmongering, witchcraft, adultery, murder and even the abandonment of God for pagan deities. Even so, and no matter how much the people suffered in consequence, it was forbidden for subjects to raise a hand to the royal person. So much was made clear when David, the heroic slayer of Goliath appointed by God to succeed the tyrant-king, Saul, had refused to strike even a monarch rejected by God: 'I will not put out my hand against my lord, because he is the Lord's anointed . . . for who shall put forth his hand against the Lord's anointed, and shall be guiltless?'[31] Even the worst of the Old Testament kings retained the divine protection entailed upon them when they were anointed with holy oil by God's prophets.

This did not mean, however, that God expected His people to suffer unjust kings. Indeed, He had established a clear solution: in the Old Testament, when a king erred He sent His prophet to reprimand him and recall him to the path of proper rule. Thus Saul, David, Solomon and their successors all received visits from prophets who pointed out the flaws in their behaviour and invited them to change their ways (it had been too late for Saul, but David and Solomon and their successors took the second chances that they were offered). This was the model for correcting illicit or improper royal behaviour that had been followed in England for centuries, with the bishops assuming the role of the Old Testament prophets. Indeed, in 1234, in very similar circumstances to 1258 – when Henry III had briefly been infatuated by a small cadre of foreign favourites (led by Peter des Roches) who had little regard for lawful rule and who had encouraged the king to rule unjustly – it had been the archbishop of Canterbury (then Edmund of Abingdon) who confronted the king in Westminster Hall, listing Henry's failings and urging him to reform himself for the sake of his kingdom and his subjects. Faced with the archbishop's public reprimand, and the threat of excommunication, the king had meekly submitted.

This, then – according to divine instruction, centuries of tradition and recent precedent – is how the king's unacceptable behaviour should have been handled in 1258, with the intervention of Archbishop Boniface. But, instead, Boniface chose to withdraw and take his bishops with him. This he perhaps did in cooperation with the baronial confederates, because he shared with them the goal of expelling the Lusignans from court. The result was that a lawful, customary and inherently non-violent process for correcting the king was bypassed in favour of one that was unprecedented and entailed a physical threat to an anointed monarch, and was by any measure illicit.

The confederates, then, without the moderating influence of the bishops, had been allowed to act freely. Amidst an atmosphere churning with resentment and dissent, they had met in secret, bound tight by oath, decrying the barbarity of the Lusignans and the king's failure to deliver justice or to govern the kingdom in its better interests, the clamours growing louder as they rebounded from one to another amongst the seven, the sense of grievance swelling until one of them, perhaps, suggested that they act to make this right. Their blood was up. They had a solution, in conciliar government, which they knew worked on the ground, no matter the rights or wrongs of forcing it upon an adult king, and they would impose it in the one way that, as they knew well, would be effective. For Henry was un-martial, and – as Simon had shown at Saintes in 1242, when he had rounded on the king who had fled in fear before the enemy and snarled that Henry ought to be taken and shut behind iron bars for his stupidity – could be cowed. So they, 'noble and strenuous' men, hardened and proven, in their sword-beaten armour, would overawe the king and seize the reins of power from his quivering hand.

As they did so, the confederates made one more decision – one that suggests that, in the making of their plans, reason marched alongside boldness: they chose the size of their council. For why choose a council of twenty-four? The number was not random. The principle that a council should comprise a set number of men was well established, though the most common size was twelve. There were twelve 'peers of France', the body of bishops and magnates who assisted in the coronation of the French king (inspired by the legendary group of twelve who counselled Charlemagne in epic literature), and twelve was a popular number for councils more broadly: boards of twelve governed various towns in England, for instance, and in Languedoc, and in 1212 Simon's father, the Count, had set up a committee of twelve to draw up the Statute of Pamiers. Twelve was seen as a propitious size for councils because it connoted the twelve apostles – a point made explicitly in the procedure of the Knights Templar for electing their Grand Master, where twelve of the Order would represent the apostles and call upon a chaplain to act as the thirteenth member of the electoral committee, in place of Christ.[32] Twenty-four was thus an unusual number to have chosen in 1258, and unusually large.

The confederates perhaps chose this number for its mystical significance.[33] The Book of Revelation describes a vision of God's celestial throne, around which a further twenty-four thrones are set. Upon these are seated twenty-four elders, wearing garments of white and crowns of gold.[34] Putting aside theological debate, past and present, about the identity of these twenty-four, we should note that the word used in the Vulgate to denote these figures is *seniores*. In a biblical context, *senior* might mean 'elder', but semantically the word provides the origin of the medieval French *seignur* or *seigneur*: 'lord', in the feudal sense.[35] By this interpretation, twenty-four was the number of lords entitled to take their seats around the king.

Yet whatever thinking lay behind the form of the new council did not detract from its illegality. The confederates, then, knew that they could not expect applause. For this reason the details of what had happened on the morning of 1 May 1258 in Westminster Hall were concealed from the wider public. The next day the confederates, with the king under their power, issued two proclamations, both in Henry's voice. The first described how Henry had met his potentates in parliament and explained that a deal had been struck: 'that if we should command the reformation of the state of our kingdom by the counsel of our faithful men', and if the pope should lighten the financial burden of the Sicilian Business, then Henry's potentates would do their best to persuade the rest of the political community (lesser barons and knights) to grant a tax. Accordingly, the proclamation continued, Henry had promised to draw up an 'ordinance' of reform, 'by the counsel of our good and faithful people of the kingdom', before the coming Christmas. He also agreed to submit himself to spiritual penalties, imposed by the pope himself, in the event that he broke these promises. His son and heir, Edward, had also sworn his agreement to these terms.

The second proclamation set out the form of the new council of twenty-four, which would be composed of two sets of twelve men:

one chosen by the king and one chosen by his potentates. It also explained that the twenty-four would convene on 9 June at Oxford, in order to ensure that 'the state of our kingdom may be ordained, rectified and reformed according to what they see to be more expedient to the honour of God and to our faith and to the utility of our kingdom'. The king's twelve, the proclamation noted, had already been chosen. They were mostly Lusignans and royal servants, including Aymer, Gui and William de Valence.[36]

The inclusion of the Lusignans in the council of twenty-four might seem at odds with the stated aim of the confederates: that the Poitevins be made to flee from the face of king and barons. But it enabled the confederates to set their plan in train. At this time so much remained unclear, not least the powers that the council would enjoy and the 'reform of the kingdom' that it would enact. Delaying the resolution of these issues for a month, after which the council would convene at Oxford, would allow the confederates to gather support and decide upon their next move, both for dealing with the Lusignans and for taking 'the state of the kingdom' in hand. Much now rested upon the forthcoming meeting at Oxford.

In all this, Simon was central: so much was shown by his ability, as revealed almost immediately, to set the council's agenda. On 5 May, within three days of the announcement that the twenty-four would convene at Oxford on 9 June, one element of their business had been decided: the council would be empowered to assign to Simon lands in place of the yearly fee and debts owed him by the king.[37] At this point the identity of the twelve 'baronial' representatives who would take their places on the council had not been decided; this provision suggests not only that Simon's voice was strong amongst the confederates in this decisive period at the turn of May, but also that he was confident in his ability, when the time came, to influence conciliar decision-making.

9

The Reform of the Kingdom

Simon could not remain in England to prepare for the Oxford parliament, for on 8 May he was commissioned to go again to France to treat with Louis IX concerning peace.* While he was away, London was engulfed by catastrophe. The cloud of volcanic ash still lingered above the kingdom, bringing relentless rain that deluged the soil and prolonged the famine. And now, as the dearth reached critical levels, it brought with it disease: dysentery, typhoid fever and tuberculosis.[1] As provisions in the countryside collapsed, the starving made their way to towns in search of food and the care offered by urban hospitals. The swelling crowds of the weak were the ideal environment for the spread of infection. In London, as Matthew Paris reports, the pestilence reached its crisis point around 19 May: 15,000 people had perished. While chroniclers are notoriously poor when it comes to estimating numbers on a large scale, it is likely that this figure is reasonably accurate, and certainly conveys a realistic order of magnitude. Excavations at St Mary Spital, a hospital located on the principal route into London from the north, have revealed the remains of 10,516 people who perished between the twelfth and sixteenth centuries, many of them buried in mass graves during the periodic bouts of famine. Archaeologists were able to study in detail 5,387 of their skeletons; of these, they

* The new embassy was empowered to negotiate a peace treaty, arriving in Paris perhaps in time for the parliament that began on 20 May, and completing its mission by 28 May (P. Chaplais, 'The making of the Treaty of Paris (1259) and the royal style', *English Historical Review*, 67 (1952), 235–53, at 239).

found, some 2,300 dated to the mid-thirteenth century, which can be attributed to the major famine of 1257–8, as well as a lesser one of 1252.[2] St Mary Spital was only one of twenty-odd hospitals and comparable institutions in London.[3]

For the confederates, therefore, the most pressing task was the provision of food for the thousands of starving and sickening people gathered in London. Most of London's hospitals and almshouses catered for only twenty or so residents at one time, and so were not capable of caring for all the needy who now descended upon them. Looking upon this scene of desperation, the potentates then in Westminster divided amongst themselves responsibility for providing emergency rations to the starving. They had proclamations made throughout the city, instructing those in need which noble they should visit to receive their bread.[4]

Such action was necessary to supplement the king's own almonry at Westminster, for it was Henry's usual practice to provide a meal for a number of poor people every day. Ten years earlier, in the 1240s, Henry was probably feeding as many as 500 people on a daily basis (or 600 in total, when those fed by the queen are taken into account), 150 at court and the rest in almshouses across England. During the same period, several times throughout the year, he would even order this number increased to thousands, either to commemorate important feast days or to speed the souls of the dead to Heaven. Indeed, there are records of 10,000 poor people being fed at the king's expense in a few instances, such as the funeral of little Katherine. Very occasionally, Henry's feeding of the poor could surpass even this: after his sister, Isabella, died in 1241, the king ordered the feeding of 102,000 poor across his kingdom. Such extravagant generosity was motivated partly by devotion – to the saints whose feast days were commemorated and to ancestors and loved ones departed – and partly by Christian duty as expounded in the Gospels. In respect of his generosity to the poor, during the 1240s, Henry had stood alone, surpassing the king of France and even the pope in the scale of his almsgiving.[5]

But, from 1250, Henry had made strides to rein in the spending of his household, hoping to save money for his planned crusade. This (as Matthew Paris noticed) impacted upon his bounty.[6] Although, admittedly, the survival of the relevant records is patchy, it seems that the number of poor fed daily fell from 500 to 100 or so. There is nothing to suggest that Henry thought to reverse this policy in the wake of the famine of 1258, let alone to make extra provision for the thousands of starving and destitute then wandering the streets of London. In this respect, the magnates' provision for the doling out of bread was a much-needed and decisive step towards rectifying Henry's deficiencies and dampening the ferocity of the famine. But in so doing, this provision also in a very public way pointed to the king's failure to respond to his people's suffering – as well as to the ability and willingness of the magnates to provide for his people instead. It created a bond between the greatest and the least of Henry's subjects from which Henry himself was excluded.

The crisis of the famine was one of many issues on the minds of the confederates as they prepared for the forthcoming parliament at Oxford, at which the council of twenty-four would establish its programme for the reform of the kingdom. Their immediate concern were the Lusignans. The confederates had made clear to the king, when they marched on Westminster Hall, that they wanted the Lusignans expelled from Henry's favour. And the grievances nursed by John fitz Geoffrey and other victims of Lusignan banditry signalled to all that the reform of the kingdom was likely to include a fixing of the flawed royal justice that had allowed the Lusignans' misdeeds to go unchecked. Clearly, the Lusignans would not simply stand back and permit such moves to be made against them. As the date set for the Oxford parliament (9 June) drew near, both sides began to gather their strength. Aymer de Valence, bishop-elect of Winchester, who could rightfully expect to be the primary target of the confederates' vengeance, sent out summonses to his men to come to Oxford with 'horses and arms' – in other words, arrayed for war.[7] Others on both sides did likewise. The excuse was given out that all were readying to ride against the Welsh, but nobody was fooled.[8]

As the armies gathered in the streets of Oxford, around 9 June, those who stood against the Lusignans and for the reform of the kingdom chose their twelve. These men would sit on the council beside Henry's contingent, already chosen.[9] At the head of the list were Walter de Cantilupe, bishop of Worcester, and Simon de

Montfort. That Simon is named at the top of the list of noblemen, immediately behind the bishop (bishops are always listed first), suggests his prominence at the opening of the Oxford parliament. So too does the inclusion of Walter, Simon's close friend. Walter would be the only bishop to join the reformers' side at Oxford, for in doing so he was taking a grave risk. Joining a party that stood against the king went against Walter's occupational identity, for bishops were expected to act as peacemakers. They were duty-bound to reprimand the king when he erred, but only with the goal of rectifying the injustices that had provoked his nobles against him. They might well sympathize with grievances against the king, but throughout any civil discord they were expected to remain loyal to their sovereign. Maintaining connections to both king and dissidents meant that the bishops would have the trust of both sides, which was essential to their role in the forging of peace. Now Walter was declared one of those chosen *ex parte* (on the side of) the earls and barons, the same confederates who had marched on the king's hall and frightened Henry into the surrender of his power.[*]

Simon and Walter were joined in the barons' twelve by another close companion, Peter de Montfort. As well as being a long-time friend of Simon, Peter was also Walter's nephew. He was of an age with Simon, who was now about fifty, while Peter was perhaps three years older, and had served him in Gascony. A fourth member of the twelve was also a friend of Simon: Hugh Despenser. Hugh's family had been tenants of Ranulf, earl of Chester, and Hugh's

---

[*] The other bishops, as we have seen, had withdrawn from court at Westminster in April, under the guidance of the archbishop of Canterbury. The only other bishop, apart from Walter, to strike out from his cohort and involve himself in events was the bishop of London, Fulk Basset. In the preceding few years, both Fulk and Walter had been members of the king's council (the small group of ministers who assisted in the day-to-day running of the kingdom). This had not stopped the two of them from opposing royal policies and doing so publicly, standing shoulder to shoulder in Church assemblies and declaring their ardent opposition to the Sicilian Business. Fulk, then, like Walter, would have felt some sympathy for the reformers' agenda, specifically their distaste for the Sicilian Business and their determination that no scheme should be advanced that required taxation without the consent of Henry's greater subjects. But, even so, Fulk was not prepared to abandon his loyalty to the king. (S. T. Ambler, *Bishops in the Political Community of England, 1213–1272* (Oxford, 2017), 96, 105–24).

father had been close to Ranulf in his service; the Despensers' loyalty had passed to Simon after the Leicester estates were ceded to him by Ranulf in 1231.[10] At that time Hugh had only been a boy, of around seven years, and five years later his father had died – so he perhaps grew up under Simon's aegis. Now, in 1258, Hugh was in his mid-thirties. He stood high in Simon's confidence and the two had become very close – we know because the following year, when Simon drew up his will, he named Hugh as one of the assistant executors.[11] The baronial twelve also included others who, like Simon and Peter, had sworn at the Westminster parliament to aid each other against the Lusignans – Richard de Clare, earl of Gloucester, Roger Bigod, earl of Norfolk and marshal of England, his brother Hugh Bigod, and John fitz Geoffrey – as well as the earl of Hereford and several other barons.

*

The baronial twelve, leading the council of twenty-four, immediately set to work on drafting an agenda for the reform of the kingdom. Their initial checklist, titled the Petition of the Barons, was probably drawn up in the first week of the parliament.[12] Its concerns fell into several categories. A handful of articles criticized Henry's behaviour as king and as a feudal lord, complaining that he had sought to expand the royal forest in contravention of the Forest Charter (first granted in 1217, and reissued in 1225 in return for a tax), and that he usurped the rights of earls and barons by claiming feudal dues from their tenants on the basis that those tenants held just a small portion of land directly from the king. The barons also complained of their treatment at the hands of the king's officers: magnates held land all over the kingdom, yet royal justices and sheriffs were demanding that they attend every local court wherever they held land, even if their holdings there were very small. To attend every local court would be almost impossible, and certainly inconvenient, and yet magnates were being amerced for non-attendance. Henry's behaviour in these cases was driven by the desire to raise money but, as the Petition implied, it was unreasonable. With the exception of the complaint about Henry's appropriation of forest rights, the baronial party was not accusing the king of treating them illegally but, rather, of advancing his rights to the very letter of the law, to the detriment of his magnates.

These articles concerned the rights of the most powerful, but also included in the Petition was a whole raft of articles that addressed the concerns of people of lesser status. In the first instance these confronted the behaviour of the sheriffs, who 'do not amerce people according to the amount of their offences, but rather force them to pay ransoms beyond their means'.* This, the Petition recognized, was ultimately the fault of the king, who tasked his sheriffs with raising unreasonably high sums. The barons were not thinking here of their own interests, since (as we have seen) the sheriffs were too intimidated to set foot within the domains of the great magnates.[13] The same was true in the case of the various articles in the Petition that addressed the iniquitous procedures of the royal courts. Royal judges imposed heavy sums for 'fair pleading': local juries, required to make presentments to royal judges who visited the county (to brief them on all legal matters that had recently occurred), were fearful of being amerced if they made a mistake or omitted something, and so might offer a fine to the judges in advance – in effect, paying out 'just in case'.[14] The complaint in the Petition that such fines were heavy suggests that judges were taking advantage of the situation to use 'fair pleading' fines as a way of raising cash. But the practice, as the barons claimed, amounted to local people being made to buy justice. On similar grounds the barons objected to new procedures for the coroners' viewing of bodies: if all men from the four neighbouring settlements failed to attend the viewing, then all those men would be amerced. By custom, only four men from each settlement were required to attend, together with the village reeve (the demand for a 100 per cent turnout was not introduced until the later 1240s).[15] It was clearly unnecessary, and existed only as a way of making money for the king. Equally, every time the king commissioned a special hearing to rule on a disputed piece of land, sheriffs proclaimed that every free tenant and knight in the district must attend the hearing at the appointed day and time, lest they face amercement. Such a demand was not

---

* Here as elsewhere, I have altered the translation taken from the published text that provides 'man/men' for *homo/homines* – the more accurate translation is person/people.

only uncustomary but also unnecessary, existing only to make money for the king to the detriment of his poorer subjects. One further such complaint stands out particularly:

> many people coming, on account of the present famine, from different parts of the land, and making their way through the different counties, die of hunger and starvation; and then according to the law of the land, the coroners hold inquest with the four nearest vills; and when the vills say that they know nothing of the people who have died in this way, save that they have died of the aforesaid cause, since there is no presentment of Englishry, the district is amerced before the justices as in a case of *murdrum*.

As we have already seen, it had long been a legal requirement that in the event of a homicide the inhabitants of the settlement in which the victim was discovered provide the identity of the deceased to authorities or face an amercement (known as *murdrum*). But, since the 1240s, under direction from the cash-strapped king, royal judges had begun to levy *murdrum* in cases of accidental death, even though legal authorities agreed that this was unjust. It was unfair to the local populations even in ordinary circumstances, but especially at a time of famine, when thousands of starving people were wandering the countryside towards the towns in search of food, and many simply collapsed at the roadside and died where they lay. Henry had made no ruling about the relaxation of the *murdrum* fine. Every corpse of every such stranger thus left hapless local people subject to an amercement. This, the barons recognized, was neither right nor just, and they were determined that it must end.

*

The barons, then, were seeking to protect lesser folk – from the gentry to the poorest – from the iniquities of royal justice. But what is most remarkable is how they were also determined to protect lesser folk even against baronial interests. Three articles of the Petition stand out in this respect. Article 1 guaranteed the right of under-tenants (anyone who held their land from a lord below the king) to inherit their estates without delay – the lord of the fee was to take only nominal possession upon the death of the previous tenant, and was not to use this as an opportunity to strip the estate of its assets for his or her own profit. If any lord did abuse their rights, 'and it is proved against them', declared the Petition, 'let them be punished in proportion to the offence; and let them at once make good all the losses which the heir may have suffered thereby'. Article 25 complained that sometimes an unscrupulous potentate bought up a Jewish debt and would not allow that debt to be paid, hoping for a chance to take possession of the estate upon which the debt was secured. And Article 29 decried the intrusion by magnates in many counties into the rightful operation of royal justice: by law, if a tenant could prove that their lord had failed to provide justice in the manorial court, they could obtain a royal writ (the writ of *praecipe*) to have the case transferred to the royal courts; but often (complained the Petition) lords were obstructing the transfer, successfully demanding their right to hear the case. The writ of *praecipe* was increasingly popular in the thirteenth century, enabling people of even low wealth and status to have their cases heard by royal judges (there was just a small administrative charge, of a few pennies, for the writ – and for the poorer petitioners the fee would be waived entirely).[16] For magnates to deny lesser people the chance to have their cases heard, simply to preserve their own rights, was 'manifestly contrary to justice', as the Petition stated.

This was a clear declaration of intent from the reformers, for in highlighting their own faults and those of their kind, and calling for those faults to be rectified against their own interests, they were breaking new ground. There had been no such drive in the last great agenda of reform, set out in Magna Carta. The original Charter granted by King John in 1215, negotiated by the barons and the king's men, had been largely concerned with protecting both the rights of magnates in regards to royal power and the rights of magnates towards their own tenants. In one chapter towards the end of the Charter, King John stated that, 'as much as it pertains to us towards our people, all the people of the kingdom . . . are to observe, as it pertains to them, to their people'.[17] But this fell a long way short of the alternative: making specific provision in the Charter itself in order to protect under-tenants from the abuses of magnate lordship. Indeed, Magna Carta was a step backward in this respect, for when John's great-grandfather had granted his Coronation Charter in 1100 (generally seen as a precursor to Magna Carta) he had made such specific provisions.[18] And later versions of the Charter more or less preserved the status quo. Indeed, when the third version of the Charter was issued in 1217 a clause was inserted to say that potentates were to pass down the Charter's liberties but only 'saving . . . the liberties and free customs which they [i.e. potentates] had before'. In other words, the earls and barons who helped to redraft the Charter in 1217 ensured that they would have an excuse for not passing down the liberties of Magna Carta to their under-tenants. In the fourth and definitive version of 1225, the 'saving' clause was emended to soften its impact, but this was balanced by various other changes that defended the interests of magnates against their own subjects.[19] Now, therefore, in 1258, the reformers were consciously striving to do better for their tenants. The inclusion of these articles in the Petition was the mark of a new era in seigneurial attitude.

It had been brought by an underlying shift in the expectations of lordship. There were various fundamentals of good lordship, ingrained through the centuries, which shaped the relationship between lord and vassal: for instance, a lord should take counsel from his or her men, they should display largesse (an easy generosity to followers), and they should defend their followers against others. But these expectations largely applied to the relationship between lords and their noble followers, rather than between lords and their poorer subjects. It was only recently, from the late 1240s, that some lords felt a growing sense of duty to rethink their treatment of their lesser tenants.

Taking the lead here was Louis IX, king of France. As we have seen, Louis had launched in 1247 a series of *enquêtes* to investigate abuses of power by his officials that had harmed his more vulnerable subjects. For the iniquities of his officials, Louis held himself personally accountable. The acuteness of his conscience was a mark of the way in which he had taken to his heart a new agenda of the Church, expounded by the clergy in the decades following the Fourth Lateran Council of 1215. The Church was setting out to improve pastoral care, and part of this programme required every

Christian to confess their sins at least once a year (in order to be in a state of grace to receive the Eucharist). This meant that all Christians had to examine their consciences, determine their sins and make satisfaction. The Church, in turn, would provide personnel with a high degree of training – in theology, moral philosophy and practical ethics – to help them do so.

These personnel were largely provided by the Franciscan and Dominican friars, the new orders that emerged in the early decades of the thirteenth century, dedicated to the apostolic ideal of poverty and to pastoral care. The friars (unlike many parish priests) were highly educated, and trained in the art of preaching and in the ministering of Confession.[20] Louis IX was supportive of the friars and made use of their expertise: not content with confessing his sins once a week as a matter of course, he kept two friars permanently in his household to act as his confessors (one would take the day shift and one the night shift, so that one would always be on hand in case Louis was so troubled by the thought of a sin that he needed to rise from bed to unburden his spirit).[21]

Louis was careful to ensure that this conscience of his, so keenly nourished, governed his treatment of his subjects. An episode recalled by his biographer, John de Joinville, was chosen to show how he was known for this trait. A knight named Renaud de Trie had approached Louis with a charter: Renaud was heir to the recently deceased countess of Boulogne, and the charter granted Renaud the right to a certain estate after the countess died. The problem was that the king's seal, appended to the charter to imbue it with legal validity, was broken in half (of the image of the king enthroned only the king's feet were visible). Louis showed the document and seal to his men, including John de Joinville, and asked for their counsel. They replied unanimously that he was not legally bound to honour the grant. But Louis would not follow their advice. 'Anyone can plainly see', he told them, 'that the imprint of the broken part of the seal is connected to the whole seal. Because of this then, I could not dare keep this county with a good conscience.'[22] The point of the anecdote was to contrast the usual attitude of a lord (represented by Louis's men) – to advance one's own rights and interests wherever possible – with Louis's new standard of lordship. This held that every lord should exercise their conscience and so conduct themselves towards their subjects according to what was morally right, rather than what was legally permissible.

Louis expected this mindset to hold even – or especially – if such conscience-driven conduct meant that the lord would suffer in respect to his own rights or finances. This is precisely the attitude that underlay his *enquêtes*: it was the reason for his appointment of Franciscan and Dominican friars (experts in the sacrament of Confession) as his *enquêteurs* and for their empowerment to pay out reparations on Louis's behalf, as a form of penance.

The *enquêtes* were conducted across the kingdom of France in 1247–8, and again between 1254 and 1258 – from Normandy in the north to Poitou (on the borders of English Gascony) and Languedoc in the south. The sheer geographical scale of Louis's *enquêtes* helped to publicize his new seigneurial mindset. And – since Louis was the mightiest of Christian kings, and also widely respected for his piety and probity – where he led, others followed: for lordship was competitive, and Louis had raised the standards of competition. His example immediately inspired his brother, Alphonse, count of Poitiers. Just before the French left in 1249 to wage holy war in Egypt, Alphonse commissioned an *enquête* in his comital lands on Louis's model, giving the same reasons: his concern for his soul and a desire to make good the wrongs of his officers.[23] And, as we have seen, Henry III was probably seeking to mimic Louis's *enquêtes* in conducting his inquiry into Simon's governorship of Gascony in 1252, like Louis, providing his subjects with the opportunity to come forward and complain about one of his officers.

But here Henry had failed. His 1252 inquiry was haphazard, lacking the clear objectives of Louis's investigations – there was no suggestion that Henry was ultimately responsible for Simon's actions, or that he intended to offer reparations. More importantly, from the perspective of the vast majority of his English subjects, Henry had offered nothing at all in this respect. In fact, quite the opposite was true. For, at the same time as Louis had been working to improve his treatment of his lesser subjects and rectify the iniquities of his officers, Henry had been pushing his judges and sheriffs to extort more and more money from the most vulnerable of his people, a drive that had encouraged exploitative and unscrupulous conduct.

Henry's determination to uphold his rights to the letter of the law in order to provide grounds for levying money from his poorer subjects ran in contradiction to Louis's ethos. The reformers of 1258, in contrast, in the Petition of the Barons, were setting out their intent to hold themselves to the new standard.

*

By 16 June they had recreated the office of justiciar and appointed Hugh Bigod to fill it.[24] The justiciar, as the name suggests, had traditionally been responsible for providing justice when the king was absent from the kingdom, but more than this had been something like a standing regent, overseeing government when the king was abroad (a very important office under the Norman and Angevin kings, who spent large portions of their time attending to their continental possessions). But the value of the justiciar even when the king was in England had been proved during Henry's minority and the early years of his personal rule, when the office was held by Hubert de Burgh. Hubert oversaw a revival of royal justice, ensuring that courts were available for petitioners at Westminster and in the localities.[25] But he had been the victim of a court coup in 1234 and since then the office of justiciar had been in abeyance. The loss had been felt deeply by the political community, and demands had been made in parliament for the restitution of the office in 1244, 1248 and 1255. The same demands insisted that the justiciar (like the chancellor) be appointed by the community of leading potentates. Now, in June 1258, the reformers finally had the opportunity to make it so. With the establishment of conciliar rule, there was less need for the justiciar to act as chief minister. But the reformers had identified manifold inadequacies and injustices in Henry's treatment of his subjects, from potentates like John fitz Geoffrey to the poorest. There was, then, an obvious role for the justiciar.

Importantly, Hugh Bigod would have the authority to deal with complaints against the king and his officers. But he would also be charged with hearing complaints against the magnates. A letter written by someone who attended the Oxford parliament recalled the conditions of Hugh Bigod's appointment: 'that he would show justice to all making complaint, and that he would not falter in this for the lord king or the queen, or for their sons, or for any one alive, or for any thing, nor from hate nor love, nor prayer nor payment'.[26] When the final programme of reform was drafted later in the parliament, the reformers were even more explicit: 'The chief justiciar has power to put right the wrongs done by all other justices, and by bailiffs, and by earls, and by barons, and by all other persons, according to the law and right of the land.'[27] In some respects these terms rested upon a long-established sense of justice. The English legal treatise known as Bracton, probably written in the circle of a high-ranking royal judge during the 1230s, stated that senior judges were empowered to correct the mistakes of other judges, while the same treatise also pointed to the verse in Deuteronomy in which Moses instructed the first judges that 'There shall be no difference of persons, you shall hear the little as well as the great: neither shall you respect any man's person, because it is the judgment of God.'[28] But at no point did Bracton demand explicitly that a judge must be prepared to rule against the king and queen, and against earls and barons. This was the design of the baronial councillors.

The plan was that Hugh Bigod would set out on a great eyre, travelling around the kingdom to hear cases. In advance of this, every shire would elect four of its knights to hear complaints 'of any trespasses and injuries whatsoever, done to any persons whatsoever by sheriffs, bailiffs, or any other persons', and attach the parties concerned (meaning they would find pledges to ensure that both plaintiff and defendant turned up to court). Everything would thus be in place to begin hearing sessions when Hugh Bigod arrived in the shire (as was standard, local men would provide the juries, using their local knowledge to determine whether the accused was innocent or guilty). But, because the initial inquiries by the knights would take some time, Hugh decided to begin a preliminary eyre immediately, hearing what cases he could as and when complainants appeared. The first he heard, during the course of the June parliament, was the plaint of John fitz Geoffrey.[29]

Hugh then set out on his preliminary circuit, hearing cases in fourteen different counties.[30] Importantly, he opened up the eyre to *querelae*. A *querela* was a procedure by which any free person with a grievance could turn up at court and make a complaint, without going to the trouble of acquiring a writ to initiate a case – Hugh wanted to make it as easy as possible for complainants to come forward. This move was extremely popular: the roll recording the activities of Hugh's preliminary eyre (operating 16 June to 29 December 1258) included fifty-four *querelae* – almost as many as contained in all the rolls of all the eyres conducted in the thirty-three years prior to 1258 (sixty-one).[31] The drive of Hugh Bigod's eyre was clearly comparable to Louis's *enquêtes*, seeking to root out corruption amongst royal and baronial officers for the benefit of the vulnerable, and both inquiries were based to some extent on *querelae* (whether or not the word was used in the technical English legal sense or simply to mean 'complaint'). The difference was that the English reformers had chosen not to use teams of friars to conduct the investigation but, rather, an established English judicial procedure (the eyre), presided over by a judge holding a venerated English office (the justiciar), with the truth of allegations determined by a jury of local men. The English reformers, then, though they were introducing something new, maintained a preference for customary procedures.

Those making use of the *querela* procedure included some of the poorest of the king's subjects, and even the destitute, who now came forward to make complaints against royal officers (indeed, one suspects that such people had been targeted by the crueller sort of officers precisely because they had not sufficient standing to complain). One was a man named Richard of Glaston, from Northamptonshire. He must have been carried into the courtroom, for he was in a wretched state. Richard was a thief who had sought sanctuary in a local church and subsequently agreed to abjure the realm (by law, a criminal could escape violent punishment if he sought sanctuary and admitted his guilt; he would then have to go directly to an assigned port and leave England, never to return). Richard was instructed to leave England via Dover. He told the court that he had set off on the highway straight to his assigned port, but had got only as far as Newport Pagnell (sixteen miles south-east of Northampton) when he was set upon by a group of men. He did not know their names, but he knew they had been sent by the sheriff of Northamptonshire, Hugh de Manneby.

These men knocked Richard to the ground. Richard, 'clinging

to the earth because of his fear', grabbed hold of the wheels of a nearby cart (perhaps he was trying to drag himself under the cart for shelter). The sheriff's men proceeded to trample all over his back and arms, and then thrashed him with bows and other weapons. The beating was so severe, Richard told the court, that 'the flesh on his back and arms is putrefied'. Following the beating, the sheriff's men 'dragged him half alive from the street' to a prison in Northampton. Richard's plight did not end there for, as he reported, 'the aforesaid sheriff in the aforesaid prison had him tormented and cruelly tortured, by hard imprisonment and other means, so that he could have no hope for his life'.

The sheriff, Hugh de Manneby, appeared in court. He claimed that his men had found Richard straying from the highway (in other words, violating the terms of his abjuration), and so had consigned him to prison. But as for the beating and the rest, the sheriff denied it. The case was put to a jury of local men.

The jurymen not only confirmed Richard's account, but also were able to add further details, not least the names of the sheriff's heavies. These men had indeed pushed Richard to the ground, the jury stated, so that he was 'clinging to the earth with his teeth'. They had then dragged Richard 'by his feet' from the road, beaten him with bows and sticks, and taken him off to a local mill, where they had raised the hue against him (in other words, giving out the story that he had absconded). They had tied Richard's hands behind his back, so that by binding him thus and thrashing him 'the flesh of his shoulder and back is thoroughly putrid'. Hugh Bigod asked the jurors if the sheriff had consented to this deed or had ordered it. As his roll records, 'they say precisely that this is so'. Indeed, the jury added that the sheriff himself had then taken Richard off to the sheriff's lodgings, where he had thrown him into the cellar beneath his bedroom. On account of this maltreatment, the jury stated, 'they in no way believed that Richard would be able to recover'.

Hugh Bigod's judgement was that the sheriff should be consigned to gaol, where he was 'to be guarded safely' until it was known whether Richard would recover or not.[32] On the following day an order was sent to the man who had been appointed by the barons to keep the royal castle of Northampton, Ralph Basset of Sapcote (one of Simon's knights). Ralph was told to take 'the former sheriff' into custody in Northampton Castle, and guard him 'safely and courteously' until his court appearance.[33] Hugh de Manneby was guilty of a crime that was, as Hugh Bigod's roll records, 'obviously – manifestly and inordinately – against the peace of the lord king and the law and custom of the kingdom' – but there would be no mistreatment of prisoners under the new regime.

Hugh Bigod would go on to hear many accounts of the cruelty and corruption suffered by poorer folk at the hands of the king's officers, once the four knights in each county had completed their investigation and he could embark upon his second eyre. Various complaints were made, for instance, against Geoffrey Norman, the king's bailiff of Southwark, who picked on the poor and vulnerable: he had levied an amercement of half a mark from a pauper named William de Barnwell; he had taken a brass pot worth three shillings from a widow named Marjery; he had extorted twenty-nine shillings from a woman named Katherine le Marbeler by telling her that her husband, who had left for Outremer, had died, and then threatening to seize her house for the king.[34] Presumably Geoffrey had been using his office to line his pockets, and others did likewise. An undersheriff in Kent had taken a bribe of twenty shillings from an outlawed murderer, in order to allow the outlaw to stay in the shire long enough to rescue his valuables; a sheriff in the same shire had taken a bribe of forty shillings to allow a family indicted for murder to go free from prison.[35] But it was not only royal officials who attracted complaints. A bailiff of the archbishop of Canterbury had used violence to distrain upon a debt; another had accused a man of harbouring criminals, tied him up and beaten him until the man offered four shillings to be free.[36] Hugh Bigod's justice was decisive. 'Not only did he amerce many bailiffs and others, who were convicted of transgressions against their subjects', wrote the London chronicler Arnold fitz Thedmar, 'but he caused them to be incarcerated, whether they were clerks or laymen.'[37]

While the lords who commanded unscrupulous or heavy-handed officials did not necessarily know of these misdeeds, others were in cahoots with them. One jury accused Richard de Grey, a member of the baronial twelve, of such behaviour. Like many lords, Richard had the right to collect amercements imposed upon his tenants by royal judges, to be handed over to the crown. But he had allowed his bailiff to take 33s 4d from the men of Aylesford, when they had owed only 20s for an amercement. The jurors reported that, of the excess, the bailiff had handed 10s over to his lord, and kept the 3s 4d for himself.[38]

In this instance, the initial complaint had been made against a baronial bailiff, and the baron was only accused indirectly. Elsewhere, cases were brought against potentates themselves. The abbot of Faversham, for instance, was one of many accused of taking money to turn a blind eye to brewing and baking in breach of the Assize of Bread and Ale, rather than meting out justice to those who broke the regulations.[39] As Hugh Bigod's eyre revealed, this practice was clearly common. Not only was it corrupt – no profit would have otherwise accrued to the lord, since the punishment for breaking the Assize was not an amercement but the pillories or ducking stool – but it also disadvantaged customers, since the point of the Assize was to provide quality control.[40] Hugh Bigod determined to put an end to it. In London, he and the earl of Gloucester held a special session in the Guildhall, summoning all the city's bakers to come before them with their bread. Any bakers whose loaves did not meet the weight demanded by the Assize were punished: they were put on the ducking stool, on which they were lowered into the Thames.[41]

One case, perhaps above all others, demonstrates Hugh Bigod's willingness to cleave to the spirit of the new reforming measures. The men of Witley (Surrey) came before him, led by one of their number, Eudes of Timperley, with a complaint against their lord, Peter of Savoy. Witley, they claimed, was 'ancient demesne', meaning that it had once been part of the crown's own estate. According to the law of 'ancient demesne', any lord who subsequently held the land by royal grant could not raise rents to a level higher than that originally charged by the king. But Peter of Savoy, since he had been granted the manor by the king five years before, had raised their rents, by £18 7s 6d per year. Peter was the queen's uncle, a great magnate, and had been one of the confederate seven at the Westminster parliament. But this did not mean that Hugh Bigod would allow him to evade justice. He appointed a day for Peter to appear in court.

Peter did indeed appear. He argued that Witley was not, as had been claimed, ancient demesne, but had always been a barony (the reason for the confusion being that it had been taken into the king's hands after 1204, because its former lord had chosen to side with the French king after the loss of Normandy). As evidence, Peter appealed to 'the book called Domesday'. The justiciar's team examined Domesday Book and found that Peter was correct: Witley had been held before the Battle of Hastings by Harold Godwinson, and had subsequently passed to a man named Gilbert son of Richer del Eagle. (For good measure, the justiciar's clerk even included in his record the details provided by Domesday about the size and value of the land.) And so Peter was acquitted. Eudes and his neighbours had lost the case, but only because the evidence stood incontrovertibly in Peter's favour (anyone in doubt can consult Domesday Book themselves). Importantly, the men of Witley had succeeded in compelling one of the greatest magnates of the land to appear in court to answer their allegations – something that would be unthinkable under Henry III.[42] And Hugh Bigod, as the Witley case proved, was determined to conduct himself according to his mission statement: 'to put right the wrongs done by all other justices, and by bailiffs, and by earls, and by barons, and by all other persons, according to the law and right of the land'.[43]

*

While Hugh was dispensing justice, the reformers at the Oxford parliament tackled an immediate concern: the Lusignans. The baronial twelve had demanded in Article 4 of the Petition of the Barons that 'royal castles shall be committed to the custody of the king's faithful subjects born in the kingdom of England, on account of many dangers which might befall or arise'.[44] The Lusignans were not named, and the nature of these envisaged dangers was not spelt out, but clearly the objective was to limit the military capacity of the king's foreign half-brothers. Next, in Article 5, the barons repeated the demand in respect to royal castles situated on harbours, and in Article 15 insisted that no castle situated on a harbour should be fortified without the consent of the council. By such means could the barons limit the ability of the Lusignans to bring in hired soldiers from abroad to further their cause.[*]

Finally, in Article 6, the barons insisted that nobles whose marriages pertained to the king (the widows or underage heirs of tenants-in-chief) should not be 'disparaged'. The demand that nobles not be disparaged was long-standing, but the issue of 'disparagement' usually concerned social status: King John had gifted the hands of wealthy heiresses to several of his low-born officers to provide a means of social and financial advancement, provoking the rebel barons in 1215 to demand that the practice be banned (as it was in Chapter 6 of the first issue of the Charter). But here, in the Petition, the reformers produced a new definition of disparagement, 'namely [marriage] to people who are not of the nation of the kingdom of England [*de natione regni Anglie*]'.[45] The wording here was careful. Clearly, it was not unusual for nobles who hailed from England to marry someone born and brought up in another country: obvious examples included Henry III and Henry's sister Eleanor (who had chosen to marry Simon, a man born in France to faithful subjects of the French king). But the wording of the article did not take issue with marriages of this sort. Simon had been born outside England but could reasonably claim to be 'of the nation of the kingdom of England', with his hereditary claim to an English earldom and his homage and service to the English king; after his marriage he was to prove his commitment: his children were brought up in England, he went with the king to war, and he refused to serve the French kingdom when offered the opportunity to act as regent in 1253. Fundamentally (and this is probably what the wording of the clause was intended to convey) he saw himself as a member of the English political community, an agent in its society, bound in the web of its culture, adhering to the expectations and laws that governed the conduct of its members and the relationships between them. It was this sense of belonging to 'the nation of the kingdom of England' that could be used to

---

[*] Matthew Paris states that this was a major concern of the reformers at the approach of the parliament, and that they had the sea ports guarded (*Matthaei Parisiensis, Monachi Sancti Albani, Chronica Majora*, ed. H. R. Luard, 7 vols. (London, 1872–83) (hereafter *CM*), V, 696).

exclude the Lusignans. These men had, in launching their various raids on the persons and property of other potentates, openly flouted the norms of conduct (not to mention the laws) that shaped the English political elite.

There were specific reasons for targeting the Lusignans through their marriages: union with wealthy heirs was their principal route to landed wealth in England, and cutting off this resource would be an important step to undermining their foothold in the kingdom. Simon had additional reasons for advancing this demand: the marriage of William de Valence to Joan de Munchensey in 1247 had provided a valuable estate to a man Simon found personally objectionable, with whom he shared an open enmity; but Joan's status as a Marshal heiress also meant that the marriage had hindered the payment of Eleanor's dower.[46] There was nothing to be done about these existing marriages, but their like could be prevented for the future.

The barons now set out to establish the apparatus through which the Lusignans could be disempowered and the kingdom could be reformed. By 22 June they had worked out the essentials, which they laid out in a draft document known simply as 'The Provisions of Oxford'. The most important step was the establishment of a new council, to run the day-to-day government of the kingdom. The councillors would be chosen by a system of election and approval by the twenty-four: the king's side chose two of the barons' twelve, and vice versa, and these four selected the final fifteen councillors, with the twenty-four as a body having the final say on appointments. Although this system appears equitable, it was the baronial element that would triumph from it: nine of the fifteen councillors appointed were men of the baronial twelve, including Simon, Walter de Cantilupe, the earl of Gloucester, John fitz Geoffrey and Peter de Montfort. They were joined by two powerful figures who, although close to the royal family, were firmly anti-Lusignan: Peter of Savoy and his brother, the archbishop of Canterbury Boniface of Savoy. None of the Lusignans found a seat on the council. Since decisions would be carried by a simple majority, the barons would face no opposition as they strode onward with their programme.

The first action taken by the newly established council was to underpin its power by means of an oath.[47] This would be much like the oath sworn by the seven confederates at the Westminster parliament in April – an oath of mutual aid – except that this time it would be sworn by the entire 'community' gathered at Oxford. The magnates had brought with them to Oxford their knightly followings, arrayed for war, and all these men would now be required to swear on the Gospels that 'each of us and all together will help each other and our people, against all men ... and if anyone opposes this, we will treat him as a mortal enemy'. The threat to those opposing the council was explicit: be with us or against us. The Lusignans refused to take the oath.[48]

The barons met in the Dominican house at Oxford to formulate their next move. They decided to seize control of royal castles. During 22 and 23 June orders were issued to the keepers of fifteen royal castles, and the warden of the Cinque Ports, to deliver custody of their charges to men appointed by the council.[49] With these castles in hand, the barons would be in a strong military position if it came to war with the Lusignans and if the Lusignans should attempt to bring in military support from overseas (the barons were certain to claim the custody of Dover and the Cinque Ports).

The next step was even bolder: a great act of resumption. 'It was agreed', recalled the eye-witness letter-writer, 'that the lord king was impoverished, to such an extent that if he or his kingdom were attacked by any neighbouring prince grave peril would threaten him and his kingdom; and so provision was made to restore to him all the lands, holdings and castles alienated from the crown by him.'[50] In accordance with the council's ruling, Simon immediately surrendered Kenilworth (granted to Eleanor and Simon jointly for life in 1255) and Odiham. He did so, Matthew Paris notes, even though 'he had repaired them just a few days earlier'.[51] But Simon's easy surrender of the castles was, in fact, a charade. The objective of the act of resumption was to dispossess the enemies of reform, chiefly the Lusignans; with this achieved, castles and other holdings could be returned to all those the council deemed friendly to its cause.

The Lusignans saw this immediately. Led by William de Valence, they swore on 'the death and wounds of Christ', as Matthew Paris records, 'that under no circumstance would they ever resign their castles, lands or wardships whilst they still drew breath'.[52]

Upon William Simon now turned. 'Know this for sure, and have no doubt: you will deliver the castles that you have from the king – or you will lose your head.'

The other earls and barons voiced their agreement in vociferous terms. The Lusignans (as Mathew Paris continues) were perturbed, for they could see that all were against them. Their first thought was to flee to one of their castles; these had not been munitioned and so could not withstand a siege, but they had little choice. Their best hope, they decided, would lie in the castles of Aymer de Valence, bishop-elect of Winchester. They would flee immediately, but do so in secret. As the assembly was preparing to take its supper, they let it be known that they planned to sit down to the meal so that nobody would suspect their design.[53]

The barons, when they realized what had happened, called their knights to arms, and rode off in pursuit. They were ready, notes the anonymous letter-writer, to besiege each and every one of the Lusignan castles in England 'and to pursue them to the farthest limits unless they would shrink from the error they had conceived against the community of the kingdom concerning the provisions of the barons'.[54]

The Lusignans were holed up in Wolvesey Castle, the mighty and palatial fortress of the bishops of Winchester that stood next to Winchester Cathedral. When the barons arrived, it was clear to both sides whose position was the stronger. The Lusignans sent out envoys, promising that they would now support the Provisions of Oxford, if only they could be reconciled to the barons. But the barons would not have it. The Lusignans, they replied, as members of the original twenty-four, had sworn to support the reform of the kingdom, but had reneged on that oath and had left Oxford 'as traitors to the lord king and to the community, and as men who had feigned faith . . . [so that] no confidence whatsoever could be placed in them'.[55] For this reason, the barons told them, 'it was necessary for all of them to leave the kingdom with their whole following'. The Lusignans would then remain abroad, the barons continued, until the reform of the kingdom had been completed, after which the king would make a decision about their future – but only 'according to the counsel that he shall have' (in other words, whatever the council of fifteen decided).

The king, who had been brought down to Winchester with the barons, offered at this point to stand surety for his brothers, so as to guarantee that they would not act against the barons or the programme of reform. But the barons would not yield: the best they would offer was a pseudo-compromise, whereby Gui and Geoffrey de Lusignan must leave the kingdom, but Aymer and William could stay 'under safe and fitting custody to be provided by the barons' until the reforms had been enacted. Effectively, under this scheme, Aymer and William would be hostages.

The four brothers chose to stick together, and agreed to leave the kingdom. They wanted to take with them the income from their lands. The barons refused. The four could have an allowance, assigned 'by the provision of the barons', and the rest of their income would be kept in England, to be returned to them at some unspecified point in the future 'if it seemed expedient' ('which is not thought likely to happen', the letter-writer notes). The Lusignans asked, then, to be allowed to take with them their treasure. The barons would allow them only 6,000 marks (£4,000) in all. This would mean £1,000 each: a paltry sum by baronial standards, amounting (for instance) to well under half Simon's annual income. The rest of the Lusignan treasure would remain in England 'to satisfy all who complain against them and their bailiffs'.[56]

The barons immediately dispatched knights to seize the Lusignan stockpiles of cash and plate from the various monasteries where they were stored. Reports reached Matthew Paris that a vast Lusignan treasure was seized at the New Temple in London, and that a sizeable hoard, which the Lusignans were attempting to smuggle out of the country, was intercepted by Richard de Grey at Dover Castle. Everything seized from the Lusignans, writes Matthew, was 'to be spent usefully to the useful advantage of the kingdom, according to the judgement of king and barons'.[57]

The Lusignans, then, left England, with only their 6,000 marks, on 14 July.* Thus the barons had achieved their initial goal: the

---

* When they arrived at Boulogne, they asked the king of France whether they could abide within his kingdom, but the French queen, Marguerite of Provence, refused on

'wretched and intolerable Poitevins' had been made to flee from the face of the king and barons.

But for one young man this was not enough. Henry de Montfort, eldest son of Simon and Eleanor, was still seething, for William de Valence had defamed his father. William's shameful words at the Westminster parliament in April – he had called Simon a traitor – could not go unpunished. And so Henry crossed the Channel in secret, prepared to pursue the Lusignans in arms. In France he told to many a sympathetic party his account of the insults thrown by William at his father, and found (as Matthew Paris reports) 'many friends who, on account of love and reverence for his father, were willingly equipped and ready to avenge the injury to the earl'. Indeed, the French he spoke to 'were amazed that a man of such noble character and born of such noble blood, pre-eminent amongst all on both the French and English sides of the sea' should have been thus defamed, and by men connected to the king of England.[58] The Lusignans heard that Henry and his friends were coming for them, and took refuge in Boulogne. Henry and his friends, thus unable or unwilling to act out their vengeance, surrounded the port town and kept the Lusignans under observation.

Whether Simon knew of the pursuit, or even gave the order, is unknown (Matthew Paris admitted that he had no idea). The result at least would work in the council's favour, for at Boulogne young Henry would be able to report on the Lusignans' movements and warn the council if the brothers were preparing to return to England with reinforcements. Yet, even if Henry's actions were moved in part by strategy, they were understood by those who saw them in plainer terms: as a demonstrable act of allegiance. Henry de Montfort was now nineteen, old enough to take his own part in the world, and his first recorded deed was a very public declaration of his unremitting loyalty and love, for his father and for his family: they

---

account of their offences against her sister, Eleanor (*CM*, V, 702–3). The queen of England, like her uncles Peter and Boniface of Savoy, stood against the Lusignans, because she was concerned about the influence they had been exerting over her eldest son, Edward (H. W. Ridgeway, 'The lord Edward and the Provisions of Oxford (1258): A study in faction', in *Thirteenth Century England I*, ed. P. R. Coss and S. D. Lloyd (Woodbridge, 1986), 89–99).

stood as one, and he was ready to fight for his family and its honour. There was nothing more Montfortian than this.

*

While his eldest son pursued the Lusignans, Simon returned to London with others of the council. Westminster was by this time established as the principal seat of government, and so London was an appropriate base for the council as it set about its programme of reform. Throughout the summer, the council would hold meetings at the New Temple and elsewhere.[59] But first it was essential to bind the powerful of London to its cause. And so, on 23 July, Simon, the earl of Norfolk and John fitz Geoffrey came to the Guildhall to meet the city's aldermen and other officials. The meeting is narrated by the chronicler Arnold fitz Thedmar, alderman of Billingsgate ward, who seems to have been present. He describes how the barons had brought with them a charter detailing how the king and Edward had sworn to adhere to 'whatever the barons should provide for the advantage and improvement of the kingdom'. The seals of the king and Edward were appended to the charter, together with the seals of several barons. Simon and his fellow barons had come to ask the Londoners to swear, similarly, to their support for the Provisions of Oxford.

The Londoners sensed, perhaps, that something was amiss – the king's absence from the Guildhall meeting had been noted, and the Londoners were refused permission to speak with the king about the swearing of the oath. Yet in the end, having discussed the matter amongst themselves, they agreed to swear as the barons had asked, and appended the city's seal to the charter. They perhaps understood – or had it explained to them – that elements of the reform programme would work in their favour. One of the most widespread grievances against Henry III was the unjust taking of prise: the king's household was entitled to take possession of food and wine from merchants, so long as the merchants were recompensed at a fair price, but it had become the norm for the royal household to offer insufficient sums or even fail to pay at all.[60] The reformers determined to halt this practice. On 30 July Simon authorized a writ to recompense a burgess of Rouen, because a royal official had seized from the man wine worth over £35. And (as Arnold fitz Thedmar notes), on 5 August, the barons issued a proclamation in the city of London that nobody of the royal household was to take anything unless by the assent of the vendor, saving the customary prise at the customary rate.* Anyone convicted of contravention of this ruling would face imprisonment.[61] These were practical acts that made a significant difference to the livelihoods of merchants.

While Simon remained in London during the latter part of July and August 1258, he stayed at the house of the bishop of Durham.[62] The residence stood on the Strand (where many of the bishops and other potentates kept townhouses), roughly where the Adelphi Theatre stands today, next door to the house of Peter of Savoy, on whose site the Savoy hotel was built. It was here, in the latter part of July, that Simon came face to face with the king once more. It was to be another of those encounters that would mark the intertwining of their lives and measure the character of one against the other: from Henry's public raging in 1239, in which he issued 'insulting and shameful words' that Simon found 'painful to recall' accusing Simon of seducing Eleanor, to Simon's brutal shaming of the king at Saintes in 1242, when he declared that Henry should be taken and shut away like Charles the Simple, to their mutual fury in 1252 that had verged on violence, when Henry had called Simon a traitor, Simon had called Henry a liar and questioned his Christianity, and Henry had declared that he regretted nothing in the world so much as allowing Simon a place in England.

This next meeting came one day when Henry had left Westminster Palace, thinking to take his meal on ship as he cruised the Thames.[63] But as the vessel approached the Strand, the clouds blackened and began to throw down torrents, and thunder rent the air. The king was frightened, and wanted to return to the safety of the shore immediately. His ship was then passing the bishop of Durham's house on the Strand, so there he landed. Simon came out to meet him.

'What is it you fear?' he asked the king. 'The storm has already passed.'

---

* The customary quantity and rate was named as 2 tuns, at forty shillings (*De Antiquis Legibus Liber. Cronica Maiorum et Vicecomitum Londoniarum*, ed. T. Stapleton (London, 1846), 39). A tun was a large vat amounting to about eight barrels.

It was 'not jokingly' that Henry answered him (as Matthew Paris reports), but 'seriously, with a severe countenance'.

'I dread thunder and lightning beyond measure,' he said. 'But, by God's head, you make me tremble more than all the thunder and lightning in the world.'

10

Rule by Conscience

Through the summer of 1258, the rain continued to pour. The time of harvest had arrived but, for the second year running, the crops were left to stand sodden and rotting in the fields. In August the people of St Albans, under the direction of the abbey's monks, processed solemnly through the streets of their town, entreating the Lord to alleviate their hardship, and soon the people of London followed their example. They found that the deluge began to ease a little, but no dramatic change in fortune was forthcoming.[1] The same was true of their condition broadly, for the reforms promised by Simon and his colleagues were not proceeding at the hoped-for pace. Hugh Bigod was doing all he could, but he was only one man, wading alone into a vast ocean of grievance. His eyre, conducted as it was with necessary breadth and thoroughness, advanced only slowly, making its way around Surrey and Kent. Perhaps the reformers now, with hindsight, recognized that the system of *enquêtes* employed by Louis IX in France, with their teams of *enquêteurs*, would have been a more efficient course. A proclamation was issued in October 1258, assuring the people of the shires that progress was continuing and promising that the same scrupulous investigation would reach each of the shires in turn.[2]

Yet other fields of reform lay firmly within the scope of progress. Many of the iniquities of Henry's government stemmed from the king's failure to steward the kingdom's finances, for it was in his quest to raise cash that he had driven his officers to extort money from his poorer subjects. It was decided, then, that a fundamental reform of the treasury was needed, overseen by a minister with drive and indubitable integrity, invested with real power to make changes. The incumbent minister, Philip Lovel, associated with Henry's oppressive and inefficient government, was deposed (after some suspiciously convenient allegations about his abuse of forest law were brought against him), and a worthier candidate brought forward on 2 November 1258.[3]

The choice of candidate was particular: John of Crakehall, archdeacon of Bedford. John had been the steward of none other than Robert Grosseteste, and had been inducted by his late master into the new way of thinking, drawn from Aristotle, that placed sound financial management at the heart of what it meant to be a ruler.[4] John was one of the two assistants who had accompanied Robert to the papal court in 1250 to make his case, together with Simon's friend Richard Gravesend. It was the thinking of this group, led by Simon as a member of the council, that underpinned John's appointment as treasurer: not only did John have experience (in managing sizeable estates to the bishop's high standards) but he also knew the ethical urgency of sound accounting. John went on to oversee a thorough reformation of treasury practice, cutting out inefficiencies, waste and extravagance as he strove to restore the royal coffers without demanding money from subjects.[5]

At the same time, the barons also took measures to halt the oppressive behaviour of the sheriffs, compelling each to swear that he would 'do justice in common to all people . . . and that he will not waver in this for love nor for hate . . . nor for any greed, but that he will do speedy justice as well and as quickly to the poor as to the rich'. News of this oath was proclaimed throughout the shires, together with a prohibition against the proffering of bribes (the council would henceforth pay each sheriff his expenses out of the royal coffers, so that 'he shall have no reason to take anything from someone else'), and a promise that sheriffs and bailiffs would henceforth hold their offices at yearly terms (rather than indefinitely) 'so that', the people of England heard, 'if hardships or wrongs are committed against you . . . you shall fear them all the less and more boldly reveal their wrongdoing'. The proclamation was issued together with another outlining the powers of the council and commanding that all 'faithful and loyal' to the king swear to support both the provisions of the council and each other against 'all men who either give or receive a bribe'.[6]

The text of both proclamations was issued in Latin, French and English, and 'sent throughout the whole kingdom of England to all shires', as the annalist at Burton Abbey notes, 'so that they could be read there by the sheriffs, and understood, to be observed henceforth firmly and inviolate by all'.[7] This means of publication was not standard. Proclamations, like other documents produced by the royal chancery, were usually issued only in Latin (the concise and precise language of governance); when the sheriff had the document read in the shire court or other public meeting place an ad hoc translation could then be made into French (and potentially English, depending upon the intended audience).* But now the council, in providing its own written translations, was assuming control of the exact words proclaimed, so that everyone listening – from Cornwall to Northumberland – would hear the same words. There would be no problem in ensuring that the sheriffs would have the proclamations read as they were ordered, for new office holders were appointed to the majority of shires later in October. The council's publication strategy was successful, as the reports of the programme of publication in chronicles attest.[8]

*

It was not long afterwards, shortly after 6 November, that Simon left England for France, in company with Richard Gravesend, Walter de Cantilupe and the earl of Norfolk.[9] Their embassy was tasked with ratifying the treaty of peace that had been negotiated – by Simon, Walter and others – between the kings of France and England. The mission failed, however, for the barons would not allow Henry to accompany the embassy, no doubt fearful of what he might say to

---

* This was probably how Magna Carta and the Forest Charter had been published throughout the kingdom since 1218 (S. T. Ambler, 'Magna Carta: its confirmation at Simon de Montfort's parliament of 1265', *English Historical Review*, 130 (2015), 801–30, at 811–12), although it seems that some written translations were produced at least of the first issue of Magna Carta in 1215 (J. C. Holt, 'A vernacular-French text of Magna Carta, 1215', *English Historical Review*, 89 (1974), 346–56).

Louis about how power had been taken from him. Louis refused to meet the ambassadors without his English counterpart, and the meeting collapsed. When the other ambassadors returned to England by the end of the month, Simon remained in France.[10]

With him were his two elder sons, Henry and Simon.[11] Young Simon was now seventeen – easily old enough to be inducted into family affairs. Henry, as we have seen, had already made his entrance onto the public stage in July, when he chased the Lusignans to France in an effort to defend his father's honour. At twenty (he celebrated his birthday in France at the end of November), he was almost of full legal age and old enough to be involved in the judicial affairs of the family, to which they were to tend in France. Indeed, Simon was to invest in his eldest son a high degree of trust.

On the first day of January 1259, Simon made his will. The original document survives (see plate 24).[12] The final sentence of the main text reads 'And I, Henry son of the aforesaid Simon, wrote these letters in my hand, and acknowledge and promise my lord my father that I, in good faith and in all my power, will attend to that which is written here.' Young Henry's hand is not as elegant as those of the highly trained clerks employed in the chanceries of bishops and kings, but it is even and clear. He took care in his work, adding the odd flourish to embellish the tops of his ascenders, and spacing his lines consistently: it is well worthy of the training he had received in the household of Robert Grosseteste. Henry wrote in French (most wills were written in Latin), perhaps because it was easier than translating on the spot, for the will would have been dictated by his father.*

In the will, Simon reveals those he trusted most – for it was his executors, and those appointed to counsel them, who would be tasked with ensuring that the terms of his testament were carried out exactly as he wished for the benefit of his soul. The principal executor was Eleanor. 'I make of her my attorney,' said Simon, 'and beseech and require and command her in the faith

---

* The making of a will in this period remained an essentially oral act, to be upheld by its witnesses, although a sealed written record, with a legal authority of its own, was increasingly desirable (M. Sheehan, *The Will in Medieval England: From the Conversion of the Anglo-Saxons to the End of the Thirteenth Century* (Toronto, 1963), 186–90).

by which she is held to me that she does it in such a manner as a good lady ought to do it for her lord to whom she is bound in faith.' That a wife should be named as an executor was not uncommon, but it was most unusual for just a single executor to be appointed.[13] The king, for instance, in his will of 1253, was to name the queen as an executor, but she was to be one of ten. That Eleanor was placed solely in charge of managing Simon's estates reflects a remarkable degree of trust between the two. Eleanor was to have 'full power', said Simon, 'that all those things that she shall do or ordain or provide to be done . . . shall be firm and stable just as if I had done it myself'. If Eleanor were to die before Simon, then their eldest son, Henry, would assume her responsibilities as executor.

Beyond Simon's immediate family, five further figures are prominent in his will. The first two are Adam Marsh and Richard Gravesend. As we have seen, Adam was a close friend of long standing, who had counselled Simon through his travails in Gascony, had been at Eleanor's side in 1251 when she was readying to give birth, and had defended him at the 1252 inquiry. Richard Gravesend, as we have also seen, had been Robert Grosseteste's second in command and a part of his circle; Adam Marsh had once described him in a letter to Simon as 'your lordship's faithful spiritual servant'.[14] But it is only from this period that he finds a regular place in our sources, for on 3 November 1258 he was consecrated bishop of Lincoln. He now became one of the most powerful men in the kingdom, ruling a diocese that reached across almost nine shires, the spiritual – and in many cases temporal – lord of perhaps one-fifth of the entire population of England. Simon must have greeted his election to the bishopric with joy; he now had a second close friend and ally amongst the bishops.[15] Richard had been part of the delegation sent to the court of France in November, and had elected to remain behind with Simon.[16]

Adam and Richard were appointed now by Simon to act as advisers to Eleanor in the execution of the will. In the event that Henry de Montfort was required to succeed his mother as executor, he was to seek the counsel of three further men (Peter de Montfort, Hugh Despenser and one Ernaut du Bois) but, 'above all', Simon decreed, 'I wish and command that he heeds the counsel of the aforementioned bishop and brother Adam, and in no manner may he act at all without the counsel of these two, if they live, and if one of them shall die, than of him who remains'. If Henry died, then the three lay counsellors were to take over, but again were to act only with the counsel of Richard and Adam.

The central terms of Simon's will were that 'the wrongs that I have done in whatever manner in whatever country . . . are to be emended, and my debts are to be paid also to all, and namely the debts of service that have been made to me are to be rendered to those who have served me'. It is not unusual to find such provision for the payment of debt and the righting of wrongs in wills, but Simon's next stipulation stands out:

> I wish that the people who make any claims of me are to benefit abundantly and readily, when they speak such reasons that it seems more likely that they are speaking the truth than a lie, for I wish that if there is any doubt, the debt will be cleared entirely on my behalf, whatever it costs, if it means that I will be entirely freed, for I do not wish to remain in debt nor under suspicion of debt to anyone.

Here Simon removed the need for a high standard of proof, and replaced it with an assessment of the claimant's delivery of their oral complaint that assumed their good faith. This was conscience-driven lordship: the insistence that tenants be treated according to what is right and not merely what was necessary. He was imposing in his will the same new standard that Louis IX and Alphonse of Poitiers had imposed in France, and that the council was imposing upon the king and barons in England. Its appearance in the context of Simon's will throws its purpose into relief – for wrongs heaped upon subjects were sins, for which the culprit would have to answer before the heavenly Lord.

*

Simon was back in England in time for the Candlemas parliament, which began in the week following 2 February.[17] He had been away for three months, and he had been missed: 'the whole of England had grieved at his long-lasting absence', writes Matthew Paris, 'being unaware of what could have happened to him in parts across the sea'.[18] The progress of reform had stalled, and meanwhile the people of England still languished in hunger and poverty. Matthew's summary of 1258 was dismal: 'the year passed most dissimilar to all previous ones', he wrote, 'namely pestilential and deadly'. In the summer it had seemed that crops would flourish, 'yet in the autumn the continual floods of rain choked the grain, fruit and pulses once again'. At Christmas, across England, barns stood empty, the crops that should have filled them festering in their fields. Vast numbers of people were still starving, and 'they wallowed in all sorts of by-ways where they would die, wretchedly exhaling their final breath . . . whence hope of rising from the abyss, which normally comforts those in despair, is now entirely snuffed out'.[19]

But with Simon's return came the next great drive of reform. By 22 February the council had issued a series of commitments binding its members to the same standard of lordship demanded of the king. The document became known as the Ordinance of the Magnates:[20]

> We wish, provide and grant [the council members proclaimed] that all wrongs which we and our bailiffs have done to our subjects or to our neighbours shall be corrected by the king and by his justiciar . . . And we will hinder no one by threats, nor by power, nor in any other manner, from freely making complaint of us and of our men, and from prosecuting their complaint, nor will we remember it against them, nor attempt any reprisal against them.

This promise echoed the insistent words of Simon's will, that those making claims be granted the benefit of the doubt. The objective in both cases was to make it as easy as possible for those with a grievance to come forward, indeed to encourage them to do so by openly adopting a sympathetic attitude. The council's promise that its members would not hinder suits pursued against themselves and their men implied that the magnates would refrain not only from intimidating complainants but also from using their legal power to obstruct the complainants' use of the *praecipe* writ to transfer cases from the baronial to the royal courts. Again, this was conscience-driven lordship.

The council decided to put these guarantees in writing as an 'official' document. The Provisions of Oxford, setting out the first great raft of reforms in the summer of 1258, exist only in draft form and were never published. This was information management: the council did not want the terms of the Provisions of Oxford to be widely known, for they stripped the king of his power – something that many would have found shocking. But the council did wish to publicize the reforms it was enacting aimed at improving the lot of ordinary people – hence why, as we have seen, it had begun to issue its own texts and translations for publication in the shires. With the Ordinance the reformers went further, for they appended their seals to the original. This imbued the document with legal authority, demonstrating the solemn commitment of the bearers of the seals to uphold its terms. Most people in the kingdom would not have seen the original version of the Ordinance, but when the text was proclaimed by the sheriffs they would have listened to its contents, which included a statement that the seals had been appended to the original. The people of the kingdom could thus be assured that these guarantees carried legal weight.

This mattered, for the Ordinance – in setting out concessions and promising a standard of lordship, freely granted by the issuing party for the benefit of subjects, and guaranteed by seal – was reminiscent of Magna Carta itself. The reformers did not actually describe the document they were issuing as a charter (they chose a term that was ambiguous: *escrit*, meaning an agreement or, more generally, just document or text). Yet the Ordinance adopts the language of a charter, beginning with a salutation to its audience, narrating the motives for making the grant and proclaiming in the voice of the issuer, 'we wish, provide, and grant (*nus voloms, grantons et otrions*)' the rights that follow.*

This was deliberate, for it seems that the text of the Ordinance

---

* The only text we now have of the Ordinance is in French. Although it is possible that the Ordinance was drawn up in Latin (as was standard for official documents),

was intended to invite comparison with Magna Carta – and, indeed, one that was favourable to the council. After promising to allow complaints against themselves and their officers, the barons proclaimed that: 'we wish and have provided, for us and for our heirs, that the articles in the Charter of Liberties . . . we will observe as regards ourselves towards our tenants and our neighbours, both in our demesnes and in our liberties'. This was the very guarantee that magnates had resisted since 1215. The reforming council now made it freely. And still the council went further. All sorts of situations – economic, legal, political – had arisen in the decades since 1215 that Magna Carta could not possibly have comprehended, hence in part the need for new legislation. Now the barons, immediately after the promise to uphold the Charter with respect to their own tenants, promised that 'whatever the king's council has established or shall establish', regarding everything from amercements to feudal rights and responsibilities 'and anything else thereafter which shall be for the reform of the state of the realm, we will uphold it as between ourselves and our subjects, both we ourselves and our heirs'. This guarantee signalled not only a volte-face in baronial attitudes as to their responsibility, but a demonstrative advance in the opposite direction. It was lavish in its generosity.

So too was the choice of audience to which the Ordinance was addressed, whose members would be the beneficiaries. This group is named in two small words in the opening sentence of the Ordinance, unobtrusive in their brevity but powerful in their implication: 'all people' (*tutte gent*). Here there was a striking contrast

---

it does seem that, unusually, it was published throughout the kingdom only in French, for only the French was enrolled and sent to the sheriffs, and this is the only version to be mentioned in the instructions for publication. This was probably a continuation of the council's experiments in communicating effectively with a broader audience. The term '*chartre*' was certainly available – it was used, for instance, in a French translation of Magna Carta in 1215 that was perhaps prepared for publication (see: Holt, 'A vernacular-French', 357; for '*chartre*', see: *Anglo-Norman Dictionary*, online edition, available at: www.anglo-norman.net/D/chartre[1], accessed 6 Aug. 2018). I have altered the translation here from that given in R. F. Treharne and I. J. Sanders (eds.), *Documents of the Baronial Movement of Reform and Rebellion, 1258–1267* (Oxford, 1973) (hereafter *DBM*), 130–7, in accordance with the translation into French from the Latin of the 1215 Magna Carta.

with Magna Carta, for 'all people' meant, literally, everyone in the kingdom, both unfree and free. Meanwhile, Magna Carta had only been granted to 'all free people' (*omnibus liberis hominibus*), ensuring that those who were unfree in the eyes of the law were excluded.[21] The unfree comprised an entire stratum of society, of unknown size but perhaps as much as 50 per cent of the population in some regions, whose status was defined by their obligation to perform labour services for their lord; someone who (in the words of the legal treatise known as Bracton) 'cannot know in the evening the service to be rendered in the morning. [He] is bound to do whatever he is bid.'[22] The unfree were not permitted to use the royal courts, and so had no recourse if they were poorly treated by their lords, though they would have no claim in any case, for they were entirely under their lord's jurisdiction. This meant that the exclusion of the unfree from the liberties granted in Magna Carta was legally justifiable. It was probably the barons who insisted upon it at Runnymede (rather than the king), for it was they who had a particular interest in keeping their tenants under their heel.[23] When the definitive version of the Charter was issued in 1225, a new opening was introduced, in which the liberties set out were said to be granted to 'archbishops, bishops, abbots, priors, earls, barons and all people of our kingdom', but this was undermined by the chapter that immediately followed, simply lifted from the 1215 version, in which the liberties granted pertained only 'to all free people'. Now, in the Ordinance, the barons removed any ambiguity, proclaiming themselves to be granting their guarantees to all, no matter their legal or social status. The text of the Ordinance was to be read out in the shire and hundred courts 'and elsewhere' (meaning public meeting places, such as markets and squares). To those listening, who would have heard Magna Carta read out on previous occasions, the contrast would surely have been striking.

Whose design, then, was this revolutionary guarantee of good lordship? It can only have been Simon's. That this assertive statement of good lordship came only with his return to England is telling, as is what happened next. Matthew Paris reports that, after the parliament's close, when the barons were drawing up 'statutes' of reform (presumably arranging for the Ordinance to be published, since it was not released until the end of March), there was an argument between Simon and the earl of Gloucester. It was these two earls who had set their seals to the Ordinance on behalf of the council, implying that it was their authority that underpinned the ruling.* But when the time came to act upon the promise of the Ordinance, the earl of Gloucester began to think again. Perhaps he had thought that a promise would suffice, or perhaps he was sobered by the reality of curtailing his own power over his subjects. Either way (as Matthew Paris reports) Simon was 'moved to rage at the other earl for wavering in regards to their common plan'.

In his anger, says Matthew, Simon left England. The earl of Gloucester, meanwhile, was reprimanded by the barons who remained: it was his fault that Simon had departed, and they would not allow the earl of Gloucester to renege on his promise. He was forced to concede and send his steward throughout his lands to implement the Ordinance.[24]

While it is clear that Simon's resolve propelled the Ordinance, there is more than meets the eye when it comes to his refusal to live 'amongst people so inconstant and false', and his storming out of England. Such a response seems illogical: if Simon was determined to see the Ordinance enacted, surely the most productive course of action when faced with opposition would have been to stay and put pressure on his fellow earl. In fact, Simon had another reason for leaving England: he was to go to France, for the next stage in

---

* At least twenty-seven nobles and prelates were party to the Ordinance, for the document notes the involvement of not only the council but also the committee of twelve appointed under the Provisions of Oxford to act as a conduit between the greater body gathered at parliament and the council (*DBM*, 104–5). Although the text of the Ordinance stated that 'we [i.e. the council and twelve] have set our seals to this document', it would have been impossible for the seals of all to be appended to the parchment, and so four men were chosen, two from the committee of twelve and two from the council, whose seals would represent themselves and their fellows. We know of their identity because, in the seventeenth century, a transcript was made of a note in a now-lost government roll, recording (in French, in the first person plural) how the four had put their seals to an *escrit* on their own behalf and that of their colleagues, on 22 February 1259 – the day that the Ordinance was issued. The two from the council were Simon de Montfort and Richard de Clare, earl of Gloucester (H. G. Richardson and G. O. Sayles, 'The Provisions of Oxford: a forgotten document and some comments', *Bulletin of the John Rylands Library*, 7 (1933), 291–321, at 300, 321).

negotiations with Louis IX concerning the Anglo-French treaty of peace.[25]

Simon might not have left because of the earl of Gloucester's recalcitrance – but what matters is why he said that this was so. 'I have no desire', Simon had declared, 'to live or keep company amongst people so inconstant and false. What we are doing now we agreed and swore together. And you, lord earl of Gloucester, as far as you are more eminent than the rest of us, so you are bound all the more to these salutary statutes.' They had given an oath, a sacred promise, to uphold a cause and were now obliged to keep that oath no matter the cost, especially no matter what it cost them personally. Those who, when they were tested, wavered or abandoned that oath were of a meaner sort, especially those who did so because they could not stomach the thought of personal sacrifice.

Simon's reading of the situation, and his presentation of it, came from his father. The Count had held fast to his oath, bearing whatever hardships had been laid upon him. He had given his fortune to carry on the fight, so that he could not even afford to feed himself, but he had borne the hunger and the shame of poverty with resolute countenance. He had been separated from his wife and children, denied the comfort of their company as each took their own part in operations. And he had not flinched from offering up his body for his oath, time and again accepting the possibility of death when he chose to take the field. It was a sacrifice he had been required to make, of course, at the end, beneath the walls of Toulouse – and a man could make no greater sacrifice to keep his oath. Meanwhile, lesser men fell away. They abandoned their oaths to fight the holy war because they lacked his resolution, his courage and his faith. They gave up the fight and went home, or joined with the enemy. The Count was left, so often, alone, alone and unmatched in worth. There was no triumph in the recognition, for it was this abandonment of oaths – and not the enemy – that had been the greatest threat to the holy cause: faithlessness.[26]

As we have seen, it was Peter of les Vaux-de-Cernay's *History* that provided material for Simon's knightly education, its stories of the Count told and retold to Simon as he grew, as an exhortation to follow in his father's footsteps. And Peter's *History* described a particular exemplar: a characterization of proper conduct as holding faithful to one's oath and suffering for it, and of the antithesis of proper conduct as abandoning one's oath for an unwillingness to suffer or for gain. And so it was that Simon turned to this exemplar when confronted by the earl of Gloucester's wavering. He characterized noble conduct, right and wrong – as he had been taught to do – according to the model of his father. Simon would be resilient and maintain his oath without regard for personal cost; others would not, and in falling so far short they deserved his scorn.

This, the first testing of the baronial resolve, is the first time (so far as we can see) that Simon gave voice to this understanding of his obligation and his role. But he was to do so again and again in the years to come, as he forged his character and his reputation in his father's image. This first recorded statement is precious in this respect, especially because the chronicler who noted it, Matthew Paris, died just a few weeks later, and can thus be cleared of any accusation of writing with the benefit of hindsight, of knowledge of Simon's later reputation.

This, in one sense, was the beginning of Simon's story.

11

Betrayal

Simon had been in the vanguard of a movement that, in its first year, had made substantial headway in combating the corruption and inefficiency of Henry's government. The coming year, however, would be a trying period, both for the movement and for Simon. It culminated, once again, with the bringing of charges against Simon by the king. The difficulties started in July 1259. Negotiations for the proposed Anglo-French peace treaty, begun some two years earlier, had stalled – the fault largely of Simon and Eleanor. By the spring of 1258 it had emerged that Louis was demanding that a new condition be added to any settlement. Not only must the king of England renounce all claim to the lands of Louis and his brothers (Normandy and Anjou, both lost by King John to the Capetians), but so too must Henry's brother, Richard, earl of Cornwall, and his sister, Eleanor, countess of Leicester. At first sight there was nothing unusual about such a stipulation. Richard and Eleanor were children of King John and were thus, like Henry, potential claimants to the lost continental lands, as would their children be; they had both been required to renounce their claims to their mother's lands as part of a deal with Hugh de Lusignan in 1242 (although Eleanor had not in fact done so).[1] But it was hard to imagine how such a situation could come about: Henry and his queen had three children (Edward, Margaret and Edmund) all of whom had passed through the perilous years of infancy. Henry's line was as good as secure, meaning that his renunciation should have been sufficient. Why, then, had Louis deemed this condition necessary? Before long Henry thought the question solved – for his brother, Richard, made the renunciation swiftly and without hesitation. His sister Eleanor, however, would not.

Eleanor was holding firm because Henry still owed her and her husband £400 worth of land, promised in 1253 as Eleanor's marriage portion. Henry had been delivering cash in lieu, but that was not enough: the 1253 agreement laid out that the land was to be heritable, meaning that it would help to form an endowment for the still-growing brood of Montfort children (a sixth child, Eleanor, was born at some point in 1258).[2] Eleanor's motives for refusing to provide her renunciation were later freely admitted by Simon: 'the countess was unwilling to make [the renunciation] until the king had assigned the land to her as he had agreed . . . and the countess showed the king that she was not bound to make the renunciation of her hereditary right [on the Continent] unless she received compensation'. The refusal was Eleanor's decision, Simon pointed out, 'for I was not in England when the countess was asked for the renunciation'.* But whether Simon was present with Eleanor at the time was, Henry believed, hardly relevant, for his absence did not preclude their plotting to make of the renunciation a bargaining counter. Indeed, Simon admitted as much, freely acknowledging the truth of the king's statement that he had 'granted by his letter that he would make his wife . . . make the renunciation if the king paid to the countess what he owed her'. In other words, Simon and Eleanor were willing – and openly so – to obstruct or delay the agreement of the Anglo-French peace treaty in order to compel the king to fulfil his promise to them.

But this was not the limit of Henry's allegations. In 1260 Henry would have the opportunity to demand Simon's answer to his charges. Their exchange was recorded.

'In the peace-treaty was included a provision,' Henry began, 'that the countess of Leicester and her two sons should make renunciation to the king of France.' (The 'two sons' were, presumably, the two

---

* In this exchange, I have changed the third-person formula given by the clerk ('the king says . . .') into the first person, recalling the words spoken by the parties rather than the scribe's mediating voice (R. F. Treharne and I. J. Sanders (eds.), *Documents of the Baronial Movement of Reform and Rebellion, 1258–1267* (Oxford, 1973) (hereafter *DBM*), 194–205).

eldest Montfort boys, Henry and Simon, who were of an age to play an active part in politics.)

'So the king of France wished it,' Simon replied.

Henry pointed out that no renunciation was demanded of his own daughters, nor from the second son of Richard of Cornwall, nor from the children of Henry's other sister, Isabella.

'This was done at the wish of the king of France,' Simon answered, 'and not by my doing.'

But Henry was not having it. 'You, both personally and through your agents,' he told Simon, 'arranged and caused to be arranged, and put it into the mind of the king of France, that renunciation should be asked from the countess and her children.'

'I neither arranged nor suggested this,' said Simon, 'nor did I get anyone else to do so, and on this charge I will stand or fall by the memory of the king of France.'

As 1259 wore on, the Montforts were still refusing to furnish Eleanor's renunciation. In July of this year, Simon and Eleanor had estimated their annual losses arising from the unpaid dower at 1,400 marks (£933), and demanded from Henry compensation to the sum of 36,400 marks (£24,267) – a sum not far off the annual royal income. They had agreed with Henry that the matter would be put to arbitration, with an outcome to be delivered by 1 November.[3]

These plans were thrown off course in October. Henry had already, in the summer, sent to his counterpart in France a draft of the treaty that did not include a demand for Eleanor's renunciation, and Louis was seemingly prepared to accept it. On 13 October the councillors issued a letter accepting the amended version. Simon was amongst those councillors: having been presented starkly with the opportunity to scupper the Anglo-French peace, he had been forced to concede.[4] But in response he raised the stakes. As Henry later reminded Simon,

'You demanded from the envoys of the king [of France] your wife's share of all the overseas territories of King John, and on account of this demand the negotiations were upset and the peace treaty delayed.' In other words, Simon was not only withholding the renunciation of Eleanor and their two eldest sons with regards to Normandy and the other old Plantagenet territories, but also actively advancing Eleanor's claim – or, rather, making a show of doing so.

Simon was unapologetic. 'If I made this demand,' he replied, 'before the king [of England] and I had come to an agreement on the issues between us, I do not see that I did anything wrong, for I believed I had right in my demand; and if I demanded it after agreement had been reached between the king and myself, I still did nothing wrong, for the promises which had been made to me had not been fulfilled, so that I was doing no wrong if I demanded my rights.'[5]

Soon, Simon would leave for France to press the matter in person. Meanwhile, he set out to secure a new ally in his quest to obtain Eleanor's dower: Edward. The heir to the throne was now twenty years old. He had disapproved of his father's willingness to surrender the familial claims to Normandy, and had only with reluctance provided his own renunciation, in May 1259.[6] Now he was persuaded to bind himself to Simon. The text of their agreement, made on 15 October, survives.[7] In it Edward states that he has 'sworn on the Holy Gospels and promised in good faith' that with 'all our power we will loyally aid and counsel our dear and faithful Simon de Montfort, earl of Leicester, and his heirs and all his friends in England in all their needs . . . against all people'. And 'by the same oath', Edward continued, 'we are held together with the aforesaid earl and with his heirs and with his friends to maintain the enterprise enacted by the barons of the land to the honour of God and to the profit of the king and his heirs and the kingdom'.

So far, Simon had persuaded Edward to commit himself to the programme of reform (which Edward, despite his initial scepticism, now professed to be in the best interests of his father, himself and England), and to support Simon and his family and friends come what may. Now Edward made another promise: he would not make a quarrel with, or make war on, anyone involved in the reforming enterprise – as long, that is, as such a person 'wished to hold to the judgement of the court of the king both in doing justice and accepting justice'. If someone refused to accept the judgement of the king's court, then 'by this oath', Edward declared, 'we are held to compel this person or these people to hold to the judgement and to make no exception'. The most likely explanation is that, with an arbitration over his family's claims in progress, Simon expected resistance to an award that favoured the Montforts, specifically from those who had a stake in the Marshal inheritance. Some of these were fellow councillors, most notably the earl of Gloucester.[8] Because Simon had apparently lost his bargaining chip – the threat of the failure of the Anglo-French peace – it would be that much easier for the earl of Gloucester to scupper Eleanor's dower settlement. Now the earl of Gloucester would have to think twice before mounting any opposition, for in so doing he would be forced to make an enemy of the heir to the throne.

With this precaution in place, Simon left England. By 19 October he was at Evreux, in Normandy, gathered with the great and the good of the kingdom of France for the consecration of the city's bishop. Amongst the congregation was King Louis.[9] Simon probably remained in and around the French court throughout November, with the aim of priming Louis before Henry arrived to ratify the treaty. Simon was confident that he had been successful: when Henry arrived in France in mid-November, Simon still refused to provide Eleanor's renunciation.[10] His confidence was justified, for Louis now took up the issue himself. As part of the treaty, Louis would have to pay Henry the costs of 500 knights for two years (an agreement that had been made with the Sicilian venture in mind).[11] From this sum, it was now decreed, he would hold back 15,000 marks until such time as Henry satisfied Eleanor's claim.[12] This agreement was probably brokered by the archbishop of Rouen, Eudes Rigaud, a friend of both Simon and Louis, and it was Eudes who, on 3 December, announced the agreement in Louis's apple orchard (like Charlemagne, Louis was known for conducting business under the trees – a sign of openness). The following day, Simon and Eleanor issued a joint declaration in which she made her renunciation in full.[13]

*

Simon's conduct in the negotiation of the treaty rankled deeply with the king – but it was what happened next, at the end of 1259 and in the early months of 1260, that sent Henry over the edge.[14] The unfurling of events is described in the charges that Henry laid before Simon in July 1260.

Henry put it to Simon that, after the renunciation was made and the treaty ratified on 4 December 1259, Simon had 'left [France] without taking leave of him'. This, as Henry implied, was an insult: Henry was a king and Simon was his vassal, and Simon should have afforded his lord this mark of respect.

'I was with the king in Paris,' Simon responded, 'until I took leave of the king of France, then I went to Normandy, where the countess my wife was, and then I went to England, where I expected that the king would have arrived as soon as myself. And whether I came back to England with or without taking leave, I do not see that I did anything wrong.' (Simon, we may note, had taken leave of Louis.)

Henry stated that, while he had remained in France, he had sent orders to Hugh Bigod, the justiciar, 'that no parliament should be held until his return'.

'The king may very well have so ordered him,' answered Simon.

Henry had indeed written to Hugh Bigod and others on 26 January, notifying them that he was delayed in France.* He knew that a parliament was scheduled for early February, for the Provisions of Oxford had decreed that three parliaments were to be held each year, on the morrow of Candlemas (3 February), 1 June and the octave of Michaelmas (6 October).† Customarily parliaments were held only when they had been summoned by the king, either to discuss some pressing issue or (particularly in Henry's case) because consent was needed to levy a tax. Here the Provisions were, for the first time, stipulating that parliaments should be integral to the running of the kingdom, whether or not the king thought them

---

* One of King Louis's sons had died, forcing postponement of the wedding of Henry's daughter, Beatrice, to the son of the duke of Brittany. The arbitration that would decide the precise sum that Louis would have to pay Henry under the terms of the treaty (to cover the 500 knights for two years) was also taking longer than expected (*DBM*, 164–7).

† The plan for the thrice-yearly parliaments echoed the tradition, reaching back centuries, of thrice-yearly major assemblies at which the king would wear his crown, in the latter case at Easter, Whitsun and Christmas. The reformers chose to spread the parliaments evenly across the year, and substituted a fixed date in June for the moveable feasts of Easter and Whitsun (J. R. Maddicott, *The Origins of the English Parliament, 924–1327* (Oxford, 2010), 238).

necessary. This principle was fundamental to the reform movement: it ensured the taking of counsel and the provision of consent were central to the process of decision-making. For committed reformers like Simon, the holding of regular parliaments was therefore non-negotiable.[*]

Hugh Bigod, however, was not so committed. He did as he was ordered by the king.

'The justiciar,' Henry put to Simon, 'forbade you and the rest of the council then present to hold any parliament until my arrival.'

'The justiciar may very well have forbidden it,' replied Simon.

'You came to London,' said Henry, 'at Candlemas and held a parliament.'

'In the common provision made by the king and by his council,' replied Simon, 'it is provided that three parliaments shall be held every year, of which one is at Candlemas; and to keep my oath I came there along with the other sound councillors who were in England.'[†]

---

[*] See: Maddicott, *Origins of Parliament*, 238–9. The first obstacle – the king's absence abroad – was not serious in itself. Assemblies could be held in the king's absence under the supervision of a regent or other appointed deputy, something that had been more common when Henry's ancestors had spent much of their time supervising their continental lands, but which had happened as recently as 1254, when Henry had been in France and parliament had met under the supervision of his queen. The problem instead was that Henry had forbidden the parliament to meet. In his letter to Hugh Bigod, Henry noted that the Welsh were in arms, were laying siege to Builth Castle, and intended to move on the Marches; in the face of 'grave and evident peril', he instructed that the council was to turn its attention to rescuing the castle and defending the March. 'Make no arrangements for a parliament and permit none to be held before our return to England', he instructed, 'for when we arrive there, we shall arrange, with your counsel and that of the magnates, for holding a parliament as may be best for us and for our kingdom' (*DBM*, 164–9).

[†] Did the Provisions' requirement for the Candlemas parliament, fortified by the oaths of the reformers, outweigh the royal prohibition? This was largely a matter of perspective. Simon was not the first to defy such a prohibition, nor to do so on moral grounds. As recently as August 1257, Boniface of Savoy, the archbishop of Canterbury and the queen's uncle, had held an ecclesiastical assembly in defiance of the king's explicit instructions. The king had justified the prohibition, as he would do in 1260, on the basis of the danger posed by the Welsh: he was at that time on campaign against them and required the prelates (who were tenants-in-chief of the crown, and thus owed military service) to join him. The archbishop, however, did

Simon continued in his answer to the king. When he came to London at Candlemas to hold the parliament, he said, 'There, at prime [the first hour of the day], came the justiciar, and told us, from the king, that we should hold no parliament until the king came, and that the king had sent to say he would be back within three weeks, and therefore the parliament was adjourned from day to day for three weeks.'

In other words, Simon professed to have followed the king's command. But this was not obvious to Henry. He challenged that while he was still in France he 'heard tell that you did not obey our commands, and did not observe the justiciar's prohibition, but held a parliament and sought allies'. The parliament might, technically, have been prorogued – but in reality those who had been summoned remained in London, where they presumably continued to discuss the business of the kingdom – in effect, a parliament was in operation. Henry had further cause for scepticism. Simon had come to the parliament, he charged, 'with horses and arms' – in other words, with his following, arrayed for war. If this were the case, Henry might well suspect that Simon was persisting with the parliament in order to muster barons, bishops and knights to oppose him.

'I did not come there with either horses or arms,' Simon answered, 'except in the manner that I usually go about the country.'

The king persisted. 'You gathered men to yourself,' he said, 'and made new alliances.'

'I did not gather any men to myself nor did I make any alliances against my fealty to the king or in any other way, save for the common undertaking.' As to the charge that he held the parliament

---

not regard the king's prohibition as binding. He consulted his prelates, asking them to consider 'whether it is right and proper and expedient for the prelates to discuss the business of the Church in a convocation of this sort or, rather, to submit to the prohibition of the king', given the pressing nature of the assembly's business (the defence of the Church's liberties from royal encroachment). They responded in the affirmative, and so the bishops and abbots met as planned. Of course, there were differences between the two cases, but both Boniface and Simon felt justified in defying their liege lord in favour of their other, sworn obligations, for the sake of the greater good of Church or kingdom (S. T. Ambler, *Bishops in the Political Community of England, 1213–1272* (Oxford, 2017), 114–15).

and sought allies, Simon said, 'Let the king or the justiciar say in what ways I disobeyed the king's commands and did not observe the justiciar's prohibition, and I will readily answer to it according to the law in parliament; and as for alliances, as I have said already.'

Henry would not let the issue drop. His land, he said, 'was greatly upset and troubled by reason of the earl's parliament and of his alliances.'

'As I have said before,' Simon replied, 'I held no parliament and made no alliance whereby your land should have been upset or troubled.'

*

During these early months of 1260, relations between the king (who remained in France) and the reformers had grown increasingly fractious. Henry wrote on 1 March to some of the leading men of the court, including Simon, noting that they had written to ask him to return. The king was 'greatly delighted by all of this . . . understanding clearly from this how completely your goodwill and the constant fidelity which you bear to us accords with your letters'. But he would be delayed further, he told them, by ongoing negotiations over the amount to be paid for the 500 knights under the terms of the Treaty of Paris. He asked that they advise him on this matter, 'which hitherto you have delayed in doing', and that they send him money for his expenses. 'We promise that, as soon as our business . . . has been settled, we intend to make our way back towards England.'[15]

Clearly, Simon and the other councillors were keen that Henry return and were unwilling to do anything (including sending funds) that might endorse his continuing delay. The danger was that the king, abroad, was now beyond their control. He was, moreover, at the French court, and it was Louis above all other potential allies who had the resources to help Henry recover his power, should he wish to do so. Simon and his comrades feared that Henry was assembling an army – just as Henry clearly feared of Simon. A few days later, on 6 March, Henry wrote again, and this time his letter dropped the pretence of affection. 'Since neither the earl of Norfolk . . . nor the others of the king's magnates have told the king anything about the state of his kingdom . . . whereat the king is really disgusted,' he ordered the earl of Norfolk do so without delay.[16] By the beginning of April, the situation had escalated further. Henry, presumably having failed to raise a response from the earl of Norfolk, targeted the earl of Gloucester, Richard de Clare. Richard had quarrelled with Simon, as we have seen, when the former had opposed the reforms enacted in 1259. By this point he had drifted from the path of hardline reform and towards the king's side. Henry wrote to him on 1 April: with the approval of the king of France, he informed him, 'we can find many knights and warriors willing to come with us into England'.

Henry had indeed been seeking to assemble an army. And he had already written to Hugh Bigod (whom he had clearly identified as malleable after the business of the Candlemas parliament) with orders to summon an English host to muster in London on 25 April.[17] Henry had prepared for Hugh a schedule listing those of his vassals to be summoned, comprising those he trusted for support and those who could be won over. The list included seven earls (excluding Simon, of course), and just three bishops and two abbots.*

The response of the reforming party was to muster its members, likewise, in London in April. They framed the gathering as a parliament but, if this assembly was much like that held after Candlemas, Simon and his allies probably came with an armed following.[18] There was now a real chance of civil war.

The prospect was only increased when, around this time, Henry heard a rumour that his own son, Edward, was plotting to depose him. This plan had apparently been made 'by the counsel of the barons and magnates of England', as the chronicler Thomas Wykes reports, 'with many of whom he had made confederations'. Edward,

---

* The chancellor, Walter de Merton, under instructions to 'keep the schedule as secret as you can', prepared the summonses and put them into the hands of messengers on 3 April. Despite the demand for secrecy, it is likely that Simon came to know of Henry's orders before long, for included in the list was at least one man who almost certainly never wavered in his support for Simon (despite Henry's evident suspicions to the contrary): Hugh Despenser (*Calendar of Patent Rolls, 1232–72*, 4 vols. (London, 1906–13), *1259–61*, 157–9). Several of those summoned were later recorded as Montfortian partisans, though it is not clear where their allegiance lay at this stage: Nicholas of Segrave, John de Burgh and Ralph de Camoys.

it was suggested, 'had begun to aspire to reigning at the cost of his father's deposition, so that if he [Henry] should come to England he would have him taken captive, to be detained in custody and as long as he should live', allowing Edward to take the crown.[19] The rumour, as the chronicler points out, was false – but it was made more credible by the truths woven through it. For Edward had allied with at least one of the baronial party: Simon, to whom he had sworn an oath guaranteeing his support in October of the previous year, as we have seen. Their alliance was probably still active, since Simon is recorded witnessing a charter of Edward in May, in the company of Walter de Cantilupe and Peter de Montfort.[20]

Henry was ready, then, to come to England with the army he had gathered. Simon tried to stop him. According to Henry's charges, Simon 'said to the justiciar that he should order the king that he should not bring with him an army of outsiders into England, that he should order the king that he would in no way allow the king to bring an army of outsiders into England, [and assured him] that if he did order the king in the manner that he had told him to' then Simon would support him come what may. Henry's allegations continued. He had written to the justiciar asking for money, but Simon had instructed the justiciar not to obey – more than this, 'he said to the justiciar that if he did send him money, he would have to pay it back himself'. Perhaps it was the justiciar, Hugh Bigod, who had also passed on to the king Simon's next comment. 'You said,' Henry charged Simon, 'that you were thinking of giving such a welcome to the army that would come with me from overseas that others would have no mind to come after them.'

'I said many words for your honour and for your profit,' Simon responded, 'to dissuade you from bringing such a following, for I knew well that it would not profit you at all, but would be damaging and against your honour and that of the whole land, for it seemed that you put your trust more in strangers than in the people of your own land, and if I spoke in this way, I would not have spoken except for your profit and for your honour, and no harm ever came of it.'

Henry might well have been disturbed by Simon's threats: as far as knew, he would be facing an army led by Simon and his own son, Edward, intent on fighting for his overthrow. The situation was eased by the decisive intervention of Henry's brother, Richard of Cornwall. He met Simon and the other barons in London, together with Edward, and persuaded them to issue letters assuring Henry that they had no designs on his crown. Henry accepted their assurances, and crossed the Channel around 23 April 1260. He still came, however, with his army: a force of 200 or 300 knights and their followings. He moved on London, and took up residence in the bishop of London's palace at St Paul's; Simon, meanwhile, remained outside the city, staying at the Hospitallers' headquarters at Clerkenwell with Edward.[21]

*

Simon's position had already begun to weaken, with the justiciar and the earl of Gloucester siding with the king. In early May Edward joined them, declaring publicly that he had never plotted against his father and submitting himself to Henry's judgement. Simon was now exposed. Henry determined to hold him to account by putting him on trial. He wanted to begin proceedings immediately, in May, but was persuaded to delay until July, when a parliament would be held.[22]

Simon would take all measures to protect himself. On 4 July his friend Eudes Rigaud, the archbishop of Rouen, landed at Dover. He came, as his own records note, 'on the business of the lord king of France'. His job was to support Simon during the trial.* Probably Simon had written to Louis and Eudes when he learned of Henry's plans – perhaps to help him mount his defence but also to add the moral force of the king of France's good opinion to his cause, and to use the presence of Eudes to ward off any attempt by Henry to subject Simon to the sort of irregular procedures employed in the Gascony inquiry of 1252.

---

* Eudes's role in defending Simon is set out in the Pershore Chronicle and substantiated by the fact that the archbishop, while in London, made a grant of a church living to Simon's son, Amaury (who was now seventeen or eighteen); Simon also made a grant to the archbishop (F. M. Powicke, 'The archbishop of Rouen, John de Harcourt, and Simon de Montfort in 1260', *English Historical Review*, 51 (1936), 108–13, at 108; J. R. Maddicott, *Simon de Montfort* (Cambridge, 1994), 198–9).

Simon's measures were successful. It was arranged that Henry would issue Simon with a schedule of accusations. Meanwhile, a committee was set up to conduct a 'diligent inquiry', taking sworn testimony from 'good and law-worthy men, through whom the truth of the matter can be better investigated'. The establishment of the committee was agreed by Henry, so the official record notes, 'at the instance of his magnates' and 'insistently requested' by Simon. It was perhaps Simon, too, or Eudes, who had suggested the committee's composition. It would be staffed by bishops, thereby taking the power of judgement from a baronial cohort that was now divided. Two were chosen by Simon (his good friends Walter de Cantilupe of Worcester and Richard Gravesend of Lincoln), two by Henry (Norwich and Exeter, his supporters) and two who had sympathies with both sides, the archbishop of Canterbury and the bishop of London.[23]

As part of their investigations, the episcopal committee listened while Henry put his accusations to Simon in full, viva voce, and Simon responded (it is the record of this exchange that we have heard throughout this chapter).[24] This was a format that played to Simon's strengths and Henry's weaknesses: reading the transcript of this exchange today, one gets a strong sense of Simon's ability to outpace Henry intellectually and, indeed, of Simon's frustration as Henry lagged behind – a frustration that emerged in his withering replies. This was also the impression created at the time. The annalist at work in Dunstable Priory reported the investigation; since he was sympathetic to Simon it is not surprising that his account is favourable to the earl, but the particular way in which he framed the episode is telling: Simon 'supported by the help of God, thus responded to all articles either through official writings or through living reason [i.e. viva voce], so that [his opponents] were struck dumb'.[25]

It is not clear whether the committee ever made a report by the appointed date of 15 July, but by 20 July the attention of the parliament was distracted by news that Builth Castle had been taken by the Welsh. The trial was postponed, in the event indefinitely.[26] Simon was then free to turn his attention, in August 1260, to the securing of his family territory of Bigorre, in the Pyrenees, which was now under threat from Gaston de Béarn. Simon called upon

Edward for support, who as lord of Gascony was well placed to act. Simon then disappears from our records until October, when he returned to the royal court for the Michaelmas parliament.[27]

Simon's position was still precarious, and he proceeded carefully.[*] This time he was willing to compromise, in order to achieve his ultimate goal: to ensure that the reforming party held the heart of government. Here he scored a great victory, first in securing his own return to court and obstructing the king's attempt to restart his trial, and second in winning the appointment of Hugh Despenser, his long-standing friend and ally, as justiciar in replacement of Hugh Bigod.[28] In order to achieve this, he was forced to make concessions to the earl of Gloucester. In particular, Simon had to draw back from some of the reforms that managed the barons' treatment of their tenants: the ease by which tenants could make complaints was diminished, and the barons themselves (rather than the justiciar) were now to address grievances made against them. It was a compromise that must have been discomforting, but it was essential if Simon were to achieve anything at all.

*

Simon had stitched the reforming movement back together, but within weeks it began to unravel. Crucially, Henry was joined almost immediately by his brother, Richard of Cornwall, and the queen's uncle, Peter of Savoy – both experienced and astute politicians who could aid Henry in planning his return to power. They were helped when Simon had to leave the court, probably in early December 1260, in order to travel to France in support of Eleanor, who had initiated a case against the Lusignans, her half-brothers, for her stake in their mother's lands in France.[†] In Simon's absence, Henry's

---

[*] For what follows, on Simon's return, see: Maddicott, *Simon de Montfort*, 201–3. The discomfort these compromises must have caused was perhaps lessened by Hugh Despenser's holding of his own investigations into magnate malpractice in Sussex at the turn of the year, though this was some way from the scale of investigations that had been expected.

[†] Around the turn of 1261 Simon had sought to forestall Henry's moves against him by seeking the intervention of the king of France, and Henry agreed on 11 January to an arbitration (Maddicott, *Simon de Montfort*, 205–6).

party began to cultivate his friends and allies, granting gifts of robes (an important symbolic act of patronage) to several in December, including Hugh Despenser.[29]

Simon returned from France by the end of February 1261. By this point Henry and his party had withdrawn behind the walls of the Tower of London, where they summoned a parliament.[30] When Simon joined the assembly he faced a renewed attack from the king, who had been marshalling his grievances against both Simon personally and against the council. Neither side was strong enough to move decisively against the other; by mid-March, both had agreed to arbitration: Henry and Simon would put their personal quarrels to the king of France, while the king's grievances against the council would be examined by a panel of six or seven arbiters.[31]

The latter arbitration took place in the final week of April. By this point, Henry had been persuaded to adopt a less hostile tone and drop the most antagonistic complaints, including a couple against Simon (for instance, that Simon had appointed a deputy to represent him at the opening of the Michaelmas parliament in October without waiting for a royal summons). The exchange between Henry and the council, recorded for the arbitration, is extensive.[32] Henry accused the council of mismanaging the kingdom, of failing to provide justice to his subjects, of failing to rebuild royal revenues, and failing to advance the Sicilian Business, to his financial loss. The council dealt with each matter in turn and did so adroitly – in many cases inviting Henry to provide hard evidence of his accusations, in others pointing to the famine as the cause of difficulty in rebuilding royal revenues, and in the matter of the Sicilian Business supplying a contemptuous response ('it is not by our counsel that you bound yourself to the papacy in the Sicilian affair, and it would be a splendid thing to our minds if you would take this problem to those who had induced you to make such a bad bargain'). One theme in particular emerges: the council's subjugation of the king.

'No argument which I put forward can prevail,' Henry complained. 'The councillors reply "We wish it to be thus", without giving any further reason.'

'It is indeed right,' replied the council, 'that when the king talks sense he should have his way more than any other person.'

'Again,' Henry continued, 'when I agreed to accept your counsel I did not make myself your ward, nor did I agree that you should give orders; and if what I say is better, then my proposal should stand, and you should not take action before I have agreed.'

'We have no intention of treating our lord as ward, and we do not wish that you should be so,' the council responded, 'and it is right and reasonable that whenever you talk sense you should be heard and listened to as the lord of us all.'

'You hold your business meetings and discussions,' Henry complained, 'in various places without informing me, and you do not ask for me at your meetings any more than you ask the humblest subject in the realm, although I am the head of the council.'

'We meet frequently in places where we think that we will be less disturbed and away from the bustle,' answered the council, 'so as to be able to attend all the better to your business, and then, when we have discussed matters, we ask you for your assent and goodwill, as is due to our lord and to our head, but we do nothing on your sole word.'

The exchange reveals the council's attitude towards its subjugation of the king as unabashed. Henry appears faintly ridiculous, comparing himself to a ward (an underage heir under guardianship) and the 'humblest subject of the realm', and opening himself up to the remark that his opinion was hardly worth hearing. In its tone the exchange is reminiscent of Simon's trial of the previous year, in which the earl ran rings around the king. And, indeed, the caustic – and sometimes sneering – replies given by the council here have a familiar air: could it have been Simon who was tasked with responding to the king?

Henry's strategy in entering this arbitration was, however, not the clumsy move it first appears. In January 1261, with Simon still absent abroad, the king had taken advantage of his freedom to dispatch a trusted follower to Rome.[33] The messenger was to reveal to the pope what had been happening in England for the past year and more. The pope held major powers that could help Henry here: the right to release a person from their oath or pronounce an oath invalid. An oath was a promise made before God, sworn upon the Gospels or a relic, that staked the soul of the one who swore it. Henry had sworn to support the Provisions of Oxford, as had the barons, and these oaths were the moral glue that held together the programme of reform, binding all in a sacred obligation.[34] As we have seen, the oath was an authority to which Simon had already appealed, in his argument with the earl of Gloucester in 1259. The difficulty was that, according to Church law, an oath extracted under duress could not be valid, and Henry had not been a free agent when he had supplied his oath in 1258: Simon and his confederates had marched on the king's hall and pressured him into submission. Henry was now in a position to inform the pope that this was the case, and remove an important moral weapon from the hands of the barons. The arbitration process was nothing more than a play for time, as Henry's party awaited the return of papal letters quashing the Provisions of Oxford. In preparation, in May the king secured the Channel coast and succeeded in depriving Simon of a major ally, winning over Edward by paying off his debts.[35]

When the messenger arrived, the news for the king was positive. Pope Alexander IV, armed with the new information about events in England, issued letters in Henry's favour over the course of April and May 1261: certain magnates and prelates, he now understood, had established the Provisions of Oxford 'under the pretext of reforming the state of the realm' but in reality to undermine the power of the king, and the oaths taken by the royal family in support of this programme had been taken 'by a kind of compulsion'. The Provisions of Oxford were declared invalid.[36] Henry published the papal letters in his great hall at Winchester on 12 June, the feast of Whitsun. This was one of the three feast days during the year (the others being Easter and Christmas) when the kings of England traditionally summoned their men for assembly and wore their crown to demonstrate their majesty, hosting a celebratory feast.[37] There could be no more fitting moment for the proclamation of the papal bulls restoring the king to his regal status.

*

But Henry had overplayed his hand. In rejecting the Provisions entirely, he provoked his magnates to unite against him. Simon was now joined by the earls of Gloucester, Warenne and Norfolk, Norfolk's brother (the failed justiciar Hugh Bigod) and Simon's friend Hugh Despenser, whom Henry had ousted from the office of justiciar during the Winchester gathering. The king, hearing of their plan to take up arms against him, withdrew speedily to London, back to the safety of the Tower.[38]

Both the barons and the king now made moves to secure support at home and abroad. In England, both attempted to control the shires: Henry replaced the sheriffs appointed by the barons with his own candidates, while Simon and his allies set up 'keepers of the counties' to oppose them.* Over the summer, Henry dispatched calls for aid to his queen's contacts on the Continent, while Simon probably went to France himself, perhaps to raise armed support and persuade Louis to endorse his cause. He also made contact with an English clerk at the papal court in an attempt to have the quashing of the Provisions overturned.[39] It was an opportune time, for Alexander IV had died in May; his successor, Urban IV, would not be elected until September: the interregnum would bring bureaucratic disarray and the new pope would be unfamiliar with the case. Meanwhile, some attempt was made to pursue a peaceful solution by diplomatic means, through arbitration, but nothing came of it.[40]

Both sides readied now for war. In early September Simon, together with Walter de Cantilupe and the earl of Gloucester, summoned a parliament (the Michaelmas parliament demanded by the Provisions). According to their instructions, three knights from each county were to gather at St Albans to discuss the business of the kingdom. The summons was a direct challenge to royal authority, declaring that a parliament could meet with no reference to the king and against his wishes. Henry countered by instructing his sheriffs to block the knights' progress to St Albans and send them instead to Windsor. Henry's swift action was successful and, maintaining his momentum, he now set to mustering an army,

---

* The situation became ugly in at least one instance, when the keeper of Gloucestershire who had been installed by the earl of Gloucester was set upon while holding a session of the shire court: the royally appointed sheriff (Matthias Bezill, the queen's steward) hauled him from his dais and slung him into the street, before dragging him off to prison (*The Metrical Chronicle of Robert of Gloucester*, ed. W. A. Wright, 2 vols. (London, 1885), II, 736–7; *Calendar of Patent Rolls, 1232–72*, 4 vols. (London, 1906–13), *1258–66*, 220).

summoning the feudal host to gather in London on 29 October, with instructions sent to his foreign troops to land the following week. The massing of troops was designed to intimidate his opposition: the baronial party was given safe conduct to come unarmed to Kingston on the same day, 29 October, to discuss terms.[41] Henry's tactic worked: the earl of Gloucester, confronted with the prospect of going against the king in arms and shaken by the size of Henry's force, backed down. Other key members of the baronial party followed him – including Walter de Cantilupe and Peter de Montfort, who now entered negotiations.

The resulting Treaty of Kingston (agreed on 21 November and ratified on 9 December) represented a dismal failure for the reforming enterprise. Its terms established a panel comprising royalists and reformers to adjudicate on the terms of the Provisions, but in the case of disagreement it was the king's brother, Richard of Cornwall, who was to rule: the proposed arbitration was nothing more than a means for the baronial party to save face in their submission.[42]

*

Simon, in the words of one chronicler, was 'disgusted' – not at the king's victory but at the capitulation of his friends and allies, especially the earl of Gloucester.[43] As in their argument of 1259, when Richard de Clare had refused to support the reforms that threatened baronial power, Simon summoned the shade of his father, comparing a willingness to hold true and suffer the consequence to an easy surrender. The annalist of Dunstable, writing quite close to the time, was perhaps picking up on Simon's presentation of events when he reported that:

> Amidst these goings on, the earl of Gloucester as good as apostatized, withdrawing from the counsel of Simon de Montfort and the other magnates, with whom he had sworn an oath of confederation, for the conservation of the good laws of the land; with these entirely abandoned, he consented to the will of the king. Upon hearing this, Simon de Montfort left England, saying that he would rather die without land, than withdraw from the truth as a perjurer.[44]

Simon was to remain in France for the greater part of 1262. In self-imposed exile from the English court, he once again sought to bolster his position by cultivating his friendship with the French king. In January he and Eleanor are recorded as Louis's guests at Pacy-sur-Eure, in Normandy. There they formally submitted their quarrel with Henry to the arbitration of Queen Marguerite. Henry agreed to comply, and set out to build a forceful case that would undermine Simon's credibility.[45] Although the records of the king's case have been lost, Simon's testimony – apparently dictated in response to Henry's accusations – was preserved in his family archive and survives today.[46] It reveals how the two men now tore open the wounds of their long dispute, reaching back to Simon's arrival on English shores: 'our lord the king' said Simon, 'says that he did me a great goodness when he took me as his man, because I was not the eldest'. Simon goes on to describe their first meeting and Henry's turning down of his request for his Leicester inheritance, the support he received subsequently from the earl of Chester, and how Henry's father, King John, had taken the lands in question 'from my father, without judgement . . . but by his will', lands which Simon had found, when he received them, to have suffered greatly at the hands of the king's men. 'All these things I point out,' said Simon, 'so that it is known what sort of goodness my lord the king did for me in these things.'

Simon's account then moves on to their dispute about the money Simon had borrowed from the count of Flanders, and the public row at the queen's churching in 1239, when Henry, Simon recalled, 'spoke insulting and shameful words to me that are painful to recall' and would have had him consigned to the Tower had not the earl of Cornwall intervened. Simon and Eleanor, seeing the 'great anger' of the king 'and that he did not want to hear reason', had then fled, while Henry had extracted the debt forcibly from Simon's lands and caused great damage, even though Simon was a sworn crusader about to depart for Outremer, compelling Simon to sell his forests to raise funds for his expedition. Three years afterwards, upon his return from Outremer, Simon had met with Henry in Poitou, and Henry had admitted to the 'great damage' he had done to Simon's lands and entreated him to stay. Later, Henry had granted Eleanor some funds as her marriage portion, but only (as Simon stressed) because the queen's mother, the countess of Provence, had berated Henry for failing to provide adequately for Eleanor in the first place.

A large part of Henry's case seems to have dwelt on Simon's government of Gascony and the subsequent dispute about damages (Henry had brought Gaillard del Soler with him to the French court to help build his case).[47] Simon responded in kind. The king and queen had entreated him to go to Gascony in order to subdue the land to their power, and guaranteed his government there for seven years, but then the people of Gascony had come to England to complain about him; Simon had asked for proper legal procedure to be followed, 'but the king, either by his will or by the counsel of another, did not wish at all to do so' and instead asked that he relinquish the governorship of Gascony. This, Simon believed, was highly irregular, 'for the king his lord had bailed it to him for a fixed term, and he, according to the great request that the king and the queen had made of him' had agreed and sworn in good faith to those terms; the validity of the first agreement was clear 'to all people, except to the king and to those of his counsel, clearly against reason'. But Simon, 'seeing that the king his lord was firm in this wish' did not want to oppose him, and accepted the offer of 7,000 marks offered by the king in compensation. But still Simon's obedience to Henry, his lord, had cost him dear, and Simon demanded proper compensation. 'If the king wishes to dwell on the affairs of Gascony', Simon finished, he could 'easily respond' with reference to the facts.

As with the Gascony inquiry of 1252 and Simon's trial of 1260, these proceedings ended prematurely – this time because, in September, Henry's court was hit by an epidemic. Several *curiales* died, and in October Henry himself was taken seriously ill.[48] Whatever Queen Marguerite might have decided, the arbitration had only served to encourage brooding resentments. Henry wrote home on 8 October to announce that the arbitration had failed, and to warn that Simon was planning to 'return to England to sow dissension between king and people'.[49]

Henry was right in his suspicions. Simon landed at Romney in Kent on 12 October, and the next day was in London for the Michaelmas parliament. This was a lightning incursion: the visit was recorded by only a single chronicler, who, from his post in

Kent, was well positioned to notice Simon's arrival despite the fact that it was made 'secretly'. Simon did not have the strength to go against the king, but he could do his best to disrupt Henry's return to power. He had procured letters from the pope confirming the Provisions, which he proceeded to publish at the parliament.[50] The letters were seemingly obtained by claiming Henry's authority at the papal court in the bureaucratic confusion that accompanied the papal succession. With the letters detonated, Simon returned to the coast at Shoreham, Sussex, to take ship for France.

*

As 1262 drew to its end, Henry's return to power was under threat, though not as a result of Simon's actions at the Michaelmas parliament. In late November a Welsh revolt erupted, spreading through the Marches as Welsh tenants took up arms. This should not have been allowed to happen. The Welsh March was a frontier zone between the English kingdom and the land of Wales, a land that English rulers in turns looked to subdue or subject to their authority. The kings of England relied upon the barons of the March both to defend the kingdom from Welsh incursions and to provide a secure base from which assaults could be launched on Wales. In order to fulfil their role the marcher barons needed to dominate the borderlands. To this end they held powers that in England were the prerogative of the king: the right to exercise justice, to build castles and to make war. They were expected to be hard, ruthless and effective. But the marcher barons were not currently of a mind to help the king. For Henry and his queen, as part of their strategy for reclaiming power, had extracted their son Edward from the friendship he had been building with the marchers, believing that these men were a bad influence.[51] The marchers were not pleased to be cut off from their friend and patron. A rumour now circulated that they had allied with the Welsh – in reality they might not have gone so far but, in their discontent, they had effectively gone on strike.[52]

The situation was worsened for Henry by his handling of the greatest of the marcher lordships: the earldom of Gloucester. Richard de Clare had died in July 1262; his son, Gilbert, was almost nineteen when his father died – strictly speaking not of an age to take possession of his father's estates, but this technicality could be waived as long as an heir was mature enough to be considered an adult.* Gilbert, accordingly, had come to France to ask the king for his inheritance – but Henry refused, thinking of the income that could be drawn from the valuable Gloucester estates while Gilbert remained in wardship. The result was Gilbert's alienation from the king and the loss of a supporter who might, when the revolt erupted, have helped to bring the marchers to heel.

Henry attempted to take a grip. Still in poor health, he returned to England in December and, in January 1263, reissued the Provisions of Westminster. This extensive set of legal reforms had been issued by the barons in October 1259 and, concerned as they were with improving the situation of ordinary men and women, had been very popular. Henry now appropriated them in an attempt to bolster his popularity.[53] But it had little impact, as the marchers moved to stir revolt across the country, attacking royal manors far and wide. Meanwhile Henry's sickness lingered, and a rumour even spread that he was dead; another rumour told that his brother, Richard, earl of Cornwall, was seeking to displace Edward and succeed Henry himself.[54] Henry's authority was collapsing around him.

It is in contexts such as these – of chaos and crisis, and a vacuum of effective power – that a new sort of leader can rise.

---

* Henry himself had taken full possession of his kingdom at the age of nineteen, without formally being declared 'of age' (D. A. Carpenter, *The Minority of Henry III* (London, 1990), 123–4).

12

Revolution

The period that followed the sealing of the Treaty of Paris in December 1259 had been turbulent: power had been snatched back and forth between king and reformers, and Simon's position, after three years of struggle, was precarious. But all this would change. In the spring of 1263 the marcher barons, seeking to raise their pressure on the royal family, asked Simon to return to England.[1]

Simon had always been central to the cause of the Provisions, prominent at the parliaments of 1258 that had seen Henry's power seized and driver of the hard-line reform of baronial as well as royal lordship in 1259. He alone had stood his ground at the end of 1261, declaring himself willing to die in poverty rather than abandon his commitment. His unremitting stand made him the one to lead a new campaign. And his character, as the marcher barons recognized, equipped him for the task: time and again he had shown himself unflinching in facing off against the king, displaying what his friend Adam Marsh had affectionately termed his 'generous nature to speak openly, freely, and boldly the thoughts in the heart, without distinction of persons'. The marchers also must have seen in Simon the quality that others had seen before: his innate ability to lead. This was the third occasion – after the invitations issued by the nobles of Jerusalem in 1241 and of France in 1253 – on which Simon was called upon to take command by those who wished to follow him.

Simon arrived on 25 April 1263. What happened next is recorded by the annalist of Dunstable Priory.[2] Simon gathered a 'parliament' at Oxford, without the knowledge of the king and his counsellors.

The annalist noted that with Simon were Gilbert de Clare, the young earl of Gloucester, and (surprisingly) Richard of Cornwall, the king's brother, as well as 'many other of the barons'. They agreed that 'all coming against the statutes of Oxford should be held as capital enemies'. This was, writes the annalist, a renewal of the oath first given at the Oxford parliament of 1258: an oath of mutual aid, the forming of a militant confederation.[3] With the oath sworn and publicly declared, Simon and his confederates sent to the king to ask whether he would now support the Provisions. Henry refused. Simon now had licence to take up arms: 'the earl', records the annalist, 'gathered an innumerable army'. He also made an alliance with the Welsh, exploiting their antipathy towards the English crown. Meanwhile, in May, the king ordered those tenants-in-chief who had not joined with Simon to assemble at Worcester: their stated intention was to march on Wales, but the muster would serve to prove Henry's strength.[4]

Simon countered at the beginning of June by launching a series of assaults on Henry's supporters. The first blow was struck against Peter d'Aigueblanche, bishop of Hereford.[5] Peter was the architect of the hated Sicilian Business, and represented Henry's clique of malign counsellors. On Simon's orders, the marcher barons rode into Hereford Cathedral. They seized the bishop and dragged him fifteen miles to Eardisley Castle, where they held him captive for twelve weeks.[6] As the summer of 1263 wore on, the moves against Henry's men continued. The bishop of Norwich, who had helped to publish the papal letters annulling the Provisions of Oxford in 1261, was forced to flee his cathedral in the face of the onslaught. The property and men of Boniface of Savoy were also targeted, since he too had complied with the papal orders.[7]

These were concerted strikes, but they rode upon a tide of violence that, inevitably, brought suffering to the wider populace. The canons of Barnwell Priory kept a record of their plight, in their *Liber Memorandorum*; the incidents they recount cannot be precisely dated, but are indicative of sufferings endured in a country in conflict. The *Liber* tells of the plundering of vills and manors, the kidnapping and killing of local people, the acts of arson. Simon's men, on one occasion, came to the prior's manor of Brunne and torched his grain store. And they intruded themselves upon the prior's hospitality, every day eating and drinking in Barnwell's hall. The canons, helpless, put on a brave face, keeping them unhappy company. One day at dawn, the leader of the intruders, one Philip le Champion, woke the prior from his bed, demanding Barnwell's entire store of victuals. Friends of the prior then arrived to tell Philip that, 'by God's wounds', he would not do this; swords were drawn and bloodshed only just averted. At another time, John de Burgh, one of Simon's lieutenants, demanded from the prior a horse for carrying his armour. With the priory's stocks depleted by the depredations, only an aged nag could be found. The response of John's men was pettily unpleasant: laughing loudly they circled round the horse, mocking it, examining its teeth, stroking it, dragging the poor creature by its tail and poking it with sticks, threatening to flay or burn it. Having returned the nag, John dispatched one of his knights, with a band of men, to harass the prior. The gang greeted the prior rudely and ordered that he deliver immediately to their lord a palfrey as a gift. The prior, duly cowed, now brought John a worthy horse.[8]

The sufferings described at Barnwell doubtless stand for those of many more who could not write their stories, for churchmen were not the only victims of the violence (just the ones keeping written records).[9] But that churchmen were victimized at all was shocking, for they were an unarmed status group and could not defend themselves. This is why it was forbidden by Church law to raise a hand against any member of the clergy and such a crime incurred automatic excommunication, meaning banishment from the Church and denial of the sacraments. Accordingly, England's senior churchmen were obliged to act against the perpetrators. The archbishop of Canterbury, Boniface of Savoy, was abroad (he had left for the papal court the previous autumn and been prevented from returning by the outbreak of violence), but wrote in anger in October 1263 to his suffragans, ordering them to move against the malefactors.[10] Having received full reports of the despoliations, Boniface could supply the names of those responsible: young Henry and Simon de Montfort were at the top of his list, followed by Roger of Leybourne and marchers such as Roger de Clifford (in whose castle the bishop of Hereford had been imprisoned), along with twenty other named individuals. 'And with bitterness of heart',

Boniface continued, 'we report that the lord Simon de Montfort, earl of Leicester, supplied his authority and assent in the aforesaid [crimes].'

For one cohort of Simon's supporters, this made for a jarring choice. Walter de Cantilupe, bishop of Worcester, was one of Simon's oldest and closest friends, and had worked for the baronial cause since the beginning, as had Richard Gravesend of Lincoln. Now, in 1263, four further bishops joined them. Here Simon enjoyed a mighty stroke of luck, for four vacancies had opened on the episcopal bench that were filled by men who chose to follow him: John Gervase, bishop of Winchester, and Stephen of Bersted, bishop of Chichester, were elected to office in 1262; Henry of Sandwich, bishop of London, and Walter de la Wyle, bishop of Salisbury, in 1263. Neither the king nor Simon had any part in their appointments: all were strong candidates and all elected or appointed without influence.[11] Their endorsement encouraged the support of a host of lesser churchmen, who preached the virtue of the reforming enterprise and so helped to garner the good opinion of women and men across the land.* But the attacks on Church persons and property, and the archbishop's instruction to excommunicate the culprits, placed these supporters in an invidious position – one that the Montfortian bishops could resolve only by evading the archbishop's orders.†

---

* Already, in 1260, the king's minister John Mansel had written to Henry to advise him that 'if only the lord king had preachers working on his behalf of the sort the opposition have, it would be better for him'. When Henry returned to power in 1262, he had felt it necessary to order the arrest of anyone who 'presumes to persuade the people or preaches against us and our honour'. Such activities were more important now, in the summer of 1263, than ever. In June, a royal supporter wrote to the king from the north of England reporting that preachers were at work and winning followers for the reforming cause (W. W. Shirley (ed.), *Royal and Other Historical Letters Illustrative of the Reign of Henry III*, 2 vols. (London, 1862–6), II, 158; P. Chaplais (ed.), *Diplomatic Documents Preserved in the Public Record Office, vol. I: 1101–1272* (London, 1964), no. 387; H. R. Luard (ed.), *Flores Historiarum*, 3 vols. (London, 1890), III, 266; *Close Rolls, 1231–72*, 14 vols. (London, 1905–38) (hereafter *CR*), 1261–4, 123).

† Simon's friends amongst the bishops eventually responded to their orders, in January 1264. They decided to evade the order to excommunicate Simon and his allies and, instead, promised the archbishop that they would do everything they could to protect the see of Canterbury from attack, and assured him that anyone found guilty by due

Meanwhile, Simon was careful to declare himself faithful to the king and avoid a direct confrontation.* In a letter of 30 June, Richard of Cornwall wrote to tell the king how, the previous day, he had sent to Simon (who was then at Reading) to request a meeting for the purpose of discussing peace: Simon had replied 'that he was not in any way able' to meet Richard, and could not change his plans. Instead, Simon broke camp the morning of 30 June and moved to Guildford and (as Richard had heard) intended to travel on to Reigate the following day.†

Simon's immediate objective was to secure the aid of the Cinque Ports, whose citizens could obstruct the landing of any foreign troops brought in by Henry. He reached Romney by 9 July where, according to a Kentish chronicler, he was successful in stirring the citizens to resist any foreigners who might 'presume to invade the English land'. The citizens swore, moreover, 'that they wished to die and live with him', if it came to that.[12] Simon then moved on to Canterbury on 12 July, to consult with some of his episcopal supporters, before heading to Dover.[13]

For the time being, Simon avoided London. He had sent letters to the Londoners in the third week of June, asking them to say 'whether they wished to observe the said ordinances and statutes, made to the honour of God, to the faith of the lord king, and to the utility of the whole kingdom, or whether they wished to adhere instead to those who wished to infringe them'.[14] In his goal of gaining their support, Simon was helped by a misguided move on

---

process in an assembly of the Canterbury bishops would be duly punished (in other words, they would not act simply upon the information supplied by their archbishop) (L. E. Wilshire, *Boniface of Savoy, Carthusian and Archbishop of Canterbury, 1207–1270* (Salzburg, 1977), 90).

* As the Montfortians put their own candidates in charge of castles seized from the king and his supporters, they reportedly 'caused all of them to swear fidelity to the lord king, and always they carried before them the banner of the lord king' (*De Antiquis Legibus Liber. Cronica Maiorum et Vicecomitum Londoniarum*, ed. T. Stapleton (London, 1846), 53).

† Richard dispatched the invitation on 29 June from his manor of Cippenham (Buckinghamshire), proposing a meeting at Loddon Bridge (Berkshire) (Shirley (ed.), *Royal Letters of Henry III*, II, no. 605). I am grateful to Adrian Jobson for his guidance on Richard of Cornwall's activities here.

Edward's part. On 29 June, Edward visited the New Temple in London. He was in desperate need of money to pay his men, and decided to target the treasure store of cash and valuables deposited by England's nobles with the Templars for safe-keeping. Telling the Templars that he wanted admittance in order to view his mother's jewels, Edward entered and, his men producing hammers brought for the purpose, began to break open the strongboxes. They made off with around £1,000.[15]

This was an egregious crime, and the citizens of London rose up in revolt against it – and agreed to offer their support to Simon.[16] Henry, shut in the Tower of London in the midst of a rioting populace, was now in a dire position. He was forced to contemplate terms.

*

On 15 July Simon and his comrades rode into the capital, where they were (according to the Dunstable annalist) 'received honourably and with the greatest joy by the citizens'.[17] Simon met with Henry and demanded that he surrender Dover Castle to the barons. Meanwhile Hugh Despenser was restored to the office of justiciar and took custody of the Tower, while other royal castles were occupied by various Montfort supporters. All that was left, on 24 July, was for Simon to move on Windsor and force Edward to yield.[18]

Simon had established the reform regime anew: Henry had been forced to issue a proclamation, on 16 July, giving notice of his agreement to observe the Provisions of Oxford. It also noted the king's agreement to a new demand: 'that the realm of England should in future be governed by native-born men, faithful and useful under us, and that aliens must depart, never to return, save those whose stay the faithful men of the realm will in common accept'.[19] The demand capitalized on growing resentment against the queen's Savoyard faction as well as the Lusignans, and concerns about Henry and Edward's use of foreign mercenaries. It also offered some satisfaction to Edward's former friends, such as Roger of Leybourne, who had been ousted by the queen, and whose animosity towards those they blamed – many of them foreign counsellors – had been unleashed in the depredations of the summer. The decree would thus win Simon political capital with a key faction of his supporters. In stirring wider suspicion of foreigners, it would also establish a core element of Montfortian propaganda, which would surface again in the coming year. The more extreme of its demands, however – the expulsion of all foreigners from England – was to be explicitly and publicly revoked before long, for it was undesirable as well as unworkable. The central objective, here as throughout Simon's programme, was the control of appointments, ensuring that only 'faithful and useful men' found a place in government, whether they were English by birth or, as in Simon's case, by loyalty and acclamation.

Despite Simon's success in securing the king's submission, he soon discovered that the new regime stood on shaky ground, for Henry had got word to the king of France. Louis responded by summoning Henry – together with Queen Eleanor, Edward, and Simon – to appear before him. Simon could not allow the royal party to leave the kingdom and sent others in their place, but Louis was not impressed.[20] Eventually, around 23 September, he travelled with them to meet Louis at Boulogne, where he reminded the king of France that he held no jurisdiction over English subjects. Louis was forced to concede the point, and Simon and Henry returned home.[21]

Back in England, Simon soon faced further problems. A parliament was scheduled for October, charged with considering the despoliations of the summer.* The meeting was marked by a rancorous atmosphere, with many of the Londoners, as well as Simon's Welsh allies, arriving armed. During the assembly, Henry, Edward and others of their party demanded that those guilty of the summer's violence be brought to justice. This Simon could not allow, given how many of his party, including his own sons, had been involved.

Edward slipped away from this meeting, giving out the line that he was off to visit his wife, and established himself at Windsor Castle. The next morning he was followed by his father. Simon and his men set themselves in the Tower of London and closed the city's

---

* This followed a first attempt to set in train the restitution of property after the despoliations, in a parliament held before Simon left for France, at St Paul's around 9 September (J. R. Maddicott, *Simon de Montfort* (Cambridge, 1994), 242–3).

gates, but soon their supporters began to desert in droves: the earl
Warenne, Henry of Almain (eldest son of Richard of Cornwall, who,
unlike his father, had hitherto supported Simon), the earl of Norfolk
and his brother Hugh Bigod and – crucially – the marchers, who
had been won round by Edward with offers of land. Simon was left
with only a clutch of faithful men. With London no longer secure,
he withdrew to his fortress of Kenilworth.[22]

Simon's response to the desertions is revealed by an important
source, the account of the St Albans monk William Rishanger (who
was writing later, in 1312, but was able to interview surviving members
of Simon's inner circle).[23] It tells how Henry of Almain, poised to
desert, made an approach to Simon. He requested that the earl 'not
harbour ill feelings', and offered him an explanation: 'against my
father . . . and my uncle the king of England, and my relations, I
cannot make further war: I withdraw under your licence. But I will
never bear arms against you.'

Simon responded (recounts the chronicler) *hillariter*, with a light
heart. 'Lord Henry, in my heart I held your character as trusted,
not on account of your arms, but because I hoped for special
constancy from you. Go, and withdraw with your arms; I do not
fear them.'

With this he turned to his closest men and said, 'I have been in
many lands and provinces of diverse peoples, pagans as well as
Christians: but in no peoples have I found such infidelity and deceit
as I have now experienced in England." Simon, now as ever, was
turning to the exemplar of his father, holding true to his oath as
the faithless fell away.

Meanwhile, Henry moved to secure his position, summoning in
mid-October an army of his faithful men to Windsor (while offering
assurances that he did not wish to undermine the Provisions of
Oxford).[24] This did not bode well for Simon: he had the support
of only a small band of barons and knights, while Henry's side had

---

* And then he added (the chronicler continues), that 'even if all men together turn
from me, I will stand fast, with my four sons, for the just cause which I have once
sworn to hold, to the honour of the Church and utility of the kingdom, nor will I
tremble to endure battle' (*The Chronicle of William de Rishanger of the Barons' War*, ed.
J. O. Halliwell (London, 1840), 17–18).

been bolstered by the defections. Simon was forced to seek a truce, sending a party of bishops to meet the king. The truce was agreed, together with a plan to submit the various issues to Louis IX for arbitration.[25]

Simon had for the time being avoided open war, but Henry's side was growing in strength. The king took his force to Winchester, taking custody of the city's castle from Simon's man.[26] He then, at the beginning of December, dispatched the marcher baron Roger Mortimer to raid Simon's manors in the Marches. Roger's men set upon Dilwyn Castle, seizing Simon's constable and holding him for ransom (he was forced to proffer 200 marks for his release), before Roger devastated Simon's crops at Dilwyn, Lugwardine and Marden, 'usurping to himself the lordship of the manor [at Dilwyn]', as Simon was to complain, 'extorting an oath of fealty from its men and tenants'.[27]

Yet Simon still held one enormously important asset: Dover Castle. While Roger Mortimer was assaulting Simon's manors in the Marches, the king and a mighty group of nobles moved on the coastal fortress. Henry demanded that the garrison deliver the castle to him, but the Montfortians held fast: their constable had been appointed by conciliar authority, they told the king, and so that authority alone could sanction the castle's delivery – so much accorded with the oath all had sworn to the Provisions.* There was little to be done: it would be a monumental feat to take the stronghold. Henry was at least able to install his own man, Roger of Leybourne, as warden of the Cinque Ports, but his principal mission had failed. This counted as a significant success for Simon: Queen Eleanor (who had remained behind in France after the meeting with Louis in September) was mustering an army on the Continent, but now Henry could not risk sailing the fleet to Kent.[28]

Still, Simon's men in Dover could not hold out indefinitely if they were besieged, and so Simon rode to their aid. Leaving the security of Kenilworth and his Midland powerbase, he headed south

---

* *The Historical Works of Gervase of Canterbury*, ed. W. Stubbs, 2 vols. (London, 1880), II, 229–30. The castle was being held by John de la Haye (the Montfortian constable recently ejected from Winchester) and a band of Montfortian knights while the constable of Dover, Richard de Grey, was away meeting with Simon.

east, via Northampton and then Dunstable. Our source for his movements here is the Dunstable annalist, who was obviously well informed (he mentions that, at Dunstable, Simon met the prior of the house and asked to be admitted into its lay fraternity, which request the prior granted). Simon then set out on the next leg of his journey, to London, with the aim of gathering troops there before heading to Dover.[29]

Simon stationed his small force at Southwark, at the southern end of London Bridge. He had assumed the Londoners were with him, but what he did not know was that a small group of citizens had been in communication with the king, agreeing to help Henry corner Simon's army. Henry was then in Croydon (some ten miles south of the capital) and, on hearing that Simon was at Southwark, headed to meet him; meanwhile Edward set out from nearby Merton. As Henry and Edward closed in, the king ordered Simon to surrender. Simon's response, reported by the Dunstable annalist, was 'that he would never do so to perjurers and apostates'.

Simon moved to enter the city – only to find that Henry's men inside had barred the gates, trapping him between the bends of the river and the oncoming royal forces. Still Simon did not surrender. Instead, he and his men confessed their sins, received the Body of Christ and armed themselves, readying for battle. Simon had them all signed with the cross. They were now *crucesignati*, crusaders, ready to wield their weapons and be martyred in a holy cause.

It could have all ended here. But Simon was saved by his supporters in London, who realized what was happening, broke the chains binding the gates and rushed out to his aid, allowing him to enter the city. Inside he held an investigation into the betrayal, identifying the four leading citizens who had conspired with the king (they were forced to pay significant fines, which were put to use in strengthening London's defences).

Simon agreed a truce with Henry of eight days, and the two sides renewed their plan to submit the whole matter to Louis of France.[30] In London, on 13 December, two days after the incident at Southwark, the Montfortians gathered to put their names to their part of the agreement; with Simon were the bishops of Worcester and London, Hugh Despenser, young Henry and Simon de Montfort, Peter de Montfort, and seventeen other barons and knights.[31] They submitted to Louis's judgement 'upon the provisions, ordinances, statutes, and all other obligations of Oxford, and upon all the disputes and disagreements which we have and have had . . . with our lord the illustrious king of England, and he with us, by occasion of the provisions'. With their hands upon the Gospels, they swore that they would 'in good faith observe whatever the lord king of France shall have ordained or decreed upon all of these matters, or on any of them, high or low'.[32] Henry's party swore likewise three days later.

Delegations from both parties would cross to France around the turn of the year. Simon, in the meantime, returned to Kenilworth. From there, when the time came, he set out on his way to the south-east coast. He had covered some twenty miles, reaching Catesby in Northamptonshire, when his fortune turned: he was thrown from his horse and his leg broken.[33] He was forced to return to Kenilworth.

*

And so it was that, in late December 1263, a small group of Montfortians set sail for France without their leader. Much rested on their mission. Louis was one of the greatest kings in Europe, and most respected. His support for the reforming enterprise would count for much, ensuring that he did not lend his sword to Henry and encouraging the approbation of the pope for the Provisions. This was a chance to build a major moral buttress for the cause – something that was needed now especially, after the depredations of the summer.

Simon's absence was a blow, for he held a strong position at the court of France. He was the last surviving son, and namesake, of the renowned crusader who had led the French to conquer Languedoc. His eldest brother, Amaury, another veteran of holy war in Languedoc and Egypt, had also been highly regarded by Louis, just as Simon himself was held in great esteem by the noblemen of France, who had invited him to be their regent ten years earlier. He had visited the French court regularly over the years, on several occasions attending court festivities or enjoying Louis's hospitality. He had felt confident enough in Louis's support to submit his quarrels to the French king's arbitration, even before now. Simon's absence would be surely felt.

Still, delegated to advance the case in Simon's stead was the strongest candidate who could be found. Thomas de Cantilupe was the nephew of Walter de Cantilupe, bishop of Worcester, and cousin of Peter de Montfort (who came with him now to France), but was also an impressive figure in his own right. A highly learned churchman, he was a Master of Arts and a doctor of Church law, and so was numbered amongst Europe's intellectual elite. He was also of a baronial family, bearing his status confidently. His personal authority, as well as his academic weight, had seen him in 1261, at the age of perhaps forty-one, appointed chancellor of Oxford.[34] There were few better qualified to make the Montfortian case.

Thomas, Peter and the rest of their small party were heading for Amiens, a thriving city whose vast cathedral would host the arbitration.[35] Here the process would begin with the drawing up of Henry's case, probably by Walter of Merton (another Master of Arts, trained in Oxford – he would later found Merton College).[36] The argument was short. The council had seized from the king customary royal prerogatives: the right to appoint ministers and keepers of castles and to remove them at the royal pleasure. Henry could not permit royal rights to be alienated from the crown, for he had sworn an oath at his coronation to preserve those rights intact. Meanwhile the barons had sworn to him oaths of fealty, which they were violating now by undermining royal power. The Provisions, furthermore, had already been 'quashed and invalidated' by the pope, with the penalty of excommunication imposed upon any who defied the papal orders.[37]

There was no great art in Henry's case, but then it needed none. His argument was based on custom (the powers in question were long held by the kings of England) and an appeal to custom made a powerful argument in a climate of thought in which the ancient and established was generally to be preferred, while anything new or radical was to be avoided.

The scale of the challenge facing Thomas, in responding to this case, was vast. The field of political ethics was thriving in Europe: since at least the late twelfth century, scholars in the schools of

Paris had been considering the rights and wrongs of kingship and the responsibility of subjects with regard to royal power.[38] More recently, as we have seen, Robert Grosseteste and his circle had examined Aristotle's arguments, as set out in the *Nicomachean Ethics*, on the kingly office. But never had these scholars been required to conjure arguments to justify a group of subjects seizing power from their king. Indeed, as we have also seen, Robert Grosseteste had considered such action and railed against it. Simon and others of his party had been close to Robert and would have known his thinking. If the greatest thinker of the age had deemed such action to be unjustifiable, how would Thomas build his case?

One possibility was to look for historical examples in which kings had been removed from power, and here there were two in recent memory. In 1245, the Holy Roman Emperor Frederick II had been denounced as a tyrant and deprived of office, his subjects absolved of their oaths of fealty to him; in the same year the king of Portugal, Sancho II, had been detached from power (though he still retained his royal rank), having been proclaimed a *rex inutilis* – literally a 'useless king'. Thomas would have been familiar with the arguments of both cases, for the actions had been taken by the pope at a general assembly of the Church, the Second Council of Lyons, which Thomas had attended. And the arguments used to justify both actions were founded upon Church law, on which Thomas was an expert.* But the cases against Frederick and Sancho could not easily be made to fit Henry III. Henry had not committed the sort of crimes of which Frederick stood accused (the emperor had attacked Church lands, and had even kidnapped a cohort of Spanish bishops who had been on their way to attend a Church council).[39] The complaints made against Sancho, in contrast, did invite comparison with Henry: Sancho was said to be *simplex* (the same adjective applied to Henry time and again – too easily led, lacking in nous), and, like Henry, he was unmartial (Sancho was said to be afflicted with 'idleness' and 'feebleness of heart').[40] But the case for

---

* In particular, the *rex inutilis* classification was based upon the action taken when a bishop was too old or infirm to wield power effectively in his diocese (E. Peters, *The Shadow King: Rex Inutilis in Medieval Law and Literature, 751–1327* (London, 1970), 131–2).

the profundity of Sancho's defects was far stronger, because the principal role of an Iberian king was to prosecute the *reconquista* against the Spanish Muslims, and so Sancho could be deemed incapable of fulfilling a fundamental duty.[41] The same could not be said of Henry. Most importantly, in both cases it had been the pope who had deprived these kings of power and not their subjects – for the right to depose rulers or to otherwise detach them from power and to absolve subjects of their oaths of fealty was a papal prerogative.* The confederates of 1258, in seizing power from Henry under their own impetus, had far exceeded their authority. And Thomas was still left with a greater problem: whatever case could be made against Henry personally did not constitute an argument for overturning the customary system of government (kingship) in favour of another (conciliar rule).

The solution Thomas arrived at was to align the Provisions of Oxford with a set of reforms that were indubitably lawful: Magna Carta.[42] The Charter had long since ceased to be radical. In 1216 it had been reissued by Henry's government with its controversial chapters taken out, a third version had been issued by the government in 1217 to mark the end of civil war, and the fourth and definitive issue had been granted by Henry in 1225 in return for a grant of taxation – in the words of the Charter, by his 'spontaneous and free will'.[43] The king had confirmed the Charter, in 1237 and 1253, and the pope himself had confirmed it in 1254. Within fifty years of its first issue, Magna Carta had been transformed from a bold and controversial statement of limited monarchy into an established measure of good government. If Thomas could bind the Provisions of Oxford to Magna Carta, he could show that the Provisions were not, in fact, radical – but rather founded upon legislation that was now hailed as customary.

And so, Thomas described at length how the king, after

---

* They had been defined as such during the period of 'Gregorian Reform' of the eleventh century, set out by Gregory VII in 1073 in his *Dictatus Papae*. In accordance with this principle, the Portuguese bishops and barons had complained to the pope about Sancho II and asked that the pope take action (Peters, *Shadow King*, 146; S. Lay, *The Reconquest Kings of Portugal: Political and Cultural Reorientation on the Medieval Frontier* (Basingstoke, 2009), 242–3, 251, 253–4).

confirming Magna Carta, had gone on to 'whittle away those liberties': he interfered in the election of bishops (contrary to chapter 1 of Magna Carta 1225), he caused damage to lands under royal wardship (contrary to chapter 4), married off baronial heirs to partners below their station (contrary to chapter 6), he delayed in giving justice and even denied it, in order to protect his favourites (contrary to chapter 29), and so on.[44] Thomas made two further points. He complained about the Sicilian Business on the basis that Henry had levied a tax from the Church in order to campaign in Outremer, only for the money to be turned toward an expedition against fellow Christians. And he described how the royal treasury had been diminished because of grants made to 'certain courtiers, aliens, and others', so that 'his store of money being utterly spent, having not the wherewithal to pay for his daily food, the lord king had to turn to seizing bread, wine and other things for the maintenance of his household . . . whereby many of his English subjects were pauperized and beggared'.[45] This was an argument that was probably inspired by the scholarship of Robert Grosseteste. As we have seen, Robert had drawn from Aristotle a definition of kingship that placed sound royal finances at the heart of what it meant to be king: a king must have a 'superabundance' of wealth in order to carry out his duties without burdening his subjects, or else he would be driven to demand resources from his subjects in order to carry out the functions of his office.

Yet Thomas still had to contend with an abiding problem. Louis might agree that Henry had failed to uphold the standards of kingship set by Magna Carta, and he might agree that the reforms established by the council – which aimed to improve the lot of ordinary subjects – were laudable. Indeed, such might be expected of a king who had done so much in his own kingdom along these very lines. But herein lay the crucial distinction. It had been the king of France who established the programme of reform in his own kingdom – no subject had taken power from him in order to achieve it. To agree that such an act was permissible would be to grant licence for any subjects to turn to radical action when they felt aggrieved. How, then, could Thomas encourage Louis to approve this seizure of royal power? All he could do was fall back upon the line that Henry had agreed to the Provisions, which 'it pleased him to grant to the leading men and the magnates of his kingdom in good faith by an oath sworn upon his soul'. The councillors, moreover, were said to be acting 'for the honour of the lord king and for the common advantage of the kingdom', helping the king to bear the burden of government. Thomas had to conclude, rather evasively, that establishing a council had been the only option, for as 'human malice grows this purpose [of reforming the realm] could be achieved in no other way'.[46]

How far had Simon and his party considered these challenges when they agreed to submit their case to Louis? Perhaps Simon had been counting on the commitment of the king of France to the shared cause of reform.[47] If so, this was a severe miscalculation. Louis, in his own words, 'heard the proposals of both sides and fully understood the replies and counter-arguments of the parties'. On 23 January he issued his judgement: 'We concluded that through the provisions, ordinances, statutes, and obligations of Oxford . . . the rights and honour of the king had been greatly harmed, the realm disturbed, churches oppressed and plundered . . . and that there was good reason to fear that still worse would follow in the future.' Louis had determined to 'quash and invalidate all these provisions, ordinances, and obligations, or whatever else they may be called, and whatever has arisen from them or has been occasioned by them'. (For good measure, Louis also pointed out that they had already been invalidated by the pope.) Nobody was to make any new provisions of this sort, he decreed, and the barons were to hand over to the king any documents that had been issued in support of the Provisions, just as they were to deliver custody of all royal castles, while the king must once again be allowed to appoint and dismiss his own ministers. Furthermore, Louis continued, 'we decree and ordain that the said king shall have full power and free authority in his kingdom and in all that pertains to it'. Louis was careful to point out that in making this ruling he did 'not wish or intend . . . to derogate in any way from the royal privileges, charters, liberties, statutes and laudable customs of the realm of England which were in force before the time of the provisions', disentangling the Provisions and Magna Carta, and thus cutting off the main thrust of Thomas's argument.[48] The ruling was unremittingly clear, leaving no room for negotiation, compromise or evasion.

Simon was now asked to abandon the Provisions and meekly to restore Henry to power. He refused to comply, and in this he was not alone. Copies of the judgement were carried back to England and news of it spread widely, causing general resentment.[49] In casting off Louis's decree, Simon could count on the support not only of his friends but also of the Londoners, the Cinque Ports and (in the words of the London chronicler Arnold fitz Thedmar) 'almost all the middling people of the kingdom'.[50]

It is possible that this was not an easy decision for Simon – nor for Walter, bishop of Worcester, Henry, bishop of London, Hugh Despenser, Peter de Montfort, Simon's sons Henry and Simon and the other men who, back in mid-December, had put their names to the agreement to submit to the arbitration. They had done so 'firmly promising and swearing, touching the holy Gospels' to 'in good faith observe whatever the lord king of France shall have ordained or decreed'.[51] To reject Louis's judgement now would be to break their oath.

But there were grounds, perhaps, to do just that – for they must by now have realized that Louis had set his mind against the Montfortians even before they arrived at Amiens – indeed, even before he had agreed to act as judge. Probably in early October, some six weeks before the parties submitted their dispute for arbitration, Louis and his queen, Marguerite, had written to the pope and asked him to send a legate to restore England to order.[52] They were acting on information supplied by Queen Eleanor and others, who had stayed on in France after the English embassy in September. Eleanor was able to tell her sister and brother-in-law how she had suffered over the summer at the hands of the Montfortians: attempting to escape the Tower by boat to rendezvous with Edward, she had been waylaid by a London mob hurling stones and rotten eggs (she was rescued by the mayor of London).[53] Her account – and that of Peter d'Aigueblanche, also on hand to describe the violence visited on Church property and how he had been kidnapped from his own cathedral – must have shocked the king and queen of France. Once they knew the situation, they had written to Pope Urban to apprise him of the facts and ask for help. Their letter does not survive, but the pope's response reports their words: in England 'dissension has arisen between the royal family and the barons and others, to the injury of royalty and danger of the kingdom; some prelates have been seized, despoiled, and imprisoned ... and crimes and excesses are committed'.[54] The pope had immediately recognized the urgency of the situation, and the very day after receiving the report had commissioned a legate. He chose the cardinal bishop of Sabina, Gui Foulquois (see plate 25). Gui was specially selected for this task, for he was close to the French royal family, having served Louis and two of his brothers as counsellor. The pope's hope was that Louis and Gui would work together in this mission to restore Henry 'to the heights of customary pre-eminence' and return the kingdom to peace. The partnership could be a military one: if necessary, Gui was to mount an expedition to secure Henry's throne, which Louis might lead – this was to be a holy war, and Louis was offered the remission of his sins if he were to cooperate.[55]

By the time Thomas de Cantilupe was laying out his case at Amiens, Louis had in all likelihood received the pope's response, and was awaiting Gui's arrival. The Montfortian case was indeed shaky – but there was nothing Thomas could have said to bring judgement in their favour. So much was certainly clear by late January or early February, when the Montfortians received reports that Louis had sent for the legate and was readying with him to invade.[56] Knowing this, they might have felt that their oath to submit to Louis's judgement, made on the mistaken premise of the king's open mind, counted for little.

*

Simon had to ready now for war against the forces of the kings of England and France. His position was more vulnerable than it had ever been, and his enemies began to whisper against him. A short pamphlet preserved in the Tewkesbury annals, written by an anonymous 'faithful Englishman' perhaps in January or February, warns 'the barons of England' about the coming of the legate and the dilemma to be faced: they could let these forces in and allow the legate to obliterate their cause, or refuse him entry and face excommunication and interdict, followed by Louis's army. 'If the noble men do not have a just cause', warned the pamphlet writer, 'or if perhaps they do not want to resist in these matters, it would be expedient for them to fall into line concerning all things before the legate arrives,' or they would have to face the consequence of making war against the king, namely disinheritance. And 'beware lord Simon de Montfort', the writer warns, pointing to Simon's grant (made on 1 August 1263) to his second son, young Simon, of the lands of John Mansel (a close counsellor of the king who had managed to escape from the Tower to the Continent).[57] Was this really a man working for the common good? The barons of England should also think on Simon's age – if he were to die, then it would be necessary to nominate a new leader.[58]

Simon was only around fifty-five, and highly active. The comment on his age was perhaps directed at the twenty-year-old earl of Gloucester, Gilbert de Clare (patron of Tewkesbury Abbey, where this pamphlet was preserved). The young earl was reported to have stayed at Simon's side in October, while so many other barons defected – but he had not put his name to the Montfortian case at Amiens, suggesting that he was not publicly committed to the cause.[59] It is not clear whether Gilbert ever took such advice seriously, or whether these whispers against Simon were widespread, but their surfacing revealed the precariousness of his position. He had the support of his friends amongst the barons, knights, and bishops, as well as the Londoners, and he also held the south-east coast, with his men in command of Dover Castle and the people of the Cinque Ports at his side, so he would be well placed to resist an invasion (Henry knew as much – he tried again, on his return to England in mid-February, to persuade Simon's men to surrender Dover Castle, but with no success).[60] But the majority of England's greatest noblemen, with their retinues, stood with the king: Simon would be outnumbered within and without the kingdom.

His response was to take the fight to the enemy, striking at the power base of the royal party: the Marches. He made a new alliance with Llywelyn ap Gruffudd, overlord of the Welsh rulers and self-styled 'prince of Wales', with whom he shared a common enemy in the marcher barons. They targeted Roger Mortimer's castle of Wigmore, as well as a castle of Roger de Clifford.[61] To Wigmore Simon sent his eldest sons, Henry and Simon. Roger, as we have seen, had raided and occupied Simon's three marcher manors during the period of truce. In sending his sons to do the job Simon was showing (as noted by the annalist of Dunstable) that they were ready to 'avenge their father', signalling the unity of the Montfort clan.[62]

At the end of February, Henry de Montfort moved on Worcester, in the company of Peter de Montfort and the earl of Derby. This city was the seat of their father's great friend, Walter de Cantilupe, and there was no obvious reason to raid the town – except to obtain funds. Reports of the sack of Worcester are cursory, but do mention that the Montfortians attacked the Jewish people of the town, imprisoning some and killing others.[63] The following month monies were seized from the Jewish people of London during a frenzied raid – a chance, while raising funds, for the perpetrators to vent their hatred and win support from those with debts to Jewish moneylenders. It is not clear whether Simon ordered the attack on Worcester, nor what response it brought from Walter de Cantilupe (the Church advocated the segregation of Jewish people but condemned violence against them).

The royal party soon struck back at this Montfortian aggression. Edward, returned from France, rendezvoused with Roger Mortimer at Hereford and took two Montfortian castles at Hay and Huntington before moving on to Gloucester. The town had been taken for the Montfortians by John Giffard, who had gained access to the town dressed as a Welsh wool merchant.* He was now laying siege to the castle. Edward was able to break through John Giffard's forces and enter the fortress, there to meet with the earl of Hereford and the wives of Roger de Clifford and Roger of Leybourne. At this point Henry de Montfort arrived from Worcester, trapping Edward inside the castle. Edward sent out messengers seeking a truce – and Henry (perhaps surprisingly) agreed, withdrawing to Kenilworth. As soon as the Montfortians had left, Edward threw off the truce and set upon the people of the town, imprisoning

---

* According to the well-informed Robert of Gloucester, John Giffard and another knight rode up to the west gate wearing cloaks over their armour and carrying bales of wool; when the porters let them in, they threw off their cloaks and the porters, in terror, threw them the keys (W. A. Wright (ed.), *The Metrical Chronicle of Robert of Gloucester*, 2 vols. (London, 1885), ll. 11, 170–9).

some and seizing their goods, before departing to rendezvous with his father in Oxford.

As the annalist of Dunstable noted, young Henry had been advised against the truce by his 'associates' (presumably the other knights present) – he was probably following the counsel of the bishop of Worcester, who mediated the agreement.[64] Simon's eldest son had recently turned twenty-five; the campaigns of 1263–4 were his first major military experience, and this episode provided a hard lesson. He now had to face his father. 'The earl,' writes the Dunstable annalist, 'because the lord Edward was thus foolishly allowed to go free, was greatly dismayed and ashamed, and rebuked his son Henry sharply for it.' Simon could at least be comforted by the successes of his second son, young Simon, who had taken the city of Northampton.[65]

The king and Edward now stepped up their offensive. On 6 March Henry issued a call to arms, ordering his faithful tenants-in-chief to muster at Oxford at the beginning of April (the call cited the need to move against Llywelyn, Simon's ally and central to his successes in the Marches).[66] Meanwhile, Simon prepared to head to London to rendezvous with Hugh Despenser, who held the Tower. Hugh had been targeting royalist property in and around the capital with the help of the Londoners, who had appointed for themselves a 'constable' and 'marshal' as military leaders: at the ringing of the bell of St Paul's, all able-bodied men were to leave the city under the banners of these two and follow wherever they might be needed. Summoning this militia, Hugh led them westward out of the city to Isleworth, where they laid low the manor of Richard of Cornwall.[67] Back in the city, royal clerks and the barons of the exchequer (in charge of the auditing of government accounts) were seized and imprisoned, ensuring Montfortian control of the machinery of government.[68]

Simon was in back in London by 31 March, with Hugh Despenser and the other leading Montfortians at his side: the earls of Gloucester and Derby, young Henry and Simon de Montfort, Peter de Montfort, Richard de Grey, Henry of Hastings, John fitz John, Nicholas of Segrave, John de Vescy and many others. They had gathered to confirm the support of London's leading citizens, who now swore with the Montfortian magnates an oath of mutual aid, promising 'to help each other against all people'. As part of the agreement, London's aldermen were to summon the assemblies of their wards, where all males of twelve years or more were to offer the same oath.[69] This was a solemn commitment by the citizens of London to take up arms in Simon's cause.

With Simon in command of London, Henry waited for the assembly of his feudal host. On 30 March he received an unpleasant surprise. In his summons, Henry had omitted the names of known Montfortians amongst the lay tenants-in-chief, but not any from amongst the bishops: such committed Montfortians as the bishops of Worcester and Lincoln, two of Simon's closest friends, as well as the bishop of London (who had put his name to the Montfortian case at Amiens) had all received the call.* These summonses must have been intended as ultimatums. Simon was known to enjoy the support of several senior churchmen – but, with the prospect of armed confrontation now very real, Henry perhaps reckoned that the prelates would not want to ride against him. The bishops of England had a traditional duty to act as peacemakers when civil conflict threatened: even if they felt sympathy to those who stood against the king, they were expected to maintain their loyalty to both sides in order to broker peace.[70] A refusal to answer a military summons from their feudal lord would constitute a major breach of their oaths of fealty, something that they would (so Henry hoped) wish to avoid. But he was to be disappointed. The bishops of Worcester, Lincoln, and London now arrived at Oxford, not as loyal vassals to join Henry's army but as loyal Montfortians. Worse still, they had brought with them two more bishops who, up to this point, Henry had thought loyal: John Gervase, bishop of Winchester, a former royal clerk, and Stephen of Bersted, bishop of Chichester.[71] These bishops approached the king in their customary role as peacemakers, but they carried from Simon unremitting terms: the Montfortians would agree to accept the Amiens judgement, but only if Henry agreed to expel all foreigners from England and govern the kingdom with the help only of his native men. The king would never comply, for agreeing to these terms would mean

---

* A number of abbots received summons as well, including the prior of Dunstable, who had recently received Simon as a lay member of the house (CR, 1261–4, 377–9).

allowing a serious constraint upon his right to choose his ministers (a crucial royal prerogative, as he had argued at Amiens). His response demonstrated his displeasure: he demanded that the bishops leave his presence immediately and ordered them not to return unless he gave them licence. He then gave instructions that the estates of the bishop of Winchester – whose changing of allegiance perhaps angered Henry most of all – should be seized if the bishop did not make satisfaction.[72]

Henry now readied his army to march towards the Montfortian heartland: the Midlands. After forty-odd miles, his force reached Northampton, a key stronghold that blocked the route to Simon's fortress of Kenilworth. Young Simon was holding the castle and the town, together with Peter de Montfort. The king arrived on the evening of 4 April and demanded entry; the garrison refused. Henry, however, knew of another way. He called on the support of the local prior, of the house of St Andrews, which occupied the northern quadrant of the town. While one contingent of the royal army attacked Northampton from the south, another knocked through a stretch of the north-western wall, which had been undermined by the prior from his garden. This assault, writes the Dunstable annalist, young Simon 'resisted manfully', repelling the royal troops. He was aided by a cohort of students, recently expelled from Oxford after a brawl with the townspeople. The students (wrote one chronicler) 'inflicted more harm upon men entering and climbing up than the rest of the barons did, with their slings, bows and catapults. For they had a standard of their own raised aloft against the king.'[73] But they could not repel another wave of royal troops. Young Simon, realizing as much, sallied out, 'holding himself manfully in the midst of them', as the Dunstable annalist records. He was toppled from his horse and captured. Peter de Montfort and the other Montfortians were soon compelled to surrender.[74]

The whole encounter took only an hour. In this brief space of time, some eighty Montfortian knights were taken – including one of Simon's sons, and one of his oldest friends.[75] Even a victory won by young Simon's brother (young Henry had redeemed himself by sallying out of Kenilworth to take Warwick Castle) could not conceal that this was a disastrous moment. And things would worsen still. From Northampton, the king's force moved swiftly northward, taking Simon's city of Leicester on 11 April, and Nottingham the following day.

The earl had left London to march to the relief of young Simon at Northampton, and had reached St Albans when he heard the news that the town and castle had fallen.[76] His men (according to the account of William Rishanger) began to lament. 'But the earl did not despair, knowing that this was the law of war, that in various events now these people, now those people are made superior.' According to the same report, as they left St Albans to return to London, Simon turned to Hugh Despenser and his close followers and told them to take comfort from the fact that, by the end of May, fortunes would be reversed and the enemy would be brought to confusion.[77]

Back in London, the Montfortians considered their next move, and determined to take Rochester Castle. Rochester lay between London and Dover, and had been seized recently by royalist forces, cutting off the Montfortians in London from their comrades in Dover Castle. Simon's forces would need to retake Rochester to ensure control of the vital region between London and the south-east coast.

Simon's difficulty was a shortage of money, needed for materials and provisions to prosecute the next stage of the war. A solution was identified: the Jewish community of London, many of whom worked as moneylenders, would have a store of funds. As at Worcester, the Montfortians would have to take the cash by force.

The assault was reported by two well-positioned chroniclers: Arnold fitz Thedmar, the London alderman who wrote his chronicle close in time to the events he describes, and Thomas Wykes, a royal clerk who lived through the war in the capital and wrote up his chronicle afterwards, perhaps in the later 1270s. The reports they give are entirely independent but similar, suggesting that the horror they describe was no exaggeration. In the week before Palm Sunday (writes Arnold fitz Thedmar), 'the Jewish religion in London was destroyed'. The goods of the Jewish people were seized, and 'any Jewish people who were found were stripped, robbed, and afterwards, by night, they were massacred'. Thomas Wykes adds detail of the frenzy: the Montfortians 'sparing neither age nor sex, perpetrating entirely unheard of murders, inhumanly butchered the aged and elderly, the suckling baby with the aged person, children wailing in the cradle, babies not yet weaned hanging from their mothers' breasts'. One man was singled out: Kok son of Abraham, a leading member of the Jewish community of London, was set upon by John fitz John. John killed Kok, Thomas Wykes reports, 'with his own hands'. Some people were saved by Hugh Despenser and the mayor of London, who got them to the Tower before the carnage started. But all the others were slaughtered: Arnold estimates five hundred people were killed, Thomas Wykes four hundred. Of the riches seized from Kok son of Abraham (writes Thomas Wykes) John fitz John 'afterwards presented, though unwillingly, no small portion to the earl of Leicester'.[78]

*

Simon now had funds to conduct what he knew would be a major operation. Rochester was a mighty fortress: its keep, at 120 feet in height, was the tallest in the kingdom, with walls eleven feet thick in places. In 1215 a garrison of one hundred rebel knights and their men had defended the keep from King John for eight weeks entire. And now it was well defended and well provisioned: the local baron Roger of Leybourne had been put in charge of Rochester in December and in January had been told to ready it for war, and his account roll survives to describe his preparations.[79] By mid-April, Roger had gathered a sizeable garrison (whose numbers of knights and mounted sergeants might be reckoned by the horses for whom Roger had to provide fodder: 164), and he was soon joined by other royalist potentates, including the earl Warenne and Henry of Almain, with their followings: some fifty-seven knights, plus sergeants, infantry and servants (some of the royalist lords also brought their wives). For this mighty garrison Roger had laid in food and drink: quantities of fodder and, for the human inhabitants, 43 oxen, as well as 50 sheep and 362½ sides of bacon, as well as many varieties of fish (for Lent began in the first week of March).[80] Simon made his own preparations. In mounting the siege of Rochester, thought Thomas Wykes, he was 'bequeathing to the English an exemplar of how assaults on castles should be conducted'. He had in London readied siege machinery for the assault, which he transported to Rochester over land and water.[81]

The castle lay in a sharp bend of the River Medway, so that it could be approached only from the north over a bridge (from the suburb of Strood on the opposite bank) or from the south through the town. In the great siege of 1215, King John had encamped in the town (even stabling his horses in the cathedral), allowing him close access to the castle – he had eventually taken the keep after undermining its southern tower. Now, in anticipation of assault, Roger of Leybourne had given orders that the town of Rochester be burned, denying the Montfortians the chance to imitate John's tactics.[82] Meanwhile, he had caused the bridge to be fortified, so that a detachment could guard it against Montfortian attack from the north.

Simon arrived at Rochester on 17 April, Maundy Thursday. It was from the north, over the bridge, that he would assault – but with his men channelled onto the narrow crossing, its defenders could easily beat them off: twice Simon attempted and failed to storm the bridge. He was forced to rethink. The solution was to build a fire ship. He had a boat brim-filled with dry wood, to which was added tar, charcoal, sulphur and pork fat: a potent mix of incendiaries. On the evening of 18 April he set a massive blaze and, helped by a strong wind, sent the boat towards the bridge. It came up alongside one of the piers and sent the defenders panicking. Simon and his men were able then to fight their way across the bridge – pushing back reinforcements led by Roger of Leybourne, who took a beating in the fray.* With the garrison called out to face Simon's assault, the town was opened up to the earl of Gloucester, who attacked from the south. The next day Simon and his forces stormed the castle's outer bailey. The day following was Easter Sunday, and so was marked by a cessation of hostilities – as well as the breaking of the Lenten fast (Roger's accounts reveal that he feasted his garrison on the meat of four and a half oxen, eight sides of bacon and eight sheep, as well as 1,400 eggs).[83]

---

* The exact sequence of events in the taking of the town is not clear, but the account of the *Flores Historiarum* describes the use of the fire ship as a stratagem devised by Simon, allowing Gilbert de Clare to fight his way into the town 'just as they had agreed between themselves' that evening (*Flores Historiarum*, II, 489–90; *Gervase of Canterbury*, II, 235).

From Easter Monday until the following Saturday, Simon maintained the siege, laying into the garrison holed up in the keep with his siege machines and crossbows, and opening mines under the walls. He made progress but could not complete his task – for he heard, on 25 April, that the king was en route to Rochester. If Simon remained here, he would be trapped between the royalist garrison and the oncoming army. Meanwhile, it was reported, Edward was heading for the earl of Gloucester's castle at nearby Tonbridge. Simon had no choice but to withdraw and return to London, which he did under cover of night. A few of the Londoners, left behind by Simon to continue the assault in token terms, were seized: some had their hands cut off, others were put to the sword.[84]

With Simon back in London, Henry set about securing the south-east. From Rochester, he covered the twenty miles south-west to Tonbridge, taking the castle there before heading south. For the next thirty miles or so, his army made its way through the woodland of the Weald, harassed by archers loyal to Simon (including men sent from Battle Abbey). From Battle, the royal force moved on to Winchelsea, where the citizens were persuaded to abandon their support for Simon and join the king. Henry had succeeded in drawing a ring around the last Montfortian stronghold in Kent: Dover Castle. He ordered the men of the region to muster at Canterbury on 12 May, probably in readiness to assault the Montfortian garrison.[85] With Rochester and Tonbridge in royalist hands, Simon would be cut off from his men in Dover, unable to come to their aid. They might hold out for weeks or months – but they could hardly be expected to, knowing they would not be relieved. If Henry were to capture Dover, he would have the entire south-east region below London: a secure landing ground for the army that Queen Eleanor was amassing on the Continent. It would be the beginning of the end.

This Simon could not allow. He mustered his forces and marched out to fight.

13

Triumph

Simon had waited in the capital, hopeful that he would be joined by the earl of Derby with his forces – but by 6 May he could wait no more and readied to move out. The army headed south, coming to a pause forty miles from the capital at Simon's manor of Fletching, in Sussex.[1] In response to news of Simon's movements, Henry moved out from his station at Battle Abbey, marching some twenty-five miles west to Lewes, only eight miles or so to the south of Fletching (see map 5). The two armies were poised for battle.

Standing with Simon as he weighed his options were the bishops of Worcester, London and Chichester, a number of Franciscan and Dominican friars, the young earl of Gloucester and the greater part of all the Montfortian barons and knights. They decided, on 12 May, to send an embassy to Henry: a party of friars headed by the bishop of Chichester, Stephen of Bersted.[2] This was, purportedly, a mission of peace – but the terms (recorded shortly afterwards by one of the bishop's household), like those offered by the bishops sent to Henry at the Oxford muster in March, showed that Simon was unwilling to give ground:

> Choose the best men, whose faith is lively, who have read canon law, or have becomingly taught theology, and sacred philosophy, and who know how to rule the Christian faith; and whatever such men shall not fear through wholesome doctrine to counsel, or whatever they shall not fear to decide, what they shall say, that shall they find

us ready to adopt; in such manner that we may not know the brand of perjury, but as sons of God may hold faith.[3]

It seemed that Simon was offering to subject the Provisions once again to arbitration, but from the royalist perspective there were two problems with the offer. The first was that there were on hand many learned churchmen qualified (by Simon's stringent criteria) to act as arbiters, but they had come to Sussex as Simon's supporters.* The second was that judgement on the Provisions had already been set down, and twice, by the pope and by the king of France.

Simon's side (this time represented by the bishops of Worcester and London) also put forward a related offer: they would pay compensation for the despoliations they had committed, to the sum of £30,000 – but still the king must agree to abide by the Provisions. This offer was no more a serious attempt to reach a settlement than was its partner (one account has Henry willing to accept the compensation, before Richard of Cornwall reminded him that an agreement to hold to the Provisions would amount to the disinheritance of Henry and his heirs and the 'depression of his power').[4] The terms were rejected, and resoundingly: 'peace is forbidden to them', Edward reportedly responded, 'unless they all bind themselves with halters on their necks and bind themselves over to us for hanging or for drawing'.[5]

The following day, 13 May, Simon moved his forces closer, covering nine miles or so to set up camp in the woodland on the northern outskirts of the town of Lewes, between the villages of Offham and Hamsey. From there Simon and the earl of Gloucester sent letters to the king:

> Since it is proven by many experiences that certain people attending on you have suggested many lies to your lordship concerning us . . .

---

* Amongst the many churchmen who supported Simon were the bishop of Chichester, Stephen of Bersted, who carried the offer here, and the bishop of London, Henry of Sandwich, who remained for now at Fletching. Both had incepted as doctors of theology at Oxford in the 1250s (A. B. Emden, *A Biographical Register of the University of Oxford to AD 1500*, 3 vols. (Oxford, 1957–9), I, 170, III, 1638).

your excellency should know that we wish to heed the health and security of your body by all strength, with the fidelity owed to you, proposing to oppress not only our enemies but also yours and those of your entire kingdom according to our power. If any other explanation seems pleasing, do not believe it. We indeed will always be found to be your faithful men.[6]

These protestations of loyalty veiled thinly the threat of force. The purpose was to avoid appearing the hostile party, and to force the king himself to announce the cutting of their feudal ties. This he did, addressing Simon, Gilbert 'and their accomplices':

Since through war and the general disturbance in our kingdom, already brought about by you by fires and other immense damages, it is manifestly clear that you do not heed the fidelity you owe to us, nor do you care for the security of our body in any way, and that immensely you have oppressed our magnates and our other faithful people adhering constantly to our faith, and propose to oppress them with your power, as you have signified to us through your letters, we consider their burden our own and their enemies to be our enemies.[7]

The response of Richard of Cornwall and Edward was set out in still plainer terms, addressed to Simon, Gilbert, 'and each and every other one of their accomplices in perfidy'. Richard and Edward were in no doubt, they said, as to the true intentions of the earls – and would treat Simon, Gilbert and all their men as public enemies and would hunt them down. Simon and Gilbert were still welcome, though, to subject themselves to royal justice: they could even have safe conduct in order to set out their lies and treacheries, and be judged accordingly.[8]

*

Simon now readied for battle. He was known to be a *vir Martius* (as Matthew Paris had once reported), a man born under the star of the god of war.[9] He had seen action in Italy, perhaps in Syria, at Saintes and certainly in Gascony – where he had 'drenched his lightning sword with the blood of many men' – and had campaigned now too in England. But it is not clear that he had ever fought a battle, that is, a pitched battle as opposed to a siege, a fighting withdrawal or a skirmish. This was not unusual, for battles were exceptional events: the most celebrated warriors of the last generation had fought hardly any (William Marshal two, Richard the Lionheart three, Philip Augustus one, Simon's father, the Count, only one).* That was by design, for a battle was a mighty risk, as every general knew – there were only so many elements under his control, and success required fortune. So much was set out in the manual of the Roman general Vegetius, much admired and copied in the Middle Ages as instruction for knights on the principles of warfare. 'It is much better', Vegetius advised, 'to overcome the enemy by famine, surprise or terror than by general actions, for in the latter instance fortune has often a greater share than valour.'[10]

For those compelled to engage in battle, though, Vegetius had much advice, which Simon would need now.

You must always endeavour [wrote Vegetius] to get the start of your enemy in drawing up in order of battle, as you will then have it in your power to make your proper dispositions without obstruction. This will increase the courage of your own troops and intimidate your adversaries. For a superiority of courage seems to be implied on the side of an army that offers battle, whereas troops begin to be fearful who see their enemies ready to attack them. You will also secure another great advantage, that of marching up in order and falling upon them while forming and still in confusion. For part of the victory consists in throwing the enemy into disorder before you engage them.[11]

---

* William Marshal: Drincourt (1167) and Lincoln (1217); Richard the Lionheart: Arsuf (1191), Jaffa (1192) and the battle that took place between St Maigrin and Bouteville against a force of Brabançons (1176); Philip Augustus: Bouvines (1214); the Count: Muret (1213); King Henry II never fought a battle (J. Gillingham, 'War and Chivalry in the History of William the Marshal', in *Thirteenth Century England II*, ed. P. R. Coss and S. D. Lloyd (Woodbridge, 1988), 1–13, at 12; J. Gillingham, 'Richard I and the science of war in the Middle Ages', in his *Richard Coeur de Lion: Kingship, Chivalry and War in the Twelfth Century* (London, 1994), 212–26, at 213–14; J. Gillingham, *Richard I* (New Haven, 1999), 54).

This, then, was Simon's plan. That night of 13 May, with Henry's forces encamped inside the town, Simon did not sleep but led his army in the early hours up the wooded hillside to the west of Lewes, to reach a site named Boxholte on the crest of the Sussex Downs (see map 5). He was claiming the high ground ('the highest ground is reckoned the best', advised Vegetius, for 'the party above their antagonists can repulse and bear them down with greater impetuosity, while they who struggle with the ascent have both the ground and the enemy to contend with').[12]

At Boxholte, around four in the morning, Simon's troops set down their packs and, as the dark dissolved, readied for battle. Before setting out Walter de Cantilupe had promised them remission of their sins if they fought hard, and they had all been signed with the cross, with which they were marked on their shoulders and chests: they were *crucesignati*, crusaders. Now Simon encouraged them to make their confessions and told them they were fighting this day for the kingdom, for God, and for the Church. He told them to keep faith. Then the entire army sank to the ground, the men laying themselves prone across the earth, stretching out their arms to form a cross, entreating God to grant them aid.[13] As crusaders, they knew that if they died today they would earn the rewards of martyrdom, gaining a place in heaven beside the saints themselves.

Simon now arrayed his troops for action. He set four divisions, the first three forming the main line: the right was commanded by Henry de Montfort and Simon's third son, Gui (young Simon was still a prisoner of the royal party), aided by John de Burgh and Humphrey de Bohun; the left – comprising the Londoners – by Nicholas of Segrave and Henry of Hastings, while the centre was led by the earl of Gloucester, together with John fitz John and William de Munchensey.[14] The fourth division, commanded by Simon himself, would form the reserve. His role would be pivotal. 'The method of having bodies of reserves in the rear of the army,' advised Vegetius, 'composed of choice infantry and cavalry, commanded by the supernumerary lieutenant generals, counts and tribunes, is very judicious and of great consequence towards the gaining of a battle.' If any part of the line were penetrated, the reserve would be ready to come to its aid, 'to keep up the courage of their fellow soldiers and check the impetuosity of the enemy'.[15] This depth of fighting power would count, especially because Simon was outnumbered, in terms of cavalry at least: the estimates of army numbers by chroniclers are notoriously unreliable, but when all are pieced together it seems likely that Simon led some 500 knights, Henry perhaps 1,500. Both sides had several thousand infantry, though how the two forces compared cannot be known.[16] If Simon followed the counsel of Vegetius for those outnumbered in mounted troops, he intermingled cavalry and infantry ('By observing this method', wrote Vegetius, 'even though the flower of the enemy's cavalry should attack you, they will never be able to cope with this mixed disposition.')[17]

Henry, meanwhile, was spending the night in Lewes Priory, while Edward was nearby at the castle (see map 5). Told in the morning twilight that Simon's army was arrayed for battle, they rushed to arm themselves and deploy their troops (Simon would have the advantage, as Vegetius predicted, in being able to fall upon the enemy while they were still in confusion). Arrangements were hastily made for the royal army to divide into three, with Henry in command of the left division and Edward of the right – the centre would be led by Richard of Cornwall.[18] As dawn began to break behind them, they looked up to the west to see Simon's army assembled upon the hill.

They had been caught off guard, but showed their resolve, raising the dragon standard.[19] The kings of England had carried a dragon banner perhaps since the Anglo-Saxon age – it had been borne by Richard the Lionheart during the Third Crusade and by Henry's father, King John, during the civil war that followed his rejection of Magna Carta. Henry, in 1244, had ordered his own dragon banner to be made: it was to be woven of red samite, picked out in gold, with eyes of sapphire and a tongue 'made as if of burning fire', always to be moving. By the thirteenth century, the raising of the dragon standard carried a particular meaning: no enemy was to be spared.[20] It was a fearsome statement. The values of chivalry dictated that noble would not seek to kill noble on the battlefield but rather to take him prisoner and ransom him for profit. In 1216 John had briefly raised his dragon banner against the invading force of Louis of France, but then had lowered it and withdrawn; after John's death, the battles of Lincoln and Sandwich were fought along chivalric lines, with nobles taken prisoner (one, the count of Perche, was killed by the rash action of one man, much to the grief of friend and foe – see p. 23). This conflict would be different. If the Montfortians lost this battle, Simon and his knights would be cut down with their men.

Simon's forces moved forward from the crest of the hill, down towards the royal army.[21] The first clash came on the Montfortian left: Edward's division crashed through its first ranks and put the Londoners to flight. Running northward, some made it back to the capital. Others in desperation tried to cross the River Ouse and there were drowned. Edward and his men pursued the fleeing men, felling any fugitive they found.

But Edward, straying perhaps as far as four miles from the field, would have done well to heed the counsel of Vegetius: 'He who rashly pursues a flying enemy with troops in disorder, seems inclined to resign that victory which he had before obtained.'[22] In Edward's absence, the Montfortian middle division collided with its counterpart, while Simon's sons, commanding the right, confronted the king's contingent. It was now that Simon entered with his reserves.

The fighting was hard – Simon's own standard-bearer was cut down – but the Montfortians forced the royal troops backward to the town. The king, according to the chronicler of the local priory, 'was much beaten by swords and maces and two horses were killed under him'. Henry's men got him to the safety of the priory; Richard of Cornwall took refuge in a nearby windmill. The Montfortians swarmed into the town. Edward, returning to the battle site after his chasing of the Londoners, at first rode up to Boxholte to set upon Simon's baggage train and hack down those who had been left with it, before moving down the slope to Lewes. There he was met by the Montfortians, and many of his men were put to flight; Edward, though, was able to move round the town to find his father in the priory.

Simon's fighting of the battle had been masterful – but the victory was not complete. Henry and Edward were holed up in the priory, together with the marchers. Simon could not storm a holy place to pull them out – but nor could Henry and Edward remain inside indefinitely. It was in the interests of both parties to come to an agreement. Negotiations were held throughout the night.

By the following morning, terms had been agreed. The final terms, known as the Mise of Lewes, have not survived, though the central points have been reconstructed.[23] Henry agreed to uphold the Provisions of Oxford, though a panel was set up to arbitrate on their contents (this was a concession on Simon's part but not a major one, given that the panel was not obliged to dilute the force of the Provisions). A further panel was envisaged, comprising French prelates and magnates; its purpose is unclear, though it might have been to arbitrate on the Mise of Amiens – the altering of Louis's judgement could provide the Provisions with an important moral buttress, though the establishment of the panel relied on Louis's cooperation, which could not be guaranteed. Finally, arrangements were made for the release and taking of prisoners. The Montfortians captured at Northampton, including young Simon, were to be released, while royalist prisoners taken at Lewes were to be ransomed. But as to the most important prisoners, Simon now had to make a most painful compromise. He would take the king and the heir to the throne into his custody, together with Richard of Cornwall (who had already been captured) and Richard's son, Henry of Almain. This would allow the Montfortians to seize control of government to a degree that had not previously been possible. But that would be permitted only if Simon agreed to let the marchers go. These were key allies of the royal party, and powerful and bellicose barons: their release would present a potent threat to the new Montfortian order. Simon, though, had little choice – there was no perfect solution. He was forced to set the marchers free.

*

The terms of the Mise of Lewes were not widely shared – the news that spread across the kingdom was that of Simon's victory. To many it was astounding. Simon had been outnumbered, and many of his knights were young and untested.[24] Such a feat could be achieved only with the aid of God. One chronicler, based in Dover, describes how 'there were indeed in the army of the king some knights who, when they came into battle, were hardly able to see their enemies, nor hold their swords in their hands'. The royal troops had said as much themselves, the chronicler records (he even names one bearing witness, the magnate Henry de Percy), 'from which it is believed that all of the aforesaid things were accomplished by divine instigation'. The same chronicler also tells how some in the Montfortian army had described seeing 'an unknown knight, clad in armour and holding before him an unknown banner, and an archbishop clothed in pontifical garb blessing the baronial army'. These were, it was believed, St George and St Thomas Becket.[25]

Their appearance was the mark of the highest divine favour, for St George was the protector of embattled crusaders (he did not become the patron saint of England until the fourteenth century, when Edward III appropriated him as patron of the Order of the Garter). Famously, he had come to the aid of the warriors of the First Crusade at Antioch in 1098. The crusaders, having seized the city, were besieged by an oncoming Muslim army and, trapped inside, had begun to starve. Deciding that it would be better to risk death in battle with the hope of victory than to perish miserably within the city's walls, they had formed up and ridden out, onto the plain beyond the city – only to be surrounded by the enemy, closing in. But then (as one who was there that day recalled) they had looked up and seen appearing atop the mountains beyond the plain 'a countless host of men on white horses, whose banners were all white'. The crusaders 'did not understand what was happening or who these men might be, until they realized that this was the succour sent by Christ, and that the leaders were St George, St Mercurius and St Demetrius'.[26] Emboldened by the presence of the saints, they beat back the enemy and overcame them.

The crusaders and their contemporaries knew that the victory at Antioch, and their later capture of Jerusalem, was most unlikely: at every stage the odds had been against them, and there were so many times when the tide might have turned and the whole enterprise been crushed. That they had triumphed nonetheless was due only in part to their own prowess, and largely to forces beyond their control. One might name these forces luck, while those believing in the power and readiness of God to intervene directly in the world might call it divine providence. Of this there was no greater demonstration than the appearance of St George at Antioch. Amongst the following generations, this was a story widely told, in the songs sung in the feasting halls to celebrate the knightly heroes of Antioch.[27] Now here, at Lewes, for those looking on to link St George with Simon's victory spoke of the status of the Montfortian army, and of Simon himself: crusaders, yes, but more than this – fit to be compared to the legendary heroes of the First Crusade.

It was also a mark of Simon's credentials that St Thomas Becket had appeared, too. His contribution is elaborated by the same Dover chronicler, who describes how around this time St Thomas had also appeared in his home city of Canterbury, in a vision to a local boy. The boy saw St Thomas rising from his bier. 'What are you doing, St Thomas, why do you rise in this way?' he asked. 'I thought you were dead.' The saint answered him, 'I was not dead, but I rested in peace; but now by necessity I have to rise and fight for my country of England.'[28] The saint's role here was as the battler of royal injustice, fearlessly confronting kings who crossed the line. In his lifetime he had followed a procession of English prelates who had reprimanded kings for their trans-gressions, though he had been unusual in suffering martyrdom for his cause.[29] His canonization, in 1173, had sanctified his stand, and he had been a talisman ever since for prelates persecuted by the king (Walter de Cantilupe had invoked his name in 1255 when leading the bishops to resist a royal tax, proclaiming his desire to follow in the footsteps of St Thomas to defend the liberty of the Church).[30] Across the wider kingdom too St Thomas was popular, with pilgrims flocking to his shrine in Canterbury. The association of St Thomas with the cause of the Provisions was not one that Simon and his party pushed (that would be problematic, given how they claimed to be acting in Henry's interests rather than attacking him). In the minds of many, though, it was clear that St Thomas was a Montfortian.

If the victory was miraculous then Simon, it seemed, was touched by God. During the weeks or months that followed, one of his supporters (seemingly a friar in the household of the bishop of Chichester) composed a poem, known as the *Song of Lewes*. Therein, through 968 lines of rhyming Latin couplets, he proclaimed Simon's virtues and his winning of God's favour, before putting forward a defence of the Provisions. Those who had cast aspersions upon Simon were now forced to eat their words: 'They call Simon a misleader and deceiver, but his deeds test him and prove him truthful.' For how could Simon, as some had claimed, have been seeking his own advantage: 'who is able to believe that he would give himself to death, would be willing to ruin his friends, that he might thus exalt himself?'

The author now proclaimed the part of Simon's character, formed on the example of his father, that was central to his identity and to his reputation: his adherence to his oath and his readiness to suffer for it:

> Hence can they, who readily swear and hesitate little to reject what they swear . . . estimate with how great care they ought to preserve their oath, when they see a man flee neither torment nor death, for the sake of his oath . . . Behold! Simon obedient scorns the loss of property, subjecting himself to penalties, that he may not let go the truth . . . Woe to the wretched perjurers, who fear not God, denying Him for the hope of earthly reward, or fear of prison or of a light penalty . . . For the earl had formerly pledged his oath . . . in the parts of Oxford . . . knowing that such canonical constitutions and such catholic ordinances for the peaceful preservation of the realm, on account of which he had previously sustained no slight persecution, were not to be scorned, and that, because he had sworn, they were to be stoutly maintained . . .

This was the most extensive declaration yet of the prime element of Simon's virtue, learned from the Count. And the author moved from here to the extolling of Simon's quality in even richer terms – for the earl's readiness to risk death on the battlefield in the preservation of his oath marked him as spectacular: Simon, 'like unto Christ, gives himself to death for the many'. Like Christ he had been denigrated by so many but 'the stone long refused by the enemy, was afterwards fitted to the two side-walls. The division of desolation of England was on our borders; but for a defence against division was present a corner-stone, the wholly singular religion of Simon.'[31]

Simon had been transformed. He had long inspired loyalty and admiration in his friends, but now his followers were seeing in him something more: a man of extraordinary virtue, who was close to the divine.

This was pure charisma – not in the mundane sense, but in the rarest: of the leader who inspires in their followers a remarkable attraction, given force by their belief that he or she is of uncommon virtue, a glowing exemplar, sent direct from God to do His work. Charisma is a force so powerful that it can pull the followers from their social or moral orbit, transforming the fundamental values upon which are built their actions, propelling them in directions that are unfamiliar.[32] This force was Simon's most potent weapon: for what he was attempting – the transformation of the known political order – was radical. Without their charismatic patron, the Provisions would have been nothing more than a flicker in the political dark, forgotten as the shock of the first coup was absorbed, and the political community settled back into a conservative and comfortable pattern. It was Simon and his magnetic power that could thrust the radical Provisions through the barrier of custom.

It is precisely at this period – when Simon's public face was fully formed, and he was transfigured by his followers into something almost superhuman – that our evidence for his inner life, and personal world, drops away. There are no more letters to him written by his intimates: Adam Marsh died in 1259 and, although his other friends – Walter de Cantilupe and Richard Gravesend, just amongst the churchmen – must have written many, none of them survives. We are thus deprived of their insights into Simon's inner struggles and his seeking of support and consolation. In the same year, 1259, Matthew Paris also died. There are other chroniclers (and amongst them Arnold fitz Thedmar is particularly valuable), but none possesses the interest in capturing a scene that marked out Matthew's work, the record of Simon's verbal spars relayed in direct speech. And Simon's testimony, which furnished in his own words his account of his relationship with Henry, finishes in 1262, when it was delivered at the court of France. We are left then, apart from a few fragments, with the image of Simon that was seen from a distance, whether those watching him looked on admiringly or disapprovingly, or were torn. It is a lacuna that is filled only at the very end of Simon's life, with one precious fragment. And, as that fragment shows, the other Simon – the 'real' Simon, so much as one can ever say that – was never lost to those who knew him well or encountered him in person. And always, through it all, there was another version of him hidden from the world – a version that Simon himself allowed no one but the closest few to see. This was to be revealed only after his end, when the testimonies were gathered and the secrets told. For now, he was the man he became in this moment of his triumph, as he forged himself leader of a new world order: a hero to his followers, and a demon to his enemies.

*

Simon's popularity spread across the kingdom after Lewes. It is not clear how widely the *Song of Lewes* was known, though it might have been picked up by the preachers who proclaimed Simon's virtues and the justness of his cause.* In this way news of Simon's victory, and the telling of his character, could be carried wide and far and, whether through such means or others, the battle and its personalities soon formed an impression on the ordinary men and women of the land. A legal case records an incident that occurred in the vill of Tonge, in Kent, on 29 May, just a couple of weeks following the battle (the Montfortians, having besieged the castle of Rochester in April, passed through Kent again shortly before the end of May).[33] The case describes how two young men, William and Guy, 'went out to play after dinner . . . with William calling himself Simon de Montfort and Guy calling himself Edward'. Although it began as a joshing fight, the two got carried away and started to throw proper punches. Things turned really nasty when another man, Walter (Guy's overseer at the hospital where he worked) moved to intervene, taking William 'by the throat, forcing him against a wall, so that he was almost strangled'. Onlookers rushed to rouse William's father, Richard, who was drinking in a

---

* Only one copy of the *Song of Lewes* survives, in British Library, Harley MS 978, ff. 107r–114r, but this sparsity of copies is not necessarily indicative of the *Song's* circulation, given that the material would later have been considered politically dangerous.

local tavern. Richard, on arriving, picked up a staff discarded in the fight and walloped Walter across the head – inflicting a wound of which Walter died eight days later.

The fight was not moved by political affiliation and, as the jurors (all local men) were keen to stress, there was no malice involved – the situation had simply got out of hand, with tragic consequences. But the beginnings of the brawl show how two young men, poor and of low status, had been inspired by impressions of the two great warriors of the day: Simon, the 'new Mattathias', as the *Song* names him, the warrior suffering for truth; and Edward, a 'lion', according even to the author of the *Song*, 'not slow to attack the strongest places, fearing the onslaught of none . . . and wherever he goes succeeding as it were at his wish, as though like Alexander he would speedily subdue the whole world, if Fortune's moving wheel should stand still for ever'.[34]

Elsewhere, other low-born people took up the cause in earnest. One report describes a woman from Gloucestershire, Margaret wife of William Mauncelle, as 'against the earl and his enemy', apparently agitating against Simon.[35] Elsewhere, others of her status took up arms against or for the earl. On 9 June the villagers of Kibworth in Leicestershire were conducting their customary procession in the week of Pentecost.[36] They were led by Wodard of Kibworth, who was the man of Saer de Harcourt (lord of Kibworth and one of Simon's knights). Wodard probably fought as a Montfortian at Lewes and, upon returning home, sought to transform the village procession into a victory rally, culminating in a special Mass in the village church. But the rally was obstructed by one William King (whose name perhaps suggests where his loyalties lay). William swung his axe and struck a blow to Wodard's head – Wodard tried to get away, but William chased him 'wishing' (so the legal record notes) 'to strike him again and kill him if he could'. Deciding to fight back, Wodard turned and swung his own axe at William's head, causing him a grievous wound, of which he later died. Ordinary men and women, whether with Simon or against him, were choosing to involve themselves in war.[37]

*

After the battle, Simon had needed to determine what to do with the captive king and the rest of the royal family. From Lewes, he had taken them sixty miles north-east, arriving on 20 May at Canterbury, where a discussion was held on the course to be taken. The result was that Simon dispatched Edward and Henry of Almain to Dover Castle, where they would be guarded by Simon's eldest son, their cousin, Henry.[38] Then, on 25 May, Simon set off from Canterbury towards the capital, taking with him the king and Richard of Cornwall. Travelling up the Roman road of Watling Street, they passed by the village of Tonge (where the fatal brawl was to take place on 29 May) and stopped, after two days, at Rochester Castle.

Simon was determined that, this time, he would take the fortress. Depositing Henry next door in the cathedral, he appeared before the garrison and put his demands: he would not eat that day, he said, until the castle had been delivered to him. When the castle's keeper refused to comply, Simon ordered his men to arms – at the sight of which the keeper speedily capitulated. He met Simon and Henry in the cathedral chapter house, where he delivered to Simon custody of Rochester.[39]

Simon entrusted the fortress to Richard de Grey (formerly keeper of Dover) and moved on to London, arriving on 28 May. Establishing Henry at St Paul's, he delivered Richard of Cornwall into the custody of Hugh Despenser in the Tower. Before long, however, he came to the decision that it would be safer to keep Richard, together with Edward and Henry of Almain, further inland, under the guard of the most reliable custodian who could be found: Eleanor de Montfort. While the king would remain at Simon's side, the other three royal prisoners were dispatched to Wallingford, to be guarded by the countess.[40]

The decision to move the prisoners from the coast might have been prompted by the arrival, on 25 May, of a messenger sent by the papal legate. Gui Foulquois, appointed by the pope at the request of the king and queen of France in November of the previous year, had been staying with Louis since his arrival at the French court. News of the Battle of Lewes had made its way to him via the earl Warenne and Hugh Bigod, who had escaped the battlefield to Pevensey in Sussex and had sailed thence across the Channel.[41] The legate, hearing their tale, now dispatched an envoy, a Franciscan named Alan, with letters asking that the legate be given safe passage into England.

Arriving at Dover, Alan had been seized immediately by men of the port. They stripped off his outer tunic to conduct a body search and rifled his baggage. They were looking for letters – if a single one, they warned Alan, were found on his possession that was damaging to the kingdom (meaning letters imposing spiritual penalties on the Montfortians) then he would face death. They then took him to the castle, where they were soon joined by Henry de Montfort. After consulting, via letter, with his father, young Henry relayed his message: Alan was to tell the legate that there was no need for him to come to England – for if his purpose was to make a peace then the barons could do this without his help and, in any case, they did not trust him to be impartial. And anyway, the legate had no authority to enter England (here the Montfortians appealed to a long-held but spurious claim that papal legates could not enter England without an invitation from the king and, as they added now, 'the community of the kingdom'). Alan was sent back to France to tell the legate that he was not welcome (Alan's report, outlining these events, is preserved in the register kept by Gui Foulquois during his legation).[42] His visit was a reminder to the Montfortians that the army of Queen Eleanor, mustered from her post at the court of France, was readying to launch – and with the help of Louis and the legate. When this happened, the coast of Kent would form the front line of the battle for England.

Meanwhile, Simon set about securing the kingdom from within. This process would begin with imposing law and order in the shires and to this end, on 4 June, keepers of the peace were appointed across the land to quell disturbances.[43] Simon would also need to build relations with the knightly class, on whom the government always relied to carry out administration on the ground. Here, Simon's party made a significant decision. In every shire new sheriffs would have to be appointed, for the new regime could not afford to keep in office men loyal to the king. One option was simply to impose upon the shires loyal Montfortians – but instead the new regime invited shire

16. The victory of Louis IX over English forces at Taillebourg and Saintes was pivotal in the Capetian campaign to conquer the Plantagenet lands on the Continent for the crown of France. The battle, subsumed into a nationalist narrative in the nineteenth century, was celebrated in a painting (1837) by Eugène Delacroix commissioned for the Galerie des Batailles at Versailles.

17. In the bottom-left-hand corner of this document, produced for the 1262 arbitration, Henry III recalls what Simon said to him two decades earlier after defeat by the king of France: 'It would be a good thing if you were taken and shut away, as was done to Charles the Simple. There are houses with iron bars at Windsor that would be good for imprisoning you securely inside.'

18. Odiham Castle, in Hampshire, was granted to Eleanor de Montfort by Henry in October 1236. She and Simon rebuilt it, erecting a mighty octagonal keep, almost seventy feet high with walls ten feet thick, encased in Caen stone (which has since been robbed). The castle would be Eleanor's base of operations during the civil war.

19. Ten miles from Odiham stands Waverley Abbey, a Cistercian house of which Eleanor was a patron. Waverley's annalist records a visit by the Montforts in 1245: Eleanor and Simon had brought their two elder sons, Henry (six) and Simon (about four), to take part in the Palm Sunday procession.

20. The tomb of Aymer de Valence's heart. Aymer was bishop of Winchester and one of Henry III's half-brothers, the son of Isabella d'Angoulême and her second husband, Hugh de Lusignan. The heart tomb, at Winchester Cathedral, is decorated with the arms of the Lusignans (below the figure of Aymer), the kings of England (three lions passant guardant) and Richard of Cornwall as king of Germany.

21. The church of St James, Shere (Surrey). The attack on the church by the men of Aymer de Valence was pivotal in the political crisis of 1258.

22. In 1258, John fitz Geoffrey's complaint against Aymer de Valence was dismissed by the king at the opening of a parliament at Westminster; shortly afterwards seven barons joined in sworn confederation, promising mutual aid against 'all people', although the real target was the Lusignans. Simon was joined by the earls of Gloucester and Norfolk, Hugh Bigod, Peter of Savoy, John fitz Geoffrey and Peter de Montfort (Simon's friend but no relation). The document recording their oath, to which the confederates attached their seals, survives only as an antiquarian sketch.

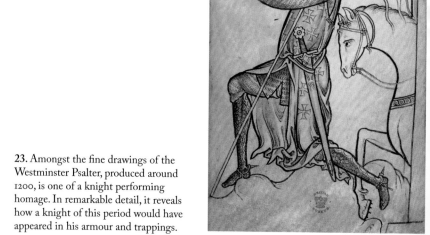

23. Amongst the fine drawings of the Westminster Psalter, produced around 1200, is one of a knight performing homage. In remarkable detail, it reveals how a knight of this period would have appeared in his armour and trappings.

24. Simon's will was drawn up on 1 January 1259, while Simon was in France together with his two eldest sons and his friend Richard Gravesend, bishop of Lincoln. The final sentence of the document testifies that it was written by Simon's eldest son, Henry (who was then twenty years old).

25. The tomb of Gui Foulquois, who served as papal legate to England in 1264 and was elected pope, as Clement IV, in February 1265. He died in 1268 and his tomb, preserved in the church of San Francesco, Viterbo, was created soon afterwards by Pietro di Oderisio. Clement's effigy reposes on an ancient sarcophagus inlaid with Cosmati mosaic.

26. Whilst almost all chronicles in this period were written by monks, Arnold fitz Thedmar's preserves the rare perspective of a layman. He seems to have attended the great Montfortian parliament of January–March 1265, and wrote up his account of it shortly afterwards. This means that his chronicle, held at the London Metropolitan Archives, preserves an account of the first parliament to which townsmen were summoned, written by one of the townsmen themselves.

27. As an inscription in the tiled floor of Westminster Abbey's Chapter House proclaims, 'As the rose is the flower of flowers, so is this the house of houses'. Key elements of its design were chosen by Henry III, who envisaged it as a venue for his speech-making.

28. The doors preserved in the east wall of St George's chapel, in Windsor Castle, were commissioned by Henry III for the original chapel, dedicated to St Edward the Confessor. Although the gilding and red ground are not original, they are true to the door's original decoration. This design was popular in the mid-thirteenth century (see image 2) and a similar one was probably used to adorn the lectern commissioned by Henry III for the Westminster Chapter House (installed in 1260).

29. On the seven hundredth anniversary of Simon's death in 1965, a monument was erected on the site of his original burial in the choir of Evesham Abbey. The monks of Evesham hosted Simon in his final hours and buried the Montfortian dead. The remains of the abbey lie at the southern end of the town, beside the River Avon.

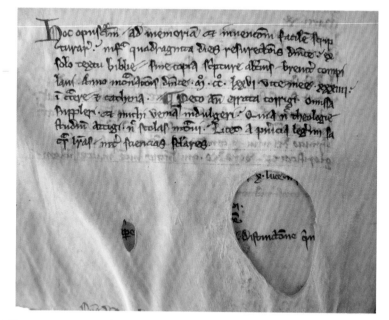

30. The treatise written by Amaury de Montfort, Simon's son, in 1276 during his imprisonment at Corfe Castle is preserved at the Bodleian Library. In this passage, Amaury gives the date of the work's composition and notes that he had only a Bible for reference, and that he undertook the task in the thirty-fourth year of his life *in carcere et cathena*, in prison and in chains. Given the circumstances, he asks for the reader's patience with his errors and omissions.

communities to elect candidates themselves from amongst their own.*
This was a risky move, but securing the good government of the
shires by sound and honest sheriffs had been an important element
of the Provisions.[44] Choosing to honour this commitment now was
a landmark statement of the new regime's intent.

The elections were orchestrated in a parliament held in London
in the fourth week of June. The assembly's other task was to establish a new system for the government of England. The goal was to
move forward from the system established in 1258 for the council
of fifteen, to one in which the process of appointment was trans-
parent and the decision-making process clearly defined. And so a
new constitution was constructed, its terms drawn up during the
parliament: three men would be appointed, and these three would
have the power to choose a further nine. The king would 'by the
counsel of these nine . . . settle and dispose of the custody of castles
and all other affairs of the realm', as well as 'appoint the justiciar,
chancellor, treasurer, and other officials, great and small, in all those
things which concern the government of the court and of the realm'.
Although here the king was named as the chief agent of government,
the constitution quickly pointed out the purely decorative nature
of his power: 'the lord king shall do all these things by the counsel
of the nine in this form, or they shall do them in place of and on
the authority of the lord king'.[45] If there was any disagreement
amongst the nine, the decision of a two-thirds majority would stand.
The three electors were to be Simon, Stephen of Bersted, bishop
of Chichester, and the earl of Gloucester. The nine included three
churchmen: a bishop (Henry of Sandwich, bishop of London), an
abbot (Henry, abbot of the Premonstratensian house St Radegund's,
near Dover), and a senior member of the scholarly community,
Thomas de Cantilupe. Joining them were six laymen. Three were
of major baronial rank – Simon's great friend Peter de Montfort,

---

* The keepers of the peace were ordered to arrange for their shires each to elect four
men, to be sent to London for 22 June to participate in a parliament. At this parliament, the representatives were apparently asked to appoint sheriffs for their shires.
The appointments produced sheriffs of local stock, of knightly or middling rank,
landowners and experienced administrators (only one can be identified as a committed
Montfortian) (R. Cassidy, 'Simon de Montfort's sheriffs, 1264–5', *Historical Research*,
91 (2018), 3–21, at 4–11).

Humphrey de Bohun (son of the earl of Hereford) and Giles de Argentin – and there were three knights: Ralph de Camoys, Roger of St John and Adam of Newmarket.[46] The council was, therefore, in its composition carefully balanced, representing the various, interlocking groups who held a stake in the new regime: the secular and monastic clergy as well as scholars, barons and knights.*

---

* On 23 June a proclamation was issued in the name of the king, empowering Simon and his two colleagues of the electoral triumvirate to nominate 'faithful, experienced and useful men of the kingdom', churchmen and laymen, to form this council. The king's mandate was confirmed two days later in a letter of two bishops and two magnates, on behalf of those present at the parliament, attaching their seals 'by the will and clear consent of all'. The decision to ratify the original order served to demonstrate that the council was founded upon a broad base of consent, rather than on Simon's military superiority. The identities of the men chosen to represent the community were important: the bishops of Exeter and Salisbury, Roger, earl of Norfolk, and John fitz John. Only two of these four – Walter de la Wyle, bishop of Salisbury, and John fitz John – were Montfortians. The earl of Norfolk had been involved in the original programme of reform back in 1258, but then had joined the king's side and had put his name to the royalist case at Amiens, while the bishop of Exeter, Walter de Bronescombe, had always remained loyal to the king. Neither was openly hostile to the Montfortian party, cooperating with it in various ways, but nevertheless the provision of their support for the establishment of the council helped to suggest that the council had a broad base of support. It was an impression clarified by the list of names appended to the full constitution, which included not only the arch-Montfortian Richard Gravesend, bishop of Lincoln, but also the bishop of Ely, Hugh Balsham – a supporter of Simon but one with no previous connection to his party, and a man whom Henry III had once described as 'a simple man of the cloister, unwarlike and feeble, who had never experienced the shrewd ways of the court'. Also putting their names to the constitution were the earl of Norfolk, the earl of Oxford, and the mayor of London, amongst others. Simon had taken power by force, but having done so he delivered it into the hands of an executive that would share power and wield it on behalf of the community (*Foedera, Conventiones, Litterae et Acta Publica*, ed. T. Rymer, new edn., I, part i, ed. A. Clark and F. Holbrooke (London, 1816), 444; J. P. Gilson, 'The parliament of 1264', *English Historical Review*, 16 (1901), 499–501, at 500; R. F. Treharne and I. J. Sanders (eds.), *Documents of the Baronial Movement of Reform and Rebellion, 1258–1267* (Oxford, 1973), 298–9; J. R. Maddicott, *Simon de Montfort* (Cambridge, 1994), 285–8; S. T. Ambler, *Bishops in the Political Community of England, 1213–1272* (Oxford, 2017), 126, 137–9, 142; K. Harvey, *Episcopal Appointment in England, c.1214–1344: From Episcopal Election to Papal Provision* (Aldershot, 2014), 94; N. Vincent, 'The thirteenth-century bishops', in *Ely: Bishops and Diocese 1109–2009*, ed. P. Meadows (Woodbridge, 2010), 26–69, at 36–9).

*

The new government now faced an immediate and major problem: the army of Queen Eleanor poised on the Continent to launch, intent on reclaiming power for the royal family. In readiness, the new regime set to mustering an army to defend the coast. Now the Montfortians held the machinery of government, including the chancery, they could issue orders in the king's name and summon the feudal host to serve for up to forty days. The summons could be published widely: there was a well-established system for publicizing royal proclamations across the kingdom, in shire courts and in public meeting places.[47] The council would exploit this system to speak directly to as broad an audience as possible, beyond the lords whose loyalty to the new regime perhaps was suspect. The call was thus addressed not only to 'bishops, abbots, priors, earls, barons' (tenants-in-chief of the crown) as well as sheriffs, but also to 'knights, free people and the entire community' of each shire. This was the same readiness to engage the population in its broadest form, including the poor and the unfree, as the first reforming council had demonstrated in 1258–9. The message, issued on 6 July, was potent:

Since it is known for sure that a great horde of foreigners is readying . . . to invade the kingdom by force of arms, to the perpetual confusion and disinheritance of us and of every single person of this kingdom . . . we order you, by the faith by which you are held to us . . . that you, knights and all free tenants, who are appointed to this task, prepare yourselves with horses and arms manfully and powerfully . . . to march thence with us against the foreigners . . . not only with the military contingent that you are held to provide for us, but as manfully and powerfully as you can . . . every vill is to send eight, six or four, at least, according to the size of the vill, of the better and more honest foot soldiers, armed with lances, bows, arrows, swords, crossbows and axes . . . Let no man plead the needs of the approaching harvest, nor the occupation of any family matter, since it is safer and better that his goods be damaged slightly and he be safe in his person, than that his lands and goods be totally destroyed and he be delivered to a cruel death by the impious hands of those who thirst for your blood, who will spare neither sex nor age if they manage to prevail.[48]

With the fears of the kingdom stirred, Simon turned to confront the enemy within: the marchers. They had failed to attend the parliament in June, to which they were supposed to have brought the Montfortians captured at Northampton to be released under the terms of the Mise of Lewes.[49] And so Simon ordered the muster of the 'knights, free people and all others' of Shropshire, Gloucestershire and Herefordshire, and headed westward (perhaps in the second week of July), together with Peter de Montfort, John fitz John and the earl of Gloucester's younger brother, Thomas de Clare.[50] This notable force, aided by Llywelyn ap Gruffudd, quickly subdued the marchers, ravaging the lands of Roger Mortimer and taking the castles of Hereford, Hay, Richard's Castle and Ludlow.[51] The marchers met Simon at Montgomery and there were compelled to promise the release of the Northampton prisoners and the delivery of the royal castles still in their possession, and to surrender hostages to guarantee their good faith: Roger Mortimer handed over his son William, and James Audley his son Nicholas.[52]

With this achieved, towards the end of July Simon returned to London, where prelates and magnates were convened at St Paul's in continued efforts to prepare their defence against the oncoming invasion. A major concern was that the papal legate, Gui Foulquois, would inflict upon the Montfortians spiritual penalties, namely that he would excommunicate them – casting them out from the community of the faithful – and place their lands under interdict. This would be a serious blow to the Montfortians, undermining their moral credibility: if the legate were to take such measures, it could turn the people of England against them. And so on 27 July, the council set out to present its version of events. Issuing a letter to the bishops of Worcester, Lincoln, Chichester, Exeter, Coventry and Lichfield, it denounced the attacks on Church property that had occurred over the previous year and denied any involvement, and gave notice of an appeal to the pope against any sentence of excommunication, suspension or interdict imposed on these erroneous grounds. The letter asked the bishops to add their seals to this statement, and instructed them to publish it, 'so that it may be revealed and be clear to all'.[53] Walter de Cantilupe, acting as leader of the English bishops, obliged: he made a speech at the assembly describing how the bishops were conducting investigations to unearth the malefactors, and how the barons had promised to make restitution for any offences – any measures taken by the legate would therefore be unnecessary, Walter pointed out, and he sent a letter to the pope to tell him so, to which many seals were appended.[54]

Meanwhile, on 27 July, a letter was directed to the papal legate from Simon, the earls of Gloucester and Norfolk, and Peter de Montfort. They told the legate that the question of his coming to England had been discussed in the parliament in London, which had decided that it would be dangerous for the kingdom 'if these matters were to be managed not in faith but under the appearance of fictitious love'. Once again, the legate was instructed that he had no authority to enter England without invitation, and told that the community did not consent to his coming. The letter writers would, however, be willing to hold discussions on the Continent – but if they were to send bishops as ambassadors, the legate must guarantee not to enjoin on them orders to impose spiritual penalties on anyone within the kingdom. They then complained about the king of France supporting the army gathered on the Continent and asked the legate to put an end to it, 'lest the envy of wicked people, thirsting without cause for life and blood' should prevail.[55] On the same day, a provision was made 'by the unanimous assent of all the magnates and potentates of the kingdom of England', that anyone carrying or publishing letters of interdict or excommunication against those sworn to observe the Provisions of Oxford would face decapitation.[56]

On 15 August, the Montfortians sent to the king of France and the papal legate a copy of the Peace of Canterbury (drawn up in the city where the Montfortians had gathered to oversee the coastal defence).[57] The Peace contained the new constitution, establishing the council of the three and the nine, but added a further stipulation, that the Peace would stand until the terms of the Mise of Lewes were fulfilled but, failing that, throughout the lifetimes of Henry III and Edward – in other words, indefinitely. The Peace therefore laid down a landmark statement: the government of England was to be operated by a council for the foreseeable future.

In sending the Peace to the legate and the king of France, the Montfortians had asked that Louis give it his approval. This was, perhaps, optimistic. In a letter to the Montfortian bishops, the legate reported Louis's words: 'We have heard the most Christian king of France say, when he heard the terms of the form of peace, that he would rather break clods of earth behind the plough than have a rule of this kind.'[58]

In England, meanwhile, the population had responded to the vitriolic call to arms. 'By this precept', wrote the London chronicler Arnold fitz Thedmar, 'an innumerable multitude of knights and foot soldiers gathered, well-armed . . . to defend the kingdom against the foreigners'. Indeed, 'such a multitude gathered together against the foreigners', wrote another chronicler, 'that you would not have believed so many men equipped for war existed in England'.* The army was mustered in London and marched south to Kent. With the chief Montfortians based at Canterbury, the army's camp was set at Barham Down, about eight miles south-east of the city, ready for deployment across the Kentish coast. This mighty host was financed by the Church: the prelates of England, many of whom supported Simon, had agreed a tax of a tenth of Church income in support of the kingdom's defence.[59]

With the Montfortians still anxious to avoid putting this army to the test, a delegation of bishops was tasked with negotiating with the legate. The bishops first tried to put forward arguments in favour of the Peace of Canterbury by letter, appealing to a threefold precedent (God's ordering of the universe, papal government and the rulership of Moses) to justify the new form of government. But

---

* *De Antiquis Legibus Liber. Cronica Maiorum et Vicecomitum Londoniarum*, ed. T. Stapleton (London, 1846), 69; H. R. Luard (ed.), *Flores Historiarum*, 3 vols. (London: 1890), II, 499. Only the people of Cambridgeshire and Huntingdonshire, and the people of Essex, were singled out by the council as having failed to attend the London muster in sufficient numbers, whereby the sheriffs of these territories were ordered to proclaim the call again; if after three or four days candidates had not been kitted out and sent by their communities, then the sheriff was to arrest lacklustre parties and imprison them, raising money from their lands for a contingent of armed men (*Calendar of Patent Rolls, 1232–72*, 4 vols. (London, 1906–13), *1258–66*, 364–5).

their arguments, produced post facto under pressure, lacked clout
and the legate demolished them with relative ease. The bishops
were locked in an invidious position: they were duty bound to obey
the papal legate, but would not abandon their loyalty to Simon and
the cause. In the end, the bishops of Worcester, London and
Winchester had no option but to meet the legate in person,
accompanied by Hugh Despenser and Peter de Montfort. The legate
was able to put the bishops on the spot, 'as to whether they would
agree with the barons, that the king of England should be bound
to having certain councillors and to following their counsel precisely'.
As the legate's clerk noted, 'each one of them responded, "yes"'.
They were sent home with orders to withdraw from their confederation with Simon, to observe the sentence of excommunication that
the legate had now pronounced against the Montfortian barons,
and to publish the sentence if the Montfortians did not submit to
the legate within a fortnight.[60] This was precisely the situation the
bishops had feared.

Before departing, the bishops had asked leave to return to the
legate – but they never did. Instead, on 11 October, at a late hour, an
English knight sailed into Wissant. He did not disembark, but from
his ship cast into the sea a chest. It was found to contain documents
for the attention of the legate. These included the Peace of Canterbury
and letters of Simon and the earl of Gloucester, to which their seals
were affixed, approving the Peace.[61] The legate, 'understanding from
what had been sent the hardened malice of the barons of England,
proceeded against them'. He renewed the sentence of excommunication
and had it published throughout France.[62]

Until this point, the legate had been preventing the launch of
Queen Eleanor's army, hoping for a peaceful resolution. Now, by
the time the talks had collapsed, it was too late: the queen had been
forced to hold the vast force for so long that her funds had run dry,
and the troops began to disband. At the same time, the legate –
much to his frustration – was recalled to Rome, for the pope who
had commissioned him had died, bringing an automatic end to his
legatine authority.

The timing of both these developments was extremely fortunate
for Simon. His own force had been kept in the field longer than
forty days (by custom the maximum term of military service).

Although the main force, mustered in Kent, had apparently remained intact under the command of the Montfortian leaders, ancillary forces gathered on the coasts of Norfolk, Suffolk and Essex had begun to disperse.[63] Now, though, Simon knew that it was safe to disband the host: with winter coming and the campaign season drawing to a close, the window for a sea-borne invasion would shut until the spring.

*

Simon could now turn to problems within the kingdom. Once again, the marchers were causing trouble for the new regime. Roger Mortimer, Roger Clifford and Roger of Leybourne (the last not a marcher by landholding, but associated with them) were ignoring the Montgomery agreement – despite the danger to the hostages – and had taken up arms in the west, capturing the castles of Gloucester, Bridgnorth and Marlborough.[64] Most worryingly, they had even attempted to break Edward free. Edward was being held at Wallingford Castle, halfway between Oxford and Reading – a site that, Simon would have reasoned, put him at a safe distance from his friends in the Welsh borderlands. But the marcher garrison of Bristol Castle had received a letter from the queen entreating her son's friends to rescue him. In response, Warin de Bassingbourne had led a force of three hundred men out of the Marches and nearly seventy miles east to Wallingford, where they managed to breach the castle's curtain wall. Probably there was never any real risk they would succeed in breaking Edward free – the keep at Wallingford was monumental and could hardly have been penetrated without serious siege machinery.[65] And as the garrison of Wallingford told Warin de Bassingbourne, they could, if threatened, simply throw Edward from the roof of the keep. It was a threat Edward certainly took seriously – he was brought out to order the marchers to withdraw, 'or he would be dead'.[66]

It was clear that Simon would need to deal with the marchers. He summoned the feudal host, which gathered at Oxford around 25 November, and moved thence to Worcester.[67] An account of what happened there is given by a local chronicler, writing at Pershore Abbey (the house lies on the direct route between Oxford and

Worcester, making it possible that Simon's force passed through Pershore on the ninety-mile journey, which would explain why the chronicler is so well informed).[68] Simon, recounts the chronicler, had been 'driven to anger by the rebellion and broken faith' of the marchers, who were to be treated as 'public enemies of the kingdom'. He moved on Worcester with a mighty force (a 'countless multitude of knights and other warriors'). The marchers, few in number but great in warlike boldness, had withdrawn to the west of Worcester and broken the city's bridge, the major crossing point across the Severn, and minor bridges too, and sunk boats up and down the river, preventing Simon's force from following them by foot or water. 'But in vain they laboured against so many nobles,' writes the chronicler, 'especially against that most astute of warriors, Simon de Montfort.' For now Simon's ally in Wales, Llywelyn ap Gruffudd, crossed eastward to attack the marchers from their rear (presumably Simon had got word to him). The marchers were trapped.[69]

Simon was now in a position to impose terms, set out on 20 December. The marchers were to deliver to Simon all their castles in the borderlands, from Bristol up to Chester. The county of Chester itself was held by Edward and this, too, would be delivered to Simon, together with the lordship and castle of the Peak, in Derbyshire. Hereford Castle would be committed to Peter de Montfort, Shrewsbury to Ralph Basset of Drayton (another dedicated Montfortian). And the marchers would be banished from the British Isles, sent to Ireland for a year. Simon, in turn, would agree to release Edward ('that distinguished young man', as the Pershore chronicler called him), and Henry of Almain.[70]

With the Peace of Worcester concluded, Simon (continues the Pershore chronicler) was 'pleased with himself in his fortune in all those things to which he had turned his mind'. Simon had not only dispelled the threat of the marchers – he had, through this resounding victory and the near-destruction of Edward's friends, been able to extract a valuable prize: the earldom of Chester and the lordship of the Peak. By the terms of the agreement, these were to be exchanged for lands of equivalent value but, tellingly, these were not specified by Simon – it was merely a device to conceal the seizing of Edward's lands. These lordships were extremely valuable: with the addition of Newcastle (taken too from

Edward in the wake of the Peace of Worcester), their total annual income amounted to something like £1,500, about three times the sum of Simon's hereditary lands in Leicester.[71] It was an extraordinary move on Simon's part. It could have been justified strategically, for the acquisition of Chester would allow Simon to oversee the Marches, while depriving Edward of perhaps a quarter of his income would significantly limit his capacity to oppose the Montfortian regime, should he find the opportunity.[72] In these terms, the seizure of Chester and the Peak could have been made as part of an act of resumption, helping to support the new regime financially. But it was not, and the lands were 'granted' to Simon himself.[73] It was an audacious move, and an act of cold aggression against the heir to the throne.

The seizure would have helped to support Simon's swelling status. The Pershore chronicler reports that, around this time, Simon was riding with a retinue of some 160 household knights, 'devoted to his allegiance'.[74] This was nothing less than a private army. It was such a sizeable household that Simon decided not to celebrate the feast of Christmas with the king – leaving Henry at Woodstock, he took his men to Kenilworth to hold his own court there. As to what to make of all of this, the Pershore chronicler was torn. He clearly admired Simon – 'that most astute of warriors' – but he also admired Edward, and was uncomfortable with the disrespect being shown to a monarch. Henry, he wrote, had been ruling for almost fifty years, but the title of king was but a 'shadow of a name'. He could not even move freely around his land, for Simon had (with the exception of Christmas) taken to leading Henry around with him.[75] The royalist chronicler Thomas Wykes spoke out more forcefully: 'the earl was carried away with his exalted status', he wrote, 'revelling in his virtue beyond measure to himself and to his sons'. As to his treatment of the king, Wykes continued, 'as the teacher is accustomed to lead his pupil, so he ignobly led the king around all the provinces of the kingdom . . . he was not ashamed to rule his king . . . so that the name of the earl utterly overshadowed the royal highness'.[76]

*

Simon could count on a dedicated cohort of friends and a devoted following of knights to aid him – but in order to stabilize the new regime and provide for its long-term success, his party needed to engage a broader constituency across the kingdom. Particularly important here were the knights of the shires – upon whom the government customarily relied to manage royal administration and implement justice on the ground – and the leading townsmen, whose prominence in society had risen through the thirteenth century to match urban growth. A decision was made, therefore, to summon a parliament in 1265, to meet around the feast of St Hilary (13 January) and to which knights and townsmen would be summoned.

There was nothing new about calling knights to parliament, for men of middling status had been attending great assemblies since at least the time of the Norman Conquest and probably before. Until the earlier thirteenth century, their qualification for this role had been based on property holding: if they held land directly from the king, they were tenants-in-chief of the crown (even if they did not hold land on a scale significant enough to put them amongst the magnates), and would thus receive a summons on significant occasions. More recently, a system had been introduced for choosing knightly representatives by local election – a procedure first employed by Henry III in 1254. But such men did not receive a summons to every great assembly: their presence was deemed necessary only when a tax would be proposed, because their support would be required for its granting and levying. The major innovation, in the tenets of the Provisions and in the summons issued in December 1264, was to call knights when no tax was on the table: their role was solely to discuss the business of the kingdom.[77]

As to the involvement of townsmen, this seems to have been entirely new. The decision to establish a place for these men in parliament was in part based on the wish to secure their support. In order to do so, the regime needed to offer them something that the king had not: a voice in the running of the kingdom. The gathering of such men also provided a singular opportunity to promote the new regime – for if they could be persuaded of the council's virtue then they would carry the sentiment home at the parliament's close, sharing their news with friends, colleagues and family, thus helping to build the regime's popularity across the kingdom.

But the impetus for the summoning of townsmen as of knights also came from an enduring commitment to the Provisions, which had decreed that three parliaments be held every year regardless of the king's wishes or immediate needs, thereby insisting that parliament's role in the running of the kingdom was fundamental. To this commitment Simon had stuck firmly, in the face of opposition from the king and conservative reformers in 1260, as we have seen. It was a commitment that Simon had maintained, in the autumn of 1261 (when he and Walter de Cantilupe had attempted to gather a parliament at St Albans) and again in the immediate aftermath of the Battle of Lewes, when the parliament at St Paul's had given its approval to the establishment of the new constitution. The holding of a parliament now, in January 1265, was thus a reaffirmation of the council's ongoing commitment to parliament's place in the new political order. And, as at St Paul's in 1264 (when attendees had approved the council of nine, and their authority had been cited in banning the papal legate's entry into England), the approval of parliament was seen as a vast moral buttress for a regime that rested on shaky theoretical foundations. The assembled men of parliament – bishops, abbots and priors, barons, knights and townsmen – represented a body that might equal or even surpass the king himself in authority: the community of the kingdom.

The parliament opened at Westminster on 20 January. It would last some seven weeks, ending around 11 March. Our most thorough account of the meetings is given by Arnold fitz Thedmar, the London chronicler. The level of detail, and his attention to the staging of the assembly's central events, imply that Arnold was present at the parliament, in his capacity as either a chronicler or, given his status as a leading alderman, one of London's representatives (most towns were to send two men, London four). An analysis of the manuscript of his chronicle suggests that he wrote up his account almost immediately afterwards.[78] This makes his telling of the Hilary parliament an incredibly precious source: an eye-witness account of the first parliament to be attended by townsmen, authored by one of the townsmen who attended, written up close to the event, in his own hand (see plate 26).

Arnold describes two key events in the course of the parliament. The first came on the feast of St Valentine, 14 February. The main meeting had probably been taking place in the grand expanse of Westminster Hall (which had a capacity of several thousand, and could thus accommodate all the churchmen, barons, knights and townsmen who had gathered), but on this day a special meeting was held in the Chapter House of Westminster Abbey. This space had been used for assemblies before (in fact, it had been built with this function in mind), though on a smaller scale, since it could accommodate only sixty-odd people sitting, or 250 standing.[79] There was a particular reason for moving the focus of the parliament (or at least as many men as possible) into the Chapter House now. Here the Montfortians announced that Henry had sworn an oath, promising that neither he nor Edward would at any time move against Simon or the earl of Gloucester, nor the citizens of London, nor anyone else who adhered to them, and that he would uphold Magna Carta and the Charter of the Forest, as well as the Montfortian constitution.[80] It is not clear whether Henry was present in the Chapter House – if he was, he was kept silent (Arnold fitz Thedmar is clear that a proclamation was made on his behalf). This was a powerful statement, for the Chapter House had been designed by Henry himself as a grand venue for his speech-making, where he envisaged himself declaiming in authoritative and dignified fashion to his bishops and barons. The architectural features on which he had insisted – from the statue of the Annunciation (the most famous speech in history) to the lectern wrought of gilded iron – were intended to emphasize this facet of Henry's personal authority (see plates 27 and 28). The Montfortians now, in appropriating the Chapter House and denying Henry the right to speak in it, were making a potent point about who was holding power.[81]

The culmination of the parliament came on the feast of St Gregory, 11 March, in Westminster Hall. Edward and Henry of Almain were, in Arnold's words, 'released to the lord king' in full view of the assembled crowd. It is not clear what form this 'release' took – perhaps the two young men were made to walk across the dais of the hall from Simon to the king. The releasing of the younger royal prisoners had been promised in the Peace of Worcester but, as must have been apparent to all involved, their 'release' now was a charade – a piece of political theatre that showed compliance with the Worcester agreement without, in reality, making any concession at all: for the hostages were being delivered to the king, and the king was still in Simon's custody.

Next, letters were read out on behalf of the king and Edward, in which they promised to observe the peace of the kingdom – again, the king was kept silent, as too now was Edward. Then, in the climax of this carefully crafted ceremony, nine bishops stepped forward in full liturgical regalia, holding lighted candles. They pronounced a sentence of excommunication against anyone who presumed to break Magna Carta or the Charter of the Forest, the Provisions of Westminster, or in any way went against the Montfortian constitution establishing the council of nine. Finally, Edward was singled out. Letters were read announcing that he had sworn to deliver custody of the Three Castles of Wales (Grosmont, Skenfrith and White Castle), to ensure that the marchers would fulfil their promises (or Edward himself was to be made a capital enemy), that he would abide in England for three years and would not seek to leave without obtaining licence from the council, and that he would not attempt to bring foreigners into England (foreign mercenaries were the target here). Edward had sworn, so the letters ran, that if he should break any of these terms his lands would be forfeit. 'And for the greater security of this matter' (Arnold recalled the announcement), 'lord Henry of Almain has put himself as a hostage, by his own free will, for lord Edward, to be held in the custody of lord Henry de Montfort up to the feast of St Peter in Chains [1 August]'. If, during this term, an army of foreigners should start preparing to invade, then Henry of Almain would remain a hostage for Edward in Henry de Montfort's custody until the feast of All Saints (1 November), until it was known whether Edward was willing to fight against the invaders.[82] The objective here was clear: to obstruct a renewed attempt by Queen Eleanor to raise a mercenary army and sail it to English shores. The naming of Henry of Almain as 'hostage' implied a serious threat: if the terms of an agreement sealed by the delivery of hostages were broken, then the lives of those hostages would be forfeit. The Montfortians might have hesitated to harm Edward himself (despite the threat of the garrison of Wallingford the previous autumn to cast him from the top of the keep), but those scruples did not necessarily apply to Edward's cousin.

The stage-managed ritual in Westminster Hall revealed the blend of principle and menace upon which the new regime was founded. The confirmation of Magna Carta and the Forest Charter, and the sentence of excommunication that enforced it, was intended to assert the legitimacy of the new regime. The establishment of the council of nine, and the imprisonment of the royal family, were profoundly radical acts – and thus potentially unsettling. In contrast, Magna Carta and the Forest Charter comprised an established political programme that contained the most venerated of principles: that government was held to operate within the law. The 1225 charters had been issued by the king, and then confirmed in 1237 and 1253, in return for grants of taxation, representing a consensual balance of power between ruler and subjects. By binding the radical programme with one that was customary and highly valued, the Montfortians hoped to imbue their constitution with legitimacy. The message was emphasized by the role of the bishops. Since 1225, the charters had been issued and then confirmed accompanied by a sentence of excommunication performed by the bishops, who had taken on the role of enforcing them. Re-enacting the ritual here and now, in the great Montfortian parliament, would associate the new programme with sacred custom.[83]

At the close of the parliament, this was the message that the bishops, abbots, priors, barons, knights and townsmen would carry home. And, in order to ensure that this message reached as wide an audience as possible, the chancery (now acting under the direction of Thomas de Cantilupe, appointed chancellor during the parliament), put together a package of documents, copies of which were sent to every shire. The package contained exemplars of the confirmation of Magna Carta and the Forest Charter, sealed with the royal seal and witnessed by Simon and his party, as well as copies of the Provisions of Westminster (reissued in December) and the Montfortian constitution. Also included was a letter in Henry's name, giving an official account of the parliament, describing the oaths sworn and the sentence of excommunication. The sheriffs were instructed to keep these documents safely, and to have them 'read aloud in full county court at least twice a year'.[84]

This was, by any standard, a masterful exercise in public

communication: a clear and powerful message, presented to the immediate audience in Westminster in a dramatic piece of theatre intended to impress upon the senses, and to a wider audience through what was, effectively, a carefully composed press release. The culmination of the Hilary parliament built upon a long-standing strength of the reforming enterprise, evident since its earliest days: a willingness and ability to communicate to a wider audience. But here this element was elevated with a subtlety and skill that was new. The man responsible was in all likelihood Thomas de Cantilupe. It had been Thomas who had first attempted to legitimize the reform programme by binding it to Magna Carta, when he had drawn up the case to be presented to the king of France at Amiens, at the turn of 1264. It was Thomas now who held the office of Chancellor, in charge of the government's writing office, overseeing the production of official documents – including the confirmations of the charters and the official account of the parliament dispatched with them to the shires. At Amiens, Thomas had constructed a detailed argument that had been dismissed; now, he set out to make the connection symbolically, in a way that was simpler and thus more powerful, precisely because it did not explain the relationship explicitly: those watching the ceremony in Westminster Hall, and those listening in the shire courts, were invited to make the association for themselves, eliminating the need to confront conflicts of interpretation and engaging the audience, by this very process, with the Montfortian programme.

As to the other side of the parliamentary ritual – the menace – this can only have been Simon. The ceremony in Westminster Hall had served to humiliate the king and the heir to the throne, who had been paraded before their subjects in a way that demonstrated their powerlessness, made to stand in silence while the terms of their submission were announced. It bore the semblance of Simon's words to the king at Saintes, that he should be imprisoned like Charles the Simple, and his fury at the king in 1252, when he had publicly cast doubt on the king's credentials as a Christian ruler, as well as the mockery he had made of him in 1261, when Simon had agreed that it was right that the king's opinion should be heard, 'when he talks sense'. This willingness to humiliate was a trait well known to his friends, and they knew the dangers it posed too. As Adam Marsh had advised Simon some years previously:

> Although it belongs to your generous nature to speak openly, freely, and boldly the thoughts in the heart, without distinction of persons, yet it is always advantageous for a generous man to use his heart to govern the utterance of his tongue, lest, while it is pleasant to speak more freely, lack of restraint causes offence . . . thoughtlessness in speaking is the downfall of both holy religion and human need.[85]

14

Disaster

The Westminster parliament had proclaimed the triumph of the Montfortian regime, and provided a means by which it could engage the wider kingdom – but its events also revealed Simon's fundamental weakness: his lack of support amongst the greatest magnates of England, the earls. At the parliament's opening, he had enjoyed the alliance of only one, Gilbert de Clare, earl of Gloucester. By the parliament's close he had lost even this – Gilbert's name does not appear on the list of witnesses to the confirmation of Magna Carta, which it certainly would have done had he been present on 11 March.[1] During the course of the parliament, Simon and Gilbert had quarrelled, although the rift did not become public knowledge until April or May, for Gilbert (according to the London annalist, who was well placed to know) had left the capital 'secretly'.[2] Chroniclers writing close to events were left to pick up rumour. Arnold fitz Thedmar could say only that it was the failure of Simon to uphold the Provisions and the Mise of Lewes that had caused the problem.[3] The Dover chronicler thought that Gilbert was angry because Simon was keeping for himself royal land and castles seized after Lewes when he, Gilbert, ought to have been entitled to half the spoils. The same is said by a later, but well-informed, chronicle written at Tynemouth: Gilbert pointed out that he had captured Richard of Cornwall at Lewes and was thus entitled to a share in the recompense, a point to which Simon 'responded all too briefly or lightly'.[4] The London annalist enjoyed the closest insight into these events (it was he who knew that Gilbert had left London secretly). He writes that Gilbert was angry because Simon 'held the kingdom in custody', having ordered that royal castles be delivered into his own lordship, and because Simon was striving 'not for the advantage of the republic . . . nor for the redemption of the captives, but entirely for himself and his sons'.[5]

The grounds for this complaint are visible, for Simon's entailing of royal and royalist lands upon his family is supported by a weight of record evidence.[6] Young Simon had already been granted the lands of John Mansel, one of Henry III's closest advisers, and after Lewes he had been allowed to dispossess the royalist baron William de Braose of his lands in Sussex. Young Gui de Montfort had been given custody of the lands of Richard of Cornwall in Devon and Cornwall, while the youngest Montfort boy, Richard, had also received land grants. Even Amaury, a clergyman, had received substantial spoils: the rectorship of one of Richard of Cornwall's churches and, on 7 February, during the course of the Westminster parliament, the treasurership of York, one of the wealthiest livings in the kingdom (previously held by John Mansel). For Henry de Montfort, the eldest of the Montfort boys, Simon had perhaps reserved the greatest prize – he seems to have planned to confer on young Henry the earldom of Chester and the lordship of the. Peak, whose seizure from Edward was enacted in the Peace of Worcester in November and confirmed during the course of the Westminster parliament.

This programme of appropriating royal lands for the Montfort family required Simon to take a further step. He had summoned to the Hilary parliament the earl of Derby, Robert de Ferrers, who had campaigned with Henry de Montfort in the Marches in the early months of 1264, helping to take Worcester, but had tarnished his Montfortian credentials by failing to appear for the Battle of Lewes. Robert answered the summons to parliament but, during the course of the assembly, before 23 February, was seized on Simon's orders and consigned to the Tower. Robert was a rival claimant to the Peak – Simon had lured him to London and arrested him so as to seize the Derbyshire estate unopposed. This act, writes the London annalist, 'stunned' the earl of Gloucester.[7]

That these actions perturbed Gilbert de Clare is not, perhaps, surprising. What is striking is that other members of the council did not, apparently, present objections – in fact, they cooperated with Simon's programme. Hugh Despenser had helped young Simon construct the scheme to dispossess William de Braose, and had witnessed the grant of 14 March by which four manors belonging to Eleanor de Montfort's dower were granted to Henry de Montfort in hereditary right, dispossessing the family of Eleanor's first husband; here Hugh was joined by the bishop of London and other members of the council, while Thomas de Cantilupe, as chancellor, authorized the act.[8] The charter issued on 20 March granting Chester and the Peak to Simon was witnessed by a similar group, with the addition of Peter de Montfort.[9] More strikingly still, when the terms of Edward's release were officially issued on 11 March – setting out, amongst other things, the 'exchange' that would deliver Chester and the Peak to Simon – the document was witnessed by the bishops of London, Worcester, Winchester, Durham, Ely, Salisbury, Coventry and Lichfield, Chichester, Bath and Wells, and Llandaff, the priors of the Hospitallers and Templars in England, and the mayor and commune of London.[10] Most of these were committed Montfortians. As we have seen, the bishops of London, Worcester, Winchester and Chichester were tightly bound to the new regime; the bishops of Ely, Salisbury and Durham were sympathetic to the cause; Roger de Vere, prior of the Hospitallers, and brother Amblard, prior of the Templars, had carried the Peace of Canterbury to the king of France on behalf of the council; the Londoners had sworn to support Simon in 1264.[11] But the bishops of Coventry and Lichfield, and Bath and Wells, despite cooperating with the Montfortian regime during the Hilary parliament, were to prove committed royalists, while the bishop of Llandaff was otherwise uninvolved in events.[12] In seizing royal and royalist estates, and bestowing them on his children, Simon had the support of an impressive cohort of senior figures – some of them his friends, others not.

It is impossible now to recover their reasoning. Were they swept along by the force of Simon's personality? Or did they find justification for these acts, perhaps in the need to strengthen Simon and his family to ensure the success of the regime on a long-term basis? As to Simon's own reasoning, it is likewise only possible to speculate. He might have justified the appropriation of some of these manors by the king's ongoing failure to provide lands in hereditary right as Eleanor's marriage portion. And the appropriation of land on a large scale could, perhaps, be justified by comparison to the situation in which he had found himself as a young man. His father had conquered an impressive reach of territories in Languedoc, and amassed a glittering parade of titles, but none had been secured for his sons: Amaury had inherited his father's rights but could have defended them only by military might, and had been forced to cede his lordships to the king of France in 1229. Amaury and Simon had been left with just their ancestral lands; and, for Simon, entry into the earldom of Leicester had not been guaranteed. Simon would have wanted to avoid a repetition of this situation. He might also have recalled the scholarship of Robert Grosseteste, who had drawn from Aristotle's work to argue that a ruler needed vast personal resources in order to govern without burdening his subjects. Yet, whatever justifications might have been offered, the dispossessions were illegal – indeed, they ran contrary to chapter 29 of Magna Carta 1225 ('No free person is to be arrested, or imprisoned, or disseised, or outlawed, or exiled, or in any other way ruined, nor will we go against them or send against them, except by the lawful judgment of their peers or by the law of the land'). The Charter had been confirmed in the course of the Hilary parliament, witnessed by many of the same men who supported the seizure of lands.

*

Simon's strategies made no dent in the affection of the churchmen, barons and knights who were his friends and followers: they knew all sides of Simon and loved him still. Amongst his allies only two men were not counted in this category – but these were the two most important of all: Gilbert de Clare and his younger brother, Thomas.

Simon cannot have realized at first the extent of the breach with the earl of Gloucester. He had been sufficiently wary of the tensions between them during the course of the parliament to cancel a tournament that had been due to take place on 17 February at Dunstable, in which Gilbert and Thomas (then twenty years old, or perhaps even younger) had planned to lead a team against Simon's sons. The event had not been Simon's idea. Young Henry and

Simon, according to one chronicler, had come to the Westminster parliament with a vast body of knights and soldiers (whom they would have planned to take with them on to Dunstable), and Simon was clearly concerned that the tournament would be an opportunity to foment trouble.[13] When he learned of the plan (writes the Tynemouth chronicler), 'he rebuked their presumption, firmly enjoining them to desist from what they had begun, threatening that unless they obeyed his order, he would put them in such a place that enjoyed the benefit of neither the sun nor the moon'.[14] By this point, Simon was not only wary of provoking trouble with Gilbert but had also grown suspicious of the young earl. Simon worried that Gilbert might, in his jealousy, conspire against him – Simon had apparently demanded that Gilbert should hand over hostages to ensure his loyalty, much to the young earl's indignation.[15]

It was likely these concerns that prompted the family conference at Odiham Castle, in Hampshire, immediately after the parliament's close. The conference is recorded in a precious source: a fragment of the household roll of Eleanor de Montfort, which lists her purchases during this period. The roll reveals the pivotal part that Eleanor played in the new regime: receiving important guests who might be wooed to the Montfortian cause and sending others gifts, dispatching messengers to members of her family and to other leading Montfortians (including Peter de Montfort, Richard Gravesend and Walter de Cantilupe) and, as here, hosting family meetings.[16] It is a part reminiscent of Alice de Montmorency in the Albigensian war – like Alice, Eleanor was her husband's trusted captain, key to the operation of the family enterprise. It is unclear how far noblewomen more broadly took on such responsibilities in times of war (though a hint that they did indeed we have already seen in the accounts of Roger of Leybourne for the siege of Rochester, which tell how the wives of the royalist lords had come with them to defend the castle when attack was imminent). But for Simon the example set him by his parents – the example they had seen inscribed in the *History* of Peter of les Vaux-de-Cernay – made it an expectation. On this occasion, at Odiham, Eleanor was required to host what amounted to a major Montfortian council. Her roll records how Gui de Montfort reached Odiham on 13 March (two days after the parliament's close), followed by his brother Henry on 17 March (bringing their cousins Edward and Henry of Almain), and Simon arrived two days later. The Montfort men brought with them too their followings: Eleanor's roll details the feeding of forty-four horses in her regular household – with young Henry's arrival, this number rose to 172 and, with Simon's, to 334.[17] Although one should not expect to extrapolate the size of a knightly force simply from the number of horses recorded, these figures accord with the private army of over 160 knights 'devoted to his allegiance' witnessed by the Pershore chronicler late in 1264. The family were together for a fortnight.

By 1 April, the Montforts had determined to bring Gilbert back into the fold. At this point Simon set out from Odiham, in the company of a 'great army', as the London annalist notes (not the feudal host, but his private force). With him too were the king and Edward, kept safely within his sight. Their destination was Northampton, where the tournament that had been postponed from Dunstable was due to take place around 19 April. Gilbert did not appear (though he sent his younger brother, Thomas, to meet Simon instead).[18] If Simon was to pursue the matter with the earl of Gloucester himself, he would have to leave the relative security of the Midlands and venture west into Gilbert's own territory. By 25 April Simon had set out to traverse the sixty miles from Northampton to Gloucester, via Long Compton and Winchcombe. He arrived on the 27th.[19]

Simon would stay at Gloucester for a little over a week. Negotiations did not progress well. Gilbert had raised an army, which loitered on the other side of the Severn in the Forest of Dean; Simon, within two days of his arrival, had decided to supplement his private force, and so had dispatched orders to the sheriffs of Worcestershire, Herefordshire and Gloucestershire to muster the feudal hosts of their shires to assemble at Gloucester.[20] Simon was able to secure terms that were highly favourable. A panel was appointed to arbitrate on the quarrel of the earls, made up of Simon's closest friends and supporters: Walter de Cantilupe, Hugh Despenser, John fitz John and William de Munchensey.[21]

But in reality Gilbert was not interested in the negotiation – indeed, in taking part he was probably just playing for time. For Gilbert was expecting the arrival of new, royalist allies. In early May

John de Warenne, earl of Surrey, and William de Valence landed
on the coast of Pembroke, in south-west Wales, with a force of 120
men.[22] Gilbert had determined to change sides. His plan had been
to lure Simon to Gloucester with the royal hostages and, with the
help of the incoming royalists, to take Simon captive and free Henry
and Edward.[23]

Simon discovered the plot in the nick of time, through his spies.[24]
He now had to determine his next move. He might have withdrawn
to the Midlands, a relatively safe distance from Gilbert's hostile
force, or further away from the Marches into the south-east. But
either option would have allowed his enemies to unite against him.
Instead, he moved twenty-file miles north-west to Hereford, where
he arrived probably on 8 May, setting his army to obstruct the
joining of the forces of Gilbert and Roger Mortimer, who was based
at Wigmore. He was now in the heart of enemy territory, and it
was here that he decided to establish his base of operations.[25]

Simon was at this stage still unaware that Thomas de Clare had
decided to withdraw his allegiance. Thomas was, so far as Simon
knew, committed to him. When Gilbert had left the Hilary
parliament in anger, Thomas had remained, and had stood witness
to the confirmation of Magna Carta at the parliament's climax.[26]
It is not clear at what point he decided to join his brother, but by
the end of May his change of sides had been revealed.

Thomas had been in contact with Roger Mortimer, who was
stationed at his castle of Wigmore, about twenty miles from
Hereford. Roger's plan is described by a local chronicler, whose
source was probably someone within Roger's circle. Roger was to
send to Edward his fastest warhorse (presumably Thomas would
lead it into Hereford Castle). Edward would then ride this horse
out when he was permitted to take his exercise. And so, on the
evening of 28 May, Edward, Thomas, and a contingent of guards
rode out of Hereford Castle to exercise in the Widemarsh meadow,
just half a mile north of the town. Roger was to send a signal: his
man would ascend a hill at Tillington, four miles to the north-west,
riding a grey horse – when Edward sighted him, he was to ride full
pelt in his direction. Edward had been instructed (as the local
chronicler notes) to trust in the speed of Roger's horse. But he

made sure that he would outstrip his guards, by asking each of them in turn if he could test their horses: after tiring each mount by hard riding, he was able to make off on the fresh speedster. At Tillington he was met by Roger Mortimer, with a force of some five hundred men, and conducted to the safety of Wigmore Castle.[27] Soon he was at Ludlow, meeting Gilbert de Clare to agree the terms of their allegiance: Gilbert had not abandoned his commitment to some of the principles of reform, insisting that Edward swear to persuade the king, in the event of victory, to banish foreigners from his council and govern through native men alone.[28]

Simon, as one chronicler notes, was 'wounded in heart' at the deception of Thomas, whom he had so trusted.[29] That Thomas was allowed oversight of Edward speaks of the profundity of that trust, for Simon had been on high alert against plots to free the prisoner. An episode recorded in the Chronicle of Melrose (clearly informed by those involved and probably dating to the period of Edward's captivity in Hereford) reveals the extent to which Simon was on his guard. The queen of Scotland, Margaret, daughter of Henry III, had sent an envoy to visit her brother in captivity. This was Oliver, abbot of Dryburgh. Simon met the abbot in person to conduct him into Edward's presence; Simon made the abbot's companion wait below while he led Oliver upstairs (several flights, notes the Melrose chronicler, so Simon was holding Edward as high up in the castle keep as possible).[30] Simon was walking ahead of the abbot, to prevent him passing any missive to the prisoner when they reached Edward's rooms. The abbot and Edward sat and talked, but for the entire meeting Simon remained standing, and 'as long as he stood thus he did not turn his eyes from one nor the other, but watched them both continuously, lest a suspect letter be delivered to Edward, or an improper word be spoken to Edward by the abbot on behalf of those who had sent him'. When the abbot was ready to leave, Simon followed him closely, again so that no surreptitious letter or words could be exchanged.[31]

Given Simon's vigilance, the only way for Roger Mortimer to make plans with Edward was through a person whom Simon trusted entirely to watch Edward as closely as he would do himself. After the Hereford escape, Simon was unwilling to take chances with the other prisoners: he dispatched orders to Kenilworth to have Richard of Cornwall and his younger son, Edmund, put in irons.[32]

*

From the crest of the Hilary parliament, Simon's position had slid to perilous within a matter of weeks. He now found himself with two formidable enemies. Gilbert de Clare, as earl of Gloucester, was the greatest magnate in the kingdom (besides the now-nullified Richard of Cornwall), and had the means in money and in manpower to confront Simon, while Edward – as the heir to the throne and a daunting opponent in the field, likened even by his enemies to a 'lion' in battle – could provide the leadership for the royal army. This new alliance soon did its work. Edward and Gilbert swept through the Marches, taking castles and towns as they went: Chester, Beeston, Shrewsbury, Bridgnorth, Ludlow, Worcester and Gloucester all fell to their forces within a couple of weeks.[33] Edward had seized the entire line of the River Severn, trapping Simon to the west.

Behind the Severn, Simon was cut off from the secondary Montfortian force, led by young Simon, who was operating between the family base at Odiham in Hampshire and Pevensey in Sussex, where he was besieging the castle held for Peter of Savoy.[34] And Simon was without an army of a size to match Edward's. He had attempted, on 30 May, to summon the feudal host, first to meet at Worcester (made impossible by the fall of the town by 7 June) and then at Gloucester – but when the town of Gloucester fell to Edward on 14 June (even though the castle would hold out for another fortnight) this plan became unworkable.[35] He dispatched an urgent message to Eleanor and young Simon at Odiham, and set out to extricate himself.

His first action, on 19 June, was to head west into Wales in order to secure the aid of Llywelyn ap Gruffudd. They met probably between Llywelyn's base at Pipton and Hereford. Llywelyn agreed to provide military and financial aid for Simon in return for considerable concessions – essentially the acknowledgement of his status as independent ruler of Wales and of his territorial conquests.[36] With Llywelyn's support secured, Simon set out to rendezvous with his second son, young Simon. Since he could not cross the Severn through the Marches, he planned to take an alternative, circuitous route to the safety of the English heartlands: he would head south from Hereford, with the aim of reaching Newport to cross the Bristol Channel, on vessels sent across by the Montfortian garrison at Bristol Castle (see map 3).

And so, on 24 June, Simon set out from Hereford, southward first to Monmouth.[37] There he found the enemy forces of John Giffard: they had pitched their tents outside the town, hoping to provoke Simon into a battle or else to encourage his withdrawal, but neither side was willing to fight and Simon was able to slip past. He now headed south-west to reach Usk on 2 July, then on to Newport two days later.[38] There he dispatched orders to the Montfortian garrison at Bristol to send as many ships as they could across to Newport to enable his crossing.

But Simon's enemies had moved faster than he would have hoped. Having taken Gloucester Castle on 29 June, Edward and Gilbert set out in pursuit of Simon. They retook Usk on 4 July and sped to cut off Simon's escape. What happened next is retailed in gleeful terms by the royalist chronicler Thomas Wykes. Gilbert had three galleys at his disposal on the western side of the Bristol Channel. These he filled with soldiers and dispatched to intercept the Montfortian vessels sailing from Bristol. The two fleets clashed on the open sea, with the Montfortians coming off worse – eleven vessels were captured or sunk, and the rest forced to withdraw. Edward and Gilbert, in triumphant mood, raised their banners and headed for Newport. The town lies on the western side of the Usk; the royalists approached from the east planning to cross the bridge into the town and meet the Montfortians in battle. But Simon, seeing the danger, burned the bridge and, under cover of darkness, on the night of 7 July, withdrew covertly.[39]

Simon had no option but to return to Hereford. He would have to take a longer route than the one that had brought him to Newport, for he would have to keep further westward to avoid the danger of Edward, Gilbert and the marchers. Over the course of the next four days, then, he and his men traversed the forty-odd miles to Hay-on-Wye, via Abergavenny, in the shadow of the Black Mountains. From here he headed east to Hereford, arriving on 16 July.[40]

*

At the end of May, following Edward's escape from custody, Simon had immediately dispatched news to young Simon and Eleanor. On 1 June they had set out together from Odiham, heading south to Portchester Castle. There they were met by more Montfortians (the number of horses to be fed, as Eleanor's household roll records, rose from twenty-eight to eighty-four).[41] From Portchester, they traversed the southern coast to Bramber Castle, then Wilmington, on to Winchelsea and finally to Dover Castle. This perhaps gave young Simon an opportunity to check on the progress of the siege of Pevensey Castle, but there must have been a greater goal – for the alternative to this coastal operation was the raising of more troops, perhaps in London; with this force amassed, young Simon could rendezvous with his father, so that the combined host could confront the royal army. One explanation has been that young Simon was looking to Eleanor's safety, heading for Dover to allow her access to a speedy Channel crossing if all else should fail.[42] But the difficulty with this explanation is the assumption that Eleanor herself, and her son, felt that she needed to be rescued.

There is an alternative explanation. The Montfort family might well have been thinking of a danger far greater than the combining of the forces of Edward and Gilbert: invasion. The previous year, the Montfortian regime had been able to see off the threat of Queen Eleanor's army, which had never set out from the Continent. But now, as spring turned into summer, Simon must have feared the approaching moment when the queen would launch a new campaign. As we have seen, this had been on the minds of the councillors at the Hilary parliament, even before a small royalist force dispatched from the Continent had landed at Pembroke in late April or early May (120 men under the command of John de Warenne, earl of Surrey, and William de Valence). At that point, Simon's concern was that 'many adversaries of the king and the realm from beyond the seas, if they knew of their landing . . . would prepare to enter the realm with more will and spirit, to disturb the peace' – such was his warning in orders to the men of Somerset and Dorset, Norfolk and Suffolk, and Kent, instructing them 'to keep their shore manfully and strongly against the invasion of anyone'.[43] Simon was now aware that his enemies might seek to land men on the coast of Wales – but it was the south-east coast, lying so near the Continent, that would always form the front line.

And so, when Eleanor and her second son set out from Odiham for the south-east coast at the beginning of June, it is likely they were acting under Simon's orders, their goal to check the defences of the coastal towns and castles, and to fortify the resolve of their defenders, before establishing Eleanor at Dover. In this scenario, Eleanor was not being rescued, and she and young Simon were not preparing her escape; rather, Eleanor was taking command of Dover Castle. This was the fortress that, when England was invaded last, in 1216, the commander of the garrison, Hubert de Burgh, had refused to surrender even in the face of apparent disaster – and when he was forced to leave the castle to lead out a fleet against the oncoming enemy armada, he had told his men: 'by the Blood of Christ, if by chance I am taken, permit me to be hanged before you surrender the castle to any Frenchman; for it is the key to England'.[44] In 1265 control of Dover was likewise essential to the defence of England from invasion, and thus the survival of the Montfortian regime. In establishing Eleanor at Dover, the Montforts were appointing a commander whose resolve would be impregnable. Again, this was a role akin to that of Simon's mother, Alice de Montmorency, in the Languedoc campaign. While the Count had led the expedition, she had been his captain, raising and moving troops and even operating on the front line, at the siege of Termes and at the end, in 1218, at Toulouse, when she and all her family had held fast in the Château Narbonnais, as captured crusaders were cut up and hurled in pieces at the castle walls.[45] This was the example set out by Alice and the Count in the pages of the *History* of Peter of les Vaux-de-Cernay: the Montfort family confronted danger as a unit, and to this enterprise the countess was vital. Now, in June 1265, the family weighed the present danger of Edward and Gilbert's army against the looming peril of invasion and the fighting of the war on a second front – a scenario that would surely doom everything Simon had built. What they cannot have expected was that the castles of the Marches would fall to Edward and Gilbert so quickly, and that Simon would therefore need young Simon's men almost immediately.

After two days at Dover, young Simon left for the capital,

travelling via Tonbridge. He rode with a force of some one hundred mounted men, and hoped to raise a greater force in London.[46] There he was able to muster perhaps sixteen knights and what the chronicler Thomas Wykes describes as 'an infinite multitude' of infantry.[47] Young Simon led his force first south-west to Winchester, where he arrived on 16 July. It is not clear why he did not make straight for his father in the Marches, or for the Montfortian stronghold of Kenilworth.[48] Thomas Wykes implies that young Simon's goal at Winchester was the raising of cash from this wealthy city: upon his arrival, young Simon met resistance from the citizens, who had closed the gates against him; he did not want to take the city by storm because the damage would diminish the sum that he could raise. In the end, young Simon found an easier route into the city (which he would have been wise to identify whatever his motives): he sent a man through a window in the buildings of the cathedral complex, which adjoined the city's walls, who was able to break the bars of the city's gates and let his comrades through. The Montfortian troops poured into the city, seizing whatever cash and plunder they could find. Young Simon also targeted Winchester's Jewish population (as his elder brother, Henry, had done at Worcester in 1264, and John fitz John had done in London). Some of them were killed.[49]

Young Simon succeeded in his goal of raising cash. He was helped on the third day of his stay, 18 July, by the receipt of £200 from the bishop of Winchester.[50] This was John Gervase, a committed Montfortian and one of several bishops willing to 'lend' Simon much-needed money to support the cause: in August 1264, John had 'lent' Simon £80; in the same period, Richard Gravesend, bishop of Lincoln, had 'lent' £100 and Henry of Sandwich, bishop of London, £133, while Walter de Cantilupe made various 'loans' that totalled perhaps £440.[51] This supply of funds from devoted friends was an essential boost to Simon's ever-emptying war chest. And now, in July 1265, the Montfortian campaign was evidently in desperate want of money. So much is made clear by young Simon's delay in rendezvousing with his father in order to sack Winchester, and in the willing role of John Gervase – who in handing over £200 to the man who had just sacked his city was implicitly condoning the actions of young Simon, and choosing to prioritize the good of the Montfortian cause. It was an act of support made all the more difficult by an unfortunate coincidence: as Arnold fitz Thedmar points out, young Simon had begun his raid of Winchester on the morrow of the feast of St Swithun – the city's patron saint.[52]

*

The morrow of St Swithun was the same day that Simon, having failed to escape from Newport across the Bristol Channel, had returned to Hereford. He then acted swiftly to neutralize the nearby marcher base at Leominster, ten miles or so to the north, setting the town alight before returning to Hereford.[53] But, trapped still behind the Severn, there was little else he could do himself. He had dispatched a message to young Simon, either during the course of his retreat or upon his return to Hereford, instructing him to take his army north into the Midlands, to head for the Montfortian stronghold of Kenilworth. This, Simon hoped, would lure Edward and Gilbert away from the Severn – allowing him to make his escape. Then, with the two Montfortian armies operating freely, they could confront the enemy together.[54] In response to his father's orders, then, young Simon led his army north from Winchester to Oxford, then on to Northampton, reaching Kenilworth on 31 July.

The castle lies to the west of Kenilworth town; young Simon's army, coming from Northampton, approached from the east. The journey from Northampton was over thirty miles and they did not reach their destination until perhaps around 9 p.m., when the sun had already set. They must have been marching for something like twelve hours. 'The army was exhausted,' writes the Worcester chronicler, 'and refused to make the effort to go any further.'[55] The men entered the town and collapsed, exhausted, into their beds.

Edward and Gilbert must have heard of young Simon's approach by the morning of 31 July, for that day they moved from Gloucester twenty miles north to Worcester. The town lay directly between Hereford and Kenilworth – the goal was to prevent Simon and his second son from joining their armies. The next day, 1 August, around mid-afternoon, Edward led a force out of Worcester to confront young Simon at Kenilworth.[56]

So far, Simon's plan had worked: although Gilbert remained in

Worcester, Edward had been lured away from the Severn. It was the best opportunity Simon would have to make his escape from Hereford. And so, on 2 August, he moved his men out of the city. They were heading for Kempsey, Walter de Cantilupe's manor, on the banks of the Severn. Kempsey lies less than four miles south of Worcester – perilously close to the enemy camp. But it was a friendly settlement, where Simon's army could cross the Severn by ford or ferry.[57] And so from Hereford, cutting through the lower northern slopes of the Malverns, they marched eastward twenty-two miles to reach Kempsey, on the eastern bank of the Severn, later that day. From here Simon would be able to lead his army on to Kenilworth: with any luck he could trap Edward before its walls, just as young Henry de Montfort had trapped Edward besieging Gloucester Castle the previous year. This time Edward would not be permitted to escape.

Edward, though, had not been fooled. He had spies in Kenilworth, who had passed him word that young Simon's forces, arriving late the previous evening, had slept not inside the castle but in the town, and they would do so again on the night of 1 August. This was Edward's opportunity to pounce. He set out in mid-afternoon, knowing that the journey of thirty miles would need the best part of the night. Wanting to conceal his objective from any Montfortian spies, he left Worcester on the northward road leading to Shrewsbury; after a couple of miles, he and his cavalry cut eastward towards their real target at speed, leaving the foot soldiers to follow.[58] As dawn began to break on 2 August, Edward and his mounted force drew up to Kenilworth.

Young Simon and his men, as Edward's spies had told him, were sleeping for a second night inside the town. Observers struggled to explain this decision. Their exhaustion on arrival the previous night would hardly be good cause to reject the safety offered by the castle walls for a second night. The chronicler of Melrose Abbey, an ardent Montfortian, did his very best to justify young Simon: the men slept in the town

> so that after they rose early in the morning from their beds, they
> would be able to have a good bath – it was on account of being able
> to bathe, indeed, that they had chosen to leave the castle, so that

being made cleaner by the grace of the baths, they would be effectual in doing battle . . . in the town, indeed, they could have access to plenty of bathtubs for bathing themselves, which they would not easily have been able to find in the castle.[59]

As these clumsy efforts show, the decision was simply a poor one. And so it was that around 5 a.m., in the final moments of darkness, young Simon's men were roused from slumber by the sound of the enemy pouring into the town. Edward's men raised a cacophony, making 'the most powerful shouts' (as the Melrose chronicler describes), in order to alarm their prey and send them into panic. It worked:

> they were terrified beyond measure; without doubt, fear and trembling, dread and fear overcame them, hearing the noise of the horses, and soldiers facing them and saying 'rise, rise, come out, come out from your beds, come outside, traitors, servants of that worst of inveterate traitors, Simon. You are all dead, by God's death!'

Young Simon's men scrambled from their beds. Not stopping to dress, let alone to arm themselves, they scattered naked or in their undergarments. Many could not even pause to fetch their horses from their stables, and had to flee the town on foot.

Edward did not pursue them: the raid had achieved its goal of nullifying the secondary Montfortian force. Meanwhile, his men could feed upon the spoils: as the morning wore on, his foot soldiers arrived, and were allowed to help themselves to all the armour and horses young Simon's men had left behind.[60]

Young Simon managed to escape the carnage. Running naked from the town, he reached the lake that stretched before the castle and was able to row across to safety.[61] But in the chaos he lost some of his most important men, who were taken prisoner: the earl of Oxford, William de Munchensey, Adam of Newmarket, Baldwin Wake, Hugh de Neville, Richard de Grey, John Despenser (cousin of Hugh), and several others.[62]

As young Simon secured himself in Kenilworth Castle, his father, unaware of his plight, was moving from Hereford to Kempsey. He arrived at some point in the afternoon. Edward, meanwhile, did not loiter at Kenilworth, but returned straight to Worcester with his captives.[63] At Kempsey, Simon discovered what had happened. He was, writes one local and well-informed chronicler, 'shaken to the core'.[64] His plan had involved two mutually dependent objectives: Edward must be lured away from Worcester long enough for Simon to escape the Marches, and the two Montfortian armies must then unite. The scattering of young Simon's army dealt both a terrible blow.

Simon, at Kempsey, now found himself less than four miles from Edward's army at Worcester. 'And so he rushed', reports the local chronicler, 'to leave those parts.' He decided that he would head still for Kenilworth, where young Simon held the castle with the remnants of his force.[65] This would mean steering widely around Worcester, to avoid the peril of meeting Edward's army. And so he determined to move first to Evesham, fifteen miles east-south-east of Kempsey – from there he could take the road north to Alcester and on to Kenilworth (see map 6).[66]

It was vital that Simon escape detection and so, as he had done in similar circumstances at Newport, when Edward's army had been dangerously close, he would move covertly, by night. He led his army out on the evening of 3 August. Their exact route is unknown. The direct route to Evesham, as the crow flies, would be through Pershore; but since the chronicler of Pershore Abbey, based in the heart of the town beside the bridge, notes that the army moved 'silently', it is more likely that they skirted the town to the north.[67] As dawn began to break, between 5 and 6 a.m. on 4 August, Simon and his army drew into Evesham, probably entering the town from the east across the bridge over the Avon. This led them straight to Evesham Abbey, which sat close to the river at the southern end of the town. There they set up camp.

Here Simon was met by his oldest friend, Walter de Cantilupe. The two had been separated probably for as long as Simon had been trapped at Hereford, but much of the action over the past few weeks had been taking place in Walter's territory. Worcester, his cathedral town and seat of his power, was under occupation by Edward's army; it had been at his manor of Kempsey that Simon had crossed the Severn, and where he had camped from 2 to 3 August; the towns of Pershore and Evesham lay within his diocese, and the Benedictine houses of these towns were under his jurisdiction.[68] As Simon's army moved out of Hereford, Walter had been close by, probably at his manor of Blockley, eleven miles south-east of Evesham. Here he would have picked up the rumours that were running through the neighbourhood (reported by the chronicler at Evesham Abbey) that the two armies were in perilous proximity and a battle was surely imminent.[69]

Walter and Simon had been friends for thirty years, from the time that Simon, as a young man in his twenties, established himself in England and Walter had been elected to the bishopric of Worcester, and the two had been drawn together in the circle of friends that included Robert Grosseteste and Adam Marsh. It was Walter along with Robert who, as Adam Marsh had once told Simon, favoured him 'amongst all men with their special friendship'.[70] Now Walter was perhaps seventy years of age, Simon perhaps fifty-seven, the only survivors of this circle.

Walter, making his way to Simon, must have stayed that night at Evesham Abbey. And so he was there, in the early dawn on 4 August, to meet Simon as he arrived. The earl was surely exhausted. The state of constant high alert, and the marching through the night, meant that he and his men had hardly slept or eaten for three days. But Simon refused to eat, and did not rest.[71] He and Walter went into the abbey church, where he made his confession to Walter, Walter celebrated Mass, and Simon received the Body of Christ. Then the two of them sat down together in the abbey precinct and talked for the next two hours.[72]

This is where we meet them when Simon's story is picked up by an account of what happened that morning at Evesham, an account that is the most valuable fragment of evidence from the whole of Simon's life. It was only discovered relatively recently, in the late 1990s, in the College of Arms. This was a fortuitous discovery: a historian consulting a fourteenth-century genealogical roll of the kings of England noticed the account copied onto the back. On examination, it proved to be a very special find indeed. The account was written within weeks or months of the events described by someone who was with Simon in the abbey precinct, probably one of the abbey's monks (the surviving copy was made years later).[73] It is so important because it supplies information that has transformed our understanding of what followed, and because the window it offers into the scene is so clear: the author writes in French, the language of his subjects, reporting Simon's words – and those of his friends – as far as we can tell as they were spoken. He describes for us, in vivid terms, the last hours of Simon de Montfort.

15

Evesham

At about 8.30, one of Simon's scouts approached him where he was sitting with Walter in the abbey precincts: the enemy was upon them. Edward and the whole royal army had left Worcester on the evening of 3 August and, like Simon, had moved through the night. They now advanced on Evesham from the north, drawing up in a meadow known as Mosham, between the road and the River Avon, just to the north-west of the town (see map 6).

The eye-witness author tells us how the news was received by the Montfortians. 'And immediately', he writes, 'everyone in the abbey and the town shouts and runs to take up arms.' But Simon remained sitting, next to Walter.

He had three options. He had cause to hope that his second son was close at hand: several chroniclers report that he had sent orders to young Simon to march out of Kenilworth with what remained of his men, so that Edward would be caught between the two Montfortian forces. It was twenty-four miles from Kenilworth to Evesham via the Alcester road: young Simon had indeed moved out that morning, but reached only as far as Alcester, nine miles short of his destination ('in this matter', sneered Evesham Abbey's regular chronicler, 'as in other orders and threats from his father, he was slow and lukewarm').[1] He was nowhere near enough to stop Edward closing in on Evesham – but if Simon were to seek sanctuary in the abbey church he could wait there for his son to come to his aid. This course was urged on him by one of his followers (as the eye-witness author tells us), who pointed out that the army had not eaten or slept in three days, 'and so we and our horses are almost done for and exhausted'. But trapped in the abbey church, and with his secondary force dreadfully weakened, Simon knew his position would be woeful. In any case, hiding in the church was not an option that appealed. Simon's reply to the suggestion was immediate: 'No, fair friend, no. One ought to seek knights on the battlefield – and chaplains in churches.'

The second option was withdrawal. Edward's forces were drawn up to the north-west of the town. The road leading east from the abbey, across the bridge over the Avon, was open. Simon could take this route and then swing north to Kenilworth (although he would probably be pursued by Edward) or head further south, to Oxford or to London. The leaving of this exfiltration route was no oversight on Edward's part – it was his design, for he was following the counsel of Vegetius. 'Generals unskilled in war think a victory incomplete unless the enemy are so straightened in their ground or so entirely surrounded by numbers as to have no possibility of escape,' Vegetius notes, but such thinking is misguided. For, as he explains, 'when men find they must inevitably perish, they willingly resolve to die with their comrades and with their arms in their hands . . . men when shut up . . . become a match for the enemy from this very reflection, that they have no resource but in despair'. On the other hand, Vegetius continues, 'when they have free room to escape they think of nothing but how to save themselves by flight and, the confusion becoming general, great numbers are cut to pieces'. Vegetius recommended the maxim of Scipio: 'a golden bridge should be made for a flying enemy'.[2]

Simon then, could choose to accept Edward's invitation and escape over the bridge. It was not that he objected to withdrawal per se. As Vegetius points out, 'Good officers never engage in general actions unless induced by opportunity or obliged by necessity.' A month or so earlier, Simon had withdrawn at Newport when confronted by the forces of Edward and the earl of Gloucester, knowing that the odds did not favour his victory.[3] But that had been a controlled withdrawal: Simon had moved his forces from the danger covertly, under the cloak of night, and had prevented the enemy's pursuit by torching the bridge that stood between them. That option was not open to him here, because of the early hour, and because there was no obstacle that he could place in the path of the pursuing enemy. Simon and his knights, on horseback, could gallop from the town across the bridge – but Simon's foot soldiers would be left at Edward's mercy.[4] It was a dilemma that Simon's eldest brother, Amaury, had faced sixteen years before and two thousand miles away, in the gorge outside Gaza. Almost surrounded by Egyptian forces, Amaury had been urged to flee, for the crusaders were outnumbered fourteen to one. But as other lords galloped to safety, Amaury had held his ground, knowing that even if the mounted men escaped 'all those on foot would be killed or taken'. Simon would have known the history of his brother's final battle and, like Amaury, he knew his answer now.

Simon's third and final option was to fight. There were clear arguments against this. As the man who had urged Simon to enclose the army in the abbey pointed out, 'we have been hard pressed for some time now, and we have not slept or eaten for three days, and so we and our horses are almost done for and exhausted'. And Simon was outnumbered, because he had been trapped for several weeks behind the Severn with no line to reinforcements. It is not possible to know how many men either he or Edward commanded, but all the chroniclers agree that Simon's army was far the smaller: the Melrose chronicler estimates that Simon was outnumbered by three to one, or more.[5] Although his force had been the smaller too at Lewes fifteen months before, there he had commanded the terrain. Fighting would be all the harder here because his men would have to fight uphill: the town of Evesham, as it stretches north into the open land beyond, rises sixty feet. His enemy would enjoy the significant advantage, as Simon had enjoyed at Lewes, of moving downwards from the higher ground. It was possible, of course, that Simon could still emerge victorious from a fight, for in battle small turns in fortune could swell to turn the tide. But Simon could not put all his hope in luck and reasonably expect to win. Fighting would most likely mean defeat.

In ordinary circumstances, defeat for noblemen like Simon would mean capture and ransom. This had been the outcome for the knights of the losing army the last time a civil war had been fought on English soil, in 1217, at the Battle of Lincoln; and it was the fate that Henry III would have met at Saintes in 1242, had Simon not fought so effectively to cover his retreat. But Simon could not hope for such forbearing treatment here. He had overturned the divinely sanctioned order, trampling on the English crown: as King Louis had remarked when he heard of the Montfortian constitution, any self-respecting king 'would rather break clods of earth behind the plough than have a rule of that kind'. And Simon had humiliated Henry and Edward personally, seizing Edward's lands and rendering him impotent, parading his and his father's subjugation in Westminster Hall before their subjects, and dragging Henry with him around the kingdom, 'as the teacher is accustomed to lead his pupil'. This humiliation would not be allowed to stand. So much had been made clear already at Lewes, before the very worst of the shaming meted out by Simon, when the royal forces had raised the dragon banner, proclaiming that no quarter would be given. Simon had lost knights that day – his standard-bearer amongst them – and the noble fallen would have probably numbered many more if his forces had not overwhelmed the king's so quickly. This time he would be defeated, and defeat would mean death.

That death, though, would be the death of a *crucesignatus*. Simon and his men had been signed with the cross, first at Southwark in December 1263 and again on the hillside above Lewes, when Walter de Cantilupe had promised to the troops the remission of their sins, and they had laid themselves down on the earth, stretching out their arms to form a cross and begging God to grant them aid. And now, at Evesham, each of Simon's men bore the white cross of the crusader on his sword arm.

In the waging of this holy war, Simon followed his mother and his father, his uncle and his brothers. Through all that had passed over the seven years since Simon and his confederates had marched on Westminster Hall and seized power from the king, it was their example he had sought to follow – and, most of all, his father's. He had already formed himself in his father's image, as he was depicted on his seal; as the French barons who had wanted Simon as their regent recognized, 'he strove to be like his father in all things'. Time and again he had sought to follow the example set for him, following the Count in declaring that he held true to his oath no matter the suffering it brought him, while others – timid and faithless souls – abandoned the obligation they had sworn. In the time of his greatest triumph, after Lewes, it was this matching of his father's otherwise inimitable standard that for Simon made his reputation: he had fled 'neither torment nor death, for the sake of his oath', as the *Song of Lewes* proclaimed. 'Behold! Simon obedient scorns the loss of property, subjecting himself to penalties, that he may not let go the truth . . . Woe to the wretched perjurers, who fear not God, denying Him for the hope of earthly reward, or fear of prison or of a light penalty.'

For Simon, there was one example left to follow: dying in battle. This was, by now, a tradition of the Montfort family. It had been inaugurated by the Count, when his head was broken open outside Toulouse in 1218. It was taken up two years afterwards by Simon's elder brother, Gui, killed besieging Castelnaudary in the course of the same war, a war that had also claimed the Count's brother, Simon's uncle Gui, eight years after that, with an arrow wound at Varilhes. And then there was Amaury, who escaped death in Languedoc and once again at Gaza only to die during the final stage of his expedition, at Otranto. This dying of the Montforts in holy war was remembered in the bodies brought back home, gathered in the family mausoleum at Haute-Bruyère and hewn in effigy. As Simon sat, on the morning of 4 August 1265, listening to the news brought by his scout and weighing up his options, perhaps he felt the day had come for him to join them.

Thus it was that on the morning of 4 August 1265, with summer rainclouds weighing heavy in the sky, Simon de Montfort decided to die.

When his men had made ready, he stood, and embraced Walter de Cantilupe. The bishop (so the eye-witness tells us) was in tears.

As Simon began to move his army out, the waiting storm was unleashed. It was only the first ill omen: as they left through the abbey gate, Simon's standard, fixed atop a lance, was smashed against the stonework. But they carried on, meeting the main road running north–south through Evesham.

Looking behind him, Simon could see that the bridge over the Avon was still unobstructed. An exit route was open. He turned to his men, so many of them so young, unknowing, others with wives and children who needed them. 'Cross the bridge,' he told them, 'and you will escape the great danger that is coming.'

'My lord Hugh,' he said to Hugh Despenser, 'think on your great age and on saving yourself. Think that your counsel can still be of great value to all the land, for you will leave behind you hardly anyone of such loyalty and such worth.'

Hugh did not hesitate. 'My lord,' he said, 'my lord, let it be. Today we shall drink from one cup, as we have done long since.'

And so they turned northward, making their way up the hill out of the town.

Edward, meanwhile, had been setting his plans. Marching east towards Evesham, he had halted his men two and a half miles outside the town, in Mosham meadow, giving all a chance to rest after their night march. He took counsel with his two lieutenants, Gilbert, earl of Gloucester, and Roger Mortimer, and planned how to purge the shames that Simon had inflicted upon him and his father. They would unleash themselves upon the earl, it was decided, and he would die.

This would not be left to chance in the chaos of battle. They would form up in three divisions on top of the hill, Gilbert's on the left flank and Mortimer's on the right, drawing Simon up to meet them, and engage. Meanwhile, a troop of twelve – of the toughest and boldest fighters, chosen now – would seek out Simon. These men would break through the ranks and stop for no one until they reached the earl and cut him down. Roger Mortimer was to lead them.

As Simon and his men took up their position on the hillside, the Welsh in Simon's army, sent by Llywelyn, now raised a great war cry, 'so that the whole ground seemed to echo against this frightful noise', as the eye-witness author recounts. But as the Montfortians formed up into battle order, Humphrey de Bohun, in command of the infantry, led his men to the rear of the formation, behind the main force of cavalry.

'Sir Humphrey, Sir Humphrey, that is no way to conduct a battle,' Simon told him, 'putting the foot soldiers at the rear. I know well how this will turn out.' And, indeed, as they waited on the hillside for the enemy, Humphrey and his men began to slip away, leaving Simon and his mounted men alone.

They watched Edward's army lining up before them. Simon, ever the general, could not help admiring the sight. 'How skilfully they are advancing,' he said. 'Our bodies are theirs. Our souls are God's.'

The first blow for Simon's side was struck by his eldest son, Henry, riding close to his father's banner. In the commotion Simon did not see what happened next, as the enemy piled upon his son and brought him down.

Gilbert de Clare's contingent, on the left flank of the royal forces, had swung round to encircle the Montfortians, as Roger Mortimer's closed in from the other side, surrounding them. Mortimer was fighting his way closer, towards Simon.

Edward, meanwhile, had been forced to halt, hearing that his father was in danger. For Simon – if he was to fall – was intent on taking Henry with him. The earl had put the king in borrowed armour and dragged him to the battle, leaving him to be cut down in the chaos. It had almost worked – a marcher had speared Henry through the shoulder. Wounded and terrified, Henry flailed through the tumbling bodies towards his son, crying out, hoping the royalists would know him – 'I am Henry of Winchester, your king!' – until at last someone pulled off his helm and saw his face. Edward, rushing towards his father's voice, took hold of him and hauled him from the field.

As Edward left, the fighting continued. Simon's few remaining men gathered around him, hoping to shield him from the worst. One by one they were hacked down. Hugh Despenser took a mortal stab wound from a dagger. Peter de Montfort had his head cut from his shoulders. As the earl's enemies closed in, they shouted that his son, Henry, was dead, hoping to dismay him. Simon fought on, raining down blows upon them from the saddle – and so they targeted his horse, killing it beneath him. Now on foot, with both hands he took up his sword and carried on. But Roger Mortimer was upon him. The marcher lowered his lance, and drove it through Simon's neck.

Simon's remaining forces scattered. They fled back down the hill, many plunging in their desperation fully armoured into the river, only to be pulled down into its depths. Others bolted back into the town, seeking the sanctuary of the abbey church, from where they had set off that morning. They clamoured around the high altar, the church's holiest point, relieved to secure sacred protection. This we know because, when the eye-witness author and his fellow monks later ventured into the church, this was where they found the greatest pile of bodies. For Edward's men had given chase. They rode down their prey, through the fields, through the town, through the abbey precinct, through the cemetery, and on into the abbey church. When the monks went in, the sight they found was sickening. The ground lay thick with broken forms no longer recognizable as human. The walls, the choir, the statues, the cross, the altars – all were soaked with blood. From the high altar, where the largest mound of corpses lay, the blood ran down in rivers to the crypt.

As the monks picked their way across the abbey precinct and beheld the carnage, they scarcely could take it in. 'And because not all the dead had been killed on the battlefield,' the eye-witness writes, 'and their bodies lay scattered all over the fields, and throughout the whole town, the entire abbey and the churches and the great garden, and some lay drowned in the river, no one knew how many there were except God.'

Back up the hill, amidst the detritus of the battle, Roger Mortimer had not finished. He set his men upon Simon's broken body. They cut off his hands and his feet. They hacked off his head, and cut off his testicles and stuffed them into his mouth. This prize was sent by Mortimer back to the Marches, as a present for his wife.

But before all the pieces of him could be made trophies, one of Simon's men, John de Vescy (amongst the few prisoners to be taken), managed to get to what was left. He rescued one of Simon's feet. John was to keep it with him and, eventually, carry it back home to Northumberland, where he would entrust it to the monks of Alnwick Priory. It was, he knew, a precious relic, not only of a leader, a warrior, and a man he loved but of a fallen saint. For, perhaps, John had seen what Mortimer's men had uncovered when they stripped Simon's body: beneath his armour and all his worldly might, hidden from the eyes of a darkening world, Simon de Montfort had been wearing a hair shirt.

Epilogue

Simon had been careful to conceal this mortifying garment, its existence discovered only by the enemies who stripped his body and then, years later, testified by the men who shared his chamber and helped him dress. He had been worried (they told the monk of Melrose who gathered their remembrances) in case reports of it seeped out – for this was a self-imposed suffering he was required to endure alone, without comment or congratulation.[1]

The hair shirt was a painful type of penitence. King Louis had worn one too – though only on important holy days – until he was told to stop by his confessor (who said it was not fitting for a king); Louis was relieved, admitting 'that a hair shirt of this sort was extremely painful to his delicate skin'.[2] For those, like Simon, who wore it day and night, through all exertion, it was agonizing. The effects are described by an attendant of a bishop, Hugh of Avalon, who wore the garment always, refusing to remove it even in his final illness: the shirt 'had become stiff as mud because of the perspiration, and was twisted like rope between his tunic and his body . . . the scratches which I saw on his skin were too numerous for me to count'.[3]

At what point Simon took to wearing one his attendants did not say, except that it was after giving his oath to the Provisions in 1258 that he grew stricter in his way of life, limiting relations with his wife and his hours of sleep, habitually rising in the darkness to pray.[4] It was a recognition of the solemnity of his commitment, and the weight of it. That Simon was prepared to suffer for his oath was central to his identity: he was the man who would 'flee neither torment nor death, for the sake of his oath', as the *Song of Lewes* proclaimed, while 'the wretched perjurers' abandoned theirs 'for the hope of earthly reward, or fear of prison or of a light penalty'. This was the ideal he had learned from his father, his exemplar and his pattern in the building of his reputation. Simon's self-mortification was the private agony to match the public face. It was the acceptance of suffering and its quiet endurance that made him worthy of his role. For suffering, as Robert Grosseteste had once told him, was a discipline. It was 'to the righteous what pruning is to vines, what cultivation is to untilled land, what washing is to dirty garments, what a healing but bitter drink is to those who are ill, what shaping with a hammer is to vessels not yet fully moulded, what proving in fire is to gold'.

After Simon's death, his self-imposed penance was seen as one of many marks of his sanctity, inviting a comparison with another felled fighting the unjust rule of an English king, Thomas Becket. 'Thomas is named a martyr', so ran a poem preserved by one of the bishop of Chichester's priests, 'just as Simon was given over to death for the sake of justice. They suffered on earth, both tormented by the same penalty, the same war. Simon suffered freely; he fell, cut down for the land, Thomas for the Church.'[5] Other signs of his saintliness were seen in the miracles worked by his relics: the foot rescued by John de Vescy and entrusted to Alnwick Priory, which healed the sick (the Alnwick monks, finding the foot uncorrupted after months, commissioned for it a silver reliquary, shaped as a shoe, which they preserved until the Reformation); and a hand seized by a marcher foot soldier who, like Roger Mortimer, thought to make of it a trophy for his wife – the hand, taken into the local church in Chester, raised itself unsupported at the elevation of the Host. These reports were collected by the same monk of Melrose who took testimony from Simon's men. In Scotland, he was well placed also to hear of the divine retribution wreaked upon the 'wretched man' who had cut off Simon's testicles: two years later he was drowned in the River Tay, near Perth. When his body was dragged from the water, it was found that crabs had dug their claws into his belly, so deep that they could not be removed.[6]

Reports of the miracles worked by Simon were collected, too, at Evesham Abbey, by the same monks who had hosted the earl in his final hours and afterwards buried the thousands slain. From the piles of bodies they retrieved all that was left of Simon – his torso – together with the remains of young Henry, his eldest son, and Hugh Despenser. These they buried in the choir of the abbey church.[7] A monument today marks the site of the burial (see plate 29), though in fact Simon's body was exhumed, maybe a year after the battle, when some local people put pressure on the monks to remove it from consecrated ground – for Simon had died excommunicate. At this time the king was striving to suppress the veneration of the earl, and it was dangerous for the monks to be seen honouring his remains. The body was reburied beyond the church, 'in a remote place', as the annalist of Oseney Abbey recorded, 'hidden and unknown except to a very few'. It was a sanction that hurt Simon's surviving children: Amaury de Montfort, in the spring of 1267, was petitioning the pope to allow his father Christian burial, though it is unclear whether the request was ever granted.[8]

Despite the danger of celebrating Simon's sainthood, the monks of Evesham diligently noted the testimony of those who prayed to him from afar or who visited the battle site. Those who journeyed to Evesham ranged from Simon's noble followers to the poorest of the kingdom, travelling in some cases for weeks to reach the place where he died, even moving by night when the king set guards on the road to stop them in the daytime. Some gathered the earth on which he had lain to mix with water for a healing drink, others were 'measured', their size taken by a string to be made into a candle burned for Simon, others washed in the well discovered on the site after the battle. Many of the pilgrims secured Simon's goodwill: in all some 190 miracles were recorded by the monks, until royal efforts to quash the cult finally won out in the late 1270s.[9]

Those of Simon's friends and family who survived him were left to play out the final, tragic act. Walter de Cantilupe had left Simon at Evesham as the earl was readying for battle 'with hot tears' (as the eye-witness noticed). He returned to his manor at Blockley. From that hour until his last – just six months later, when his broken spirit finally gave out – he was to grieve a few short miles from the carnage.[10] Eleanor de Montfort was inconsolable (as Thomas Wykes reported); her household roll records her assumption of mourning garments and her withdrawing from the company of the great hall to the solitude of her chamber. She had remained at Dover Castle, and from there she was able to get two of her sons, Amaury and Richard, away to France. In October 1265 she herself left with her daughter, Eleanor, who was then around seven years old. Within a few months they were joined by young Simon, who had carried on the fight initially before he was compelled to surrender, and Gui, who had been taken captive at Evesham but later escaped. Eleanor retired to the Montfort family lands of the Île-de-France and enclosed herself in the Dominican convent of Montargis. The house had been founded by Simon's sister, Amicia, and was close to La Ferté-Alais, seat of the line of Simon's uncle Gui. There she died, in 1275.[11]

Young Simon and Gui would go on to serve in the army of Charles of Anjou, together with their cousin Philip (son of the Philip de Montfort who had crusaded with the earl and his brother Amaury in 1239–41). Charles, a brother of the king of France, had replaced Henry III as papal choice to take the throne of Sicily, and led to Italy a winning campaign of conquest. Gui de Montfort, with all the warlike qualities he had inherited, impressed. He fought in the great Battle of Tagliacozzo in 1268, where 'for his outstanding quality', wrote one chronicler, 'he ought to be praised above all the others', for he was 'like a wild boar amongst a company of dogs, who strikes them and cuts them to their bone'. As Gui hacked through the enemy lines, the chronicler continued, 'he called out the battle-cry of his father'. His elder brother, Simon, joined him in Italy later the same year, and the two rose high in the ranks of Charles's lieutenants, rewarded with prosperous lands, Gui with appointment as vicar-general in Tuscany and *podesta* of Florence, and marriage to a wealthy heiress.[12]

It was in the service of Charles of Anjou that, on 12 March 1271, Gui and Simon entered Viterbo. There they heard that Henry of Almain, son of Richard of Cornwall, had come to the town as well. Henry had been dispatched by Edward on a mission to make peace with their Montfort cousins. But, to Gui and Simon, Henry of Almain was the man who had abandoned his fealty to their father, and who was now serving the one guilty of their father's death and desecration. The next day they hunted Henry down. They found him in the church of San Silvestro, where he was hearing Mass. Gui stormed the church and set upon his cousin with his sword, dragging his broken body into the street for further maltreatment. It was a crime at which the whole of Europe shuddered. Dante was to immortalize the sacrilege in his *Inferno*, where Gui stands in the seventh circle of hell, condemned to dwell for ever throat-deep in a river of boiling blood.[13]

Edward (who ascended the throne in 1272) was as furious as he was distraught. Gui submitted himself in 1273 to papal justice but escaped from his prison on Lake Como, and Edward undertook to track him down. In 1280 he received intelligence that Gui was in Norway, and Edward's agents engaged a group of Norwegian barons to secure his capture, but with no result. By 1281 Gui had returned to the service of Charles of Anjou.[14] Although he and young Simon had escaped Edward's wrath, towards the end of 1275 the king was able to visit his vengeance on two other children of the earl, Amaury and Eleanor. Amaury had been studying in Padua, but now returned to England to escort his sister for her marriage: the earl, in his alliance with Llywelyn, had promised the Welsh prince his daughter. The voyage was a melancholy one, for their mother had recently died. As their ship drew into Bristol, they were seized by the men of the port, who handed them over to Edward. Eleanor was consigned to Windsor Castle, where she remained for the best part of three years, until Llywelyn was able to secure her release. Amaury was held first at Corfe, then Sherborne, then Taunton, for more than six years. His experience was recorded in a remarkable account, for during his long imprisonment he resolved to spend his time productively: he begged a Bible from his gaolers, ink and some scraps of parchment, and set to writing a treatise on theology. His 'little work', as he calls it, is preserved in the Bodleian Library (see plate 30). In its shabby pages Amaury's experience breaks through: he tells, for instance, of his efforts to comfort his sister during their voyage and how, during his lengthy incarceration, he fought against depression, despairing of his release, before finally resolving to endure. Edward was eventually persuaded to let him go in April 1282, but only on the condition of Amaury's permanent banishment from England.[15] This was not the limit of the animosity between the Montfort boys and their royal cousin. Three years later, in 1285, a priest was accused of spying at the royal court: allegedly conspiring with Gui and Amaury, together with Llywelyn, he was said to have passed on to them by letter whatever he discovered, with treasonous intent.[16] The mention of Llywelyn dates the alleged espionage to before the prince's death in December 1282 – in the midst of Edward's campaign to conquer Wales. The Montforts were suspected, it seems, of plotting in support of Welsh resistance.

The events surrounding the murder in Viterbo came in the turning of the tide. For two and a half centuries the killing of a Christian noble by his fellows was the scarcest of occurrences. In the 1260s and 1270s, it once again became contemplatable. The Battle of Evesham, with the deliberate killing of Simon and his cadre, was a landmark in this respect – although, as we have seen, such action had been planned at Lewes but not implemented. Four years after Evesham, following the Battle of Tagliacozzo, Charles of Anjou executed four noble opponents – including Conradin, grandson of Frederick II and king of Jerusalem and Sicily.[17] The Viterbo killing followed less than three years later, and 1306 brought another such act in Scotland: Robert Bruce, earl of Carrick and claimant to the Scottish throne, attacked John Comyn, lord of Badenoch, in the Franciscan church of Dumfries. According to tradition, upon discovering that he had left his victim alive, Robert gave orders that the man be dragged from his sick-bed in the vestry and finished at the altar.[18]

From here the kinetic energy of noble violence would increase. During his war in Scotland, Edward I killed his noble opponents concertedly: in 1306 he executed the earl of Atholl and several others of high status, variously by hanging, beheading, and hanging, drawing and quartering, followed by the public exhibition of their bodies (or parts thereof).[19] The reign of his son, Edward II, was to be studded and then ended by political executions, while the continental battlefields of the Hundred Years War, opened by Edward III, offered possibilities for noble killing on a grander scale. The totality of the change can be seen in 1346, in the French casualty figures for the Battle of Crécy: the English king himself estimated that eighty French nobles of high rank were killed, together with 1,542 knights and squires – as well as the king of Bohemia, a friend of the French king and one of the great chivalric figures of his age.[20] The killing of noblemen – on and off the battlefield – in the fifteenth century, particularly during the Wars of the Roses, would be tiresome to list.

How could such a change in mentality come about? Simon's story, we might suggest, helps unlock the answer: the boundaries between 'holy' and 'normal' war broke down. In the twelfth century, knights fought political enemies at home, in Europe, governed by the shared expectation of forbearance; they fought enemies of the faith in Outremer, expecting to kill regardless of status and knowing they could die. On the Celtic fringes of Christendom, too, knightly culture was not shared and so its staying influence did not apply.[21] Mental boundaries – sanctioning or forbidding lethal violence against noble targets – aligned with geographical ones.

This began to change in the early thirteenth century. It came in part with war against the infidel within Europe, the *reconquista*: in 1212 the campaign of French as well as Spanish troops against the forces of the Almohad Caliphate culminated in the Battle of Las Navas de Tolosa and the annihilation of the Muslim army; James I of Aragon then led his troops first to Majorca, in 1229, and then Valencia to claim these territories for Christendom. At just this time, Christian knights were also asked to direct their martial energies within Europe against heretics, in the Albigensian Crusade. This was a war that, as we have seen, saw for the first time in the age the torture and killing of nobles, as both sides agreed that the rules of European warfare did not apply.

But, above all, what brought the crumbling of chivalric boundaries was the application of crusader vows, and the benefits that accompanied them, to wars against Christian enemies. This concept was not wholly new: in 1166, for instance, at the Synod of Segovia, the bishops of Castile had sought to defend their kingdom from invasion and forestall civil conflict by offering the remittance of enjoined penance to all those who appeared in arms to defend Castile, while threatening those who failed in their duty with excommunication and interdict. It is not clear, though, how far this measure was applied.[22] The same is true of the first papal use of crusading indulgences against Christian enemies in Europe. This came in 1199, when the papal territories in Italy – and thus the papacy's independence – came under threat from the Hohenstaufen dynasty, rulers of the Holy Roman Empire, who had taken control of the kingdom of Sicily and thus closed in on papal lands from the south as well as the north. Innocent III declared the leader of the German forces, Markward of Anweiler, 'another Saladin' and offered to the people of Sicily ready to resist him the same indulgences granted to those defending the Holy Land.[23] Innocent was a pioneer in almost every sphere of papal operation, and where he led his successors followed: eight popes in the thirteenth century were to use crusading sanctions against Christian enemies within Europe.[24]

The impact of these measures was not profound at first. In the civil war that followed King John's rejection of Magna Carta, the leader of the rebels, Robert fitz Walter, attempted to sanctify their cause by assuming the title Marshal of the Army of God and Holy Church. The papal legate sent to secure the throne of the young Henry III sought to overwrite this message: having been authorized to suspend the crusading vows of those willing to fight for Henry, he exceeded his mandate and granted them remission of their sins, signing them with the cross. According to one monastic chronicler, the legate's actions transformed perceptions of the enemy's status: 'those who once called themselves the army of God, and boasted that they fought for the liberties of the Church and the kingdom, were reputed to be the sons of Belial and compared to infidels'.[25] But, in reality, while the rebel cause suffered a moral blow, Robert fitz Walter and his comrades maintained their chivalric standing and the protection it afforded: at the Battle of Lincoln all but one were captured for ransom – and the death of the count of Perche, as we have seen, was the cause of grieving regret.[26] But mentalities began to change when, in the mid-thirteenth century, the application of crusading sanctions to intra-Christian conflict became the hallmark of European war. In the 1250s, when Innocent IV sought a means of crushing the power of the dangerous house of Hohenstaufen in Italy, he turned to the most effective means possible of persuading a European ruler to lead an army to Sicily: the conqueror would not only win a crown but also satisfy the vow of a crusader. Henry III, in fact, never commuted his vow to campaign in Outremer in favour of his planned expedition against the Hohenstaufen, but his subjects believed otherwise – a view encouraged by papal permission to use taxes already raised for a campaign in Outremer for the Sicilian conquest.[27] When the right to conquer Sicily was transferred to Charles of Anjou in the early 1260s, his army was granted crusading indulgences. The Battle of Tagliacozzo, in August 1268, followed a papal campaign of preaching across Italy against Conradin, 'ward of slander and damnation'.[28]

Indeed, the period between 1255 and 1268 saw the undertaking of a Europe-wide campaign of preaching, in which the papacy brought to bear the rhetorical powers and organizational might of the Franciscans and Dominicans, in conjunction with local clergy and papal representatives, to proclaim a holy war against the Hohenstaufen and their Italian allies, across England in 1255 and throughout the lands of Italy over the following years, and then, in 1263, at the instigation of Charles of Anjou, throughout the kingdom of France, as well as Provence and the dioceses bordering Germany along with northern Italy and the Papal State.[29] The terms of war in Outremer were being applied concertedly in Europe by the greatest of authorities, the people of Europe exhorted to take up arms in holy war against Christian enemies for the benefit of their souls. It was in this context that Gui Foulquois was empowered in 1263 to preach a holy war to restore Henry III to power, and Louis IX offered the remission of his sins if he would assist the legate militarily. It is in this context too that Simon de Montfort's army took the cross and Walter de Cantilupe promised the remission of sins to all who fought and died in their righteous cause. The Montfortians might have lacked papal authority but, in applying the terms of holy war to a conflict against fellow Christians, they were riding the papal tide.

This policy has had its critics amongst historians, but important justifications could be offered. The papacy was charged with defending the Church and the faithful and, ultimately, overseeing the good and peaceful government of Christendom. This sometimes required taking measures against European rulers or their unruly subjects.[30] Yet, unlike the kings they oversaw, the popes did not have sheriffs to distrain or arrest recalcitrants or a feudal host to march against them. They relied on moral sanctions, through which they could isolate dangerous individuals and persuade others to enforce their decrees. Operating within a culture in which fighting in holy war was so highly valued, the offer of spiritual benefits to those who would defend the Church, her interests and her policies at home was a potent incentive – and the success of the papal alliance with Charles of Anjou in eliminating the Hohenstaufen threat shows how productive it could be.

But this policy encouraged a dangerous inference: if knights were now authorized and encouraged to fight fellow Christian knights for the benefit of their souls, as if they were fighting Muslims in Outremer, then was the killing of their opponents on these same terms not now permissible? No matter whether individual campaigns in future were decreed holy causes, the impact would be transform-ative: for, after two and a half centuries, the geographical and ethical boundaries governing the conduct of war had been collapsed in on one another. Later knightly generations would write and talk of 'chivalry', and acknowledge a shared code of conduct in warfare, but they meant something very different. In their life and in their death, Simon de Montfort, his friends and his sons were caught in the end of the first age of chivalry.

As for the earl, in his dying he was remembered as he would have wished to be. 'Simon', the Melrose author concluded, 'was descended from warlike men, namely his father' and all his fore-fathers, 'of which ancestors he was no inferior but was created the semblance of them, a warlike man, passing into the tomb of death in battle for the sake of justice, just as they went to their graves in battle for the cause of justice'. Simon could not be laid beside his father, his mother and his brothers at Haute-Bruyère – but he was remembered by the sisters who kept the Montfort family mausoleum, and who sang prayers for his soul every year on the day of his death.[31] They were singing him to heaven. It was a place, as Robert Grosseteste had once described, where 'the most precious thing will be a light combined with no shadows, interrupted by no changes, restricted by no boundaries, and defined by no limits. There will be an abundance there of all good things without depletion, a perfection without defect, and an undivided and undiminished sharing by participants in a particular good.' In heaven, Robert concluded, bodies will have 'a lightness that cannot be weighed, a mobility that knows no hindering, [and] a strength that knows not how to suffer pain . . . There we shall rest from all activity and look upon God.'[32]

Bibliography

Manuscript Primary Sources

Cambridge, Corpus Christi College
MS. 016II (Matthew Paris, *Chronica Majora*)

Evreux, Archives départementales de l'Eure
H 793 (*Petit Cartulaire de l'abbaye Saint-Taurin d'Evreux*)

Leicester, Leicestershire Record Office
BRI/I/II (charter of Simon de Montfort, s.xiii)

London, British Library (BL)
Additional 8877 (Eleanor de Montfort's household roll, 1265)
Additional Charter 3298 (complaints of Gaillard del Soler, s.xiii)
Additional Charter 3299 (complaints of Sault, s.xiii)
Additional Charter 3300 (complaints of Bazas, s.xiii)
Additional Charter 3301 (complaints of viscount de Soule, s.xiii)
Additional Charter 3302 (complaints of William de Ermandars, s.xiii)
Additional Charter 3303 (complaints of Gaston de Béarn, s.xiii)
Additional Charter 11234 (complaints of Gaillard, dean of St Severin, s.xiii)
Additional Charter 11236 (complaints of Gosse, s.xiii)
Additional Charter 11237 (complaints of Ayquilin de Lesparre, s.xiii)
Additional Charter 11238 (complaints of Bayonne, s.xiii)
Additional Charter 11240 (complaints of Arnauld de Blanquefort, s.xiii)
Cotton Vespasian F I (diplomatic correspondence, s.xiii–s.xvii)
Cotton Vespasian A VI (miracles of Simon de Montfort)
Harley 978 (literary miscellany, including *Song of Lewes*, s.xiii)

London, Metropolitan Archives

COL/CS/01/001/01 (chronicle of Arnold fitz Thedmar)

London, The National Archives (TNA)

C 47/24/1/11 (complaints of viscount de Tartas, s.xiii)

C 47/24/1/12 (complaints of Amanieu d'Albret, s.xiii)

C 47/24/1/13 (complaints of Bordeaux, s.xiii)

C 47/24/1/14 (complaints of Dax, s.xiii)

C 47/24/1/15 (two unidentified fragments of complaints, s.xiii)

C 47/24/1/16 (defence of William Pigorel, Simon de Montfort's seneschal, s.xiii)

C 66/81 (Patent Rolls, 1263–4)

E 36/274 (Liber A, s.xiii)

E 101/3/3 (accounts of Roger of Leybourne for Rochester Castle, 1263–7)

E 159/17 (Memoranda Roll, 1238–9)

E 372/86 (Pipe Roll, 1241–2)

Just 1/710 (Oxfordshire eyre, 1285)

Just 1/1187 (Hugh Bigod's eyre, 1258–9)

Oxford, Bodleian Library

Bodleian Library: MS. Auct. D. 4. 13 (thirteenth-century codex, including the theological tract of Amaury de Montfort)

Paris, Archives nationales

J 192B no. 13 (complaints of the people of Carcassonne, 1247)

J 318 nos. 87, 93, 96, 99, 101 (complaints of the people of Carcassonne, 1247)

J 896 no. 35 (complaints of the people of Carcassonne, 1247)

JJ 274 (complaints of the people of Touraine, Poitou and Saintonge, 1247)

J 1028/B no. 13 (complaints of Gaillard del Soler and responses of Simon de Montfort, s.xiii)

J 1031 no. 5 (complaints of Sault, Dax, Gosse and Bayonne, s.xiii)

Paris, Bibliothèque nationale

Clairambault 1188 (Montfort archive, originals and transcripts)

Latin 9016 (response of Simon de Montfort to complaints of numerous individuals and towns, s.xiii)

Vatican City, Archivio Segreto Vaticano

Registra Vaticana 28 (register of Urban IV, 1263–4)

Vatican City, Biblioteca Apostolica Vaticana

Reg.lat.491 (copy of Peter of les Vaux-de-Cernay's *History of the Albigensian Crusade*, s.xvi–s.xvii)

Printed Primary Sources

Adam of Eynesham, *The Life of St Hugh of Lincoln*, ed. and trans. D. L. Douie and H. Farmer, 2 vols. (Oxford, 1961–2).

Adam Marsh, *The Letters of Adam Marsh*, ed. and trans. C. H. Lawrence, 2 vols. (Oxford, 2006–10).

Alfonso X, *Las Siete Partidas*, trans. S. Parsons Scott and ed. R. I. Burns, 5 vols. (Philadelphia, 2001).

Annales Placentini Gibellini, *Monumenta Germaniae Historica; Scriptores*, ed. G. H. Pertz et al., 39 vols. (Hanover, 1826–2009), XVIII.

Annals of Chester, *Annales Cestrienses; Chronicle of the Abbey of S. Werburg, At Chester*, ed. R. Copley Christie (London, 1887), 60–79, provided by *British History Online*, available at: http://www.british-history.ac.uk/lancs-ches-record-soc/vol14/pp60-79 (accessed 25 Oct. 2018).

Annals of London, *Annales Londonienses*, in *Chronicles of the Reigns of Edward I and Edward II*, ed. W. Stubbs, 2 vols. (London, 1882), I.

Annales Monastici, ed. H. R. Luard, 5 vols. (London, 1864–9).

Arab Historians of the Crusades, ed. and trans. F. Gabrieli, trans. from the Italian by E. J. Costello (London, 1969).

Arnold Fitz Thedmar, *De Antiquis Legibus Liber. Cronica Maiorum et Vicecomitum Londoniarum*, ed. T. Stapleton (London, 1846).

Aubri of Trois-Fontaines, 'Chronica Albrici Monachi Trium Fontium', *Monumenta Germaniae Historica; Scriptores*, ed. G. H. Pertz et al., 39 vols. (Hanover, 1826–2009), XXIII.

Barnwell, *Liber Memorandorum Ecclesie de Bernewelle*, ed. J. W. Clark (Cambridge, 1907).

Bayonne, J. Balasque, *Études historiques sur la ville de Bayonne*, 2 vols. (Bordeaux, 1869).

Bernard of Clairvaux: Sermons for Lent and the Easter Season, trans. I. Edmonds (Collegeville, MN, 2013).

'Bracton', G. E. Woodbine (ed.) and S. E. Thorne (trans.), *Bracton: On the Laws and Customs of England*, 4 vols. (Cambridge, MA, 1968–77).

Bulletin de la Société des archives historiques de la Saintonge et de l'Aunis, 12 (Paris and Saintes, 1892).

Calendar of Charter Rolls, 1226–1300, 2 vols. (London, 1903–6).

Calendar of Entries in the Papal Registers Relating to Great Britain and Ireland, I, 1198–1304, ed. W. H. Bliss (London, 1893).

Calendar of the Fine Rolls of the Reign of Henry III, 1216–72, available on the Henry III Fine Rolls Project website at: https://finerollshenry3.org.uk

Calendar of Liberate Rolls, 1226–72, 6 vols. (London, 1916–64).

Calendar of Patent Rolls, 1232–72, 4 vols. (London, 1906–13).

Cambridgeshire, W. Farrer, *Feudal Cambridgeshire* (Cambridge, 1920).

The Charters of the Anglo-Norman Earls of Chester, c.1071–1237, ed. G. Barraclough (Gloucester, 1988).

Clement IV, J. Heidemann (ed.), *Papst Clemens IV: Das Vorleben des Papstes und sein Legationregister* (Münster, 1903).

Close Rolls, 1231–72, 14 vols. (London, 1905–38).

The Conquest of Jerusalem and the Third Crusade, ed. P. W. Edbury (Abingdon, 2016).

Corpus Iuris Canonici, ed. E. J. Friedberg, 2 vols. (Leipzig, 1879–81).

Councils and synods: with other documents relating to the English Church, II, *1205–1313*, ed. F. M. Powicke and C. R. Cheney, 2 vols. (Oxford, 1964).

Crusade and Christendom: Annotated Documents in Translation from Innocent III to the Fall of Acre, 1187–1291, ed. J. Bird, E. Peters and J. M. Powell (Philadelphia, 2013).

Decrees of the Ecumenical Councils, ed. N. P. Tanner, 2 vols. (London, 1991).

Dialogus de Scaccario, and Constitutio Domus Regis (The Dialogue of the Exchequer, and The Disposition of the Royal Household), ed. Emilie Amt and S. D. Church (Oxford, 2007).

Diplomatic Documents Preserved in the Public Record Office, vol. I: 1101–1272, ed. P. Chaplais (London, 1964).

Documents of the Baronial Movement of Reform and Rebellion, 1258–1267, ed. R. F. Treharne and I. J. Sanders, (Oxford, 1973).

English Episcopal Acta 13: Worcester 1218–1268, ed. P. M. Hoskin (Oxford, 1997).

English Episcopal Acta 38, London 1229–1280, ed. P. M. Hoskin (Oxford, 2011).

Eudes Rigaud, *The Register of Eudes of Rouen*, ed. J. F. O'Sullivan, trans. S. M. Brown (New York and London, 1964).

Flores Historiarum, ed. H. R. Luard, 3 vols. (London, 1890).

Foedera, Conventiones, Litterae et Acta Publica, ed. T. Rymer, new edn., I, part i, ed. A. Clark and F. Holbrooke (London, 1816).

A Formulary of the Papal Penitentiary in the Thirteenth Century, ed. H. C. Lea (Philadelphia, 1892).

Frederick II, *Historia Diplomatica Friderici Secundi*, ed. J.-L.-A. Huillard-Bréholles, 7 vols. (Paris, 1852–61).

'Geoffrey of Beaulieu's Life and Saintly Comportment of Louis, Former King of the Franks, of Pious Memory', *The Sanctity of Louis IX: Early Lives of Saint Louis by Geoffrey of Beaulieu and William of Chartres*, ed. M. C. Gaposchkin and S. L. Field, trans. L. F. Field (New York, 2014).

Gervase of Canterbury, *The Historical Works of Gervase of Canterbury*, ed. W. Stubbs, 2 vols. (London, 1880).

Gesta Francorum et Aliorum Hierosolimitanorum, ed. R. Hill (Oxford, 1962).

Gregory IX, *Les Registres de Grégoire IX*, ed. L. Auvray et al., 4 vols. (Paris, 1896–1955).

Guillaume le Breton, *Gesta Regis Philippi: Oeuvres de Rigaud et de Guillaume le Breton*, ed. H.-F. Delaborde, 2 vols. (Paris, 1882–5).

Histoire générale de Languedoc, ed. C. de Vic and J. Vaissète, rev. edn., 16 vols. (Toulouse, 1872–1904).

History of William Marshal, ed. A. J. Holden, trans. S. Gregory, notes by D. Crouch, 3 vols. (London, 2002–6).

James I of Aragon, *The Book of Deeds of James I of Aragon: A Translation of the Medieval Catalan Llibre dels Fets,* trans. D. Smith and H. Buffery (Farnham, 2010).

Jean de Vignay, 'La chronique de Primat', *Monumenta Germaniae Historica; Scriptores*, ed. G. H. Pertz et al., 39 vols. (Hanover, 1826–2009), XXVI.

John de Joinville, *The Memoirs of the Lord of Joinville: A New English Version by Ethel Wedgwood*, trans. Ethel Wedgwood (London, 1906).

John de Joinville, 'The life of Saint Louis', *Joinville and Villehardouin: Chronicles of the Crusades,* trans. C. Smith (London, 2008).

John of Oxnead, *Chronica Johannis de Oxenedes,* ed. H. Ellis (London, 1859).

Layettes du Trésor des Chartes, ed. A. Teulet, H.-F. Delaborde and E. Berger, 5 vols. (Paris, 1863–1909).

Li Livres de Jostice et de Plet, ed. L. N. Rapetti (Paris, 1850).

Manners and Household Expenses of England in the Thirteenth and Fifteenth Centuries, ed. T. H. Turner (London, 1841).

Matthew Paris, *Matthaei Parisiensis, Monachi Sancti Albani, Chronica Majora*, ed. H. R. Luard, 7 vols. (London, 1872–83).

Melrose, *Chronica de Mailros*, ed. J. Stevenson (Edinburgh, 1835).

Monasticon Anglicanum, ed. W. Dugdale, J. Caley, H. Ellis and B. Bandinel, 6 vols. in 8 (London, 1817–30).

Peter of Blois, 'Passion of Reginald, prince of Antioch', in *Petri Blesensis Tractatus Duo: Passio Raginaldi principis Antiochie, Conquestio de dilatione vie Ierosolimitane*, ed. R. B. C. Huygens (Turnhout, 2002).

Peter of Les Vaux-de-Cernay, *Petri Vallium Sarnaii monachi Hystoria albigensis*, ed. P. Guébin and E. Lyon, 3 vols. (Paris, 1926–39).

Peter of Les Vaux-de-Cernay, *The History of the Albigensian Crusade: Peter of les Vaux-de-Cernay's Historia Albigensis*, trans. W. A. and M. D. Sibly (Woodbridge, 1998).

Philippe de Nanteuil, 'En chantant vueil mon dueil faire', available on the website of the project *Troubadours, Trouvères and the Crusades*, at: https://warwick.ac.uk/fac/arts/modernlanguages/research/french/crusades/texts/of/rs164/#page1 (accessed 12 Oct. 2018).

Porrois, *Cartulaire de l'Abbaye de Porrois*, ed. A. de Dion (Paris, 1903).

Quadro elementar das relações políticas e diplomáticas de Portugal com as diversas potencias do mundo, desde o principio da monarchia portugueza até aos nossos dias, ed. M. F. de Barros e Sousa, Visconde de Santarém, L. A. Rebello da Silva, and J. J. da Silva Mendes Leal, 18 vols. (Paris, 1842–1976).

Quinti belli sacri scriptores minores, ed. R. Röhricht (Geneva, 1879).

Raffaello Maffei, *Commentariorum rerum urbanarum libri XXXVIII* (Rome, 1506).

Ramon Lull, *The Book of the Order of Chivalry*, trans. N. Fallows (Woodbridge, 2013).

Recueil des historiens des Gaules et de la France, ed. M. Bouquet, 24 vols. (new edn., 1869–1904).

Regesta pontificum romanorum inde ab anno post Christum natum 1198 ad annum 1304, ed. A. Potthast, 2 vols. (Berlin, 1874–5, repr. Graz, 1957).

Robert of Gloucester, *The Metrical Chronicle of Robert of Gloucester*, ed. W. A. Wright, 2 vols. (London, 1885).

Robert Grosseteste, *The Letters of Robert Grosseteste, Bishop of Lincoln*, ed. F. A. C. Mantello and J. Goering (eds.), (Toronto, 2010).

Roger of Howden, *Gesta regis Henrici secundi Benedicti abbatis*, ed. W. Stubbs, 2 vols. (London, 1867).

Roger of Wendover, *Chronica, sive Flores Historiarum*, ed. H. O. Coxe, 5 vols. (London, 1841–4).

Rôles Gascons, ed. Francisque-Michel and C. Bémont, 4 vols. (Paris, 1885–1906).

'The Rothelin Continuation', *Crusader Syria in the Thirteenth Century: The Rothelin Continuation of the History of William of Tyre with part of the Eracles or Acre Text*, trans. J. Shirley (Aldershot, 1999).

Rotuli Litterarum Patentium in Turri Londinensi Asservati, ed. T. Duffus Hardy (London, 1835).

The Royal Charter Witness Lists of Henry III (1226–1272) from the Charter Rolls in the Public Record Office, ed. M. Morris, 2 vols. (Chippenham, 2001).

Royal and Other Historical Letters Illustrative of the Reign of Henry III, ed. W. W. Shirley, 2 vols. (London, 1862–6).

Saint Louis et Alfonse de Poitiers, ed. E. Boutaric (Paris, 1870).

Sens, *Obituaires de la province de Sens,* ed. A. Molinier, 3 vols. (Paris, 1902–9).

The Song of Lewes, ed. and trans. C. L. Kingsford (Oxford, 1963).

Thibaut de Champagne, 'Seignor, sachiez, qui or ne s'an ira', available on the website of the project *Troubadours, Trouvères and the Crusades,* at: https://warwick.ac.uk/fac/arts/modernlanguages/research/french/crusades/texts/of/rs6/#page1 (accessed 12 Oct. 2018).

Urban IV, *Les Registres d'Urbain IV (1261–1264),* ed. J. Guiraud, 4 vols. (Paris, 1896–1906).

Vegetius, *De Re Militari,* trans. J. Clarke (London, 1767, reprinted by Oakpast, 2012).

William of Newburgh, *Historia rerum Anglicarum,* in *Chronicles of the Reigns of Stephen, Henry II, and Richard I,* ed. R. Howlett, 4 vols. (London, 1884–9).

William of Puylaurens, *The Chronicle of William of Puylaurens,* trans. W. A. Sibly and M. D. Sibly (Woodbridge, 2003).

William Rishanger, *The Chronicle of William de Rishanger of the Barons' War,* ed. J. O. Halliwell (London, 1840).

William Rishanger, *Willelmi Rishanger Chronica et Annales,* ed. H. T. Riley (London, 1865).

William of Tudela and his anonymous continuator, *The Song of the Cathar Wars: A History of the Albigensian Crusade,* trans. J. Shirley (Farnham, 1996).

The 1258–9 Special Eyre of Surrey and Kent, ed. A. Hershey, (Woking, 2004).

Secondary Sources

Allen, D., and Stoodley, N., et al., 'Odiham Castle, Hampshire: Excavations 1981–85', *Proceedings of Hampshire Field Club and Archaeological Society,* 65 (2010), 23–101.

Ambler, S. T., 'On kingship and tyranny: Grosseteste's memorandum and its place in the baronial reform movement', *Thirteenth Century England XIV,* ed. J. Burton, P. Schofield and B. K. Weiler (Woodbridge, 2013), 115–28.

——, 'Magna Carta: Its confirmation at Simon de Montfort's parliament of 1265', *English Historical Review,* 130 (2015), 801–30.

——, *Bishops in the Political Community of England, 1213–1272* (Oxford, 2017).

Aurell, M., *Le chevalier lettré: Savoir et conduite de l'aristocratie aux XIIe et XIIIe siècles* (Paris, 2011).

Baldwin, J. W., *Masters, Princes and Merchants. The Social Views of Peter the Chanter and his Circle*, 2 vols. (Princeton, 1970).

Barber, M., *The New Knighthood* (Cambridge, 1994).

——, 'The Albigensian Crusades: Wars like any other?', *Dei Gesta per Francos. Crusade Studies in Honour of Jean Richard*, ed. M. Balard, B. Z. Kedar and J. Riley-Smith (Aldershot, 2001), 45–55.

Bémont, C., *Simon de Montfort* (Paris, 1884).

——, 'La campagne de Poitou, 1242–1243. Taillebourg & Saintes', *Annales du Midi*, 5 (1893), 289–314.

Bienvenu, J.-M., 'L'ordre de Fontevraud et la Normandie au XIIe siècle', *Annales de Normandie*, 25, 3–15.

Borchardt, P., 'The sculpture in front of the Lateran as described by Benjamin of Tudela and Magister Gregorius', *Journal of Roman Studies*, 26 (1936).

Boyle, L. E., 'E cathena et carcere: The imprisonment of Amaury de Montfort, 1276', *Medieval Learning and Literature, Essays presented to R. W. Hunt*, ed. J. J. G. Alexander and M. Gibson (Oxford, 1976), 379–97.

Brand, P., *King, Barons, Justices. The Making and Enforcement of Legislation in Thirteenth-Century England* (Cambridge, 2003).

Brand, P., 'Bigod, Hugh (b. in or before 1220, d.1266), baron and justiciar', in *Oxford Dictionary of National Biography* (hereafter *ODNB*), online edn. (2008), available at: http://www.oxforddnb.com/view/10.1093/ref:odnb/9780198614128.001.0001/odnb-9780198614128-e-2377 (accessed 15 Oct. 2018).

Brunn, M. B., 'Procession and contemplation in Bernard of Clairvaux's first sermon for Palm Sunday', *The Appearances of Medieval Rituals: The Play of Construction and Modification*, ed. N. H. Petersen, M. B. Brunn, J. Llewellyn and E. Oestrem (Turnhout, 2004), 67–82.

Buc, P., *L'ambiguïté du Livre: prince, pouvoir, et peuple dans les commentaires de la Bible au Moyen Âge* (Paris, 1994).

Cam, H. M., and Jacon, E. F., 'Notes on an English Cluniac chronicle', *English Historical Review*, 44 (1929).

Campbell, B. M., 'Global climates, the 1257 mega-eruption of the Samalas volcano, Indonesia, and the English food crisis of 1258', *Transactions of the Royal Historical Society*, 27 (2017), 87–121.

Carley, J. P., 'William Rishanger's chronicles and history writing at St Albans', *A Distinct Voice: Medieval Studies in Honor of Leonard E. Boyle*, ed. J. Brown and W. P. Stoneman (Notre Dame, 1997), 71–102.

Carpenter, D. A., *The Battles of Lewes and Evesham, 1264/65* (Keele, 1987).

——, *The Minority of Henry III* (London, 1990).

——, 'Justice and jurisdiction under King John and Henry III', D. A. Carpenter, *The Reign of Henry III* (London, 1996), 17–44.

——, 'Chancellor Ralph de Neville and plans of political reform, 1215–58', *Reign of Henry III*, 61–73.

——, 'King, magnates and society: the personal rule of King Henry III, 1234–58', *Reign of Henry III*, 75–106.

——, 'Matthew Paris and Henry III's speech at the exchequer in October 1256', *Reign of Henry III*, 137–50.

——, 'The decline of the curial sheriff in England, 1194–1258', *Reign of Henry III*, 151–82.

——, 'The lord Edward's oath to aid and counsel Simon de Montfort, 15 October 1259', *Reign of Henry III*, 241–52.

——, 'An unknown obituary of King Henry III from the year 1263', *Reign of Henry III*, 253–9.

——, 'Henry III's "statute" against aliens: July 1263', in his *The Reign of Henry III*, 261–80

——, 'English peasants in politics, 1258–1267', *Reign of Henry III*, 309–48.

——, 'The beginnings of parliament', *Reign of Henry III*, 381–408.

——, *The Struggle for Mastery, Britain 1066–1284* (London, 2003).

——, 'The household rolls of King Henry III of England (1216–72)', *Historical Research*, 80 (2007), 22–4.

——, 'King Henry III and Saint Edward the Confessor: The origins of the cult', *English Historical Review*, 122 (2007), 865–91.

——, 'King Henry III and the Chapter House of Westminster Abbey', in *Westminster Abbey Chapter House: The History, Art and Architecture of 'a Chapter House Beyond Compare'*, ed. R. Mortimer (London, 2010), 32–9.

——, 'A Peasant in politics during the Montfortian regime of 1264–5: The Wodard of Kibworth case', *Fine of the Month* (September 2010), *Henry III Fine Rolls Project*, available at: http://www.finerollshenry3.org.uk/content/month/fm-09-2010.html (accessed 16 Nov. 2018).

——, 'Archbishop Langton and Magna Carta: His contribution, his doubts and his hypocrisy', *English Historical Review*, 126 (2011), 1041–65.

——, 'King Henry III and the Sicilian Affair', *Fine of the Month* (February 2012), 6, *Henry III Fine Rolls Project*, available at: http://www.finerollshenry3.org.uk/content/month/fine_of_the_month.html (accessed 16 Nov. 2018).

——, 'The Pershore *Flores Historiarum*: An unrecognised chronicle from the period of reform and rebellion in England, 1258–65', *English Historical Review*, 127 (2012), 1343–66.

——, 'Feature of the month: December 2015 – The saving clause in Magna Carta: new light shed on its meaning by the copies of the 1225 Charter at Burton Abbey', *The Magna Carta Project*, available at: http://magnacartaresearch.org/read/feature_of_the_month/ Dec_2015_3 (accessed 7 Aug. 2017).

——, *Magna Carta* (London, 2015).

——, 'The secret revolution of 1258', *Baronial Reform and Revolution in England, 1258–1267*, ed. A. Jobson (Woodbridge, 2016), 30–42.

Cassidy, R., 'The reforming council takes control of fines of gold, 1258–59', *Fine of the Month* (October 2011), *Henry III Fine Rolls Project*, available at: http://www.finerollshenry3.org.uk/content/month/fm-10-2011.html (accessed 25 Nov. 2011).

——, 'William Heron, "hammer of the poor, persecutor of the religious", sheriff of Northumberland, 1246–58', *Northern History*, 50 (2013), 9–19.

——, 'Bad sheriffs, custodial sheriffs and control of the counties', *Thirteenth Century England XV* (Woodbridge, 2015), 35–49.

——, 'Simon de Montfort's sheriffs, 1264–5', *Historical Research*, 91 (2018), 3–21.

Chaplais, P., 'The making of the Treaty of Paris (1259) and the royal style', *English Historical Review*, 67 (1952), 235–53.

Chenard, G., 'Les enquêtes administratives dans les domaines d'Alphonse de Poitiers', *Quand gouverner c'est enquêter. Les pratiques politiques de l'enquête princière* (Occident, XIIIe–XIVe Siècles), ed. T. Pécout (Paris, 2010), 157–68, at 158.

——, *L'Administration d'Alphonse de Poitiers (1241–1271)* (Paris, 2017).

Church, S. D., *King John: England, Magna Carta and the Making of a Tyrant* (London, 2015).

Connell, B., Gray Jones, A., Redfern, R., and Walker, D., *A Bioarchaeological Study of Medieval Burials on the Site of St Mary Spital: Excavations at Spitalfields Market, London E1, 1991–2007* (London, 2012).

Constable, G., 'The historiography of the Crusades', *The Crusades from the Perspective of Byzantium and the Muslim World*, ed. A. E. Laiou and R. P. Mottahedeh (Washington DC, 2001), 1–22.

Cox, D. C., *The Battle of Evesham: A New Account* (Evesham, 1988).

——, 'The Battle of Evesham in the Evesham chronicle', *Historical Research*, 62 (1989), 337–45.

Crook, D., and Wilkinson, L. J. (eds.), *The Growth of Royal Government Under Henry III* (Woodbridge, 2015).

Crouch, D., *The Image of Aristocracy in Britain, 1000–1300* (London, 1992).

——, 'Siward, Sir Richard (*d.*1248)', *Oxford Dictionary of National Biography, online edn.* (Oxford, 2004), available at: www.oxforddnb.com/view/article/37971 (accessed 18 Nov. 2016).

——, *The Birth of Nobility: Constructing Aristocracy in England and France, 900–1300* (Harlow, 2005).

——, *The English Aristocracy, 1070–1272: A Social Transformation* (New Haven, 2011).

——, 'The battle of the countesses: the division of the Honour of Leicester, March–December 1207', in *Rulership and Rebellion in the Anglo-Norman World*, ed. P. Dalton and D. E. Luscombe (Farnham, 2015), 179–211.

Crump, J., 'Mortimer, Roger de, lord of Wigmore (1231–1282), magnate', *ODNB*, online edn. (2004), available at: http://www.oxforddnb.com/view/10.1093/ref:odnb/9780198614128.001.0001/odnb-9780198614128-e-19352 (accessed 4 Mar. 2018).

d'Avray, D., 'Authentication of marital status: A thirteenth-century English royal annulment process and late medieval cases from the papal penitentiary', *English Historical Review*, 120 (2005), 987–1013.

——, D., *Medieval Marriage: Symbolism and Society* (Oxford, 2005).

——, D., *Rationalities in History: A Weberian Essay in Comparison* (Cambridge, 2010).

——, D., *Papacy, Monarchy and Marriage, 860–1600* (Cambridge, 2015)

Dejoux, M., *Les enquêtes de Saint Louis: Gouverner et sauver son âme* (Paris, 2014)

de Laborderie, O., Maddicott, J. R., and Carpenter, D. A., 'The Last Hours of Simon de Montfort: A New Account', *English Historical Review*, 115 (2000), 378–412.

Dixon-Smith, S., 'The image and reality of alms-giving in the great halls of Henry III', *Journal of the British Archaeological Association*, 152 (1998), 79–96, at 86–7.

Doherty, J., 'Remembering the crusading past in late medieval England: the Worksop priory tabula' (forthcoming).

Dunbabin, J., *Charles of Anjou: Power, Kingship and State-Making in Thirteenth-Century Europe* (London and New York, 1998).

Durand, G., *Monographie de l'église Notre-Dame, cathédrale d'Amiens*, 3 vols. (Paris, 1901–3).

Edbury, P., 'The de Montforts in the Latin East', *Thirteenth Century England VIII*, ed. M. Prestwich, R. Britnell and R. Frame (Woodbridge, 2001), 23–31.

Emden, A. B., *A Biographical Register of the University of Oxford to AD 1500*, 3 vols. (Oxford, 1957–9).

Frame, R., 'Clare, Thomas de (1244x7–1287), magnate and administrator', *ODNB*, online edn. (2004), available at: www.oxforddnb.com/view/10.1093/ref:odnb/9780198614128.001.0001/odnb-9780198614128-e-50023 (accessed 10 Mar. 2018).

Gaposchkin, M. C., *Invisible Weapons: Liturgy and the Making of Crusade Ideology* (Ithaca and London, 2017).

Garnett, G., 'Braybrooke [Braybroc], Henry of (d.1234), sheriff and justice', *Oxford Dictionary of National Biography*, online edn. (2010), available at: http://www.oxforddnb.com/view/10.1093/ref:odnb/9780198614128.001.0001/odnb-9780198614128-e-3300 (accessed 15 Oct. 2018).

Gillingham, J., 'War and Chivalry in the History of William the Marshal', *Thirteenth Century England II*, ed. P. R. Coss and S. D. Lloyd (Woodbridge, 1988), 1–13.

——, 'Richard I and the science of war in the Middle Ages', J. Gillingham, *Richard Coeur de Lion: Kingship, Chivalry and War in the Twelfth Century* (London, 1994), 212–26.

——, *Richard I* (New Haven, 1999).

——, 'The beginnings of English imperialism', J. Gillingham, *The English in the Twelfth Century: Imperialism, National Identity and Political Values* (Woodbridge, 2000), 3–18.

——, '1066 and the introduction of chivalry into England', *The English in the Twelfth Century*, 209–231.

Gilson, J. P., 'An unpublished notice of the Battle of Lewes', *English Historical Review*, 11 (1896), 520–2.

——, 'The parliament of 1264', *English Historical Review*, 16 (1901), 499–501.

Gransden, A., *Historical Writing in England, II, c. 1307 to the Early Sixteenth Century* (London, 1982).

Grant, L., *Blanche of Castile* (New Haven and London, 2016).

Guébin, P., and Lyon, E., 'Les manuscrits de la chronique de Pierre des Vaux-de-Cernay (texte et traductions)', *Le Moyen Âge*, 23 (1910), 221–34.

Harding, A., 'Walton [Wauton], Simon of (d. 1265/6), justice and bishop of Norwich', *ODNB*, online edn. (2004), available at: http://www.oxforddnb.com/view/10.1093/ref:odnb/9780198614128.001.0001/odnb-9780198614128-e-28902 (accessed 8 Feb. 2018).

Harvey, K., *Episcopal Appointment in England, c.1214–1344: From Episcopal Election to Papal Provision* (Aldershot, 2014).

Haskins, C. H., 'The Sources for the history of the papal penitentiary', *American Journal of Theology*, 9 (3) (1905), 421–50.

——, 'Robert le Bougre and the beginnings of the Inquisition in Northern France', *The American Historical Review*, 7 (1902), 437–57.

Hawkyard, A., 'From Painted Chamber to St Stephen's Chapel: The meeting places of the House of Commons at Westminster until 1603', *Parliamentary History*, 21 (2002), 62–84.

Hershey, A., 'Success or failure? Hugh Bigod and judicial reform during the baronial movement, June 1258–February 1259', *Thirteenth Century England V*, ed. P. R. Coss and S. D. Lloyd (Woodbridge, 1993), 65–88.

Hey, J., 'Two oaths of the community in 1258', *Historical Research*, 88 (2015), 213–29.

Holt, J. C., 'A vernacular-French text of Magna carta, 1215', *English Historical Review*, 89 (1974), 346–56.

——, *The Northerners: A Study in the Reign of King John* (2nd edn., Oxford, 1992).

Holt, J. C., rev. Hudson, J., and Garnett, G., *Magna Carta* (3rd edn., Cambridge, 2015).

Housely, N., *The Italian Crusades: The Papal–Angevin Alliance and the Crusades against Christian Lay Powers, 1254–1343* (Oxford, 1982).

Howell, M., *Eleanor of Provence: Queenship in Thirteenth-Century England* (Oxford, 1998).

Jacob, E. F., 'A proposal for arbitration between Simon de Montfort and Henry III in 1260', *English Historical Review*, 37 (1922).

Jobson, A., 'John of Crakehall: The "Forgotten" baronial treasurer, 1258–60', *Thirteenth Century England XIII*, ed. J. Burton, F. Lachaud and P. Schofield (Woodbridge, 2009), 83–99.

——, *The First English Revolution: Simon de Montfort, Henry III and the Barons' War* (London, 2012).

Jones, M., *The Black Prince* (London, 2017).

Jordan, W. C., *Louis IX and the Challenge of the Crusade: A Study in Rulership* (Princeton, NJ, 1979).

Keats-Rohan, K. S. B., '"Most securely fortified": Wallingford Castle 1071–1540', *Wallingford: The Castle and the Town in Context*, ed. K. S. B. Keats-Rohan, N. Christie and D. Roffe (Oxford, 2015), 34–115.

Keen, M., *Chivalry* (New Haven and London, 1984).

Kennan, E., 'Innocent III and the first political crusade: a comment on the limitations of papal power', *Traditio*, 27 (1971), 231–49.

Kienzle, B. M., *Cistercians, Heresy and Crusade in Occitania 1145–1229: Preaching in the Lord's Vineyard* (York, 2001).

Kjær, L., 'Matthew Paris and the royal Christmas: Ritualised communication in texts and practice', *Thirteenth-Century England XIV*, ed. J. Burton, P. Schofield and B. Weiler (Woodbridge, 2013), 141–54.

——, 'Writing reform and rebellion', *Baronial Reform and Revolution in England, 1258–1267*, ed. A. Jobson (Woodbridge, 2016), 109–124.

Knowles, C. H., 'Despenser, Sir Hugh (*c*.1223–1265)', *ODNB*, online edn. (2004), available at: http://o-www.oxforddnb.com.catalogue.libraries.london.ac.uk/view/article/7552 (accessed 3 Aug. 2017).

Lawrence, C. H., 'The university of Oxford and the chronicle of the Barons' Wars', *English Historical Review*, 95 (1980), 99–113.

——, *The Friars: The Impact of the Early Mendicant Movement on Western Society* (London, 2013).

Lay, S., *The Reconquest Kings of Portugal: Political and Cultural Reorientation on the Medieval Frontier* (Basingstoke, 2009).

Le Goff, J., 'The symbolic ritual of vassalage', J. Le Goff, *Time, Work and Culture in the Middle Ages*, trans. A. Goldhammer (Chicago, 1980), 237–87.

——, *Saint Louis*, trans. G. E. Gollrad (Paris, 2009).

Linehan, P. A., 'The Synod of Segovia (1166)', *Bulletin of Medieval Canon Law*, New Ser., 10 (Berkeley, 1980), 31–44, reprinted P. A. Linehan, *Spanish Church and Society 1150–1300* (London, 1983).

Lippiatt, G. E. M., *Simon V of Montfort and Baronial Government, 1195–1218* (Oxford, 2017).

Lloyd, S., 'King Henry III, the crusade and the Mediterranean', *England and her Neighbours 1066–1453: Essays in Honour of Pierre Chaplais*, ed. M. Jones and M. Vale (London, 1989), 97–119.

Lower, M., *The Barons' Crusade: A Call to Arms and its Consequences* (Philadelphia, 2005).

Lunt, W. E., *Financial Relations of the Papacy with England to 1327* (Cambridge, Mass., 1939).

Maddicott, J. R., 'Magna Carta and the local community 1215–1259', *Past and Present*, 102 (1984), 25–65.

——, 'Follower, leader, pilgrim, saint: Robert de Vere, earl of Oxford, at the shrine of Simon de Montfort, 1273', *English Historical Review*, 109 (1994), 641–53.

——, *Simon de Montfort* (Cambridge, 1994).

——, 'Montfort, Guy de (c.1244–1291/2), soldier and administrator', *ODNB*, online edn. (2006), available at: www.oxforddnb.com/view/10.1093/ref:odnb/9780198614128.001.0001/odnb-9780198614128-e-19047 (accessed 7 Aug. 2018).

——, *The Origins of the English Parliament, 924–1327* (Oxford, 2010).

——, 'Politics and the people in thirteenth-century England', *Thirteenth Century England XIV*, ed. J. Burton, P. Schofield and B. Weiler (Woodbridge, 2013), 1–13.

Maitland, F. W., 'A song on the death of Simon de Montfort', *English Historical Review*, 11 (1896), 314–18.

McAuley, F., 'Canon law and the end of the ordeal', *Oxford Journal of Legal Studies*, 26 (2006), 473–513.

McLeish, T. C. B., Bower, R. G., Tanner, B. K., Smithson, H. E., Panti, C., Lewis, N., and Gasper, G. E. M., 'History: A medieval multiverse', *Nature* 507 (12 March 2014), 161–3.

Moore, R. I., *The Formation of a Persecuting Society: Authority and Deviance in Western Europe, 950–1250* (2nd edn., Oxford, 2006).

Moore, T. K., 'The Fine Rolls as evidence for the expansion of royal justice during the reign of Henry III', *The Growth of Royal Government Under Henry III*, ed. D. Crook and L. J. Wilkinson (Woodbridge, 2015), 55–71.

Morris, M., *Castle: A History of the Buildings that Shaped Medieval Britain* (London, 2003).

——, *A Great and Terrible King: Edward I and the Forging of Britain* (London, 2008).

——, M., *King John: Treachery, Tyranny and the Road to Magna Carta* (London, 2015).

Murray, S., *Notre-Dame, Cathedral of Amiens: The Power of Change in Gothic* (Cambridge, 1996).

Page, W. (ed.), *A History of the County of London* (London, 1909).

Page, W., and Willis-Bund., J. W. (eds.) *A History of the County of Worcester*, 5 vols. (London, 1901–26).

Paul, N., *To Follow in Their Footsteps: The Crusades and Family Memory in the High Middle Ages* (Ithaca, 2013).

——, 'In search of the Marshal's lost crusade: the persistence of memory, the problems of history and the painful birth of crusading romance', *Journal of Medieval History*, 40 (2014), 292–310.

Peltzer, J., 'The marriages of the English earls in the thirteenth century: A social perspective', *Thirteenth Century England XIV*, ed. J. Burton, P. Schofield, and B. Weiler (Woodbridge, 2011), 61–86.

Peters, E., *The Shadow King: Rex Inutilis in Medieval Law and Literature, 751–1327* (London, 1970).

Piper, A. J., 'Kirkham, Walter of (d. 1260), administrator and bishop of Durham', *ODNB*, online edn. (2003), available at: http://www. oxforddnb.com/view/10.1093/ref:odnb/9780198614128.001.0001/odnb-9780198614128-e-15668 (accessed 8 Nov. 2018).

Poleg, E., *Approaching the Bible in Medieval England* (Manchester, 2013).

Power, D., *The Norman Frontier in the Twelfth and Early Thirteenth Centuries* (Cambridge, 2004).

——, 'Who went on the Albigensian Crusade?', *English Historical Review*, 128 (2013), 1047–85.

Powicke, F. M., 'Guy de Montfort (1265–71)', *Transactions of the Royal Historical Society*, 18 (1935), 1–23.

——, 'The archbishop of Rouen, John de Harcourt, and Simon de Montfort in 1260', *English Historical Review*, 51 (1936), 108–13.

Rawcliffe, C., 'The hospitals of later medieval London', *Medical History*, 28 (1984), 1–21.

Richardson, H. G., and Sayles, G. O., 'The Provisions of Oxford: A forgotten document and some comments', *Bulletin of the John Rylands Library*, 7 (1933), 291–321.

Richardson, H. G., 'Glanville continued', *Law Quarterly Review*, 54 (1938), 381–99.

Ridgeway, H. W., 'The lord Edward and the Provisions of Oxford (1258): A study in faction', *Thirteenth Century England I*, ed. P. R. Coss and S. D. Lloyd (Woodbridge, 1986), 89–99.

——, 'King Henry III's grievances against the council in 1261', *Historical Research*, 61 (1988), 227–42.

——, 'Foreign favourites and Henry III's problems of patronage, 1247–1258', *English Historical Review*, 104 (1989), 590–610.

Roquebert, M., *L'Épopée cathare*, 4 vols. (Toulouse and Paris, 1970–89).

Sayles, G. O., *The Functions of the Medieval Parliament of England* (London, 1988).

Sheehan, M., *The Will in Medieval England: From the Conversion of the Anglo-Saxons to the End of the Thirteenth Century* (Toronto, 1963).

Southern, R. W., *Robert Grosseteste: The Growth of an English Mind in Medieval Europe* (Oxford, 1986).

Stacey, R. C., 'Crusades, crusaders, and the baronial *Gravamina* of 1263–4', *Thirteenth Century England III*, ed. P. R. Coss and S. D. Lloyd (Woodbridge, 1991), 137–50.

——, 'The conversion of Jews to Christianity in thirteenth-century England', *Speculum*, 67 (1992), 263–83.

Sternberg, M., *Cistercian Architecture and Medieval Society* (Leiden, 2013).

Stone, I., 'The rebel barons of 1264 and the commune of London: An oath of mutual aid', *English Historical Review*, 129 (2014), 1–18.

Strickland, M., 'A law of arms or a law of treason? Conduct in war in Edward I's campaign in Scotland, 1296–1307', *Violence in Medieval Society*, ed. R. W. Kaeuper (Woodbridge, 2000).

——, 'Killing or clemency? Ransom, chivalry and changing attitudes to defeated opponents in Britain and Northern France, 7th–12th centuries', *Krieg im Mittelalter*, ed. H-H. Kortüm (Berlin, 2001), 93–122.

——, 'Treason, feud and the growth of state violence: Edward I and the "war of the earl of Carrick", 1306–7', *War, Government and Aristocracy in the British Isles, c.1150–1500: Essays in Honour of Michael Prestwich*, ed. C. Given-Wilson, A. Kettle and L. Scales (Woodbridge, 2008), 84–113.

Summerson, H., 'The 1215 Magna Carta: Clause 14, Academic commentary', *The Magna Carta Project*, available at: http://magnacartaresearch.org/read/magna_carta_1215/Clause_14?com=aca (accessed 11 Oct. 2018).

——, 'The siege of Rochester in 1264 and its impact in North Kent' (forthcoming).

——, 'Repercussions from the Barons' Wars: A Kentish inquest of 1264', *Historical Research* (forthcoming).

Suppe, F., 'The cultural significance of decapitation in high medieval Wales and the Marches', *Bulletin of the Board of Celtic Studies*, 36 (1989), 147–60.

Timbal, P., *Un conflit d'annexion au Moyen Âge: L'Application de la coutume de Paris au pays d'Albigeois* (Paris, 1949).

Tolan, J., 'The first imposition of a badge on European Jews: The English royal mandate of 1218', *The Character of Christian–Muslim Encounter: Essays in Honour of David Thomas*, ed. D. Pratt, J. Hoover, J. Davies and J. Chesworth (Leiden, 2016), 145–66.

Treharne, R. F., *The Baronial Plan of Reform, 1258–1263* (rev. edn., Manchester, 1971).

Tyreman, C., *England and the Crusades* (Chicago, 1996).

Verdon, J., *Travel in the Middle Ages* (Notre Dame, IN, 2003).

Vincent, N., 'Simon de Montfort's first quarrel with King Henry III', *Thirteenth Century England IV*, ed. P. R. Coss and S. D. Lloyd (Woodbridge, 1992), 167–77.

——, *Peter des Roches: An Alien in English Politics, 1205–1238* (Cambridge, 1996).

——, 'Two papal letters on the wearing of the Jewish badge, 1221 and 1229', *Jewish Historical Studies*, 34 (1997), 209–24.

——, 'Savoy, Peter of, count of Savoy and de facto earl of Richmond (1203?–1268), magnate', *ODNB*, online edn. (2004), available at: http://www.oxforddnb.com/view/10.1093/ref:odnb/9780198614128.001.0001/odnb-9780198614128-e-22016 (accessed 8 Feb. 2018).

——, 'Aubigny, Philip d' [Philip Daubeney] (d. 1236), knight and royal councillor', *ODNB*, online edn. (2006), available at: http://www.oxforddnb.com/view/10.1093/ref:odnb/9780198614128.001.0001/odnb-9780198614128-e-47227 (accessed 14 Nov. 2018).

——, 'Lovel, Philip (d. 1258), administrator and royal counsellor', *ODNB*, online edn. (2006), available at: http://www.oxforddnb.com/view/10.1093/ref:odnb/9780198614128.001.0001/odnb-9780198614128-e-17052 (accessed 8 Nov. 2018).

——, 'Lacy, John de, third earl of Lincoln (*c*.1192–1240)', *ODNB*, online edn. (Oxford, 2010), available at: www.oxforddnb.com/view/article/15855 (accessed 18 Nov. 2016).

——, 'The thirteenth-century bishops', *Ely: Bishops and Diocese 1109–2009*, ed. P. Meadows (Woodbridge, 2010), 26–69.

——, *Magna Carta: A Very Short Introduction* (Oxford, 2012).

——, 'Feature of the month: April 2015 – Leopards, lions and dragons: King John's banners and battle flags', *The Magna Carta Project*, available at: http://magnacartaresearch.org/read/feature_of_the_month/Apr_2015_4 (accessed 27 Feb. 2018).

——, 'King John's Diary & Itinerary: Disaster at La Roche-aux-Moins, 29 June 1214–5 July 1214', *The Magna Carta Project*, available at: http://magnacarta.cmp.uea.ac.uk/read/itinerary/Disaster_at_La_Roche-aux-Moins (accessed 25 Oct. 2018).

——, 'Henry of Bratton (alias Bracton)', *Great Christian Jurists in English History*, ed. M. Hill and R. Helmholz (Cambridge, 2017), 19–44.

——, 'The Plantagenets and the priories of Fontevraud: Old connections, new resonances?', *Fontevraud et ses prieurés*, ed. C. Andrault-Schmitt (Presses universitaires de Rennes, forthcoming).

Weiler, B., 'The *rex renitens* and the medieval idea of kingship, *c*.900–1250', *Viator* 31 (2000), 1–42.

——, 'Matthew Paris on the writing of history', *Journal of Medieval History*, 35 (2009), 254–78.

——, 'Bishops and kings in England, c.1066–1215', *Religion and Politics in the Middle Ages: Germany and England by Comparison*, ed. L. Körntgen and D. Wassenhoven (Berlin, 2013), 157–203.

Wiedemann, B. G. E., '"Fooling the court of the lord pope": Dafydd ap

Llywelyn's petition to the curia in 1244', *Welsh History Review*, 28 (2) (2016), 209–32.

Wildhaber, B., 'Catalogue des établissements cisterciens de Languedoc aux XIIIe et XIVe siècles', *Cahiers de Fanjeaux*, 21 (1986), 21–44.

Wilkinson, L. J., *Eleanor de Montfort: A Rebel Countess in Medieval England* (London, 2012).

Wilshire, L. E., *Boniface of Savoy, Carthusian and Archbishop of Canterbury, 1207–1270* (Salzburg, 1977).

Woolgar, C., *The Culture of Food in England, 1200–1500* (New Haven and London, 2016).

Zerner, M., 'L'Abbé Gui des Vaux-de-Cernay, prédicateur de croisade', *Cahiers de Fanjeaux*, 21 (1986), 183–204.

——, 'L'Epouse de Simon de Montfort et la croisade albigeoise', *Femmes – mariages – lignages. XIIe–XIVe siècles. Mélanges offerts à Georges Duby*, ed. J. Dufournet, A. Joris, P. Toubret and D. Barthélemy (Brussels, 1992), 449–70.

Unpublished Theses

Cassidy, R., 'The 1259 Pipe Roll' (King's College London Ph.D. thesis, 2012).

Dixon-Smith, S., 'Feeding the poor to commemorate the dead: the pro-anima almsgiving of Henry III of England, 1227–72' (University College London Ph.D. thesis, 2002).

Hope, A., 'Hireling shepherds: English bishops and their deputies, c. 1186 to c. 1323' (University College London Ph.D. thesis, 2013).

Knowles, C. H., 'The Disinherited, 1265–80. A political and social study of the supporters of Simon de Montfort and the resettlement after the Barons' War' (University of Wales Aberystwyth Ph.D. thesis, 1959).

Pélissié du Rausas, A., 'Voices from the archives: reassembling the dossier of Gascon complaints against Simon de Montfort (1252). A study in Anglo-Gascon history' (King's College London MA thesis, 2013).

Stone, I., 'The Book of Arnold fitz Thedmar' (King's College London Ph.D. thesis, 2016).

Websites

Anglo-Norman Dictionary: http://www.anglo-norman.net/gate/

Digital Dante: https://digitaldante.columbia.edu/dante/divine-comedy/inferno

The Historical Gazetteer of England's Place-Names: http://placenames.org.uk/index.php

Notes

Introduction

1 C. Bémont, *Simon de Montfort* (Paris, 1884); J. R. Maddicott, *Simon de Montfort* (Cambridge, 1994).

2 In his letter to Garnier of Rochefort, abbot of Clairvaux (1 October 1191), in P. W. Edbury (ed.), *The Conquest of Jerusalem and the Third Crusade* (Abingdon, 2016), 179–81.

3 G. Constable, 'The historiography of the Crusades', in *The Crusades from the Perspective of Byzantium and the Muslim World*, ed. A. E. Laiou and R. P. Mottahedeh (Washington DC, 2001), 1–22, at 11–12.

4 Various modern historians have exercised themselves in defining a 'crusade': is it only expeditions to Outremer that deserve the title, or is it only those with papal endorsement that can be said to count? See: Constable, 'The historiography of the Crusades', 12–15.

5 For an introduction to chivalry in this period, see: D. Crouch, *The Birth of Nobility: Constructing Aristocracy in England and France, 900–1300* (Harlow, 2005), 29–86; J. Gillingham, 'War and chivalry in the history of William the Marshal', in *Thirteenth Century England II*, ed. P. R. Coss and S. D. Lloyd (Woodbridge, 1988), 1–13.

6 For an introduction to the administrative records of Henry III's reign, see: *The Growth of Royal Government Under Henry III*, ed. D. Crook and L. J. Wilkinson (Woodbridge, 2015).

7 D. A. Carpenter, 'Matthew Paris and Henry III's speech at the exchequer in October 1256', in his *The Reign of Henry III* (London, 1996), 137–50, at 137–41. For an overview of Matthew Paris's work,

see: B. Weiler, 'Matthew Paris on the writing of history', *Journal of Medieval History*, 35 (2009), 254–78.

8 I. Stone, 'The Book of Arnold fitz Thedmar' (King's College London Ph.D. thesis, 2016), 21–35.

9 O. de Laborderie, J. R. Maddicott and D. A. Carpenter, 'The last hours of Simon de Montfort: A New Account', *English Historical Review*, 115 (2000), 378–412.

10 F. A. C. Mantello and J. Goering (eds.), *The Letters of Robert Grosseteste, Bishop of Lincoln* (Toronto, 2010).

11 C. H. Lawrence (ed. and trans.), *The Letters of Adam Marsh*, 2 vols. (Oxford, 2006–10).

12 Bémont, *Simon de Montfort*, 332–43; for the dating of the deposition to 1262, see: Maddicott, *Simon de Montfort*, 218, n.110.

13 L. J. Wilkinson, *Eleanor de Montfort: A Rebel Countess in Medieval England* (London, 2012); G. E. M. Lippiatt, *Simon V of Montfort and Baronial Government, 1195–1218* (Oxford, 2017).

14 *Petri Vallium Sarnaii monachi Hystoria albigensis*, ed. P. Guébin and E. Lyon, 3 vols. (Paris, 1926–39), translated in *The History of the Albigensian Crusade: Peter of les Vaux-de-Cernay's Historia Albigensis*, trans. W. A. and M. D. Sibly (Woodbridge, 1998) – in what follows I have given references for the translation; 'The Rothelin Continuation', in *The Rothelin Continuation of the History of William of Tyre with Part of the Eracles or Acre Text*, trans. J. Shirley (Aldershot, 1999); A. Molinier (ed.), *Obituaires de la province de Sens*, 3 vols. (Paris, 1902–9), II, 224–5.

15 N. Paul, *To Follow in Their Footsteps: The Crusades and Family Memory in the High Middle Ages* (Ithaca, 2013).

1. A Way of Living, and a Way of Dying

1 On use of the term 'count', see: D. Crouch, *The Image of Aristocracy in Britain, 1000–1300* (London, 1992), 41–6.

2 *The History of the Albigensian Crusade: Peter of les Vaux-de-Cernay's Historia Albiensis*, trans. W. A. and M. D. Sibly (Woodbridge, 1998) (hereafter *PVC*), ch. 609. See too the account by the anonymous successor to William of Tudela in *The Song of the Cathar Wars: A History of the Albigensian Crusade*, trans. J. Shirley (Farnham, 1996), laisse 205.

3 *Song of the Cathar Wars*, laisse 205.

4 Ibid.

5 *PVC*, ch. 612; *Song of the Cathar Wars*, laisse 205.

6 *Song of the Cathar Wars*, laisse 183 and 123, n.3.

7 D. Crouch, *The Birth of Nobility: Constructing Aristocracy in England and France, 900–1300* (Harlow, 2005), 46–55; N. Paul, *To Follow in Their Footsteps: The Crusades and Family Memory in the High Middle Ages* (Ithaca, 2013), 55–89.

8 Crouch, *Birth of Nobility*, 56–80.

9 *PVC*, ch. 299.

10 M. Zerner, 'L'Abbé Gui des Vaux-de-Cernay, prédicateur de croisade', *Cahiers de Fanjeaux*, 21 (1986), 183–204, at 185; G. E. M. Lippiatt, *Simon V of Montfort and Baronial Government, 1195–1218* (Oxford, 2017), 82–3; for the education of noble children by monks, see: M. Aurell, *Le chevalier lettré: savoir et conduite de l'aristocratie aux XIIe et XIIIe siècles* (Paris, 2011), 62–5.

11 *PVC*, ch. 106, in which the Count steps in to prevent the Venetians murdering Gui; M. Zerner, 'L'Abbé Gui des Vaux-de-Cernay, prédicateur de croisade', *Cahiers de Fanjeaux*, 21 (1986), 183–204, at 185, 188–90 (highlighting the divergence of Peter's account, which gives a prominent place in events to the Count, with that of Geoffrey of Villehardouin); G. E. M. Lippiatt, *Simon V of Montfort and Baronial Government, 1195–1218* (Oxford: 2017), 82–5.

12 *PVC*, chs. 51, 299; B. M. Kienzle, *Cistercians, Heresy and Crusade in Occitania 1145–1229: Preaching in the Lord's Vineyard* (York, 2001), 136–8, 161–4; Zerner, 'L'abbé Gui des Vaux-de-Cernay', 194–9.

13 *PVC*, ch. 300.

14 Lippiatt, *Simon V of Montfort*, 56.

15 Paul, *To Follow in Their Footsteps*, 21–53.

16 Evreux, Archives départementales de l'Eure, H 793 (*Petit Cartulaire de l'abbaye St-Taurin d'Evreux*), f.75r no.69; see too: ibid., f.75r–v no.70. I am grateful to Daniel Power for bringing these entries in the St-Taurin cartulary to my attention.

17 The expedition of Roger de Mowbray and Hugh de Beauchamp to Jerusalem is described in Roger of Howden, *Gesta regis Henrici secundi Benedicti abbatis*, ed. W. Stubbs, 2 vols. (London, 1867), I, 359, and, II, 22; for the plight of the Templars at Hattin, see the letter of brother Terricus, who escaped the battle, preserved by Roger of Howden, given in M. Barber, *The New Knighthood* (Cambridge, 1994), 115–16, and the account of Imad al-Din, which describes the beheadings, given in F. Gabrieli (ed. and trans.), *Arab Historians of the Crusades*, trans. from the Italian by E. J. Costello (London, 1969), 138. There is no evidence for Amaury's presence in Normandy after Hattin, nor is he mentioned in the accounts of the Third Crusade, suggesting his demise at Hattin (for this point I am grateful again to Daniel Power).

18 N. Paul, 'In search of the Marshal's lost crusade: the persistence of memory, the problems of history, and the painful birth of crusading romance', *Journal of Medieval History*, 40 (2014), 292–310.

19 Paul, *To Follow in Their Footsteps*, 64–74.

20 *PVC*, ch. 101. For episcopal elections, see: K. Harvey, *Episcopal Appointments in England, c. 1214–1344. From Episcopal Election to Papal Provision* (Aldershot, 2014), 36.

21 For the Count's conduct at the siege of Carcassonne, see: *PVC*, ch. 96.

22 Ibid., ch. 180.

23 For example: ibid., chs. 106, 115, 125, 134, 135, 136, 140, 156, 167, 182, 187, 228, 246, 266, 267, 269, 280, 318, 358. On the forty-day term of service, see: D. Power, 'Who went on the Albigensian Crusade?', *English Historical Review*, 128 (2013), 1047–85, at 1048 n.4.

24 *PVC*, ch. 136.

25 Crouch, *Birth of Nobility*, 63–6; M. Strickland, 'Killing or clemency? Ransom, chivalry and changing attitudes to defeated opponents in Britain and Northern France, 7th–12th centuries', in *Krieg im Mittelalter*, ed. H-H. Kortüm (Berlin, 2001), 93–122.

26 *History of William Marshal*, ed. A. J. Holden, trans. S. Gregory, notes by D. Crouch, 3 vols. (London, 2002–6) (hereafter *HWM*), II, ll. 19072–3, 19084.

27 *HWM*, II, ll. 16733–68.

28 M. Barber, 'The Albigensian crusades: wars like any other?', in *Dei Gesta per Francos. Crusade Studies in Honour of Jean Richard*, ed. M. Balard, B. Z. Kedar and J. Riley-Smith (Aldershot, 2001), 45–55.

29 *PVC*, ch. 227.

30 Ibid., ch. 142.

31 Ibid., ch. 107.

32 Ibid., chs. 181, 339, 606B; see too: *Song of the Cathar Wars*, laisse 183 and 123 n.3.

33 M. Zerner, 'L'Épouse de Simon de Montfort et la croisade albigeoise', in *Femmes – mariages – lignages. XIIe–XIVe siècles. Mélanges offerts à Georges Duby*, ed. J. Dufournet, A. Joris, P. Toubret and D. Barthélemy (Brussels, 1992), 449–70, at 450.

34 *PVC*, ch. 258.

35 Ibid., ch. 305.

36 Ramon Lull, *The Book of the Order of Chivalry*, trans. N. Fallows (Woodbridge, 2013), 62.

37 Lull, *Order of Chivalry*, 62; M. Keen, *Chivalry* (New Haven and London, 1984), 64–5.

38 *PVC*, ch. 430.

39 Alfonso X, *Las Siete Partidas*, trans. S. Parsons Scott and ed. R. I. Burns, 5 vols. (Philadelphia, 2001), II, 425.

40 *PVC*, ch. 430.

41 Ibid., chs. 362–4.

42 C. de Vic and J. Vaissète (eds.), *Histoire générale de Languedoc*, rev. edn., 16 vols. (Toulouse, 1872–1904), VIII, c. 626.

43 M. Roquebert, *L'Épopée cathare*, 4 vols. (Toulouse and Paris, 1970–89), III, 467 n.21.

44 A. Molinier (ed.), *Obituaires de la province de Sens*, 3 vols. (Paris, 1902–9), II, 224–5. For the retrieval of Gui's body at Castelnaudary, see: *The Chronicle of William of Puylaurens*, trans. W. A. and M. D. Sibly (Woodbridge, 2003), ch. 29.

45 For the importance of the mausoleum to crusading families, see: Paul, *To Follow in Their Footsteps*, 145–50.

2. A New Kingdom

1 C. Bémont, *Simon de Montfort* (Paris, 1884), 333.

2 S. T. Ambler, *Bishops in the Political Community of England, 1213–1272* (Oxford, 2017), 50–1.

3 J. C. Holt, *The Northerners: A Study in the Reign of King John* (2nd edn., Oxford, 1992), 81; J. C. Holt, rev. J. Hudson and G. Garnett, *Magna Carta* (3rd edn., Cambridge, 2015), 8–9.

4 For an account of John's reign, see the narratives and varied interpretations of D. A. Carpenter, *Magna Carta* (London, 2015); S. D. Church, *King John: England, Magna Carta and the Making of a Tyrant* (London, 2015); M. Morris, *King John: Treachery, Tyranny and the Road to Magna Carta* (London, 2015). For the early years of Henry's reign, see: D. A. Carpenter, *The Minority of Henry III* (London, 1990).

5 Carpenter, *Magna Carta*, 4–5.

6 Bémont, *Simon de Montfort*, 333.

7 Ibid.

8 *Rotuli Litterarum Patentium in Turri Londinensi Asservati*, ed. T. Duffus Hardy (London, 1835), 150; *Calendar of Patent Rolls, 1232–72*, 4 vols. (London, 1906–13) (hereafter *CPR*), *1225–32*, 124.

9 *CPR*, *1225–32*, 325.

10 *Close Rolls*, *1231–72*, 14 vols. (London, 1905–38) (hereafter *CR*), *1227–31*, 316.

11 N. Vincent, 'Simon de Montfort's first quarrel with King Henry

III', in *Thirteenth Century England IV*, ed. P. R. Coss and S. D. Lloyd (Woodbridge, 1992), 167–77, at 168.

12 W. W. Shirley (ed.), *Royal and Other Historical Letters Illustrative of the Reign of Henry III*, 2 vols. (London, 1862–6) (hereafter *Royal Letters*), I, 362–4; for the career of Philip d'Aubigny, see: N. Vincent, 'Aubigny, Philip d' [Philip Daubeney] (d. 1236), knight and royal councillor', *Oxford Dictionary of National Biography*, online edn. (2006), available at: http://www.oxforddnb.com/view/10.1093/ref:odnb/9780198614128.001.0001/odnb9780198614128-e-47227 (accessed 14 Nov. 2018).

13 *Royal Letters*, I, 362–4; *The Royal Charter Witness Lists of Henry III (1226–1272) from the Charter Rolls in the Public Record Office*, ed. M. Morris, 2 vols. (Chippenham, 2001) (hereafter *RCWL*), I, 96.

14 Bémont, *Simon de Montfort*, 333.

15 *CPR, 1232–47*, 185; Vincent, 'First quarrel', 169; for the wardship of Dodderford (Dadford, Bucks), to hold during the minority of the son and heir of William de Caignes, see: *CPR, 1232–47*, 3.

16 Bémont, *Simon de Montfort*, 333.

17 *Layettes du Trésor des Chartes*, ed. A. Teulet, H.-F. Delaborde and E. Berger, 5 vols. (Paris, 1863–1909), II, 194–5.

18 *The Charters of the Anglo-Norman Earls of Chester, c.1071–1237*, ed. G. Barraclough (Gloucester, 1988), no. 436; Vincent, 'First quarrel', 167 n.2.

19 *RCWL*, I, 105–6; *CR, 1227–31*, 543; Bémont, *Simon de Montfort*, 333.

20 *RCWL*, I, 105–6.

21 TNA: E 372/86 m.17 (a reference I owe to Richard Cassidy).

22 TNA: E 159/17 m. 6 (a reference I owe to Richard Cassidy).

23 G. E. M. Lippiatt, *Simon V of Montfort and Baronial Government, 1195–1218* (Oxford, 2017), 108; Vincent, 'First quarrel', 175.

24 J. R. Maddicott, *Simon de Montfort* (Cambridge, 1994), 47–9.

25 Leicestershire Record Office, BRI/I/II, a photograph of which is printed in Maddicott, *Simon de Montfort*, plate 1.

26 For Simon's affinity, see: Maddicott, *Simon de Montfort*, 61–9.

27 William of Newburgh, *Historia rerum Anglicarum*, ed. R. Howlett in *Chronicles of the reigns of Stephen, Henry II, and Richard I*, 4 vols. (London, 1884–9), I, 312–22.

28 As argued in the seminal work of R. I. Moore, *The Formation of a Persecuting Society: Authority and Deviance in Western Europe, 950–1250* (2nd edn., Oxford, 2006).

29 'Hospitals: Domus conversorum', in *A History of the County of London: vol. 1, London Within the Bars, Westminster and Southwark*, ed. W. Page (London, 1909), 551–4; *British History Online*, available

at: www.british-history.ac.uk/vch/london/vol1/pp551–4 (accessed 15 Mar. 2018); R. C. Stacey, 'The conversion of Jews to Christianity in thirteenth-century England', *Speculum*, 67 (1992), 263–83, at 267.

30 M. Zerner, 'L'Épouse de Simon de Montfort et la croisade albigeoise', in *Femmes – mariages – lignages. XIIe–XIVe siècles: Mélanges offerts à Georges Duby*, ed. J. Dufournet, A. Joris, P. Toubret and D. Barthélemy (Brussels, 1992), 449–70, at 461.

31 Canon 68 (N. P. Tanner (ed.), *Decrees of the Ecumenical Councils*, 2 vols. (London, 1991), I, 266).

32 J. Tolan, 'The first imposition of a badge on European Jews: the English Royal Mandate of 1218', in *The Character of Christian– Muslim Encounter: Essays in Honour of David Thomas*, ed. D. Pratt, J. Hoover, J. Davies and J. Chesworth (Leiden, 2016), 145–66, at 145.

33 N. Vincent, 'Two papal letters on the wearing of the Jewish badge, 1221 and 1229', *Jewish Historical Studies*, 34 (1997), 209–24.

34 Tolan, 'The first imposition of a badge on European Jews', 153–7.

35 See Grosseteste's description of his visitations, in a speech to the papal court in 1250, translated in R. W. Southern, *Robert Grosseteste: The Growth of an English Mind in Medieval Europe* (Oxford, 1986), 258.

36 Ambler, *Bishops in the Political Community*, 35–7.

37 C. H. Lawrence (ed. and trans.), *The Letters of Adam Marsh*, 2 vols. (Oxford, 2006–10), II, 339.

38 F. A. C. Mantello and J. Goering (eds.), *The Letters of Robert Grosseteste, Bishop of Lincoln* (Toronto, 2010), 66–9.

39 H. G. Richardson, 'Glanville continued', *Law Quarterly Review*, 54 (1938), 381–99, at 393.

40 D. A. Carpenter, *The Struggle for Mastery, Britain 1066–1284* (London, 2003), 488.

41 Stacey, 'Conversion of Jews to Christianity', 269–71.

3. Love

1 *The Royal Charter Witness Lists of Henry III (1226–1272) from the Charter Rolls in the Public Record Office*, ed. M. Morris, 2 vols. (Chippenham, 2001) (hereafter *RCWL*), I, 125.

2 *Matthaei Parisiensis, Monachi Sancti Albani, Chronica Majora*, ed. H. R. Luard, 7 vols. (London, 1872–83) (hereafter *CM*), III, 336.

3 The description of the ceremony is provided by Matthew Paris, *CM*, III, 337–8; for the sword known as Curtein, see Paris's drawing at Corpus Christi College, Cambridge, MS. 016II f. 99r.

4 On the washing of hands and its accoutrements, see: C. Woolgar, *The Culture of Food in England, 1200–1500* (New Haven and London, 2016), 174.

5 Through Ranulf's sister, John's mother-in-law, Hawise (N. Vincent, 'Lacy, John de, third earl of Lincoln (*c.*1192–1240)', *Oxford Dictionary of National Biography*, online edn. (Oxford, 2010), available at: www.oxforddnb.com/view/article/15855 (accessed 18 Nov. 2016).

6 H. Summerson, 'The 1215 Magna Carta: Clause 14, Academic commentary', *The Magna Carta Project*, available at: http://magnacartaresearch.org/read/magna_carta_1215/Clause_14?com=aca (accessed 11 Oct. 2018).

7 D. A. Carpenter, 'Justice and jurisdiction under King John and Henry III', in his *The Reign of Henry III* (London, 1996), 17–44, at 38–42; N. Vincent, *Peter des Roches: An Alien in English Politics, 1205–1238* (Cambridge, 1996), 429–45; S. T. Ambler, *Bishops in the Political Community of England, 1213–1272* (Oxford, 2017), 62–5.

8 *CM*, III, 362.

9 Ibid., 369.

10 D. Crouch, 'Siward, Sir Richard (*d.*1248)', *Oxford Dictionary of National Biography*, online edn. (Oxford, 2004), available at: www.oxforddnb.com/view/article/37971 (accessed 18 Nov. 2016).

11 *CM*, III, 380–5; J. R. Maddicott, *The Origins of the English Parliament, 924–1327* (Oxford, 2010), 457.

12 *RCWL*, I, 161.

13 *CM*, III, 418.

14 Ibid., 476.

15 *Calendar of the Fine Rolls of the Reign of Henry III* (henceforth *CFR*), *1236–7*, 21/nos. 134, 142, available on the Henry III Fine Rolls Project website at: https://finerollshenry3.org.uk/content/calendar/roll_004E.html (accessed 16 Nov. 2018); *Close Rolls, 1231–72*, 14 vols. (London, 1905–38) (hereafter *CR*), *1234–7*, 451.

16 L. J. Wilkinson, *Eleanor de Montfort: A Rebel Countess in Medieval England* (London, 2012), 28–9.

17 W. W. Shirley (ed.), *Royal and Other Historical Letters Illustrative of the Reign of Henry III*, 2 vols. (London, 1862–6) (hereafter *Royal Letters*), I, 364–5.

18 Eleanor's motives are suggested by Wilkinson, *Eleanor de Montfort*, 44–7.

19 J. R. Maddicott, *Simon de Montfort* (Cambridge, 1994), 17–18; L. Grant, *Blanche of Castile* (New Haven and London, 2016), 113.

20 *CM*, III, 470–1.

21 Wilkinson, *Eleanor de Montfort*, 21.

22 *Royal Letters*, I, 244–6; Wilkinson, *Eleanor de Montfort*, 22.

23 *Royal Letters*, I, 244–6; Wilkinson, *Eleanor de Montfort*, 22.

24 C. Bémont, *Simon de Montfort* (1st edn., Paris, 1884), 334.

25 *CM*, III, 566–7.

26 *Calendar of Patent Rolls, 1232–72*, 4 vols. (London, 1906–13) (hereafter *CPR*), *1232–47*, 209.

27 *RCWL*, I, 166; *Calendar of Liberate Rolls, 1226–72*, 6 vols. (London, 1916–64) (hereafter *CLR*), *1226–40*, 311, 312.

28 *CM*, III, 478.

29 Ibid., 478–9.

30 D. d'Avray, *Medieval Marriage: Symbolism and Society* (Oxford, 2005), 105.

31 *CM*, III, 478–9, 487.

32 D. d'Avray, *Medieval Marriage*, 124–9.

33 D. d'Avray, 'Authentication of marital status: a thirteenth-century English royal annulment process and late medieval cases from the papal penitentiary', *English Historical Review*, 120 (2005), 987–1013, at 989.

34 *CM*, III, 487.

35 D. d'Auvray, 'Authentication of marital status', 990–5.

36 J. Verdon, *Travel in the Middle Ages* (Notre Dame, IN, 2003), 8.

37 *CPR*, *1232–47*, 214; L. Auvray et al. (eds.), *Les Registres de Grégoire IX*, 4 vols. (Paris, 1896–1955), II, nos. 4329, 4330 (10 May 1238).

38 Maddicott, *Simon de Montfort*, 28, connects Simon's dealings with a burgess of Leicester, Simon Curlevache, to a need to fund the trip, following Matthew Paris's remark that Simon extorted 500 marks from the burgess, but these dealings with the burgess might well date to 1237, as suggested by F. A. C. Mantello and J. Goering (eds.), *The Letters of Robert Grosseteste, Bishop of Lincoln* (Toronto, 2010), 171 n.6, where it is pointed out that Matthew Paris does not make a strong chronological link between the taking of the 500 marks and the journey, and secondly that Grosseteste's concern in this affair is Simon's failure to temper justice with mercy in exercising a judicial judgement and punishment, i.e. that Simon had levied an arbitrary and excessive fine, in anger.

39 Maddicott, *Simon de Montfort*, 26–7; see too Henry's speech to Simon in 1239, in which he notes Edmund told 'the truth' to the pope (*CM* III, 567).

40 *CPR*, *1232–47*, 214; *CM*, III, 479–80.

41 *Registres de Grégoire IX*, II, nos. 4329, 4330.

42 *CM*, III, 479–80.

43 Ibid., 485, 491.

44 *Historia Diplomatica Friderici Secundi*, ed. J.-L.-A. Huillard-
Bréholles, 7 vols. (Paris, 1852–61), V, i, 188, 192, 196, 197.

45 *Annales Placentini Gibellini*, in *Monumenta Germaniae Historica*, ed.
G. H. Pertz et al., 39 vols. (Hanover, 1826–2009), XVIII, 479 (read
May for April); *Historia Diplomatica Friderici Secundi*, V, i, 200, 201,
203, 210–15.

46 Ibid., 207–8.

47 *Annales Placentini Gibellini*, 479.

48 Ibid., 480.

49 *CM*, III, 498.

50 Ibid. The king was at Westminster by 13 October, in order to attend
the celebrations of the feast of the Translation of St Edward the
Confessor (D. A. Carpenter, 'King Henry III and Saint Edward the
Confessor: The origins of the cult', *English Historical Review*, 122
(2007), 865–91, at 869.

51 Wilkinson, *Eleanor de Montfort*, 69.

4. Holy War

1 *Matthaei Parisiensis, Monachi Sancti Albani, Chronica Majora*, ed. H.
R. Luard, 7 vols. (London, 1872–83) (hereafter *CM*), III, 518.

2 *Calendar of Liberate Rolls, 1226–72*, 6 vols. (London, 1916–64)
(hereafter *CLR*), *1226–40*, 356.

3 *CLR, 1226–40*, 360; L. Kjær, 'Matthew Paris and the royal
Christmas: ritualised communication in texts and practice', in
Thirteenth-Century England XIV, ed. J. Burton, P. Schofield and B.
Weiler (Woodbridge, 2013), 141–54, at 153.

4 *CM*, III, 522–3; Kjær, 'Matthew Paris and the royal Christmas', 145,
153.

5 TNA: E 159/17 m.6. I am grateful to Richard Cassidy for bringing
this to my attention. The grant of the third penny is also noted by
D. Crouch, *The English Aristocracy, 1070–1272: A Social
Transformation* (New Haven, 2011), 262 n.27.

6 L. Auvray et al. (eds.), *Les Registres de Grégoire IX*, 4 vols. (Paris,
1896–1955), II, nos. 4329, 4330.

7 *CM*, III, 524.

8 *The Royal Charter Witness Lists of Henry III (1226–1272) from the
Charter Rolls in the Public Record Office*, ed. M. Morris, 2 vols.
(Chippenham, 2001) (hereafter *RCWL*), I, 169.

9 *Layettes du Trésor des Chartes*, ed. A. Teulet, H.-F. Delaborde and E.
Berger, 5 vols. (Paris, 1863–1909), II, no. 4789.

10 *Calendar of Charter Rolls, 1226–1300*, 2 vols. (London: 1903–6)
(hereafter *CChR*), *1226–57*, 242, 243; *RCWL*, I, 171. For the
parliament, see: J. R. Maddicott, *The Origins of the English
Parliament 924–1327* (Oxford, 2010), 458. Other marks of Simon's
exaltation were also made publicly: already his name had been
elevated in the witness lists to royal charters above that of John de
Lacy (*RCWL*, I, 169, 170, 171 (4 March 1239, 4 April 1239, 24 May
1239)).

11 M. Howell, *Eleanor of Provence: Queenship in Thirteenth-Century
England* (Oxford, 1998), 27.

12 D. A. Carpenter, 'King Henry III and Saint Edward the Confessor:
the origins of the cult', *English Historical Review*, 122 (2007), 865–91,
at 872.

13 D. d'Avray, *Papacy, Monarchy and Marriage, 860–1600* (Cambridge,
2015), 113–19.

14 *CM*, III, 539–40.

15 The intricacies of Simon's financial problems are unpicked by J. R.
Maddicott, *Simon de Montfort* (Cambridge, 1994), 24–5.

16 C. Bémont, *Simon de Montfort* (Paris, 1884), 263–4.

17 Ibid., 333–4; Maddicott, *Simon de Montfort*, 25.

18 Bémont, *Simon de Montfort*, 334.

19 Ibid.; *CM*, III, 566–7; H. R. Luard (ed.), *Annales Monastici*, 5 vols.
(London, 1864–9) (hereafter *AM*), III, 152.

20 F. A. C. Mantello and J. Goering (eds.), *The Letters of Robert
Grosseteste, Bishop of Lincoln* (Toronto, 2010), 264–6.

21 For Frederick's treaty, see: *Historia Diplomatica Friderici Secundi*, ed.
J.-L.-A. Huillard-Bréholles, 7 vols. (Paris, 1852–61), III, 86–90.

22 J. Bird, E. Peters and J. M. Powell (eds.), *Crusade and Christendom:
Annotated Documents in Translation from Innocent III to the Fall of
Acre, 1187–1291* (Philadelphia, 2013), 271.

23 Bird, Peters and Powell (eds.), *Crusade and Christendom*, 280 (from
CM, III, 287), 271.

24 *CM*, III, 368–9; 'The Rothelin Continuation', in *The Rothelin
Continuation of the History of William of Tyre with Part of the Eracles
or Acre Text*, trans. J. Shirley (Aldershot, 1999), ch. 20; Lower,
Barons' Crusade, 42–4.

25 Thibaut de Champagne, 'Seignor, sachiez, qui or ne s'an ira', available
on the website of the project *Troubadours, Trouvères and the Crusades*,
at: https://warwick.ac.uk/fac/arts/modernlanguages/research/french/
crusades/texts/of/rs6/#page1 (accessed 12 Oct. 2018).

26 *Calendar of Patent Rolls, 1232–72*, 4 vols. (London, 1906–13) (hereafter
CPR), *1232–47*, 155.

27 'The Rothelin Continuation', ch. 20; M. Lower, *The Barons' Crusade: A Call to Arms and its Consequences* (Philadelphia, 2005), 162.

28 'The Rothelin Continuation', ch. 20.

29 Bémont, *Simon de Montfort*, 334; *Dialogus de Scaccario, and Constitutio Domus Regis* (*The Dialogue of the Exchequer, and The Disposition of the Royal Household*), ed. Emilie Amt and S. D. Church (Oxford, 2007), 164–7.

30 *Dialogue of the Exchequer*, 166–7.

31 Bémont, *Simon de Montfort*, 334.

32 Ibid.

33 *CM*, IV, 7.

34 For the importance of woodland in the Montfort family estates, see: G. E. M. Lippiatt, *Simon V of Montfort and Baronial Government, 1195–1218* (Oxford, 2017), 116.

35 'The Rothelin Continuation', ch. 23.

36 Ibid., ch. 26.

37 Ibid.

38 Ibid., ch. 27.

39 Ibid.

40 Ibid., chs. 27–8. That an escape route was left open is suggested by Lower, *Barons' Crusade*, 169–70.

41 'The Rothelin Continuation', ch. 29.

42 Lower, *Barons' Crusade*, 173–4.

43 Philippe de Nanteuil, 'En chantant vueil mon dueil faire', available on the website of the project *Troubadours, Trouvères and the Crusades*, at: https://warwick.ac.uk/fac/arts/modernlanguages/research/french/crusades/texts/of/rs164/#page1 (accessed 12 Oct. 2018).

44 *CM*, IV, 25–6.

45 Ibid., 44.

46 Ibid., 138–44.

47 Corpus Christi College, Cambridge, MS 016II, f. 137r.

48 Maddicott, *Simon de Montfort*, 43.

49 *AM*, III, 152.

50 For the Furnival brothers, see: J. Doherty, 'Remembering the crusading past in late medieval England: the Worksop priory tabula' (forthcoming) – I am very grateful to James Doherty for allowing me to see a draft of this article in advance of publication; *Calendar of the Fine Rolls of the Reign of Henry III* (hereafter *CFR*), *1235–6*, nos. 21, 22, available on the Henry III Fine Rolls Project website at: www.finerollshenry3.org.uk/content/calendar/roll_035.html#it021_018 (accessed 15 Oct. 2018).

51 G. Garnett, 'Braybrooke [Braybroc], Henry of (d.1234), sheriff and justice', *Oxford Dictionary of National Biography* (hereafter *ODNB*), online edn. (2010), available at: http://www.oxforddnb.com/view/10.1093/ref:odnb/9780198614128.001.0001/odnb-9780198614128-e-3300 (accessed 15 Oct. 2018).

52 *CFR, 1239–40*, no. 32, available at: https://finerollshenry3.org.uk/content/calendar/roll_007E.html (accessed 15 Oct. 2018).

53 P. Brand, 'Bigod, Hugh (b. in or before 1220, d.1266), baron and justiciar', in *ODNB*, online edn. (2008), available at: http://www.oxforddnb.com/view/10.1093/ref:odnb/9780198614128.001.0001/odnb-9780198614128-e-2377 (accessed 15 Oct. 2018); *CFR, 1241–42*, nos. 91, 92, 98, 105, available at: https://finerollshenry3.org.uk/content/calendar/roll_038.html#it092_011 (accessed 15 Oct. 2018).

54 *Registres de Grégoire IX*, II, no. 4507.

55 Brand, 'Bigod, Hugh', *ODNB*.

56 *CM*, III, 539–40.

57 Lower, *Barons' Crusade*, 45, notes their origins but provides no references.

58 For Simon's affinity, see: Maddicott, *Simon de Montfort*, 61–9.

59 William had been paid 40 marks (just short of £27) per annum since at least 1228, while Gerard had received £20 yearly since perhaps 1238 (*CLR, 1226–40*), 108, 156, 217, 242–3, 356, 360, 419, 463, 471; Lower, *Barons' Crusade*, 142.

60 H. C. Lea (ed.), *A Formulary of the Papal Penitentiary in the Thirteenth Century* (Philadelphia, 1892), 52–3. For discussion of the formulary, see: C. H. Haskins, 'The Sources for the history of the papal penitentiary', *American Journal of Theology*, 9 (1905), 421–50, at 429–32.

61 C. H. Haskins, 'Robert le Bougre and the beginnings of the Inquisition in Northern France', *American Historical Review*, 7 (1902), 437–57, at 453–4.

62 Lea, *A Formulary of the Papal Penitentiary*, 52–3.

63 'The Rothelin Continuation', ch. 36.

64 *CM*, IV, 174–5; for the death of Thomas de Furnivall, see: Doherty, 'Worksop priory tabula'.

65 BL: Cotton MS Vespasian F I f. 131r.

66 P. Edbury, 'The de Montforts in the Latin East', in *Thirteenth Century England VIII*, ed. M. Prestwich, R. Britnell and R. Frame (Woodbridge, 2001), 23–31, at 23–5.

67 A. Molinier (ed.), *Obituaires de la province de Sens*, 3 vols. (Paris, 1902–9), II, 224–5. His death is given here as 28 August, though he was remembered at Haute-Bruyère on 22 August.

68 R. Maffei, *Commentariorum rerum urbanarum libri XXXVIII* (Rome, 1506), book 22.

69 For the importance of claiming bodies for burial, see: N. Paul, *To Follow in Their Footsteps: The Crusades and Family Memory in the High Middle Ages* (Ithaca, 2013), 134–70.

70 Molinier (ed.), *Obituaires de la province de Sens*, II, 224–5.

5. An Exemplar of Defeat

1   C. Bémont, *Simon de Montfort* (Paris, 1884), 334, n.3.

2   C. Bémont, 'La campagne de Poitou, 1242–1243. Taillebourg & Saintes', *Annales du Midi*, 5 (1893), 289–314, at 296.

3   *Calendar of the Fine Rolls of the Reign of Henry III* (hereafter *CFR*), 26 (20 May 1242–27 October 1242), no. 561, available on the Henry III Fine Rolls Project website at: https://finerollshenry3.org.uk/content/calendar/roll_039b.html (accessed 25 Oct. 2018).

4   Bémont, *Simon de Montfort*, 334.

5   *Bulletin de la Société des archives historiques de la Saintonge et de l'Aunis*, 12 (Paris and Saintes, 1892), 312–15, 411–12.

6   *Matthaei Parisiensis, Monachi Sancti Albani, Chronica Majora*, ed. H. R. Luard, 7 vols. (London, 1872–83) (hereafter *CM*), IV, 209–10.

7   *CM*, IV, 210–11.

8   Bémont, 'La campagne de Poitou', 305.

9   N. Vincent, 'King John's diary & itinerary: disaster at La Roche-aux-Moins, 29 June 1214–5 July 1214', *The Magna Carta Project*, available at: http://magnacarta.cmp.uea.ac.uk/read/itinerary/Disaster_at_La_Roche-aux-Moins (accessed 25 Oct. 2018).

10 *CM*, IV, 212–13.

11 *Close Rolls, 1231–72*, 14 vols. (London, 1905–38) (hereafter *CR*), *1242–7*, 31.

12 *The Memoirs of the Lord of Joinville: A New English Version by Ethel Wedgwood*, trans. Ethel Wedgwood (London, 1906), 42.

13 Bémont, *Simon de Montfort*, 341.

14 D. A. Carpenter, *The Struggle for Mastery, Britain 1066–1284* (London, 2003), 338–40; S. T. Ambler, *Bishops in the Political Community of England, 1213–1272* (Oxford, 2017), 172, n.144.

15 C. H. Lawrence (ed. and trans.), *The Letters of Adam Marsh*, 2 vols. (Oxford, 2006–10), II, 349.

16 *CM*, IV, 217–20.

17 Ibid., 231; J. R. Maddicott, *Simon de Montfort* (Cambridge, 1994), 32.

18 *CM*, IV, 231–2.

19 There is no royal charter recorded between 14 and 26 November, but Simon witnessed the latter (*The Royal Charter Witness Lists of Henry III (1226–1272) from the Charter Rolls in the Public Record Office*, ed. M. Morris, 2 vols. (Chippenham, 2001) (hereafter *RCWL*), I, 189); *CM*, IV, 263.

20 It is unclear whether he stayed until the end of the Christmas festivities at Epiphany – there is no charter recorded between 27 December and 20 January (*RCWL*, I, 189–90).

21 Bémont, *Simon de Montfort*, 335.

22 Maddicott, *Simon de Montfort*, 43.

23 *Calendar of Patent Rolls, 1232–72*, 4 vols. (London, 1906–13) (hereafter *CPR*), *1232–47*, 419; Maddicott, *Simon de Montfort*, 32–3, 51–5.

24 Maddicott, *Simon de Montfort*, 43.

25 They received gifts from the king of deer from both the forest of Chute in Wiltshire, in order to stock their nearby park of Everleigh, and the forest of Savernake, fifteen miles north-west, near Marlborough (*CR, 1242–7*, 268, 288).

26 *CPR, 1232–47*, 161, 166; L. J. Wilkinson, *Eleanor de Montfort: A Rebel Countess in Medieval England* (London, 2012), 55. That the octagonal keep was the work of King John has been disproved by recent excavations: D. Allen and N. Stoodley et al., 'Odiham Castle, Hampshire: excavations 1981–85', *Proceedings of Hampshire Field Club and Archaeological Society*, 65 (2010), 23–101, at 92–4.

27 M. B. Brunn, 'Procession and contemplation in Bernard of Clairvaux's first sermon for Palm Sunday', in *The Appearances of Medieval Rituals: The Play of Construction and Modification*, ed. N. H. Petersen, M. B. Bruun, J. Llewellyn and E. Oestrem (Turnhout, 2004), 67–82, at 80. The sermon was read out to the assembled guests before the start of the procession every year.

28 *Bernard of Clairvaux: Sermons for Lent and the Easter Season*, trans. I. Edmonds (Collegeville, MN, 2013), 99–100.

29 For this and the description that follows, see: Brunn, 'Bernard of Clairvaux's first sermon for Palm Sunday', 71–2, and E. Poleg, *Approaching the Bible in Medieval England* (Manchester, 2013), 14–58.

30 Matthew 21:1–9.

31 *Letters of Adam Marsh*, I, 58, n.4; ibid., II, 336–7, 338–9, 350–1, 386–7, 390–1.

32 Ambler, *Bishops in the Political Community*, 35–7.

33 *CM*, IV, 295–6; Carpenter, *Struggle for Mastery*, 363–4; B. G. E. Wiedemann, "Fooling the court of the lord pope": Dafydd ap Llywelyn's petition to the curia in 1244', *Welsh History Review*, 28

(2016), 209–32, at 213–15 (which points out that Dafydd did not, as had previously been thought, offer himself as vassal to the pope).

34 'The chronicle: 1235–61', in *Annales Cestrienses: Chronicle of the Abbey of S. Werburg, at Chester*, ed. R. Copley Christie (London, 1887), 60–79, *British History Online*, available at: http://www.british-history.ac.uk/lancs-ches-record-soc/vol14/pp60-79 (accessed 25 Oct. 2018).

35 M. Morris, *Castle: A History of the Buildings that Shaped Medieval Britain* (London, 2003), 110–12.

36 'The chronicle: 1235–61', in *Annales Cestrienses*; *RCWL*, II, 6.

37 *CM*, IV, 481–4.

38 J. Gillingham, 'The beginnings of English imperialism', in his *The English in the Twelfth Century: Imperialism, National Identity and Political Values* (Woodbridge, 2000), 3–18, at 14–15.

39 S. A. Dixon-Smith, 'Feeding the poor to commemorate the dead: the pro-anima almsgiving of Henry III of England, 1227–72' (University College London Ph.D. thesis, 2002), 244–5.

6. Ruler of Gascony

1 J. R. Maddicott, *Simon de Montfort* (Cambridge, 1994), 106 and n.1.

2 W. C. Jordan, *Louis IX and the Challenge of the Crusade: A Study in Rulership* (Princeton, NJ, 1979), 65–104.

3 E. Boutaric, *Saint Louis et Alfonse de Poitiers* (Paris, 1870), 69–77, at 72–3.

4 Bibliothèque Nationale, Paris, MS Clairambault 1188, f. 7 (August 1248).

5 C. H. Lawrence (ed. and trans.), *The Letters of Adam Marsh*, 2 vols. (Oxford, 2006–10), II, 335.

6 C. Bémont, *Simon de Montfort* (Paris, 1884), 341.

7 *Letters of Adam Marsh*, II, 335.

8 Bémont, *Simon de Montfort*, 358; Leicestershire Record Office, BRI/I/II.

9 The following account of the Count's seals follows G. E. M. Lippiatt, *Simon V of Montfort and Baronial Government, 1195–1218* (Oxford, 2017), 105–7.

10 Bémont, *Simon de Montfort*, 298.

11 MS Clairambault 1188, f. 78, printed in Bémont, *Simon de Montfort*, 264–5, with the terms also set out by Simon in the documents that record the arbitration between himself and the king (ibid., 341–2).

12 Bémont, *Simon de Montfort*, 342.

13 *Matthaei Parisiensis, Monachi Sancti Albani, Chronica Majora*, ed. H. R. Luard, 7 vols. (London, 1872–83) (hereafter *CM*), V, 290.

14 *Letters of Adam Marsh*, II, 341, 343 (Exodus 23: 20–3, 27, 29–30).

15 Ibid., 343 (Deuteronomy 7: 17–24).

16 Ibid., 347.

17 Adam Marsh dates the arrival of the Gascons to around the time of the feast of the Ascension (9 May 1252), and states that they stayed, laying out their complaints, until around the feast of St Barnabas (11 June) (*Letters of Adam Marsh*, I, 78–9).

18 A. Hawkyard, 'From painted chamber to St Stephen's Chapel: the meeting places of the House of Commons at Westminster until 1603', *Parliamentary History*, 21 (2002), 62–84, at 70–4.

19 The following is not a comprehensive survey of the surviving documents recording the complaints against Simon, but only those I have examined. The task of tracking down the various documents and analysing this corpus is being undertaken by Amicie Pélissié du Rausas, for which see her 'Voices from the archives: reassembling the dossier of Gascon complaints against Simon de Montfort (1252). A study in Anglo-Gascon history' (King's College London MA thesis, 2013). Archives Nationales, Paris, MS J 1028/B (no. 13) (complaints of Gaillard del Soler and responses of Simon), J 1031 no. 5 (complaints of Sault, Dax, Gosse and Bayonne); BL: Add. Ch. 3298 (complaints of Gaillard del Soler), Add. Ch. 3299 (complaints of Sault), Add. Ch. 3300 (complaints of Bazas), Add. Ch. 3301 (complaints of viscount de Soule), Add. Ch. 3302 (complaints of William de Ermandars), Add. Ch. 3303 (complaints of Gaston de Béarn), Add. Ch. 11234 (complaints of Gaillard, dean of St Severin), Add. Ch. 11236 (complaints of Gosse), Add. Ch. 11237 (complaints of Ayquilin de Lesparre), Add. Ch. 11238 (complaints of Bayonne), Add. Ch. 11240 (complaints of Arnauld de Blanquefort); TNA: C 47/24/1/11 (complaints of viscount de Tartas), C 47/24/1/12 (complaints of Amanieu d'Albret), C 47/24/1/13 (complaints of Bordeaux), C 47/24/1/14 (complaints of Dax), C 47/24/115 (two unidentified fragments).

20 Only men could undertake trial by combat. The difficulties this presented in cases where females made accusations are discussed in D. A. Carpenter, *Magna Carta* (London, 2015), 106–7.

21 Simon's responses are recorded in: Bibliothèque Nationale, Paris, MS Latin 9016 (responses of Simon to the complaints of Gaston de Béarn, Blanquefort, Castillon, Soule, Gramont, Fronsac, and (in French) Gaston de Béarn, Blanquefort, Castillon, Soule, Gramont, Fronsac, Albret, Dax, Bayonne, Sault); Archives Nationales, Paris:

MS J 1028/B no. 13 (complaints of Gaillard del Soler and responses of Simon); TNA: C 47/24/1/16 (the defence of William Pigorel, Simon's seneschal).

22 *History of William Marshal*, ed. A. J. Holden, trans. S. Gregory, notes by D. Crouch, 3 vols. (London, 2004), ll. 13077–270.

23 The composition of the royal witness lists fluctuates considerably during the period of the inquiry, which is not perhaps surprising, given that the process provoked heated debates and moved several *curiales* to take sides, many in Simon's favour; this list of episcopal attendees is taken from charters dated to the early days of the inquiry, 11 and 16 May (*The Royal Charter Witness Lists of Henry III (1226–1272) from the Charter Rolls in the Public Record Office*, ed. M. Morris, 2 vols. (Chippenham, 2001), II, 64–5); the presence of the earls is attested in several charters during this period, and in the accounts of Adam Marsh and Matthew Paris.

24 *CM*, V, 289.

25 M. Bouquet, *Recueil des historiens des Gaules et de la France*, 24 vols. (new edn., 1869–1904), XXIV, 4.

26 M. Dejoux, *Les enquêtes de Saint Louis: gouverner et sauver son âme* (Paris, 2014), 75–6.

27 Those of Louis's *enquêtes* that I have examined include: Archives Nationales, Paris: J 192B no. 13 (complaints of the people of Carcassonne, 1247), J 318 nos. 87, 93, 96, 99, 101 (complaints of the people of Carcassonne, 1247), J 896 no. 35 (complaints of the people of Carcassonne, 1247), JJ 274 (complaints of the people of Touraine, Poitou and Saintonge, 1247). The corpus is outlined in Dejoux, *Les enquêtes de Saint Louis*, 41–3.

28 Dejoux, *Les enquêtes de Saint Louis*, 30, 416.

29 Gaston's complaints were various. He began by describing how he had left Gascony for a time (in December 1249 – in fact, Simon had seized him and sent him to England for judgement, on account of his various transgressions), entrusting Simon to respect the peace and rights of his men, particularly 'his dear knight and companion', one Arnaud Bernardi. But, as soon as Gaston left, Simon, 'without any reasonable cause', seized Arnaud's castle of Lados, 'violently, without judgement'. Simon then ordered Arnaud to appear before him in his court, even though Arnaud's affairs lay outside Simon's jurisdiction. There he forced the knight to agree to a judicial duel (Gaston does not say why – though in fact Arnaud had been accused of homicide). Arnaud pointed out that Simon had no right to make such a demand, especially because Gaston, and not Simon, was Arnaud's 'true lord', whose right it was to exercise justice over

him. But Simon would not brook any objection. At this point
Gaston returned to Gascony, approached Simon, and 'entreated him
in friendly fashion' not to do him such an injury, promising the earl
that 'if he had done wrong in these matters he would make
emends', at least if the matter were to be judged in court. But 'the
earl did not wish to heed him'. Gaston then persuaded the
combatants to agree to a treaty of peace, but Simon compelled them
to enter the ring armed and ready to fight – only then to insist
upon a treaty detrimental to Arnaud and Gaston, namely that
Arnaud would give Simon 100 marks 'for expenses' and agree to
take the cross and depart from Gascony. Even this agreement
Simon had then violated, by seizing Arnaud's horse and arms.
Simon's response tells a different story. Another knight, William
Arnaud de Werros, had alleged that Arnaud Bernardi had killed his
father. And so Simon, according to the custom of the land,
summoned Arnaud to appear before him, but Arnaud failed to
come and stand to right. Simon made inquiries and was informed
clearly by the whole community that Arnaud's castle of Lados was
of the king's lordship (not Gaston's), and that Arnaud had always
been accustomed to stand to right before the king's seneschal. And
so Simon took the rightful step of punishing the default by seizing
the castle. When Arnaud was thus compelled to appear before
Simon, he refuted the allegation of homicide. Therefore, 'by the
judgement of the court and by the customs of the country', the
parties agreed to trial by combat to determine who was telling the
truth. Both had presented themselves on the appointed day as
planned. Gaston was in attendance and, according to his wish and
that of his man Arnaud, a peace was made between the parties,
according to which Arnaud would take the cross and head to
Outremer. 'But he never went, nor did he wish to hold the peace,
and because he was summoned to come to the court [for this
breach of the agreement] and he did not wish to come nor to stand
to right', Simon seized his castle of Lados a second time. And 'all
these things', Simon continued, he 'did by right and by reason and
by the view of a court'. To complicate matters, Arnaud was now
claiming that Simon should never have proceeded against him at
all, because the matter of the homicide had been settled by the king
and previous governors, who had given Arnaud letters clearing him
of the allegation. To this Simon replied that he 'never knew
anything about such letters, nor had they been shown to him'. And
as to Arnaud's claim that he had been obliged to give Simon 100
marks, 'this is a lie; never did he give him money' (Bémont, *Simon*

de Montfort, 313–14 (for Gascon's complaints); J. Balasque, *Études historiques sur la ville de Bayonne*, 2 vols. (Bordeaux, 1869), II, 575–6 (for Simon's responses)). The king had written, on 28 December 1249, that he had pardoned Gaston and his partisans 'all damage and murders that he inflicted upon us and our men' (*Royal and Other Historical Letters Illustrative of the Reign of Henry III*, ed. W. W. Shirley, 2 vols. (London, 1862–6), II, 57).

30 Bémont, *Simon de Montfort*, 316; Balasque, *Études historiques sur la ville de Bayonne*, II, 577.

31 Bémont, *Simon de Montfort*, 316.

32 Balasque, *Études historiques sur la ville de Bayonne*, II, 578.

33 Bémont, *Simon de Montfort*, 316; Balasque, *Études historiques sur la ville de Bayonne*, II, 578.

34 Bémont, *Simon de Montfort*, 316; Balasque, *Études historiques sur la ville de Bayonne*, II, 577.

35 BL: Add. Ch. 3298. It runs across three sheets of parchment, sewn end to end (the scribe, realizing the length of the complaint by the time he reached the second sheet, had to make his writing smaller). A summary version was made in French, to which Simon's responses were appended (Archives Nationales, Paris: MS J 1028/B no. 13). The Latin complaint is printed in Bémont, *Simon de Montfort*, 279–85, and the French summary with Simon's responses in ibid., 286–96. The relationship between the two is unpicked by A. Pélissié du Rausas, 'Voices from the archives', 23–4, 76.

36 Bémont, *Simon de Montfort*, 311.

37 *Letters of Adam Marsh*, I, 79.

38 Ibid., I, 79, 81.

39 *The Royal Charter Witness Lists of Henry III (1226–1272) from the Charter Rolls in the Public Record Office*, ed. M. Morris, 2 vols. (Chippenham, 2001), II, 66.

7. A New Enemy

1 C. H. Lawrence (ed. and trans.), *The Letters of Adam Marsh*, 2 vols. (Oxford, 2006–10), I, 85.

2 Ibid., I, 85–9.

3 *Matthaei Parisiensis, Monachi Sancti Albani, Chronica Majora*, ed. H. R. Luard, 7 vols. (London, 1872–83) (hereafter *CM*), V, 313.

4 *Letters of Adam Marsh*, I, 88–9, n.11.

5 C. Bémont, *Simon de Montfort* (Paris, 1884), 343; *CM*, V, 313.

6 *Letters of Adam Marsh*, II, 326–7.

7 E. Boutaric, *Saint Louis et Alfonse de Poitiers* (Paris, 1870), 69–77, at 72–3.

8 *Letters of Adam Marsh*, II, 384–5.

9 *CM*, V, 313; Bémont, *Simon de Montfort*, 343.

10 *CM*, V, 315–16.

11 *The History of the Albigensian Crusade: Peter of les Vaux-de-Cernay's* Historia Albigensis, trans. W. A. and M. D. Sibly (Woodbridge, 1998) (hereafter *PVC*), ch. 96 (with an alteration to the translation, from 'virtue' to 'probity' (*probitas*).

12 *PVC*, chs. 270–1.

13 Bibliothèque Nationale, Paris, MS Clairambault 1188, f. 8v.

14 *Calendar of Patent Rolls, 1232–72*, 4 vols. (London, 1906–13) (hereafter *CPR*), *1247–58*, 161; Bémont, *Simon de Montfort*, 343.

15 *CM*, V, 334–5.

16 Ibid., 337–8.

17 Bémont, *Simon de Montfort*, 337.

18 Ibid., 321–4.

19 *CM*, V, 365; Bémont, *Simon de Montfort*, 338.

20 *CM*, V, 365.

21 Bémont, *Simon de Montfort*, 342.

22 *CM*, V, 370.

23 Ibid., 383.

24 *Rôles Gascons*, ed. Francisque-Michel and C. Bémont, 4 vols. (Paris, 1885–1906), I, no.3540; *CM*, V, 366.

25 J. R. Maddicott, *Simon de Montfort* (Cambridge, 1994), 120.

26 *Rôles Gascons*, I, no. 2111, preserved in the Montfort family archive and copied into MS Clairambault 1188, ff. 8v–9r.

27 *CM*, V, 366, 371–2.

28 W. C. Jordan, *Louis IX and the Challenge of the Crusade* (Princeton, 1979), 116–21.

29 Aubri of Trois-Fontaines, 'Chronica Albrici Monachi Trium Fontium', in *Monumenta Germaniae Historica Scriptores*, ed. G. H. Pertz et al., 39 vols. (Hanover, 1826–2009), XXIII, ed. P. Scheffer-Boichorst (Hanover, 1874), 631–950, at 940; L. Grant, *Blanche of Castile* (New Haven, 2016), 113.

30 Grant, *Blanche of Castile*, 175.

31 John de Joinville, 'The life of Saint Louis', in *Joinville and Villehardouin: Chronicles of the Crusades*, trans. C. Smith (London, 2008), ch. 518.

32 Boutaric, *Saint Louis et Alfonse de Poitiers*, 69–77, at 73.

33 *CM*, V, 415.

34 Ibid., 366, 372, 415.

35 Bémont, *Simon de Montfort*, 265–6.

36 *CM*, V, 415–16.

37 Ibid., 407–9.

38 *CPR, 1247–58*, 246.

39 Ibid., 249.

40 *Foedera, Conventiones, Litterae et Acta Publica*, ed. T. Rymer, new edn., I, part i, ed. A. Clark and F. Holbrooke (London, 1816), 295.

41 *CM*, V, 440; J. R. Maddicott, *The Origins of the English Parliament 924–1327* (Oxford, 2010), 469–70. Simon was, perhaps, aware that Henry had already, in early February, entered into peace negotiations with the king of Castile (*Foedera*, I, part i, 295).

42 Morris, *A Great and Terrible King: Edward I and the Forging of Britain* (London, 2008), 18.

43 *CPR, 1247–58*, 270.

44 *CM*, V, 383.

45 M. Morris, *Great and Terrible King*, 19–20.

46 D. A. Carpenter, 'King Henry III and the Sicilian affair', *Fine of the Month* (February 2012), 6, *Henry III Fine Rolls Project*, available at: http://www.finerollshenry3.org.uk/content/month/fine_of_the_month.html (accessed 16 Nov. 2018).

47 S. T. Ambler, *Bishops in the Political Community of England, 1213–1272* (Oxford, 2017), 96.

48 *CM*, V, 623. Matthew Paris dates the presentation of Edmund to the parliament of March 1257, but it more likely took place in October 1255 (Maddicott, *Origins of Parliament*, 472).

49 This is according to the calculations of Richard Cassidy who, with various caveats, estimates crown income to be at least £37,000 in 1249–50; £31,000 in 1250–1; and £33,000 in 1251–2. I am very grateful to Dr Cassidy for sharing his findings, which will be presented in a forthcoming article.

50 Maddicott, *Origins of Parliament*, 173–4.

51 Ambler, *Bishops in the Political Community*, 95.

52 *CM*, V, 525.

53 Ambler, *Bishops in the Political Community*, 95–8.

54 S. T. Ambler, 'On kingship and tyranny: Grosseteste's memorandum and its place in the baronial reform movement', in *Thirteenth Century England XIV*, ed. J. Burton, P. Schofield and B. K. Weiler (Woodbridge, 2013), 115–28, at 115, n.2.

55 Ambler, *Bishops in the Political Community*, 155–6.

56 Ibid., 42, 50–51, 156.

57 *Letters of Adam Marsh*, I, 56–7, 62–3; Ambler, 'Grosseteste's memorandum', 115–16.

58 Ambler, *Bishops in the Political Community*, 23.

59 J. R. Maddicott, 'Magna Carta and the local community 1215–1259', *Past and Present*, 102 (1984), 25–65, at 47.

60 Maddicott, 'Magna Carta and the local community', 47; P. Brand, *King, Barons, Justices. The Making and Enforcement of Legislation in Thirteenth-Century England* (Cambridge, 2003), 77–80.

61 R. Cassidy, 'Bad sheriffs, custodial sheriffs and control of the counties', *Thirteenth Century England XV* (Woodbridge, 2015), ed. J. Burton, P. Schofield and B. Weiler, 35–49, at 37.

62 Maddicott, 'Magna Carta and the local community', 47.

63 D. A. Carpenter, 'The decline of the curial sheriff in England, 1194–1258', in his *The Reign of Henry III* (London, 1996), 151–82, at 172; see too: Cassidy, 'Bad sheriffs', 38–9.

64 Maddicott, 'Magna Carta and the local community', 44.

65 Ibid., 35.

66 Cassidy, 'Bad sheriffs', 39.

67 R. Cassidy, 'William Herón, "hammer of the poor, persecutor of the religious", sheriff of Northumberland, 1246–58', *Northern History*, 50 (2013), 9–19, at 15.

68 Cassidy, 'Bad sheriffs', 39–40; Cassidy, 'William Heron', 15–16.

69 Cassidy, 'Bad sheriffs', 38.

70 Maddicott, *Origins of Parliament*, 173–4.

71 Ambler, *Bishops in the Political Community*, 82–104, especially at 84.

72 Carpenter, 'Decline of the curial sheriff', 166–71.

73 D. A. Carpenter, 'King, magnates and society: the personal rule of King Henry III, 1234–58', in his *Reign of Henry III*, 75–106, at 76–85, 100.

74 Ibid., 88–93.

75 Maddicott, *Simon de Montfort*, 130–5.

76 *CPR, 1247–58*, 609; Maddicott, *Simon de Montfort*, 137.

77 Maddicott, *Simon de Montfort*, 130.

78 *CM*, V, 348–51; A. Hershey (ed.), *The 1258–9 Special Eyre of Surrey and Kent* (Woking, 2004), no. 163.

79 *CM*, V, 343–4.

80 Matthew Paris dates this incident only roughly, as concurrent with incidents in early May (*CM*, V, 634); Simon and William de Valence are both recorded at court on 18 April and 12 May 1257 (*The Royal Charter Witness Lists of Henry III (1226–1272) from the Charter Rolls in the Public Record Office*, ed. M. Morris, 2 vols. (Chippenham, 2001) (hereafter *RCWL*), II, 107.

81 *CM*, V, 632.

82 S. Dixon-Smith, 'Feeding the poor to commemorate the dead: the

pro-anima almsgiving of Henry III of England, 1227–72' (University College London Ph.D. thesis, 2002), 218–19.

83 L. J. Wilkinson, *Eleanor de Montfort: A Rebel Countess in Medieval England* (London, 2012), 84.

84 *CM*, V, 634.

85 *CPR, 1247–58*, 590.

86 Ibid., 609.

87 *Calendar of the Fine Rolls of the Reign of Henry III, 1257–58*, 42/no. 147, available on the Henry III Fine Rolls Project website at: https://finerollshenry3.org.uk/content/calendar/roll_055.html (accessed 16 Nov. 2018).

88 *CPR, 1247–58*, 563, 564, 567–8, 594; *CM*, V, 649–50, 659, 663; *RCWL*, II, 114, 116.

8. The Seizure of Power

1 *Matthaei Parisiensis, Monachi Sancti Albani, Chronica Majora*, ed. H. R. Luard, 7 vols. (London, 1872–83) (hereafter *CM*), V, 674.

2 B. M. Campbell, 'Global climates, the 1257 mega-eruption of the Samalas volcano, Indonesia, and the English food crisis of 1258', *Transactions of the Royal Historical Society*, 27 (2017), 87–121, at 114.

3 *CM*, V, 690.

4 Ibid., 673, 690.

5 *Close Rolls, 1231–72*, 14 vols. (London, 1905–38) (hereafter *CR*), *1256–59*, 212.

6 H. R. Luard (ed.), *Annales Monastici*, 5 vols. (London, 1864–9) (hereafter *AM*), I, 390–1; F. M. Powicke and C. R. Cheney (eds.), *Councils and Synods: With Other Documents Relating to the English Church*, II, *1205–1313*, 2 vols. (Oxford, 1964), part I, 526–7.

7 *CM*, V, 708; TNA: Just 1/1187, m.1; D. A. Carpenter, 'What happened in 1258?', in his *The Reign of Henry III* (London, 1996), 183–97, at 192–3.

8 Carpenter, 'What happened in 1258?', 192–3.

9 *CM*, V, 708–9.

10 Bibliothèque Nationale, Paris: MS Clairambault 1188, f. 10, printed in C. Bémont, *Simon de Montfort* (Paris, 1884), 327–8.

11 J. Hey, 'Two oaths of the community in 1258', *Historical Research*, 88 (2015), 213–29, at 218–19.

12 *CR, 1256–59*, 294–6.

13 *CM*, V, 676.

14 Ibid., 676–7.

15 Ibid., 666.

16 J. R. Maddicott, *The Origins of the English Parliament 924–1327* (Oxford, 2010), 173.

17 D. A. Carpenter, 'The secret revolution of 1258', in *Baronial Reform and Revolution in England, 1258–1267*, ed. A. Jobson (Woodbridge, 2016), 30–42, at 37.

18 Carpenter, 'What happened in 1258?', 188–9.

19 S. T. Ambler, *Bishops in the Political Community of England, 1213–1272* (Oxford, 2017), 113–18.

20 Psalm 67:2: *Exsurgat Deus, et dissipentur inimici ejus; et fugiant qui oderunt eum, a facie ejus*; compare to Roger Bigod's *Sed fugiant captivi et intolerabiles Pictavenses, et omnes alienigenae a facie vestra et nostra tanquam a facie leonis* (*AM*, I, 163–5). All biblical references are given for the Vulgate, and quotations in the Douay-Rheims translation.

21 M. C. Gaposchkin, *Invisible Weapons: Liturgy and the Making of Crusade Ideology* (Ithaca and London, 2017), 207, 296–7.

22 Compare Luke 2:14: *Gloria in altissimis Deo, et in terra pax hominibus bonae voluntatis* with Roger Bigod's words: *erit gloria in excelsis Deo et in terra vestra pax hominibus bonae voluntatis* (*AM*, I, 164).

23 D. A. Carpenter, 'Chancellor Ralph de Neville and plans of political reform, 1215–58, in his *The Reign of Henry III*, 61–73, at 66–71.

24 Ibid., 62 (quoting Matthew Paris (*CM*, III, 364)).

25 Ambler, *Bishops in the Political Community*, 94–5.

26 Ibid., 42.

27 Ibid., 57–8.

28 F. A. C. Mantello and J. Goering (eds.), *The Letters of Robert Grosseteste, Bishop of Lincoln* (Toronto, 2010), 401–2.

29 T. C. B. McLeish, R. G. Bower, B. K. Tanner, H. E. Smithson, C. Panti, N. Lewis and G. E. M. Gasper, 'History: a medieval multiverse', *Nature*, 507 (12 March 2014), 161–3.

30 *Letters of Robert Grosseteste*, 446.

31 1 Samuel / Kings 24: 11–13; 1 Samuel / Kings 26: 9–11; Ambler, *Bishops in the Political Community*, 33.

32 Ambler, *Bishops in the Political Community*, 202; M. Barber, *The New Knighthood* (Cambridge, 1994), 185–6.

33 It is possible that they conceived of a council of twenty-five in total (twenty-four councillors plus the king). Since at least the days of St Augustine, the number twenty-five had been held to represent the law of the Old Testament (because it was achieved by squaring the number five, which in turn represented the first five books of the

Old Testament that were, according to tradition, written by Moses).
This is, perhaps, why twenty-five barons had been chosen in 1215 to
enforce the first issue of Magna Carta (N. Vincent, *Magna Carta: A
Very Short Introduction* (Oxford, 2012), 67–9).

34 Revelation 4: 4 Vulgate: *Et in circuitu sedis sedilia viginti quatuor: et
super thronos viginti quatuor seniores sedentes, circumamicti vestimentis
albis, et in capitibus eorum coronae aureae.*

35 'seigneur', *Anglo-Norman Dictionary*, online edn., available at: www.
anglo-norman.net/D/seigneur (accessed 2 Nov. 2018).

36 R. F. Treharne and I. J. Sanders (eds.), *Documents of the Baronial
Movement of Reform and Rebellion, 1258–1267* (Oxford, 1973)
(hereafter *DBM*), 74–7, 100–1.

37 *Calendar of Patent Rolls, 1232–72*, 4 vols. (London, 1906–13), *1247–58*,
627.

9. The Reform of the Kingdom

1 B. Connell, A. Gray Jones, R. Redfern and D. Walker, *A
Bioarchaeological Study of Medieval Burials on the Site of St Mary
Spital: Excavations at Spitalfields Market, London E1, 1991–2007*
(London, 2012), 230.

2 Ibid., 19–20, 229.

3 C. Rawcliffe, 'The hospitals of later medieval London', *Medical
History*, 28 (1984), 1–21, at 4–5.

4 *Matthaei Parisiensis, Monachi Sancti Albani, Chronica Majora*, ed. H.
R. Luard, 7 vols. (London, 1872–83) (hereafter *CM*), V, 693–4.

5 S. Dixon-Smith, 'The image and reality of alms-giving in the great
halls of Henry III', *Journal of the British Archaeological Association*, 152
(1998), 79–96, at 86–7, 90.

6 D. A. Carpenter, 'The household rolls of King Henry III of
England (1216–72)', *Historical Research*, 80 (2007), 22–46, at 36.

7 G. O. Sayles, *The Functions of the Medieval Parliament of England*
(London, 1988), 64.

8 See the comments by Matthew Paris: *CM*, V, 695–6.

9 While the date set for the parliament in the proclamation issued at
the end of the Westminster parliament was 9 June, Matthew Paris
dates the Oxford assembly as 'with the feast of St Barnabas
approaching' – the feast of St Barnabas is 11 June (R. F. Treharne and
I. J. Sanders (eds.), *Documents of the Baronial Movement of Reform and
Rebellion, 1258–1267* (Oxford, 1973) (hereafter *DBM*), 74–5; *CM*, V,
695).

10 C. H. Knowles, 'Despenser, Sir Hugh (*c.*1223–1265)', *Oxford Dictionary of National Biography*, online edn. (2004), available at: http://0-www.oxforddnb.com.catalogue.libraries.london.ac.uk/view/article/7552 (accessed 3 Aug. 2017); J. R. Maddicott, *Simon de Montfort* (Cambridge, 1994), 63–4.

11 C. Bémont, *Simon de Montfort* (Paris, 1884), 328–30.

12 *DBM*, 76–91; P. Brand, *King, Barons, Justices. The Making and Enforcement of Legislation in Thirteenth-Century England* (Cambridge, 2003), 20–4.

13 D. A. Carpenter, 'King, magnates and society: the personal rule of King Henry III, 1234–58', in his *The Reign of Henry III* (London, 1996), 75–106, at 76–85, 100.

14 Brand, *King, Barons, Justices*, 87–90.

15 Ibid., 81–2.

16 T. K. Moore, 'The Fine Rolls as evidence for the expansion of royal justice during the reign of Henry III', in *The Growth of Royal Government Under Henry III*, ed. D. A. Carpenter, D. Crook and L. J. Wilkinson (Woodbridge, 2015), 55–71, 61, 63–4, 65–6.

17 Chapter 60, from D. A. Carpenter, *Magna Carta* (London, 2015), 62–3, 143 (I have altered the translation from 'men' to the gender-neutral 'people', which conveys the meaning of the Latin *omnes . . . suos*).

18 Carpenter, *Magna Carta*, 151–3.

19 D. A. Carpenter, 'Feature of the month: December 2015 – the saving clause in Magna Carta: new light shed on its meaning by the copies of the 1225 Charter at Burton Abbey', *The Magna Carta Project*, available at: http://magnacartaresearch.org/read/feature_of_the_month/Dec_2015_3 (accessed 7 Aug. 2017); Carpenter, *Magna Carta*, 425–7.

20 For the classic survey, see: C. H. Lawrence, *The Friars: The Impact of the Early Mendicant Movement on Western Society* (London, 2013).

21 J. Le Goff, *Saint Louis*, trans. G. E. Gollrad (Paris, 2009), 625.

22 Ibid., 623.

23 The *enquête* of Alphonse, however, pursued a broader governmental agenda than that of Louis, perhaps having learned from the experiences of the king's *enquête* (G. Chenard, 'Les enquêtes administratives dans les domaines d'Alphonse de Poitiers', in *Quand gouverner c'est enquêter. Les pratiques politiques de l'enquête princière (Occident, XIIIe–XIVe siècles)*, ed. T. Pécout (Paris, 2010), 157–68, at 158; G. Chenard, *L'Administration d'Alphonse de Poitiers (1241–1271)* (Paris, 2017), 494–524).

24 A. Hershey (ed.), *The 1258–9 Special Eyre of Surrey and Kent* (Woking, 2004), xxv.

25 Ibid., xxviii.

26 *DBM*, 91.

27 Ibid., 106–7 (amending *dreit* from 'justice' to 'right').

28 G. E. Woodbine (ed.) and S. E. Thorne (trans.), *Bracton: On the Laws and Customs of England*, 4 vols. (Cambridge, MA, 1968–77), II, 307, 302; for the argument in favour of the foundation of the 1258 prerogatives in Bracton, see: Hershey, *The 1258–9 Special Eyre*, xxiv n.7. For Bracton, see: N. Vincent, 'Henry of Bratton (alias Bracton)', in *Great Christian Jurists in English History*, ed. M. Hill and R. Helmholz (Cambridge, 2017), 19–44.

29 TNA: Just 1/1187 m.1.

30 Hershey, *The 1258–9 Special Eyre*, xli n.24.

31 A. Hershey, 'Success or failure? Hugh Bigod and judicial reform during the baronial movement, June 1258–February 1259', in *Thirteenth Century England V*, ed. P. R. Coss and S. D. Lloyd (Woodbridge, 1993), 65–88, at 66, 71.

32 TNA: Just 1/1187 m.14d. Hugh Bigod ruled that Richard was to be sent to a local hospital – if he did recover, he would have to resume his abjuration.

33 *Close Rolls, 1231–72*, 14 vols. (London, 1905–38) (hereafter *CR*), *1256–59*, 262; R. Cassidy, 'The 1259 Pipe Roll' (King's College London Ph.D. thesis, 2012), 90.

34 Hershey, *The 1258–9 Special Eyre*, nos. 170, 171.

35 Ibid., nos. 337, 364.

36 Ibid., nos. 335, 370.

37 *De Antiquis Legibus Liber. Cronica Maiorum et Vicecomitum Londoniarum*, ed. T. Stapleton (London, 1846), 39.

38 Hershey, *The 1258–9 Special Eyre*, no. 313.

39 Ibid., no. 361, and see too nos. 100, 379, 391.

40 *Bracton*, II, 340, which states that pecuniary penalties are only appropriate 'sometimes', and cf. Hershey, *The 1258–9 Special Eyre*, no. 391.

41 *De Antiquis Legibus Liber*, 40–1.

42 D. A. Carpenter, 'King, magnates and society: the personal rule of King Henry III, 1234–58', in his *Reign of Henry III*, 75–106, at 76–85, 80–5.

43 *DBM*, 106–7.

44 Ibid., 80–1. I have amended the translation slightly, supplying 'kingdom' for *regno*.

45 Ibid. (The translation in *DBM* imposes a gendered reading where the Latin implies none, and so I have altered the translation to provide the gender-neutral 'people'). For the marriages of the Poitevins, see: H. W. Ridgeway, 'Foreign favourites and Henry III's problems of patronage, 1247–1258', *English Historical Review*, 104 (1989), 590–610, at 595–6; J. Peltzer, 'The marriages of the English earls in the thirteenth century: A social perspective', in *Thirteenth Century England XIV*, ed. J. Burton, P. Schofield, and B. Weiler (Woodbridge, 2011), 61–86, at 66.

46 Ridgeway, '*Foreign favourites*', 595.

47 J. Hey, 'Two oaths of the community in 1258', *Historical Research*, 88 (2015), 213–29, at 213–20.

48 *DBM*, 100–1; *CM*, V, 696–7.

49 Winchester Castle was later delivered to Simon, after the man to whom it was committed, William de Clare, died (*Calendar of Patent Rolls, 1232–72*, 4 vols. (London, 1906–13) (hereafter *CPR*), *1247–58*, 638).

50 *DBM*, 90–3.

51 *CM*, V, 697.

52 Ibid.

53 Ibid., 697–8.

54 *DBM*, 92–3, with slight alterations in translation.

55 Ibid., with slight alterations in translation.

56 The comment of Treharne and Sanders (*DBM*, 94 n.9) that 'the negotiations with the Lusignans show the determination of the nobles to reach a fair solution of the problem. The absence of hatred and vindictiveness is worthy of note', seems completely misplaced. See too the account of Arnold fitz Thedmar, who confirms the letter writer's account (*De Antiquis Legibus Liber*, 38).

57 *CM*, V, 704.

58 Ibid., 703.

59 *De Antiquis Legibus Liber*, 39.

60 Ibid., 38–9; *DBM*, 276–7; *CM*, V, 371, 538.

61 *CPR*, *1247–58*, 643; *De Antiquis Legibus Liber*, 39.

62 For Walter of Kirkham, bishop of Durham, see: A. J. Piper, 'Kirkham, Walter of (d. 1260), administrator and bishop of Durham', *Oxford Dictionary of National Biography*, online edn. (2003), available at: http://www.oxforddnb.com/view/10.1093/ref:odnb/9780198614128.001.0001/odnb-9780198614128-e-15668 (accessed 8 Nov. 2018).

63 *CM*, V, 706.

10. Rule by Conscience

1 *Matthaei Parisiensis, Monachi Sancti Albani, Chronica Majora*, ed. H. R. Luard, 7 vols. (London, 1872–83) (hereafter *CM*), V, 710–12.

2 R. F. Treharne and I. J. Sanders (eds.), *Documents of the Baronial Movement of Reform and Rebellion, 1258–1267* (Oxford, 1973) (hereafter *DBM*), 118–21.

3 N. Vincent, 'Lovel, Philip (d. 1258), administrator and royal counsellor', *Oxford Dictionary of National Biography*, online edn. (2006), available at: http://www.oxforddnb.com/view/10.1093/ref:odnb/9780198614128.001.0001/odnb-9780198614128-e-17052 (accessed 8 Nov. 2018).

4 S. T. Ambler, 'On kingship and tyranny: grosseteste's memorandum and its place in the baronial reform movement', in *Thirteenth Century England XIV*, ed. J. Burton, P. Schofield and B. Weiler (Woodbridge, 2013), 115–28, at 124–5.

5 A. Jobson, 'John of Crakehall: the "forgotten" baronial treasurer, 1258–60', in *Thirteenth Century England XIII*, ed. J. Burton, F. Lachaud and P. Schofield (Woodbridge, 2009), 83–99, at 91–4; R. Cassidy, 'The reforming council takes control of fines of gold, 1258–59', *Fine of the Month* (October 2011), *Henry III Fine Rolls Project*, available at: http://www.finerollshenry3.org.uk/content/month/fm-10-2011.html (accessed 25 Nov. 2011); R. Cassidy, 'The 1259 Pipe Roll' (University of London Ph.D. thesis, 2012), 123–82.

6 *DBM*, 116–23.

7 H. R. Luard (ed.), *Annales Monastici*, 5 vols. (London, 1864–9) (hereafter *AM*), I, 453–6.

8 *DBM*, 118, n.*.

9 *CM*, V, 720–1. Matthew Paris gives a date of 'around the feast of St Leonard' (6 November), but three of the four ambassadors (not Richard Gravesend) are listed as witnesses to a royal charter on 6 November (*The Royal Charter Witness Lists of Henry III (1226–1272) from the Charter Rolls in the Public Record Office*, II, 122).

10 *CM*, V, 720–1; *English Episcopal Acta 13: Worcester 1218–1268*, ed. P. M. Hoskin (Oxford, 1997), 161.

11 We know of their presence because they were party to documents issued by Simon during their sojourn in France (C. Bémont, *Simon de Montfort* (Paris, 1884), 328–30; Bibliothèque Nationale, Paris: MS Clairambault 1188, f. 81 (original manuscript), f. 10v.).

12 MS Clairambault 1188, f. 81 (original manuscript), printed in Bémont, *Simon de Montfort*, 328–30.

13 M. Sheehan, *The Will in Medieval England: From the Conversion of the Anglo-Saxons to the End of the Thirteenth Century* (Toronto, 1963), 179, 184, 185.

14 C. H. Lawrence (ed. and trans.), *The Letters of Adam Marsh*, 2 vols. (Oxford, 2006–10), II, 341.

15 R. W. Southern, *Robert Grosseteste: The Growth of an English Mind in Medieval Europe* (Oxford, 1986), 235, 237.

16 *AM*, III (Dunstable), 211; H.-F. Delaborde and E. Berger (eds.), *Layettes du Trésor des Chartes*, 5 vols. (Paris, 1863–1909), III, no. 4454 (22 November 1258, Paris). It is very likely that Richard was still with Simon and Henry when the will was drawn up at the beginning of January, for he is only recorded back in England on 14 February (at the bishop of Lincoln's London townhouse at the Old Temple, suggesting that he returned with Simon for the February parliament) (A. Hope, 'Hireling shepherds: English bishops and their deputies, c. 1186 to c. 1323' (University College London Ph.D. thesis, 2013), 277–8). I am very grateful to Aaron Hope for providing me with a copy of his doctoral thesis.

17 *RCWL*, II, 122 (there is no charter witness list between 8 January and 10 February, when Simon's name is listed).

18 *CM*, V, 737.

19 Ibid., 728.

20 *DBM*, 130–7.

21 D. A. Carpenter, *Magna Carta* (London, 2015), 111–15.

22 Ibid., 107–9.

23 Ibid., 113–15.

24 *CM*, V, 744–5.

25 *Calendar of Patent Rolls, 1232–72*, 4 vols. (London, 1906–13), *1258–66*, 18.

26 *The History of the Albigensian Crusade: Peter of les Vaux-de-Cernay's Historia Albigensis*, trans. W. A. and M. D. Sibly (Woodbridge, 1998), chs. 106, 115, 125, 134, 135, 136, 140, 156, 167, 182, 187, 228, 246, 266, 267, 269, 280, 281, 318, 358.

11. Betrayal

1 L. J. Wilkinson, *Eleanor de Montfort: A Rebel Countess in Medieval England* (London, 2012), 104.

2 J. R. Maddicott, *Simon de Montfort* (Cambridge, 1994), 44.

3 Ibid., 183.

4 D. A. Carpenter, 'The lord Edward's oath to aid and counsel Simon

de Montfort, 15 October 1259', in his *The Reign of Henry III* (London, 1996), 241–52, at 245.

5 R. F. Treharne and I. J. Sanders (eds.), *Documents of the Baronial Movement of Reform and Rebellion, 1258–1267* (Oxford, 1973) (hereafter *DBM*), 204–5.

6 P. Chaplais, 'The making of the Treaty of Paris (1259) and the royal style', *English Historical Review*, 67 (1952), 235–53, at 244.

7 Carpenter, 'The lord Edward's oath', 251.

8 Ibid., 247–8.

9 M. Bouquet and L. Delisle (eds.), *Recueil des Historiens des Gaules et de la France*, 24 vols. (Paris, 1738–1904), xxiii, 467.

10 He is recorded in Paris in November, advising his cousin Philip in making an agreement with Philip's sisters, Alice and Agnes, Cistercian nuns in the house of Port-Royal, concerning the rights of their father, Gui, in Languedoc (*Cartulaire de l'Abbaye de Porrois*, ed. A. de Dion (Paris, 1903), 260–1); *DBM*, 202–3. A date of 26 November was set for their meeting and Henry sailed for France on 14 November (Chaplais, 'Treaty of Paris', 247).

11 H.-F. Delaborde and E. Berger (eds.), *Layettes du Trésor des Chartes*, 5 vols. (Paris, 1863–1909), III, no. 4416.

12 Ibid., no. 4564.

13 Eudes Rigaud had been in Paris since 10 November for the *parlement* summoned to manage the treaty, and had been at Louis's side to greet Henry upon his arrival (*The Register of Eudes of Rouen*, ed. J. F. O'Sullivan, trans. S. M. Brown (New York and London, 1964), 396–7; *Layettes du Trésor des Chartes*, III, no. 4564.) For Louis's arboreal kingship, see: J. Le Goff, *Saint Louis*, trans. G. E. Gollrad (Paris, 2009), 386.

14 Simon's next actions provoked the accusation (as one chronicler understood it) of lèse-majesté (F. M. Powicke, 'The archbishop of Rouen, John de Harcourt, and Simon de Montfort in 1260', *English Historical Review*, 51 (1936), 108–113, at 108).

15 *DBM*, 172–5.

16 Ibid., 176–7.

17 *DBM*, 178–81.

18 Ibid., 180–3.

19 R. F. Treharne, *The Baronial Plan of Reform, 1258–1263* (rev. edn., Manchester, 1971), 225.

20 H. R. Luard (ed.), *Annales Monastici*, 5 vols. (London, 1864–9) (hereafter *AM*), IV, 123–4.

21 Maddicott, *Simon de Montfort*, 197.

22 Treharne, *Baronial Plan*, 227–32.

23 Ibid., 233–4.

24 E. F. Jacob, 'A proposal for arbitration between Simon de Montfort and Henry III in 1260', *English Historical Review*, 37 (1922), 80–2; Maddicott, *Simon de Montfort*, 197.

25 Bibliothèque Nationale, Paris: MS Latin 9016 no. 5, which appears to be a fair copy of the working document. It is printed in C. Bémont, *Simon de Montfort* (Paris, 1884), 343–53, and reprinted with translation in *DBM*, 194–211.

26 *AM*, III, 215.

27 Maddicott, *Simon de Montfort*, 199.

28 Ibid., 199–200. The witness lists put Simon at Westminster from 20 October (*RCWL*, II, 130–1). He had missed the beginning of the parliament and had, on 8 October, appointed his nephew, Henry of Almain, as his representative (before he had received an official summons to the parliament – a violation of protocol that caused offence (H. W. Ridgeway, 'King Henry III's grievances against the council in 1261', *Historical Research*, 61 (1988), 227–42, at 230)).

29 Maddicott, *Simon de Montfort*, 200–1.

30 Ibid., 204.

31 *Close Rolls, 1231–72*, 14 vols. (London, 1905–38) (hereafter *CR*), *1259–61*, 457.

32 Maddicott, *Simon de Montfort*, 207–8.

33 Ridgeway, 'King Henry III's grievances against the council', 236–7; *DBM*, 218–39. In what follows I have changed the dialogue from the scribe's third person to the original first person.

34 Maddicott, *Simon de Montfort*, 207.

35 For the oaths taken in 1258, see: J. Hey, 'Two oaths of the community in 1258', *Historical Research*, 88 (2015), 213–29.

36 *Calendar of Patent Rolls, 1232–72*, 4 vols. (London, 1906–13) (hereafter *CPR*), *1258–66*, 185; Treharne, *Baronial Plan*, 257.

37 *DBM*, 238–43.

38 *AM*, IV, 128.

39 Maddicott, *Simon de Montfort*, 209.

40 *CR*, *1269–61*, 489–90; P. Chaplais (ed.), *Diplomatic Documents Preserved in the Public Record Office, I, 1101–1272* (London, 1964), nos. 330, 331; M. Howell, *Eleanor of Provence: Queenship in Thirteenth-Century England* (Oxford, 1998), 183–4.

41 Maddicott, *Simon de Montfort*, 209–10.

42 *DBM*, 246–9; *CR*, *1259–61*, 496–9; *CPR*, *1258–66*, 179.

43 Maddicott, *Simon de Montfort*, 214.

44 From the fragment of the chronicle produced at Battle Abbey, printed in Bémont, *Simon de Montfort*, 373–80, at 374.

45 *AM*, III, 217.

46 Maddicott, *Simon de Montfort*, 217.

47 Bibliothèque Nationale, Paris: MS Clairambault 1188, f. 80 (original manuscript), printed in Bémont, *Simon de Montfort*, 332–5.

48 *CR, 1261–64*, 130.

49 A. Jobson, *The First English Revolution: Simon de Montfort, Henry III and the Barons' War* (London, 2012), 80.

50 Maddicott, *Simon de Montfort*, 219. The continuator of Gervase of Canterbury states that Simon arrived at Romney on the ides of October (15 October), but that he arrived in London for the feast of St Edward (13 October) – I have followed Maddicott, *Simon de Montfort*, 219 in suggesting he arrived in Kent on 12 October (*The Historical Works of Gervase of Canterbury*, ed. W. Stubbs, 2 vols. (London, 1880), II, 217).

51 M. Morris, *A Great and Terrible King: Edward I and the Forging of Britain* (London, 2008), 52.

52 Jobson, *First English Revolution*, 82.

53 P. Brand, *King, Barons, Justices: The Making and Enforcement of Legislation in Thirteenth-Century England* (Cambridge, 2003), 161–4.

54 D. A. Carpenter, 'An unknown obituary of King Henry III from the year 1263', in his *The Reign of Henry III* (London, 1996), 253–9; Jobson, *First English Revolution*, 83.

12. Revolution

1 J. R. Maddicott, *Simon de Montfort* (Cambridge, 1994), 223.

2 H. R. Luard (ed.), *Annales Monastici*, 5 vols. (London, 1864–9) (hereafter *AM*), III, 221–2.

3 J. Hey, 'Two oaths of the community in 1258', *Historical Research*, 88 (2015), 213–29, at 215.

4 *Close Rolls, 1231–72*, 14 vols. (London, 1905–38) (hereafter *CR*), *1261–64*, 302–5.

5 *AM*, III, 222.

6 H. R. Luard (ed.), *Flores Historiarum*, 3 vols. (London, 1890), II, 480; III, 256; *Calendar of Entries in the Papal Registers Relating to Great Britain and Ireland, I, 1198–1304*, ed. W. H. Bliss (London, 1893), 411; J. Guiraud (ed.), *Les Registres d'Urbain IV (1261–1264)*, 4 vols. (Paris, 1896–1906), III, no. 1454.

7 A. Harding, 'Walton [Wauton], Simon of (d. 1265/6), justice and bishop of Norwich', *Oxford Dictionary of National Biography*, online edn. (2004), available at: http://www.oxforddnb.com/view/10.1093/

ref:odnb/9780198614128.001.0001/odnb-9780198614128-e-28902 (accessed 8 Feb. 2018); S. T. Ambler, *Bishops in the Political Community of England, 1213–1272* (Oxford, 2017), 117, n.79, 142–3; L. E. Wilshire, *Boniface of Savoy, Carthusian and Archbishop of Canterbury, 1207–1270* (Salzburg, 1977), 88–9.

8 *Liber Memorandorum Ecclesie de Bernewelle*, ed. J. W. Clark (Cambridge, 1907), 121–2, 126–7.

9 The lands of Peter of Savoy, for instance, were plundered while he was abroad (N. Vincent, 'Savoy, Peter of, count of Savoy and de facto earl of Richmond (1203?–1268), magnate', *Oxford Dictionary of National Biography*, online edn. (2004), available at: http://www.oxforddnb.com/view/10.1093/ref:odnb/9780198614128.001.0001/odnb-9780198614128-e-22016 (accessed 8 Feb. 2018)).

10 Wilshire, *Boniface of Savoy*, 88–9.

11 Ambler, *Bishops in the Political Community*, 138.

12 *The Historical Works of Gervase of Canterbury*, ed. W. Stubbs, 2 vols. (London, 1880), II, 223.

13 The bishops of London, Lincoln, and Coventry and Lichfield (*Gervase of Canterbury*, II, 223; *AM*, III, 223–4).

14 *De Antiquis Legibus Liber. Cronica Maiorum et Vicecomitum Londoniarum*, ed. T. Stapleton (London, 1846), 53–4.

15 *AM*, III, 222.

16 Ibid., 222–3; *De Antiquis Legibus Liber*, 55.

17 *AM*, III, 224.

18 Ibid., 224; *Gervase of Canterbury*, II, 223–4; *De Antiquis Legibus Liber*, 55; *Calendar of Patent Rolls, 1232–72*, 4 vols. (London, 1906–13) (hereafter *CPR*), *1258–66*, 270–2.

19 D. A. Carpenter, 'Henry III's "statute" against aliens: July 1263', in his *The Reign of Henry III* (London, 1996), 261–80.

20 *CPR, 1258–66*, 275; *Gervase of Canterbury*, II, 224.

21 *Gervase of Canterbury*, II, 224–5; *AM*, III, 225; *De Antiquis Legibus Liber*, 57.

22 *De Antiquis Legibus Liber*, 58; *AM*, III, 225; *Gervase of Canterbury*, II, 225–6.

23 *The Chronicle of William de Rishanger of the Barons' War*, ed. J. O. Halliwell (London, 1840), 17–18; Maddicott, *Simon de Montfort*, 87–90, 245–6.

24 *CPR, 1258–66*, 290.

25 Ibid., 296; *De Antiquis Legibus Liber*, 58.

26 R. F. Treharne and I. J. Sanders (eds.), *Documents of the Baronial Movement of Reform and Rebellion, 1258–1267* (Oxford, 1973) (hereafter *DBM*), 264–5.

27 Ibid., 266–7.

28 *Gervase of Canterbury*, II, 229–30.

29 *AM*, III, 226.

30 Ibid., 226; *Gervase of Canterbury*, II, 231; *William Rishanger*, 15–16.

31 *DBM*, 284–5.

32 Ibid., 284–7.

33 *AM*, III, 227.

34 Ambler, *Bishops in the Political Community*, 147–8.

35 S. Murray, *Notre-Dame, Cathedral of Amiens: The Power of Change in Gothic* (Cambridge, 1996), 148–50. While Louis's judgement at Amiens is simply dated to 'Amiens', and hence it cannot be known whether the arbitration took place in the cathedral, it is the most likely candidate (G. Durand, *Monographie de l'église Notre-Dame, cathédrale d'Amiens*, 3 vols. (Paris, 1901–3), I, 37; Murray, *Cathedral of Amiens*, 96, 104).

36 R. C. Stacey, 'Crusades, crusaders, and the baronial *Gravamina* of 1263–4', in *Thirteenth Century England III*, ed. P. R. Coss and S. D. Lloyd (Woodbridge, 1991), 137–50, at 141, 142. Walter de Merton was appointed on 5 January to present the case in Henry's stead at Amiens on 8 January, for the king had been taken ill (*CPR, 1258–66*, 376).

37 *DBM*, 252–7; Ambler, *Bishops in the Political Community*, 152–3.

38 The classic works on the Paris schools are: J. W. Baldwin, *Masters, Princes and Merchants. The Social Views of Peter the Chanter and His Circle*, 2 vols. (Princeton, 1970), and P. Buc, *L'ambiguïté du Livre: prince, pouvoir, et peuple dans les commentaires de la Bible au Moyen Âge* (Paris, 1994).

39 M. F. de Barros e Sousa, Visconde de Santarém, L. A. Rebello da Silva, and J. J. da Silva Mendes Leal (eds.), *Quadro elementar das relações políticas e diplomáticas de Portugal com as diversas potencias do mundo, desde o principio da monarchia portugueza até aos nossos dias*, 18 vols. (Paris, 1842–1976), IX, 141–2; N. P. Tanner (ed.), *Decrees of the Ecumenical Councils*, 2 vols. (London, 1991), I, 278–83.

40 E. J. Friedberg (ed.), *Corpus Iuris Canonici*, 2 vols. (Leipzig, 1879–81), II, cols. 971–4.

41 Ambler, *Bishops in the Political Community*, 54.

42 Stacey, 'The baronial *Gravamina*', 141–2; Maddicott, *Simon de Montfort*, 260–2; Ambler, *Bishops in the Political Community*, 153; S. T. Ambler, 'Magna Carta: its confirmation at Simon de Montfort's parliament of 1265', *English Historical Review*, 130 (2015), 801–30, at 806–7.

43 D. A. Carpenter, 'Archbishop Langton and Magna Carta: His

contribution, his doubts and his hypocrisy', *English Historical Review*, 126 (2011), 1041–65, at 1055.

44 *DBM*, 268–77. The Montfortian case is made up of two documents, which in *DBM* are labelled 37B and 37C (*DBM*, 256–79); the latter is titled 'Grievances which oppressed the land of England', while 37B sets out the remedies put in place by the reformers. As Stacey points out, the order of these documents ought to be reversed (Stacey, 'The baronial *Gravamina*', 138–41).

45 *DBM*, 277.

46 Ibid., 256–7, 262–5.

47 For an evaluation of different explanations of why the Montfortians agreed to submit to Louis's arbitration, see: Maddicott, *Simon de Montfort*, 258–60. While acknowledging the skill with which the case was put together by the Montfortian side, Maddicott suggests that the substitution of Thomas de Cantilupe for Montfort was the cause of the Montfortians' failure, for Thomas 'lacked Montfort's weight' and worldly experience. While Thomas might have lacked Montfort's charisma, the analysis here suggests that the major obstacle to Montfortian success at Amiens was the strength of opinion that had built up against the party at the French court and, moreover, fundamental objections to their violent actions, and the weaknesses of their case.

48 *DBM*, 286–9.

49 The text of Louis's judgement was copied by Arnold fitz Thedmar and the Tewkesbury annalist into their chronicles, and reports are given elsewhere (*De Antiquis Legibus Liber*, 59–61; *AM*, I, 177–9; *Gervase of Canterbury*, II, 232; *Flores Historiarum*, II, 486; *AM*, III, 227; H. M. Cam and E. F. Jacon, 'Notes on an English Cluniac chronicle', *English Historical Review*, 44 (1929), 102 (the Northampton chronicle).

50 *De Antiquis Legibus Liber*, 61.

51 *DBM*, 284–7.

52 *Registres d'Urbain IV*, I, nos. 586 (the pope's letter to Louis, in which he states that he determined to send a legate the day after receiving news from Louis and Marguerite) and 581 (the legate's commission, dated 22 November 1263).

53 For Eleanor's activities in France, see: M. Howell, *Eleanor of Provence: Queenship in Thirteenth-Century England* (Oxford, 1998), 196–7, 199–205.

54 *Registres d'Urbain IV*, I, no. 586.

55 Archivio Segreto Vaticano, Registra Vaticana 28, f. 56v; *Registres d'Urbain IV*, I, nos. 581, 586, 596.

56 *AM*, I, 179–80.

57 *CPR, 1258–66*, 273; *AM*, III, 223.

58 *AM*, I, 179–80.

59 *Gervase of Canterbury*, II, 226; *DBM*, 284–5.

60 *Gervase of Canterbury*, II, 232–3.

61 Ibid., II, 233.

62 *AM*, III, 227.

63 *AM*, IV, 448–9; *Flores Historiarum*, II, 486–7; *William Rishanger*, 20.

64 *AM*, III, 227–8.

65 Ibid., III, 228; *AM*, IV, 143–4; Cam and Jacon, 'Notes on an English Cluniac chronicle', 102.

66 *CR, 1261–64*, 377–9.

67 *De Antiquis Legibus Liber*, 61.

68 *Flores Historiarum*, II, 487.

69 I. Stone, 'The rebel barons of 1264 and the Commune of London: an oath of mutual aid', *English Historical Review*, 129 (2014), 1–18, at 4–5.

70 Ambler, *Bishops in the Political Community*, 61–81.

71 W. Stubbs (ed.), *Annales Londonienses*, in *Chronicles of the Reigns of Edward I and Edward II*, 2 vols. (London, 1882), I, 61. The account of 1264 in the London annals draws from an independent source that has since been lost (*Annales Londonienses*, xvii–xviii; A. Gransden, *Historical Writing in England, II, c. 1307 to the Early Sixteenth Century* (London, 1982), 23–5).

72 *CR, 1261–64*, 383; Ambler, *Bishops in the Political Community*, 126–7.

73 Walter of Guisborough, quoted in C. H. Lawrence, 'The university of Oxford and the chronicle of the Barons' Wars', *English Historical Review*, 95 (1980), 99–113, at 100.

74 *AM*, III, 229; *Gervase of Canterbury*, II, 234; *De Antiquis Legibus Liber*, 62. For the chroniclers' treatment of the battle, see: L. Kjær, 'Writing reform and rebellion', in *Baronial Reform and Revolution in England, 1258–1267*, ed. A. Jobson (Woodbridge, 2016), 109–124, at 114.

75 Madddicott, *Simon de Montfort*, 267.

76 *Gervase of Canterbury*, II, 235; *William Rishanger*, 24.

77 *William Rishanger*, 24.

78 *De Antiquis Legibus Liber*, 62; *AM*, IV, 141–3. For the treatment of this event by the Dunstable annalist (who has Simon foiling a plot by the Jewish population to burn the city on Palm Sunday using Greek Fire), see: Kjær, 'Writing reform and rebellion', 115.

79 TNA: E 101/3/3, discussed in a forthcoming article by Henry Summerson, 'The siege of Rochester in 1264 and its impact in North Kent' – I am very grateful to Dr Summerson for allowing me to see the article in advance of publication.

80 Summerson, 'The siege of Rochester in 1264'.
81 *William Rishanger*, 25.
82 *Gervase of Canterbury*, II, 235.
83 Summerson, 'The siege of Rochester in 1264'.
84 *Gervase of Canterbury*, II, 236; *AM*, IV, 147; Summerson, 'The siege of Rochester in 1264'.
85 Jobson, *First English Revolution*, III.

13. Triumph

1 D. A. Carpenter, *The Battles of Lewes and Evesham, 1264/65* (Keele, 1987), 18.
2 Ibid., 20–2.
3 *The Song of Lewes*, ed. and trans. C. L. Kingsford (Oxford, 1963), ll. 198–206, and see too: J. P. Gilson, 'An unpublished notice of the Battle of Lewes', *English Historical Review*, 11 (1896), 520–2, at 521.
4 *The Chronicle of William de Rishanger of the Barons' War*, ed. J. O. Halliwell (London, 1840), 29–30; H. R. Luard (ed.), *Annales Monastici*, 5 vols. (London, 1864–9) (hereafter *AM*), IV, 148–9.
5 *Song of Lewes*, ll. 250–2.
6 *William de Rishanger*, 27–8; *De Antiquis Legibus Liber. Cronica Maiorum et Vicecomitum Londoniarum*, ed. T. Stapleton (London, 1846), 64.
7 *William Rishanger*, 28; *De Antiquis Legibus Liber*, 64.
8 *William Rishanger*, 29; *De Antiquis Legibus Liber*, 64–6.
9 *Matthaei Parisiensis, Monachi Sancti Albani, Chronica Majora*, ed. H. R. Luard, 7 vols. (London, 1872–83), V, 365.
10 Book Three, 'General maxims', Vegetius, *De Re Militari*, trans. J. Clarke (London, 1767, reprinted by Oakpast, 2012), 103.
11 Book Three, 'The post of the general and of the second and third in command', Vegetius, *De Re Militari*, 92–3.
12 Carpenter, *Battles of Lewes and Evesham*, 26; Book Three, 'Choice of the field of battle', Vegetius, *De Re Militari*, 88.
13 *Chronica Johannis de Oxenedes*, ed. H. Ellis (London, 1859), 221–2; *William Rishanger*, 30; H. R. Luard (ed.), *Flores Historiarum*, 3 vols. (London, 1890), 495; *William Rishanger, Chronica et Annales*, ed. H. T. Riley (London, 1865), 25–6.
14 Carpenter, *Battles of Lewes and Evesham*, 31.
15 Book Three, 'Reserves', Vegetius, *De Re Militari*, 91.
16 Carpenter, *Battles of Lewes and Evesham*, 23.
17 Ibid., 32 suggests the possibility that each division was led by cavalry with infantry following, which might be one variation on

Vegetius' mixed disposition (Book Three, 'Disposition of the cavalry', Vegetius, *De Re Militari*, 90–1).

18 Carpenter, *Battles of Lewes and Evesham*, 30.

19 Gilson, 'An unpublished notice', 521; *The Historical Works of Gervase of Canterbury*, ed. W. Stubbs, 2 vols. (London, 1880), II, 237, *Chronica Johannis de Oxenedes*, 223.

20 *Close Rolls, 1231–72*, 14 vols. (London, 1905–38) (hereafter *CR*), *1242–7*, 201; N. Vincent, 'Feature of the month: April 2015 – Leopards, lions and dragons: King John's banners and battle flags', *The Magna Carta Project*, available at: http://magnacartaresearch.org/read/feature_of_the_month/Apr_2015_4 (accessed 27 Feb. 2018); M. Strickland, 'A law of arms or a law of treason? Conduct in war in Edward I's campaign in Scotland, 1296–1307', in *Violence in Medieval Society*, ed. R. W. Kaeuper (Woodbridge, 2000), 56–7; and as noted in Gilson, 'An unpublished notice', 521; *Chronica Johannis de Oxenedes*, 223; *William Rishanger Chronica et Annales*, 26.

21 The following account of the engagement is drawn from Carpenter, *Battles of Lewes and Evesham*, 32–3.

22 Book Three, 'General maxims', Vegetius, *De Re Militari*, 104.

23 For what follows on the Mise, see J. R. Maddicott, *Simon de Montfort* (Cambridge, 1994), 272–8.

24 *Song of Lewes*, ll. 79–96.

25 *Gervase of Canterbury*, II, 237–8.

26 *Gesta Francorum et Aliorum Hierosolimitanorum*, ed. R. Hill (Oxford, 1962), 69.

27 S. T. Ambler, *Bishops in the Political Community of England, 1213–1272* (Oxford, 2017), 135–6.

28 *Gervase of Canterbury*, II, 238; Ambler, *Bishops in the Political Community*, 132–3.

29 For the long tradition of prelates chastising kings, see: B. Weiler, 'Bishops and kings in England, c.1066–1215', in *Religion and Politics in the Middle Ages: Germany and England by Comparison*, ed. L. Körntgen and D. Wassenhoven (Berlin, 2013), 157–203.

30 *CM*, V, 525–6.

31 *Song of Lewes*, ll. 79–82, 325–38, 207–38, 346, 261–6.

32 Charisma, as Max Weber wrote, is 'the great revolutionary power in epochs that are in the grip of tradition' (M. Weber, *Wirtschaft und Gesellschaft*, ed. J. Winckelmann, 3 vols. (5th edn. Tübingen, 1976) I, 142, translated in D. d'Avray, *Rationalities in History: A Weberian Essay in Comparison* (Cambridge, 2010), 104–5).

33 For this incident, see: H. Summerson, 'Repercussions from the

barons' wars: a Kentish inquest of 1264', *Historical Research* (forthcoming). I am very grateful to Henry Summerson for providing me with a draft of his article prior to publication.

34 *Song of Lewes*, ll. 76–7, 417–26.

35 *William Rishanger*, 99–100 (from the miracle collection of Simon de Montfort gathered at Evesham), in which Simon appears to her in a vision, saying: 'Why do you disparage me, and always speak ill of me?'

36 For Wodard of Kibworth, see: D. A. Carpenter, 'A peasant in politics during the Montfortian regime of 1264–5: the Wodard of Kibworth case', *Fine of the Month* (September 2010), *Henry III Fine Rolls Project*, available at: http://www.finerollshenry3.org.uk/content/month/fm-09-2010.html (accessed 16 Nov. 2018).

37 For the involvement of the peasantry, see: D. A. Carpenter, 'English peasants in politics, 1258–1267', in his *The Reign of Henry III* (London, 1996), 309–48.

38 *Gervase of Canterbury*, II, 238; *AM*, III, 232–3.

39 *Gervase of Canterbury*, II, 238, as noticed in H. Summerson, 'The siege of Rochester in 1264 and its impact in North Kent' (forthcoming).

40 *De Antiquis Legibus Liber*, 63; *Annales Londonienses*, 64; *AM*, IV, 232–3; L. J. Wilkinson, *Eleanor de Montfort: A Rebel Countess in Medieval England* (London, 2012), 105–6.

41 *Annales Londonienses*, 64; *Chronica Johannis de Oxenedes*, 224; *AM*, IV, 151–2.

42 J. Heidemann (ed.), *Papst Clemens IV: Das Vorleben des Papstes und sein Legationregister* (Münster, 1903), no. 12.

43 R. Cassidy, 'Simon de Montfort's sheriffs, 1264–5', *Historical Research*, 91 (2018), 3–21, at 6.

44 Ibid., 4–5.

45 *DBM*, 294–9.

46 For biographies of several of these, see: S. T. Ambler, 'Magna Carta: its confirmation at Simon de Montfort's parliament of 1265', *English Historical Review*, 130 (2015), 801–30, at 816–18.

47 For the extent and antiquity of this system, see: J. R. Maddicott, 'Politics and the people in thirteenth-century England', in *Thirteenth Century England XIV*, ed. J. Burton, P. Schofield and B. Weiler (Woodbridge, 2013), 1–13.

48 *CPR, 1258–66*, 362; *Foedera, Conventiones, Litterae et Acta Publica*, ed. T. Rymer, new edn., I, part i, ed. A. Clark and F. Holbrooke (London, 1816), 444; *De Antiquis Legibus Liber*, 67–9.

49 *CPR, 1258–66*, 362.

50 Ibid. In the calendar, this summons appears to have been issued on 18 July – in reality its enrolment on the dorse of the membrane is not dated, and cannot be dated by the surrounding entries because it has been entered in the middle of a large space amongst the commissioning of inquests (TNA: C 66/81 m.8d). There has been some confusion over the dating of this expedition and the personnel involved. The summons instructed the men of the Marches to rendezvous with Simon and the earl of Gloucester, but the earl of Gloucester is not mentioned as having been part of the expedition in the account given by *Flores Historiarum*, II, 496–7, nor is he mentioned as being part of the agreement at Montgomery that resulted (although his younger brother, Thomas, is: *CPR, 1258–66*, 344). The *ODNB* entry for Roger de Mortimer incorrectly dates this expedition to early winter 1264, apparently based on Rishanger, but Rishanger has borrowed the account of the *Flores* and inserted it into a later chronology, following Simon's quarrel with Gloucester later in the year (*William Rishanger*, 35; *Flores Historiarum*, II, 498–9; J. Crump, 'Mortimer, Roger de, lord of Wigmore (1231–1282), magnate', *Oxford Dictionary of National Biography*, online edn. (2004), available at: http://www.oxforddnb.com/view/10.1093/ref:odnb/9780198614128.001.0001/odnb-9780198614128-e-19352 (accessed 4 Mar. 2018). There was a second expedition later in the year, when the marchers failed to keep to the peace terms imposed at Montgomery (*Flores Historiarum*, II, 502–3).

51 *Flores Historiarum*, II, 498–9.

52 *CPR, 1258–66*, 344; *Flores Historiarum*, II, 498–9.

53 J. P. Gilson, 'The parliament of 1264', *English Historical Review*, 16 (1901), 499–501, at 500–1.

54 *Gervase of Canterbury*, II, 239–42. The bishops identified the earl of Gloucester and wrote to him asking him to desist lest the legate should lay a sentence of excommunication (*English Episcopal Acta 38, London 1229–1280*, ed. P. M. Hoskin (Oxford, 2011), 102–3).

55 Heidemann, *Legationregister*, no. 14.

56 Gilson, 'The parliament of 1264', 501.

57 *CPR, 1258–66*, 366; Heidemann, *Legationregister*, nos. 2, 3b.

58 Heidemann, *Legationregister*, no. 29c.

59 F. M. Powicke and C. R. Cheney (eds.), *Councils and Synods: With Other Documents Relating to the English Church*, 2 vols. (Oxford, 1964), II, part I (1205–1265), 695, 698–9.

60 Heidemann, *Legationregister*, nos. 28, 29, 43; Ambler, *Bishops in the Political Community*, 163–7.

61 Heidemann, *Legationregister*, no. 45.

62 Ibid., nos. 49, 50.

63 *CPR, 1258–66*, 367–8.

64 Maddicott, *Simon de Montfort*, 306–7.

65 K. S. B. Keats-Rohan, '"Most securely fortified": Wallingford Castle 1071–1540', in *Wallingford: The Castle and the Town in Context*, ed. K. S. B. Keats-Rohan, N. Christie and D. Roffe (Oxford, 2015), 34–115, at 40, n.1, 44.

66 *The Metrical Chronicle of Robert of Gloucester*, ed. W. A. Wright, 2 vols. (London, 1885), II, 751–2.

67 The original muster point was Northampton, but this was changed to Oxford at the eleventh hour (*CPR, 1258–66*, 389; *AM*, III, 234–5; *Flores Historiarum*, 503).

68 *Flores Historiarum*, II, 503–4; for the attribution of this section of the *Flores* to Pershore, see: D. A. Carpenter, 'The Pershore *Flores Historiarum*: an unrecognised chronicle from the period of reform and rebellion in England, 1258–65', *English Historical Review*, 127 (2012), 1343–66.

69 *Flores Historiarum*, II, 503–4.

70 Ibid., 504; *De Antiquis Legibus Liber*, 70–1; *CPR, 1258–66*, 396–7.

71 Maddicott, *Simon de Montfort*, 321.

72 Ibid., 321–2.

73 *CPR, 1258–66*, 397.

74 *Flores Historiarum*, II, 504.

75 Ibid., 503–5.

76 *AM*, IV, 153.

77 J. R. Maddicott, *The Origins of the English Parliament 924–1327* (Oxford, 2010), 198–206, 259–60.

78 London Metropolitan Archives: COL/CS/01/001/01; *De Antiquis Legibus Liber*, 71–2. A new edition of Arnold fitz Thedmar's chronicle is currently in preparation by Dr Ian Stone for Oxford Medieval Texts; for Arnold, see: I. Stone, 'The Book of Arnold fitz Thedmar' (King's College London Ph.D. thesis, 2016), 46. I am very grateful to Dr Stone for sharing his thoughts on this passage.

79 D. A. Carpenter, 'King Henry III and the Chapter House of Westminster Abbey', in *Westminster Abbey Chapter House: The History, Art and Architecture of 'a Chapter House Beyond Compare'*, ed. R. Mortimer (London, 2010), 32–9, at 38.

80 *De Antiquis Legibus Liber*, 71.

81 S. T. Ambler, 'Magna Carta: its confirmation at Simon de Montfort's parliament of 1265', *English Historical Review*, 130 (2015), 801–30, at 828–9.

82 *De Antiquis Legibus Liber*, 71–2.

83 Ambler, 'Simon de Montfort's parliament of 1265', 807–9.

84 *Foedera*, I, pt. I, 452–3; *DBM*, 308–15; Ambler, 'Simon de Montfort's parliament of 1265', 809.

85 C. H. Lawrence (ed. and trans.), *The Letters of Adam Marsh*, 2 vols. (Oxford, 2006–10), II, 349.

14. Disaster

1 S. T. Ambler, 'Magna Carta: its confirmation at Simon de Montfort's parliament of 1265', *English Historical Review*, 130 (2015), 801–30, at 820–1.

2 W. Stubbs (ed.), *Annales Londonienses*, in *Chronicles of the Reigns of Edward I and Edward II*, 2 vols. (London, 1882), 67.

3 *De Antiquis Legibus Liber. Cronica Maiorum et Vicecomitum Londoniarum*, ed. T. Stapleton (London, 1846), 73.

4 *The Historical Works of Gervase of Canterbury*, ed. W. Stubbs, 2 vols. (London, 1880), II, 242; *William Rishanger Chronica et Annales*, ed. H. T. Riley (London, 1865) (the Tynemouth chronicle), 32–3. For the Tynemouth chronicle, see: J. P. Carley, 'William Rishanger's chronicles and history writing at St Albans', in *A Distinct Voice: Medieval Studies in Honor of Leonard E. Boyle*, ed. J. Brown and W. P. Stoneman (Notre Dame, 1997), 71–102.

5 *Annales Londonienses*, 67.

6 The following account of the Montfortian appropriations is drawn from J. R. Maddicott, *Simon de Montfort* (Cambridge, 1994), 324–7.

7 Maddicott, *Simon de Montfort*, 322–3; *Annales Londonienses*, 67.

8 Maddicott, *Simon de Montfort*, 325–6; *Calendar of Charter Rolls, 1226–1300*, 2 vols. (London, 1903–6) (hereafter *CChR*), *1257–1300*, 54; *RCWL*, II, 148.

9 *CChR*, *1257–1300*, 54; *RCWL*, II, 148.

10 *Foedera, Conventiones, Litterae et Acta Publica*, ed. T. Rymer, new edn., I, part i, ed. A. Clark and F. Holbrooke (London, 1816), 451–2. For the dating of this act, see: Ambler, 'Simon de Montfort's parliament', 806, n.26.

11 *Calendar of Patent Rolls, 1232–72*, 4 vols. (London, 1906–13) (hereafter *CPR*), *1258–66*, 366; Ambler, 'Simon de Montfort's parliament', 813–14.

12 Ambler, 'Simon de Montfort's parliament', 814–16.

13 *Annales Londonienses*, 67; H. R. Luard (ed.), *Annales Monastici*, 5 vols. (London, 1864–9) (hereafter *AM*), IV, 238; *William Rishanger Chronica et Annales*, 32; R. Frame, 'Clare, Thomas de (1244x7–1287), magnate and administrator', *Oxford Dictionary of National*

Biography, online edn. (2004), available at: www.oxforddnb.com/
view/10.1093/ref:odnb/9780198614128.001.0001/odnb-
9780198614128-e-50023 (accessed 10 Mar. 2018).

14 *William Rishanger Chronica et Annales*, 32.

15 *Annales Londonienses*, 66–7.

16 BL: Add. MS 8877, printed in *Manners and Household Expenses of
England in the Thirteenth and Fifteenth Centuries*, ed. T. H. Turner
(London, 1841), 3–85. A new edition of Eleanor's roll is being
prepared for publication by the Pipe Roll Society by Professor
Louise Wilkinson. For discussion of the roll and the light it throws
on Eleanor's role, see: Wilkinson, *Eleanor de Montfort* (London,
2012), xi–xii, 109–25.

17 *Manners and Household Expenses*, 12–14; Wilkinson, *Eleanor de
Montfort*, 111. Henry of Almain was sent on a mission to the king of
France in April (*CPR, 1259–66*, 418, 425).

18 *Annales Londonienses*, 67; *AM*, IV, 238.

19 *CPR, 1258–66*, 420.

20 *AM*, II, 361; the initial order gave Hereford as the muster point but
this was changed almost immediately to Gloucester (*Close Rolls,
1231–72*, 14 vols. (London, 1905–38), *1264–68*, 115–16.

21 *AM*, II, 361–2.

22 *CPR, 1258–66*, 423–4; *William Rishanger Chronica et Annales*, 33; H.
R. Luard (ed.), *Flores Historiarum*, 3 vols. (London, 1890), III, 1–2.

23 *AM*, II, 362.

24 Ibid.

25 Ibid.; Maddicott, *Simon de Montfort*, 333, n.214.

26 Ambler, 'Simon de Montfort's parliament', 810, 820.

27 The Wigmore chronicler, in W. Dugdale, *Monasticon Anglicanum*,
ed. J. Caley, H. Ellis and B. Bandinel, 6 vols. in 8 (London, 1817–
30), VI, 351.

28 *AM*, IV, 164–5.

29 Ibid., 163.

30 Hereford Castle stands no longer, having been pulled down in the
seventeenth century. For a survey of the castle and its remains, see:
'Hereford Castle' (List entry number 1005530), *Historic England*,
available at: https://historicengland.org.uk/listing/the-list/list-
entry/1005530 (accessed 12 Nov. 2018).

31 *Chronica de Mailros*, ed. J. Stevens.n (Edinburgh, 1835), 215.

32 Maddicott, *Simon de Montfort*, 335.

33 Ibid., 334–5.

34 D. A. Carpenter, *The Battles of Lewes and Evesham, 1264/65* (Keele,
1987), 38–9; *Manners and Household Expenses*, 41–2.

35 Carpenter, *Lewes and Evesham*, 38–9; Maddicott, *Simon de Montfort*, 335.

36 Carpenter, *Lewes and Evesham*, 38; Maddicott, *Simon de Montfort*, 337–8.

37 *Flores Historiarum*, III, 3.

38 *AM*, IV, 166–7; Carpenter, *Lewes and Evesham*, 39.

39 *AM*, IV, 167–8; Carpenter, *Lewes and Evesham*, 39.

40 Carpenter, *Lewes and Evesham*, 39, 49.

41 Wilkinson, *Eleanor de Montfort*, 116.

42 *Manners and Household Expenses*, 42–8; Maddicott, *Simon de Montfort*, 336.

43 *CPR, 1258–66*, 423–4.

44 *Matthaei Parisiensis, Monachi Sancti Albani, Chronica Majora*, ed. H. R. Luard, 7 vols. (London, 1872–83), III, 28.

45 *The History of the Albigensian Crusade: Peter of les Vaux-de-Cernay's Historia Albigensis*, trans. W. A. and M. D. Sibly (Woodbridge, 1998), chs. 181, 606C.

46 Wilkinson, *Eleanor de Montfort*, 116; Maddicott, *Simon de Montfort*, 339.

47 *AM*, IV, 169.

48 *AM*, II, 102; *AM*, II, 363; *AM*, IV, 454. For discussion see: Maddicott, *Simon de Montfort*, 339.

49 *AM*, IV, 169; *AM*, IV, 454; *AM*, II, 363; *De Antiquis Legibus Liber*, 74.

50 Maddicott, *Simon de Montfort*, 339, n.244.

51 S. T. Ambler, *Bishops in the Political Community of England, 1213–1272* (Oxford, 2017), 143.

52 *De Antiquis Legibus Liber*, 74.

53 Carpenter, *Lewes and Evesham*, 39, 49; *Flores Historiarum*, III, 3–4.

54 O. de Laborderie, J. R. Maddicott and D. A. Carpenter, 'The last hours of Simon de Montfort: a new account', *English Historical Review*, 115 (2000), 378–412, 396.

55 *AM*, IV, 454; *AM*, IV, 170.

56 Laborderie, Maddicott and Carpenter, 'The last hours of Simon de Montfort', 396.

57 Ibid.

58 *AM*, IV, 454; *AM*, IV, 170; D. C. Cox, 'The Battle of Evesham in the Evesham chronicle', *Historical Research*, 62 (1989), 337–45, at 341; Carpenter, *Lewes and Evesham*, 50–51. That the foot soldiers did follow is revealed by the Melrose chronicle, which records their arrival at Kenilworth the next morning (*Chronica de Mailros*, 199).

59 *Chronica de Mailros*, 199.

60 Ibid.

61 *AM*, IV, 170.

62 Carpenter, *Lewes and Evesham*, 51; for a full list and references, see: C. H. Knowles, 'The Disinherited, 1265–80. A political and social study of the supporters of Simon de Montfort and the resettlement after the Barons' War' (University of Wales Aberystwyth Ph.D. thesis, 1959), appendix I.

63 Carpenter, *Lewes and Evesham*, 51.

64 Cox, 'The Evesham chronicle', 341.

65 Ibid.; Laborderie, Maddicott and Carpenter, 'The last hours of Simon de Montfort', 397.

66 Laborderie, Maddicott and Carpenter, 'The Last Hours of Simon de Montfort', 397.

67 *Flores Historiarum*, III, 4; 'The borough of Pershore', in *A History of the County of Worcester*, vol. IV, ed. W. Page and J. W. Willis-Bund (London, 1924), 151–5, available at: www.british-history.ac.uk/vch/worcs/vol4/pp151-155 (accessed 12 Nov. 2018). The author of the Pershore chronicle was sympathetic to the Montfortian cause but ambivalent about an enterprise that, while admirable, had brought the misery of civil war and the degradation of a king (D. A. Carpenter, 'The Pershore *Flores Historiarum*: an unrecognised chronicle from the period of reform and rebellion in England, 1258–65', *English Historical Review*, 127 (2012), 1343–66, at 1362–3).

68 Walter had dedicated the church of Pershore Abbey in 1239, when it was rebuilt following a fire ('Houses of Benedictine monks: Abbey of Pershore', *A History of the County of Worcester*, vol. 2, ed. W. Page and J. W. Willis-Bund (London, 1971), 127–36, available at: www.british-history.ac.uk/vch/worcs/vol2/pp127-136 (accessed 12 Nov. 2018)); 'Houses of Benedictine monks: Abbey of Evesham', ibid., 112–27, available at: www.british-history.ac.uk/vch/worcs/vol2/pp112-127 (accessed 12 Nov. 2018).

69 Cox, 'The Evesham chronicle', 341, which first narrates Simon's arrival at Evesham and his dispatch of orders to young Simon to join him, before stating that 'Walter de Cantilupe then bishop of Worcester arrived on the same day at Evesham to speak with the king, and the earl confessed his sins to him' – a phrasing that suggests Walter was not hitherto with Simon's army. The eyewitness account produced at Evesham describes Simon and Walter sitting in counsel since Simon's arrival at Evesham, so it seems that Walter was recently arrived – probably, like Simon, having travelled through the night (Laborderie, Maddicott and Carpenter, 'The last hours of Simon de Montfort', 410).

70   C. H. Lawrence (ed. and trans.), *The Letters of Adam Marsh*, 2 vols. (Oxford, 2006–10), II, 339.

71   Laborderie, Maddicott and Carpenter, 'The last hours of Simon de Montfort', 410; *AM*, II, 364.

72   Cox, 'The Evesham chronicle', 341; Laborderie, Maddicott and Carpenter, 'The last hours of Simon de Montfort', 410.

73   Laborderie, Maddicott and Carpenter, 'The last hours of Simon de Montfort', 378–9, 385.

15. Evesham

1   D. C. Cox, 'The Battle of Evesham in the Evesham chronicle', *Historical Research*, 62 (1989), 337–45, at 341; D. A. Carpenter, *The Battles of Lewes and Evesham, 1264/65* (Keele, 1987), 52, 54. Unless otherwise stated, the following account of the battle is drawn from: O. de Laborderie, J. R. Maddicott and D. A. Carpenter, 'The last hours of Simon de Montfort: a new account', *English Historical Review*, 115 (2000), 378–412, at 407–12 (with some slight amendments to translation); and D. C. Cox, *The Battle of Evesham: A New Account* (Evesham, 1988), 11–19. The references in this chapter to sources concerning Simon's life before the battle that have been discussed and referenced in the foregoing chapters are not repeated here.

2   Book Three, 'The flight of an enemy should not be prevented but facilitated', Vegetius, *De Re Militari*, trans. J. Clarke (London, 1767, reprinted by Oakpast, 2012), 97.

3   Book Three, 'General maxims', Vegetius, *De Re Militari*, 105; Laborderie, Maddicott and Carpenter, 'The last hours of Simon de Montfort', at 405.

4   Laborderie, Maddicott and Carpenter, 'The last hours of Simon de Montfort', 405.

5   Carpenter, *Lewes and Evesham*, 58.

Epilogue

1   *Chronica de Mailros*, ed. J. Stevenson (Edinburgh, 1835), 208. The references in this chapter to sources that have been discussed and referenced in the foregoing chapters are not repeated here.

2   'Geoffrey of Beaulieu's life and saintly comportment of Louis, former King of the Franks, of pious memory', in *The Sanctity of Louis IX: Early Lives of Saint Louis by Geoffrey of Beaulieu and*

William of Chartres, ed. M. C. Gaposchkin and S. L. Field, trans. L. F. Field (New York, 2014), ch. 17.

3 Adam of Eynsham, *The Life of St Hugh of Lincoln*, ed. and trans. D. L. Douie and H. Farmer, 2 vols. (Oxford, 1961–62), II, 190.

4 *Chronica de Mailros*, 207–8.

5 F. W. Maitland, 'A song on the death of Simon de Montfort', *English Historical Review*, 11 (1896), 314–18, at 314–15, 317.

6 *Chronica de Mailros*, 202–5, 213.

7 D. C. Cox, *The Battle of Evesham: A New Account* (Evesham, 1988), 18.

8 H. R. Luard (ed.), *Annales Monastici*, 5 vols. (London, 1864–9), IV, 176–7; *Calendar of Entries in the Papal Registers Relating to Great Britain and Ireland 1198–1304*, ed. W. H. Bliss (London, 1893), 434.

9 The miracle collection is preserved in the British Library, as Cotton MS Vespasian A VI, printed in *The Chronicle of William de Rishanger of the Barons' War*, ed. J. O. Halliwell (London, 1840), 67–110; J. R. Maddicott, 'Follower, leader, pilgrim, saint: Robert de Vere, earl of Oxford, at the shrine of Simon de Montfort, 1273', *English Historical Review*, 109 (1994), 641–53, at 647–8; Cox, *New Account*, 21–5.

10 S. T. Ambler, *Bishops in the Political Community of England, 1213–1272* (Oxford, 2017), 189.

11 L. J. Wilkinson, *Eleanor de Montfort: A Rebel Countess in Medieval England* (London, 2012), 123–31, 135.

12 Jean de Vignay, 'La chronique de Primat', in *Monumenta Germaniae Historica Scriptores*, ed. G. H. Pertz et al., 39 vols. (Hanover, 1826–2009), XXVI, 662; F. M. Powicke, 'Guy de Montfort (1265–71)', *Transactions of the Royal Historical Society*, 18 (1935), 1–23, at 10–12.

13 Powicke, 'Guy de Montfort', 15–17; 'He pointed out one shade, alone, apart, and said: "Within God's bosom, he impaled the heart that still drips blood upon the Thames"' (Dante, *Inferno*, canto XII, from the *Digital Dante*, available at: https://digitaldante.columbia. edu/dante/divine-comedy/inferno/inferno-12/ (accessed 13 Nov. 2018). Henry of Almain's heart was interred at Westminster Abbey – hence the heart upon the Thames.

14 For Gui's career, see: J. R. Maddicott, 'Montfort, Guy de (c.1244–1291/2), soldier and administrator', *Oxford Dictionary of National Biography*, online edn. (2006), available at: www.oxforddnb.com/view/10.1093/ref:odnb/9780198614128.001.0001/odnb-9780198614128-e-19047 (accessed 7 Aug. 2018); for his supposed flight to Norway see: TNA: E 36/274 f. 445v., printed in *Foedera, Conventiones, Litterae et Acta Publica*, ed. T. Rymer, new edn., I, part

II, ed. A. Clark and F. Holbrooke (London, 1816), 577 (two letters). I am most grateful to Nicholas Vincent for bringing this reference to my attention.

15 Bodleian Library: MS. Auct. D. 4. 13 ff. 129–225; L. E. Boyle, '*E cathena et carcere*: The imprisonment of Amaury de Montfort, 1276', in *Medieval Learning and Literature: Essays Presented to R.W. Hunt*, ed. J. J. G. Alexander and M. Gibson (Oxford, 1976), 379–97.

16 TNA: Just 1/710 m. 55. I am very grateful to Henry Summerson for bringing this entry to my attention.

17 J. Dunbabin, *Charles of Anjou: Power, Kingship and State-Making in Thirteenth-Century Europe* (London and New York, 1998), 23.

18 M. Strickland, 'Treason, feud and the growth of state violence: Edward I and the "war of the earl of Carrick", 1306–7', in *War, Government and Aristocracy in the British Isles, c.1150–1500: Essays in Honour of Michael Prestwich*, ed. C. Given-Wilson, A. Kettle and L. Scales (Woodbridge, 2008), 84–113, at 97–8.

19 Ibid., 85. Strickland's interpretation of the turn towards intra-noble violence differs from that presented in this chapter, being centred on the British Isles and the Anglo-Scottish wars in particular. My suggestion is that this is part of a European phenomenon.

20 M. Jones, *The Black Prince* (London, 2017), 106–7.

21 The seminal scholarship on the norms that limited noble violence within Europe includes: M. Strickland, 'Killing or clemency? Ransom, chivalry and changing attitudes to defeated opponents in Britain and Northern France, 7th–12th centuries', in *Krieg im Mittelalter*, ed. H.-H. Kortüm (Berlin, 2001), 93–122; J. Gillingham, '1066 and the introduction of chivalry into England', reprinted in his *The English in the Twelfth Century: Imperialism, National Identity and Political Values* (Woodbridge, 2000), 209–231; J. Gillingham, 'The beginnings of English imperialism', ibid., 3–18, at 14–15.

22 P. A. Linehan, 'The Synod of Segovia (1166)', *Bulletin of Medieval Canon Law*, New Ser., 10 (Berkeley, 1980), 31–44, reprinted in his *Spanish Church and Society 1150–1300* (London, 1983).

23 E. Kennan, 'Innocent III and the first political crusade: a comment on the limitations of papal power', *Traditio*, 27 (1971), 231–49, at 231.

24 N. Housely, *The Italian Crusades: The Papal–Angevin Alliance and the Crusades against Christian Lay Powers, 1254–1343* (Oxford, 1982), 2.

25 D. A. Carpenter, *The Minority of Henry III* (London, 1990), 28; S. T. Ambler, *Bishops in the Political Community of England, 1213–1272* (Oxford, 2017), 70. For discussion of the title 'Marshal of the Army of God', see the introduction to the third edition of Professor Sir James Holt's *Magna Carta* by Professors George Garnett and John

Hudson: J. C. Holt, rev. J. Hudson and G. Garnett, *Magna Carta* (3rd edn., Cambridge, 2015), 1–32, at 9.

26 For the taking of prisoners, see: Carpenter, *Minority of Henry III*, 40.

27 S. Lloyd, 'King Henry III, the crusade and the Mediterranean', in *England and her Neighbours 1066–1453: Essays in Honour of Pierre Chaplais*, ed. M. Jones and M. Vale (London, 1989), 97–119, at 113; W. E. Lunt, *Financial Relations of the Papacy with England to 1327* (Cambridge, MA, 1939), 263.

28 *Regesta pontificum romanorum inde ab anno post Christum natum 1198 ad annum 1304*, ed. A. Potthast (Berlin, 1874–5, repr. Graz, 1957), II, no. 20318; Housley, *The Italian Crusades*, 19.

29 Housley, *The Italian Crusades*, 16–18, 113–18.

30 Ibid., 3–6, 35–70.

31 *Chronica de Mailros*, 216; A. Molinier (ed.), *Obituaires de la province de Sens*, 3 vols. (Paris, 1902–9), II, 225.

32 F. A. C. Mantello and J. Goering (eds.), *The Letters of Robert Grosseteste, Bishop of Lincoln* (Toronto, 2010), 71–2.

Index